AI
in the
Classroom

Adaptive technology delivering tailored instructions by integrating real-time insights into personalized learning pathways

Ross Smith

Mayte Cubino

Emily McKeon

bpb

www.bpbonline.com

First Edition 2026

Copyright © BPB Publications, India

ISBN: 978-93-65891-492

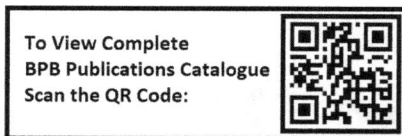

To View Complete
BPB Publications Catalogue
Scan the QR Code:

Dedicated to

My rapidly growing and always inspiring family.

– Ross Smith

My family, my anchor, and my everyday motivation.

– Mayte Cubino

Colin and Riley, with love

– Emily McKeon

Foreword

For the past thirty-six years, I have devoted my life to public education, leading innovative STEM programs and seeking new ways to ignite creativity and innovation in students. My journey has taken me from running one of the world's premier STEM labs to working internationally with schools and government bodies to integrate artificial intelligence responsibly. In 2016, I was honored to be named one of the Top 10 Teachers in the World. The opportunities that came from that honor affirmed a lifelong mission: preparing students with the skills, resilience, and vision they will need to thrive in an uncertain future. Today, I continue this pursuit as I complete research for my doctorate, focusing on the synthetic relationships that develop between children and intelligent tutoring systems and social robots, which is an area that highlights both the promise and complexity of AI in education.

This book arrives at a pivotal moment. Education is increasingly shaped by technology, from digital learning platforms to remote instruction. Artificial intelligence now offers personalized learning, streamlined tasks, and deeper student engagement. Yet, alongside this potential, we must consider risks. For example, young children may form unhealthy attachments to social robots or intelligent systems, confusing programmed interactions with genuine relationships. As AI becomes more common in classrooms, these developmental and ethical concerns must stand alongside issues of security, privacy, and equity. This book addresses these challenges directly, offering both practical insights and a responsible framework for implementation.

Across its eleven chapters, the book explores the history of technology in the classroom, the rise of personalized learning, and the growing role of AI in assessment, feedback, and professional development. It presents case studies of successful AI use, strategies for supporting diverse learning needs, and thoughtful discussions on parental concerns and ethical considerations. The later chapters look ahead, examining how students can prepare for an AI-driven workforce and how educators can build their own AI fluency. Together, these themes provide a comprehensive roadmap for schools seeking to embrace AI while safeguarding trust and human connection.

Reading this book, I was struck by its balance of inspiration and practicality. It speaks to educators, technologists, and parents alike, offering vision while grounding its insights in real-world examples. Most importantly, it reinforces what I have witnessed throughout my career: when thoughtfully applied, technology has the power to unleash creativity, resilience, and potential within every student. For those seeking to understand how AI can responsibly shape the future of education, this book is both timely and essential.

Joseph Fatheree | Innovation specialist
Top 10 Finalist 2016 Global Teacher Prize
NEA National Award for Teaching Excellence 2009
Illinois State Teacher of the Year 2007

About the Authors

- **Ross Smith** is a **Fellow of the Royal Society of Arts (FRSA).** Ross is a published author and holds seven software patents. He co-founded the Future World Alliance, a nonprofit committed to responsible AI for the next generation and is also a co-founder of the Seattle Women in Tech – a non-profit dedicated to connecting Women in Tech across industries in Seattle. He is currently the worldwide support leader of the AI First Team at Microsoft and Ph.D. scholar at University College Dublin, focused on AI, automation, worker displacement, and the future of work.

- **Mayte Cubino** is a published author and the director of strategy and programs in the AI First team at Microsoft and serves as the site lead and board member of Microsoft Portugal. With 20 years of experience in customer service and support roles at Cisco and Microsoft, Mayte is an AI enthusiast and patent holder. Her passion for people and technology has driven her to lead and sponsor numerous award-winning initiatives around diversity and inclusion, being recognized in 2016 with the European Disability Champion award for her work in raising awareness about hidden disabilities and workplace adjustments.

- **Emily McKeon** is a published author and communication director at Microsoft focused on global strategic business and executive communications designed to strengthen employee engagement and drive value for the customer service and support business. She has vast communication experience and a strong depth of knowledge in customer support, global diversity and inclusion, and employee engagement.

About the Reviewers

❖ **Joshua M. Paiz**, Ph.D., is the assistant dean for the School of Technology, Trades, Business, and Hospitality at Frederick Community College in Frederick, Maryland. He is an applied linguist who has studied inclusive and equitable teaching practices as well as AI literacy in teacher education. More recently, his work has focused on the intersection of applied linguistics and applied computer science.

❖ **James Hutson** is an interdisciplinary researcher and academic leader specializing in artificial intelligence, neurohumanities, and the intersection of digital innovation with the arts. His scholarly practice spans the integration of generative AI, immersive realities, and gamification within education, emphasizing the advancement of human-centered AI applications across domains. With terminal degrees in both art history and artificial intelligence, James has served in roles such as department head, program chair, and lead XR disruptor, consistently bridging technology with the humanities in teaching and research. He has authored several books on AI in education and cultural heritage, with research interests encompassing the design and implementation of generative media, ethical frameworks for automated systems, and strategies for upskilling professionals for the rapidly evolving digital economy. James is currently based at Lindenwood University, where he directs initiatives in AI research, digital humanities, and curriculum innovation.

Acknowledgements

○ **Ross Smith:** Dedicated to my grandmother, Deane Smith, a librarian who changed my life with her appreciation for books and truly helped to build my dream of reading and writing! And to the next generation(s) who will live, hopefully in harmony, and co-exist with our AI partners: Dear Smith Kids! - Maddy, Emma, Clara, Roo – and the next generation - Scarlett, Sela, Paz, Daisy, Jules – and to their support network – Tim, Bruno, Max, Mal and Lynsey.

I cannot share enough special gratitude for my incredible co-authors, Mayte and Emily – you are the most amazing people I have ever met and worked with, and I would never ever embark on this journey without you both! I am so grateful for our life and work together! Life-long friends!

○ **Mayte Cubino:** To my parents, whose hard work, sacrifices, and love paved the way for my education and shaped me into the person I am today. To my husband João, for being my rock. To our children Sofia, Tiago, and Laura, for always being my endless source of inspiration—watching you embrace AI in your classrooms and in your lives is truly rewarding, and I cannot wait to see the incredible things you will do with the future that lies ahead!

And to my incredible co-authors, Ross and Emily, thank you for being the best in the world. I am deeply grateful for your friendship and support, no matter the distance or special day on the calendar. I could not have asked for better partners on this journey!

○ **Emily McKeon :** To my family and especially my husband Kevin, and our boys, Colin and Riley, who sparked the passion to embark on this transformative journey of research and learning into AI in the Classroom!

To my co-authors, Ross and Mayte, the late nights and weekends were more than worth it to get the opportunity to co-create with both of you. Thank you for your dedication, creativity and amazing friendship!

We want to express our deepest gratitude to our family and friends for their unwavering support and encouragement throughout this books writing. This is our second authoring adventure in the past few years, and this passion has taken away many weekends and evenings from our social activities, toiling in the research and development of what we hope is a useful text for many.

We are also grateful to BPB Publications for their guidance and expertise in bringing this book to fruition. Their patience, coordination and belief in our vision, along with the collaboration of reviewers, technical experts, and editors, is what makes this book come to life.

We would also like to acknowledge the valuable contributions of our colleagues and co-workers during many years working in the tech industry, who have taught us so much and provided valuable feedback, empowering us to be the best we can be.

For all the people who have shaped our thinking about life and specifically around AI in the Classroom! Including: Joe Fatheree, Holly Kelly, Xin Deng, Iro Stefopoulou, Wendy Norman, Koen Timmers, Ivy Zhang, Paul Watkins, Dyane Smokorowski, Phaedra Boinodiris, Yu Kai Chou, Daniel Englebretson, Ishita Pai Raikar, Heidi Spiess, Lizbeth Goodman, Anthony Ventresque, Julian Birkenshaw, Gary Hamel, Christine Delos Reyes and Melanie Jackson. Ross's late close friends who shaped his thinking - Mihaly Csikszentmihaly and Warren Miller.

Finally, we would like to thank all the readers who have taken an interest in our book and for their support in making it a reality. Your encouragement has been invaluable!

Preface

Education is increasingly shaped by technology, from digital learning platforms to remote education systems. As **artificial intelligence (AI)** becomes more embedded in our daily lives, its role in education continues to grow. AI tools offer personalized instruction, streamlined administrative tasks, and enhanced student engagement, creating a learning environment tailored to individual needs. As AI becomes more integrated into the classroom, it is crucial to implement these tools with responsible AI practices, ensuring that security, privacy, and ethical considerations are prioritized. This book explores how AI can become an integral part of the classroom, helping students and instructors succeed in an AI-driven future, while safeguarding trust and compliance every step of the way.

Chapter 1: AI and Personalized Learning – Explores how different learning methods have evolved over time and the role AI plays in today's more personalized learning approach to education.

Chapter 2: History of Technology in the Classroom – Covers the history of technology in the classroom from clay tablets to the use of television and explores how advances in technology as teaching tools have led to improvements in how we educate and acquire knowledge.

Chapter 3: AI-driven Assessment and Feedback Tools – Shares the impact AI has on both student and teacher assessment practices, along with the challenges faced with implementation.

Chapter 4: Successful AI Implementations – Looks at multiple case studies and best practices in how to successfully implement AI in the classroom.

Chapter 5: Addressing Parental Concerns – Discusses what teachers should consider when supporting their students through their AI journey, including: privacy, security, screen time, AI tools access and the need for ongoing collaboration with parents and guardians.

Chapter 6: AI for Diverse Learning Needs – shares the benefits and challenges of AI inclusion for students with diverse learning needs, exploring early AI intervention techniques and curriculum personalization.

Chapter 7: Preparing for an AI-driven Workforce – Shows students how to prepare for their future in an AI-driven workforce, from understanding the basics of AI to applying this knowledge for success, bringing the classroom and real world together.

Chapter 8: AI-enhanced Professional Development for Educators – Dives into how educators can enhance their AI skills, learn best practices and become instructors of the future.

Chapter 9: AI in Supporting Social-emotional Learning – Discusses how AI can support students' social-emotional learning in new and interesting ways through classroom strategies and implementation techniques.

Chapter 10: Data Security and Ethical Considerations in AI – Explores the core themes of security, fairness, transparency, accountability, inclusiveness, and privacy.

Chapter 11: Future of AI in the Classroom – Discusses what the future holds for AI in the classroom and how human and AI solutions come together to offer students a comprehensive roadmap to academic and social-emotional growth.

Coloured Images

Please follow the link to download the
Coloured Images of the book:

https://rebrand.ly/d8715b

We have code bundles from our rich catalogue of books and videos available at https://github.com/bpbpublications. Check them out!

Errata

We take immense pride in our work at BPB Publications and follow best practices to ensure the accuracy of our content to provide an indulging reading experience to our subscribers. Our readers are our mirrors, and we use their inputs to reflect and improve upon human errors, if any, that may have occurred during the publishing processes involved. To let us maintain the quality and help us reach out to any readers who might be having difficulties due to any unforeseen errors, please write to us at :

errata@bpbonline.com

Your support, suggestions and feedback are highly appreciated by the BPB Publications' Family.

At www.bpbonline.com, you can also read a collection of free technical articles, sign up for a range of free newsletters, and receive exclusive discounts and offers on BPB books and eBooks. You can check our social media handles below:

Instagram

Facebook

Linkedin

YouTube

Get in touch with us at: business@bpbonline.com for more details.

Piracy

If you come across any illegal copies of our works in any form on the internet, we would be grateful if you would provide us with the location address or website name. Please contact us at business@bpbonline.com with a link to the material.

If you are interested in becoming an author

If there is a topic that you have expertise in, and you are interested in either writing or contributing to a book, please visit www.bpbonline.com. We have worked with thousands of developers and tech professionals, just like you, to help them share their insights with the global tech community. You can make a general application, apply for a specific hot topic that we are recruiting an author for, or submit your own idea.

Reviews

Please leave a review. Once you have read and used this book, why not leave a review on the site that you purchased it from? Potential readers can then see and use your unbiased opinion to make purchase decisions. We at BPB can understand what you think about our products, and our authors can see your feedback on their book. Thank you!

For more information about BPB, please visit www.bpbonline.com.

Join our Discord space

Join our Discord workspace for latest updates, offers, tech happenings around the world, new releases, and sessions with the authors:

https://discord.bpbonline.com

Table of Contents

Chapter 1
AI and Personalized Learning

I am always ready to learn although I do not always like being taught.

-Winston Churchill

Introduction

For centuries, educators have faced the challenge of crafting truly personalized lesson plans. Understanding each student's strengths, growth areas, and unique interests requires not just teaching expertise but a deep commitment to individualized learning. Given the diversity of student needs, creating tailored learning experiences has long seemed like an unattainable dream. Too many students and too few educators. Instead, most lesson plans today focus on aligning with standardized curricula, often overlooking the opportunity to meet students exactly where they are and spark genuine curiosity.

Enter **artificial intelligence (AI)**, the game-changer in today's education. AI does not just make personalized learning possible; it makes it practical, scalable, and achievable. With AI-powered insights and assistance, educators can now adapt lessons in real-time, responding to each student's learning style, pace, and engagement. Imagine a system that identifies when a student struggles with a certain concept and instantly suggests alternative explanations, interactive exercises, or even real-world applications tailored to their interests. AI-driven tutoring and self-help do not just provide answers; they cultivate curiosity, guiding students toward mastery in a way that feels natural and exciting.

With AI in the classroom, education is shifting from a one-size-fits-all model to a dynamic, student-centered experience. Every learner moves at their ideal pace, building confidence, deep understanding, and learning progress like never before. The impact extends far beyond the classroom, instilling a lifelong love of learning and equipping students with the skills they need to thrive in an ever-evolving world. The future of education is not just digital; it is intelligent, adaptive, and inspiring.

Structure

This chapter covers the following topics:

- Evolution of education and learning methods
- Personalized learning and AI
- Plato's vision of education
- Balance of individuality and collective good
- Developing a complete child through AI

Objectives

By the end of this chapter, you will have a thorough understanding of how different learning methods have evolved over time and the role AI plays in today's more personalized learning approach to education. You will learn how adaptive learning systems and technologies influence personalized learning and understand how these systems benefit teachers and students, along with introducing some challenges. We will wrap up with sharing a unique view of ancient philosophies on education and how they are juxtaposed with AI and personalized learning practices. For the ideal reader, whether a forward-thinking teacher, an engaged parent or guardian, or a passionate advocate for educational innovation, this chapter provides both inspiration and practical guidance. By embracing adaptive technologies responsibly, we can create classrooms where every student has a unique opportunity to reach their full potential.

Evolution of education and learning methods

For centuries, education has largely followed a more traditional, one-size-fits-all approach. This model goes back to early humans learning from elders. There was no specialization; everything was about survival. In *Ancient Greece* and *Rome*, the wealthy were all educated similarly. It was very different for women and slaves, who were only educated in the basics. Today's modern education was shaped by the industrial revolution, designed to produce a standardized workforce, with students progressing through rigid curricula based on age and grade levels rather than individual ability or interest. However, as societies evolved and technology advanced over the last few decades, the limitations of this method have become increasingly evident, paving the way for a shift toward personalized learning. The concept is built on the idea that education should adapt to the learner, rather than expecting the learner to adapt to a predefined curriculum.

For generations, the conventional education system has operated like a well-oiled machine; it has been structured, standardized, and uniform. Students' progress through the curriculum at the same pace, absorbing identical lessons, regardless of their unique strengths, interests, or learning styles. Teachers, so often constrained by rigid schedules and standardized tests, deliver their best lessons in a lecture-based format, while assessments prioritize memorization over understanding.

While this model has provided foundational education for millions over the years, it comes with undeniable flaws. Some students struggle to keep up, feeling overwhelmed and discouraged. Other students find the material too easy and quickly lose interest. The result? Frustration, disengagement, and, in many cases, an increased risk of dropping out. Meanwhile, educators are stretched thin, trying to support diverse learning needs without the flexibility or resources to do so effectively.

However, in 2025, education is evolving. We are seeing the entrance of AI-based personalized learning, a transformative approach that recognizes students do not all learn the same way or at the same speed. Instead of forcing everyone into a one-size-fits-all system, personalized learning adapts the curriculum to individual needs, abilities, and interests. Imagine a classroom where each student receives instruction tailored to their strengths, where learning feels more like an adventure than a chore.

Beyond customization, AI can revolutionize the way students receive feedback. No longer do students need to wait for test results or progress reports as AI offers immediate, data-driven insights, highlighting areas for improvement and celebrating successes in the moment. It can recommend supplementary resources, track progress and tendencies over time, and help teachers refine their strategies to support every learner effectively.

What is driving this shift is technology. With AI-powered tutoring, adaptive learning software, and real-time data analytics, educators can now track student progress with unprecedented accuracy. Gamified lessons make learning more interactive and engaging, while digital platforms adjust content dynamically, ensuring students grasp concepts before moving forward.

With the wide availability of new generative AI and language models, such as ChatGPT, Claude, and Gemini, new possibilities in learning are now available to society at large. These **large language models** (**LLMs**) open up a world of generative technologies that have the ability to create new and valuable outputs with little to no input. These outputs include text, video, art, and music. While these LLM developments assist in the creation of a large range of natural language tasks such as translation, question answering, and summarization, there are challenges that we will explore throughout this book related to security, privacy, and bias.

Personalized learning is not just an educational trend; it is an AI revolution. By meeting students where they are and empowering them to take ownership of their education, AI is redefining what is possible in the classroom. The question is: Are we ready to embrace the future of learning?

Real-time insights for tailored instruction

Personalized learning has long been a cornerstone of effective education and an aspirational goal for educators. The historical dream of tailoring learning to the unique needs, preferences, and pace of each student has often been out of reach due to logistical challenges. However, with the integration of AI into education, this vision is finally becoming a reality. AI opens the door to a new era of individualized learning, overcoming longstanding barriers and reshaping how we think about education, as celebrated in the following figure:

Figure 1.1: Personalized learning: Teacher, student, and AI working together

Historically, education systems have struggled to balance individuality with the scalability and standardized goals of curricula. During the *Industrial Revolution*, education mirrored the factory system, focusing on efficiency and uniformity to prepare students the same way the system prepared workers for a growing industrial economy. Classrooms were structured to manage large groups of students, with standardized instruction designed to ensure consistent delivery and predictable outputs. While this model expanded access to education, it came at a significant cost. The rigidity of the system often stifled creativity and failed to address diverse learning styles, paces, and the interests of individual students.

Teachers have always recognized the value of personalized learning, but have always been constrained by time, resources, and the sheer size of their classrooms. Addressing the unique needs of each student required more time and attention than most teachers had the capacity to realistically provide. Additionally, traditional tools for assessing progress, such as standardized tests, offered limited insight into a student's understanding, leaving educators with an incomplete picture of individual needs.

During the global COVID-19 pandemic, students and educators were challenged to shift their status quo. Many educational institutions quickly pivoted from in-person instruction to online only. Students were given, or required to purchase, computer devices, and leverage meeting software such as Zoom or Microsoft Teams in order to connect with instructors and other students in a virtual classroom setting. Teachers were challenged to adapt to new instruction styles and pay attention to students in virtual settings, and students were challenged to sit through hours of virtual instruction without much personal interaction with others. These challenges were a catalyst for the creation of additional AI-powered solutions, allowing both educators and students to learn and thrive in new ways. While most teachers and students are back in an in-person classroom setting, the learning, adaptation, and adoption of AI solutions continue to excel. Even if the use of technology for in-class instruction is less than during the pandemic, teachers are now more apt to include the use of educational technologies in their curriculum.[1]

Today, AI is revolutionizing this dynamic by introducing adaptive technologies that can easily customize learning experiences in real time. AI-powered platforms analyze vast amounts of data that provide insights into how students engage with material, providing detailed insights into their strengths, weaknesses, and preferences. These systems use this information to adjust content delivery, student pacing, and teaching methods that suit the individual, helping to ensure that learning is truly tailored to the individual at each stage in their development. For example, AI-based adaptive learning systems can help refine lesson plans on the fly, allowing students who excel in a subject to advance quickly while ensuring those who struggle receive targeted support.

Real-time insights generated by AI systems can further enhance the learning experience. Intelligent tutors, for instance, monitor a student's progress and offer immediate feedback or supplemental resources, much like a dedicated personal tutor. This ensures that students remain engaged and supported, fostering an environment where curiosity and mastery can flourish. Ironically, AI can also support the human experience that students are familiar with. These AI tools also help teachers identify patterns that might otherwise go unnoticed, such as a student consistently struggling with a specific concept, enabling timely intervention.

AI also addresses significant historical challenges in education, particularly in terms of accessibility and inclusivity. Traditional classrooms often struggle to accommodate students with disabilities or language barriers, leaving these learners at a disadvantage. AI-powered tools like speech-to-text systems, language translation applications, computer vision, and customizable content delivery ensure that all students can participate fully in the learning process. Additionally, remote learning platforms powered by AI can help to extend educational opportunities to underserved and geographically isolated communities, breaking down barriers that once seemed insurmountable.

Another area where AI is making notable progress is in enhancing the role of teachers. While technology provides tailored instruction, it can also free educators from repetitive tasks, such as grading and basic content delivery. This allows teachers to focus their time on higher-order

1 Pozo, J., Cabellos, B., & Del Puy Pérez Echeverría, M. (2024). Has the educational use of digital technologies changed after the pandemic? A longitudinal study. PLoS ONE, 19(12), e0311695. https://doi.org/10.1371/journal.pone.0311695

tasks like mentoring, fostering critical thinking, and nurturing creativity. Far from replacing teachers, AI will serve as a powerful ally in the future, amplifying their ability to connect with and support students.

The integration of AI into education also helps align personalized learning with broader curriculum goals. By helping to harmonize individual learning paths with established milestones, AI can ensure that students meet critical objectives while still pursuing their unique interests and strengths. A study conducted by the *International Journal of Innovative Science and Research Technology* explores how multimodal AI, the integration of different forms of AI such as audio, video, and language, influences learning. By using different AI modalities during instruction, the AI systems have the ability to personalize and provide more accurate feedback to students.[2] This is crucial for preparing students to thrive in a complex and interconnected world.

Despite all of its promises, the use of AI in education is not without challenges. Ethical considerations, such as model transparency, data privacy and algorithmic bias, must be carefully managed to ensure equitable outcomes. Moreover, the human element of education, empathy, understanding, and the cultivation of social skills, must remain central in a world of AI. It cannot replace the role of a teacher in inspiring, motivating, and guiding students, but it can augment these efforts in meaningful ways.

Squirrel AI, a case study on personalized learning

Squirrel AI[3], an AI-powered education company based in China, offers an exemplary case study of how AI can enhance personalized learning. Squirrel AI's platform uses AI to assess students' current knowledge level, identify learning gaps, and continuously adjust content to address those gaps. The system applies machine learning algorithms to analyze student behavior and provides individualized recommendations and lessons, ensuring that each student is always challenged at the appropriate level.

In the study, *Performance comparison of an AI-based Adaptive Learning System in China*[4], the authors evaluate the effectiveness of Squirrel AI compared to traditional classroom instruction and another adaptive learning platform, BOXFiSH[5]. The results show that students using the

Squirrel AI system performed better in both English and math learning than those receiving traditional instruction from expert human teachers or those using BOXFiSH. This suggests that AI-powered adaptive learning systems can enhance student performance by providing personalized, real-time feedback and adapting to individual learning needs.

---

2 Arjunan, G. (2024). AI Beyond Text: Integrating vision, audio, and language for multimodal learning. In International Journal of Innovative Science and Research Technology (Vol. 9, Issue 11, pp. 1911–1912) [Journal-article]. https://ijisrt.com/assets/upload/files/IJISRT24NOV1542.pdf
3 Home - Squirrel AI. (2025, February 11). Squirrel AI. https://squirrelai.com/
4 Cui, W., Xue, Z., & Thai, K. (2019, January 29). Performance comparison of an AI-based Adaptive Learning System in China. arXiv.org.https://arxiv.org/abs/1901.10268?utm_source=chatgpt.com
5 Teaching Method - BOXFiSH. (n.d.). https://www.boxfish.cn/en/guide.html

In 2020, *Squirrel AI Learning* by *Yixue Group* received the prestigious *UNESCO AI Innovation Award* for its groundbreaking work in adaptive learning technology. This award, under the theme *Artificial Intelligence and Inclusion,* affirmed Squirrel AI Learning's role as a leader in promoting personalized high-quality learning with AI recognition of learning patterns and its contribution towards the direction of more inclusion and equity in education.

Squirrel AI continues to make strides in adaptive learning by using vast amounts of learning behavior data to fine-tune their first all-subject **Large Adaptive Model (LAM)**, resulting in their ability to correctly represent students' learning profiles and provide customized learning solutions.[6] They have since expanded beyond *China* to the global market, with the founder, *Derek Li,* seen as one of the world's premier AI education thought leaders.[7] While benefits abound in AI platforms that are able to deliver personalized learning, challenges are also apparent. Chief among the challenges is maintaining personal data privacy and security. With the vast amounts of data needed to train the model, it has become apparent that keeping the private data of students safe and secure is paramount to the success of the platform.

In the age of AI, personalized learning is no longer a distant ideal but a real-life, evolving practice that redefines what is possible in education. It transforms classrooms into dynamic, student-centered environments where every learner can unlock their potential in new and unique ways. By addressing historical challenges and leveraging cutting-edge technologies, AI can help foster and usher in a generation better equipped to navigate the complexities of the modern world. The future of education is here, and it is as individualized as the students it serves.

Personalized learning and AI

Today, instructors are often stretched thin, trying to address individual needs while managing large groups of students. This is a prime situation where adaptive technologies, powered by AI, have emerged as transformative tools for supporting personalized learning. The diverse needs of each student necessitate a unique learning plan that draws on their strengths and bolsters opportunities for excelling in any setting. With the power of AI, teachers now have the ability to better meet the needs of each individual student while ensuring larger classroom sizes can easily move forward with skill development together. The following figure showcases AI instruction:

---

6 Squirrel Ai Learning. (2024, March 12). Squirrel Ai Speaks at Harvard + MIT Joint Symposium on the Future of AI-based Adaptive Learning. PR Newswire. https://www.prnewswire.com/news-releases/squirrel-ai-speaks-at-harvard--mit-joint-symposium-on-the-future-of-ai-based-adaptive-learning-302086461.html
7 Flannery, R. (2025, February 18). Derek Li and Squirrel Ai aim to lead the future of AI-Driven education. Forbes. https://www.forbes.com/sites/forbeschina/2025/02/18/derek-li-and-squirrel-ai-aim-to-lead-the-future-of-ai-driven-education/

Figure 1.2: AI can help teach every student

Adaptive learning systems and AI-driven platforms

Adaptive learning systems leverage AI to create a personalized learning environment that adjusts in real time to a student's performance. These platforms are designed to deliver content that matches the learner's current ability level, continually challenging them without overwhelming them. As a student works through exercises, the AI platform analyzes responses and tailors subsequent questions to better align with their skill level. DreamBox Math[8] (K-8), for example, is an AI-powered platform that adapts math lessons for students based on their individual responses, providing real-time adjustments in difficulty and learning pace. Think of adaptive technologies as AI tools that help students accomplish their learning goals in the way that is best for them as an individual.

Examples of adaptive technologies include:

- **Tailored content delivery**: As a student learns, the content platform adapts to the learner's progress by delivering customized lessons, quizzes and activities. It helps the student keep pace with the educational objectives while challenging them and assisting with areas where they may need additional assistance.

- **Real-time feedback**: As students learn, real-time feedback provides immediate insights. For example, when a student answers a question incorrectly, they are notified immediately and provided with additional context and similar problems to help reinforce the learning and concepts being taught.

- **Dynamic learning paths**: Customized and personalized learning designed to guide students on a path toward subject mastery. This AI-driven system helps to identify gaps in a student's knowledge and provides the flexibility to learn with a non-rigid educational plan.

8 DreamBox by Discovery Education. (2025, January 8). Online math & reading programs for students | DreamBox by Discovery Education. https://www.dreambox.com/

Recent advances in adaptive learning are made possible by the ability of AI to enhance personalization through the integration of LLMs into the learning platforms, making interactive tutors, multimodal capabilities, real-time adaptation, and collaborative learning a reality. The natural interaction these LLMs, such as with ChatGPT, can enable through conversational dialogue with students allows for greater engagement and effective learning experiences.

Elementary and secondary education

Adaptive learning platforms such as *Khan Academy*[9], *DreamBox*[10] and *Smart Sparrow*[11] provide differentiated instruction at the elementary and secondary level, revolutionizing how students interact with core subjects like math, reading, and science. They provide the right level of instruction and challenge based on where the student is in their knowledge journey. By meeting students where they are, the tools help prevent both frustration and boredom and ensure progress through a fun and engaging experience.

Higher education

Personalized learning platforms like **Assessment and Learning in Knowledge Spaces (ALEKS)**[12] are increasingly being used in higher education settings. The individualized problems, constructive feedback, and practice allow students to learn at their own pace while instructors can track both individual and group progress through detailed dashboards. This ensures that the educator can best monitor the progress of the full class and ensure the overall pace progresses, giving students specialized instruction to deepen their understanding.

Additional tools such as ChatGPT[13] and Claude AI[14] are being adopted and integrated into higher education classrooms to assist with:

- Personalized tutoring (interactive learning, adaptive feedback and 24/7 availability on demand).

- Research assistance (summary generation and providing insights).

- Writing assistance (content generation, error detection, grammar and style support, and plagiarism detection).

The integration of adaptive learning systems in higher education is not without challenges. Ethical concerns, including data privacy, accessibility, bias in AI models and the autonomy of

9 Khan Academy. (n.d.). https://www.khanacademy.org/
10 DreamBox by Discovery Education. (2025b, February 12). Online math & reading programs for students | DreamBox by Discovery Education. https://www.dreambox.com/
11 Smart Sparrow. (n.d.). Smart Sparrow. https://www.smartsparrow.com/
12 ALEKS | Learning Solutions | McGraw Hill Higher Education. (n.d.). https://www.mheducation.com highered/aleks.html
13 Naznin, K., Mahmud, A. A., Nguyen, M., & Chua, C. (2025). ChatGPT Integration in Higher Education for Personalized Learning, academic writing, and coding Tasks: A Systematic review. Computers, 14(2), 53. https://doi.org/10.3390/computers14020053
14 Praxis AI pioneers AI-driven education with Claude in Amazon Bedrock. (n.d.). Anthropic. Retrieved March 30, 2025, from https://www.anthropic.com/customers/praxis

teachers and students, is discussed in detail in *Chapter 10, Data Security and Ethical Considerations in AI*. Academic integrity, another concern with the adoption of AI in education, is core to maintaining quality learning free from bias, trust and a strong reputation. Educational institutions are learning and adapting established practices and policies to best protect their academic integrity with the inclusion of AI tools. Updated standards around plagiarism are a prime example of how academic institutions are working to protect their reputation and integrity.[15]

Special education

Adaptive technologies such as text-to-speech and speech-to-text features, visual aids, **augmented reality (AR)**, **virtual reality (VR)** and gamified learning lessons assist students with learning disabilities, ensuring they can more easily keep pace with their traditional learner peers. Through the use of adaptive technologies, a student with dyslexia, for example, can use AI tools to improve reading fluency by receiving audio prompts and instant corrections, giving them more confidence in their learning abilities. Students with **attention deficit hyperactivity disorder (ADHD)** or autism can benefit from AR through behavioral interventions where real-time prompts and feedback are given, helping the student stay on task and better manage their behavior. Similarly, students on the autism spectrum could benefit from VR environments that generate real-life scenarios that create a safe space for these kids to practice their social interactions and develop their communication skills.[16] This topic is covered in detail in *Chapter 6, AI for Diverse Learning Needs*.

Empowering educators

While modern adaptive technologies primarily focus on enhancing the student's personal experience, they also empower educators to make data-driven decisions on what and how the student experiences content. Here is how:

- **Insights into student performance**: AI platforms help generate detailed analytics, highlight trends, strengths, and areas of improvement for individual students, as well as entire classes, schools, districts, and states. Educators can use this data to design targeted interventions, such as forming small groups for peer collaboration or adjusting lesson plans to address widespread trends and challenges.

- **Time savings**: By automating routine tasks like grading and progress tracking, AI-based adaptive technologies can help free up educators to focus on fostering meaningful human connections with students and exploring creative teaching methods.

15 Ahmad, H., & Fauzi, M. A. (2024). Plagiarism in academic writing in Higher Education Institutions: A Bibliometric analysis. International Journal on Social and Education Sciences, 6(1), 64–84. https://doi.org/10.46328/ijonses.623

16 Manu, & Author_Name. (2025, March 18). Top 5 immersive technology trends for the upcoming 2025. YORD | XR & AI Creative Studio. https://yordstudio.com/top-5-immersive-technology-trends-for-the-upcoming-2025-year/

- **Professional development**: AI-based adaptive systems can also support teachers' growth by identifying areas where they might benefit from additional training or **professional development (PD)** resources, offering personalized PD pathways similar to those provided for students.

Overall, teachers have reported that the use of generative AI in the classroom is beneficial, especially for reducing time spent on administrative tasks, adaptive learning support, improving student engagement and helping to enhance a student's learning.[17] In a study published in the *IAFOR Journal of Education: Technology in Education,* it was noted that instructors who perceive AI to be useful are more likely to use AI for educational purposes. This study also indicates that a supportive educational institution is key to the adoption of AI in the educational setting, helping to better train and support instructors.[18]

Fostering student autonomy

One of the most significant advantages of adaptive learning is its potential to cultivate self-directed learners. By providing students with immediate personal feedback and control over their learning paths, these tools encourage and empower students to take ownership of their education. This aligns closely with Montessori principles[19] of fostering independence and respect for individual development.

For example, a high school student preparing for standardized tests might use an AI-driven platform to identify weak areas, set personal goals, and monitor their own progress. The system not only adapts to their pace but also builds their confidence by showing tangible improvement over time.

Challenges and considerations

While these AI-based adaptive technologies hold immense promise, they are not without challenges. Some of these challenges include:

- **Equity and access**: The digital divide remains a significant barrier to widespread adoption. Even in today's climate, students in under-resourced schools may lack access to the necessary devices or internet connectivity to benefit from these tools. Policymakers and educators must work to address these disparities to ensure all learners can access personalized resources.

---

17 Slagg, A. (2024, September 30). AI in Education in 2024: Educators Express Mixed Feelings on the Technology's Future. Technology Solutions That Drive Education. https://edtechmagazine.com/k12/article/2024/09/ai-education-2024-educators-express-mixed-feelings-technologys-future-perfcon
18 Bakhadirov, M., Alasgarova, R., & Rzayev, J. (2024). Factors influencing teachers' use of artificial intelligence for instructional purposes. In IAFOR Journal of Education, IAFOR Journal of Education: Technology in Education (Vol. 12, Issue 2). https://files.eric.ed.gov/fulltext/EJ1440077.pdf
19 Natalie. (2021, September 24). What is Montessori? 7 Principles of the Montessori Method. Montessori Up! https://www.montessoriup.com/what-is-montessori/

- **Algorithmic bias**: AI systems are only as good as the data they are trained on. If training data reflects biases, whether cultural, gender-based, socioeconomic, or otherwise, if deliberate efforts are not made, these adaptive technologies risk perpetuating those biases. Developers and educators must prioritize fairness, safety, security, and inclusivity in AI design.

- **Over-reliance on technology**: While AI can enhance learning, it should not replace the human touch that educators bring to the classroom. Teachers can play a crucial role in guiding students, fostering critical thinking, and addressing emotional and social needs, areas where technology cannot yet replicate human interaction.

- **Privacy concerns**: Adaptive technologies collect vast amounts of data on students, raising questions about how and where this information is stored, used, and protected. As a result, educational institutions need to be more diligent than ever. In March 2025, a widely used *Student Information System*, *PowerSchool*, experienced a global privacy breach that exposed millions of sensitive student and teacher records.[20] This breach remained undetected for nine days, giving the perpetrators the benefit of time to dig into children's sensitive information. Data breaches continue to raise questions about what needs to be done to secure our students' information. It likely is a multipronged approach where advocacy groups, government and schools must define and implement robust data security measures and communicate transparently with parents or guardians about privacy policies.

Many organizations and governments around the world are working to better regulate and provide guidance to help mitigate many of these challenges. One such framework, developed by UNESCO, called **Rights, Openness, Access and Multi-stakeholder Governance (ROAM)**, works to ensure AI in education addresses concerns such as ethical issues and human rights.[21]

Best practices for implementation

To maximize the benefits of AI-based adaptive technologies while addressing potential pitfalls, educators and administrators can consider the following strategies:

- **Blend AI-based learning with traditional methods**: Rather than relying solely on AI tools, combine them with teacher-led instruction to create a balanced and holistic learning environment.

- **Invest in professional development**: Provide teachers with AI training to effectively integrate adaptive technologies into their classrooms and interpret the data these tools generate.

20 Fioccola, D. (2025, March 27). The PowerSchool Breach: A Privacy Lesson on Third-Party Risk Exposure | Proskauer on Privacy. Proskauer on Privacy. https://privacylaw.proskauer.com/2025/03/articles/data-breaches/the-powerschool-breach-a-privacy-lesson-on-third-party-risk-exposure/
21 PDF.js viewer. (n.d.). https://unesdoc.unesco.org/in/documentViewer.xhtml?v=2.1.196&id=p::usmarc-def_0000376709&file=/in/rest/annotationSVC/DownloadWatermarkedAttachment/attach_import_761b-cdad-d1e3-40c9-819d-03c4ac725f26%3F_%3D376709eng.pdf&locale=en&multi=true&ark=/ark:/48223/pf0000376709/PDF/376709eng.pdf#AI%20in%20education_pages.indd%3A.14137%3A1018

- **Engage stakeholders**: Involve parents, students, business, and community members in discussions about AI adoption to build trust and ensure alignment with educational goals.

- **Monitor and evaluate**: Continuously assess the effectiveness of adaptive technologies, gather feedback from teachers and students to refine implementation strategies. Reinforcement learning is a key strategy here.

UNESCO produced guidelines for AI in education which included a human-centered approach to responsible AI implementation.[22] These guidelines detail steps for not only governments to consider for the regulation of AI in educational settings, but also for the roles teachers play in helping students learn and understand the appropriate use of AI technologies in the classroom.

Future of AI-based adaptive technologies

As AI continues to evolve, personalized learning using AI will continue to evolve. Emerging trends include:

- **Emotion-sensing AI**: AI Tools that can adjust lessons based on students' emotional states, helping to promote engagement and reducing frustration.

- **Collaborative AI platforms**: Systems that help to facilitate peer learning by intelligently grouping students for collaborative projects.

- **Lifelong learning support**: AI-based adaptive technologies designed to support learners at all stages of life, from preschool to professional development.

These advancements promise to make education more inclusive, engaging, impactful, and effective, empowering students and educators to thrive in an AI-driven world. According to a Forbes article, AI will take the lead in developing personalized learning paths for students from identification of need to analysis to the deployment of content. This **decision intelligence**, whereby AI has the ability to analyze vast amounts of data and make informed recommendations, has the potential to assist both the instructors and students through an adaptable personalized learning plan.[23]

AI-based adaptive technologies represent a paradigm shift in education, offering personalized learning experiences that empower students and support educators. By tailoring content, pacing, and feedback to individual needs, AI-driven tools make learning more accessible and engaging for a broad set of diverse learners. Their successful implementation requires careful consideration of equity, ethics, and teacher engagement.

---

22 Guidance for generative AI in education and research. (2024, June 19). UNESCO. Retrieved March 31, 2025, from https://www.unesco.org/en/articles/guidance-generative-ai-education-and-research
23 Ravaglia, R. (2024, December 28). AI in education innovators identify directions expected in 2025. Forbes. https://www.forbes.com/sites/rayravaglia/2024/12/28/innovators-see-ai-in-education-unlocking-digital-promise-in-2025/

Plato's vision of education

The legendary Plato envisioned education as the foundation of a just and virtuous society. In Plato's Republic, he proposed a model where education nurtures the soul, cultivating wisdom, courage, and temperance to achieve harmony within individuals and the state[24]. For Plato, true education goes beyond mere knowledge acquisition; it helps shape character and fosters critical thinking, guiding individuals toward the ideals of the good and the just. He emphasized the role of philosophers as educators, entrusted with enlightening the guardians of society. Plato's vision endures as a call to view education not as a tool for utility, but as a path to virtue and justice for future generations.

Plato's vision of education can be seen as the foundation of today's ethical debates involving AI integration in education. New courses are being developed and taught in some of the most prestigious universities, where the debate ensues regarding whether computer programs or technologies, specifically AI, can distinguish right from wrong. One example is MIT's ethics of computing course, where philosophy meets technology through an interdisciplinary approach to ethical questions.[25]

Role of education in a just society

Education plays a fundamental role in shaping a just society by cultivating virtue, rational thought, and a sense of shared responsibility among its members. Rooted in the ideals of philosophers like Plato, education is not merely a mechanism for acquiring knowledge but can help to contribute to a transformative process that will nurture the moral and intellectual capacities necessary for justice. A well-educated populace understands and values principles of fairness, equity, and collaboration, laying the foundation for a harmonious and balanced society. And to be frank, an uneducated populace will not.

Central to this vision is the cultivation of virtue, qualities like honesty, empathy, and courage, through education. By encouraging critical thinking, perspective, and rational discourse, education can help empower individuals to engage with diverse perspectives and make informed decisions. This fosters not only personal growth but also the ability to contribute meaningfully to the collective good.

Personalized learning can help amplify the role of education in a just society by addressing the unique needs and potential of each individual. Tailored approaches ensure that every learner, regardless of background or ability, has equitable access to opportunities for intellectual growth. By embracing diversity and inclusiveness, personalized education can help to promote fairness and strengthen societal cohesion.

---

24 What does Plato say about education in The Republic? - WisdomShort.com. (2024, February 7). WisdomShort.com. https://wisdomshort.com/philosophers/plato/on-education-in-the-republic
25 Bridging philosophy and AI to explore computing ethics. (2025, February 11). MIT News | Massachusetts Institute of Technology. https://news.mit.edu/2025/bridging-philosophy-and-ai-to-explore-computing-ethics-0211

In essence, education serves as both a mirror and a compass for a just, functioning society, reflecting its values while guiding its progress.

AI's potential to foster virtue and wisdom

AI has the potential to transform education by serving as a powerful guide in fostering both moral and intellectual virtues in students. Traditionally, nurturing virtues such as empathy, integrity, and critical thinking has relied on an individual educator's ability to tailor lessons to the diverse needs of their students. However, with AI's adaptive capabilities, educators now have tools to assist them in deepening and personalizing this process, unlocking pathways for student character development and intellectual growth that were previously unattainable.

AI excels in identifying individual strengths and weaknesses, enabling it to craft personalized learning experiences that encourage self-awareness and mastery. For instance, intelligent systems can employ AI tools to assess a student's progress in real time, offering challenges that stretch their abilities while reinforcing areas of need. This tailored approach cultivates perseverance, self-discipline, and a sense of accomplishment, qualities foundational to wisdom and virtue.

Beyond academics, AI can facilitate the exploration of moral reasoning through simulations and ethical dilemmas, providing students with curated opportunities to reflect on their values and decision-making processes. It can also help bridge cultural and social divides, offering tailored insights into diverse perspectives and fostering empathy.

By aligning learning paths with each student's personal background and potential, AI can leverage their background to nurture both their intellect and character. Far from being a mere tool for knowledge acquisition, AI emerges as a wise mentor for holistic growth, guiding students toward a deeper understanding of themselves, others, and the world. In this new era, AI enables education to inform minds and help virtuous, wise individuals ready to contribute to a better society.

Tests of wisdom and virtue

In exploring this concept, the idea of these four classic thought experiments was intriguing, with the potential application of AI:

- **The prisoner's dilemma**: A classic exercise. Two individuals are arrested and interrogated separately. Each can either betray the other (known as defecting) or remain silent (cooperating). If both remain silent, they receive a light sentence. If one defects and the other cooperates, the defector goes free while the cooperator receives a harsh sentence. If both defect, they receive moderate sentences. The dilemma highlights the tension between individual rationality (defection) and collective benefit (cooperation), often used to explore trust, collaboration, and competition in social and strategic contexts.

- **The tragedy of the commons**: This thought experiment illustrates the conflict between individual and collective interests over shared resources. Imagine a group of farmers using a common pasture. Each benefits from adding more livestock, but if everyone overuses the pasture to serve their own personal needs, it becomes depleted, harming all. The tragedy explores how unregulated self-interest can lead to the overexploitation of communal goods, raising questions about sustainability, governance, and cooperation.

- **The ultimatum game**: One participant (the proposer) decides how to divide a sum of money between themselves and another participant (the responder). The responder can accept or reject any offer. If rejected, neither participant gets anything. Rationally, the responder should accept any non-zero offer, but emotions and perceptions of fairness often drive rejections of unequal splits. This game probes the interplay between self-interest, fairness, and social behavior.

- **Newcomb's paradox**: A player faces two boxes: one transparent, containing $1,000, and one opaque, which may contain $1,000,000 or nothing. A predictor, who has a near-perfect record, places the $1,000,000 in the opaque box only if it predicts the player will take only the opaque box. If the player takes both boxes, the opaque box is empty. This paradox explores trust, rationality, free will, and decision-making in the face of predictive certainty and uncertainty. The following figure indicates the question of uncertainty in this thought experiment:

Figure 1.3: AI is not always right and can hallucinate

These thought experiments are meant to invite educators to think about their relationship with AI and AI-based tools. Human-AI-based partnerships will be a part of our human future and we can learn and develop our own perspectives from these thought experiments.

Balance of individuality and collective good

The tension between personal growth and the collective good has been a persistent theme in philosophy, education, and governance throughout history. On one hand, fostering individual potential unlocks creativity, innovation, and fulfillment; on the other, societal progress depends on cooperation, cohesion, shared goals, and collective community effort. This duality presents a challenge: how can we reconcile these seemingly opposing needs to create a harmonious society? With the advent of AI, there is a growing belief that technology can bridge this gap through tailored learning and societal alignment.

Case for personal growth

Personal growth has been the basis of self-actualization and the engine of societal progress. History has shown us that individual achievement often leads to breakthroughs that benefit the collective. Innovators like *Marie Curie*, who discovered *polonium and radium,* leading to medical advances such as radiation therapy for cancer[26], and *Nikola Tesla*, who changed the power industry by developing AC systems and the invention of the AC induction motor[27], pursued personal intellectual growth, yet their discoveries transformed entire fields and improved countless lives through medical advancements and energy technologies.

A focus on individual development can help nurture creativity, resilience, and critical thinking, equipping people to solve complex problems. Education that prioritizes personal growth empowers learners to explore their interests and strengths, fostering intrinsic motivation and lifelong learning. This approach acknowledges and respects the diversity of human potential, ensuring that individuals are not limited by one-size-fits-all systems that stifle unique talents.

Personal growth contributes to mental health and well-being. When individuals feel empowered to pursue their passions and develop their skills, they are more likely to contribute meaningfully to society. A fulfilled, self-actualized individual often becomes an engaged citizen, actively participating in the community and supporting its collective goals.

Case for the collective good

While personal growth is vitally important, societies thrive on collaboration, shared values, and a shared, collective purpose. A purely individualistic approach risks fragmenting this societal cohesion, where self-interest overshadows the common good. Historically, from the agricultural revolution to modern democratic systems, civilizations have succeeded by building on a shared vision to foster cooperation.

The needs of society often require individuals to prioritize collective goals over personal aspirations. For example, during crises like global pandemics or natural disasters, society depends on shared sacrifice and collective action from individuals joining together. Education systems have traditionally emphasized standardized curricula to instill shared knowledge, values, and social norms essential for maintaining order and mutual understanding.

Furthermore, society's infrastructure, from healthcare to public safety, relies on collective effort and a commitment to the greater good. If individuals exclusively pursue personal

26 Marie Curie the scientist | Bio, facts & quotes. (n d.). Marie Curie. https://www.mariecurie.org.uk/about-us/our-history/marie-curie-the-scientist
27 Tesla Memorial Society of New York. (n.d.). Tesla Society. Retrieved April 3, 2025, from https://www.teslasociety.com/hall_of_fame.htm

interests, essential societal functions may be neglected, leading to inequality, instability, and inefficiency. Striking a balance between individuality and societal needs ensures equitable access to resources and opportunities, fostering a sense of fairness and unity. The same is true in education.

Reconciliation through AI by bridging the divide

Artificial intelligence offers unprecedented opportunities to harmonize personal growth with societal needs. By leveraging adaptive technologies, AI can tailor education and skill development to individual student strengths, preferences, and learning styles while ensuring alignment with the collective objectives of society.

AI-powered personalized learning platforms can provide students with custom pathways that cater to their personal learning interests while embedding core societal values and knowledge. For instance, a student passionate about environmental science could receive an education that not only deepens their expertise but also emphasizes the broader importance of sustainability and community responsibility. AI can help make this connection.

Additionally, AI can analyze societal trends and workforce demands, ensuring that individualized learning aligns with the collective needs of the labor force. It can help balance personal aspirations with practical considerations, preparing individuals for meaningful roles in society without sacrificing their unique potential. For example, AI could guide students toward professions that match their abilities and passions while addressing critical skill shortages in diverse fields like healthcare or renewable energy.

AI can also foster empathy and collaboration by exposing learners to diverse perspectives through simulations, virtual exchanges, and curated content. This approach bridges cultural and social divides, reinforcing the idea that personal growth and societal well-being are interconnected.

Path forward

Striking the balance between personal growth and the needs of society requires a nuanced approach. Education systems and policymakers must avoid framing the two as mutually exclusive, as well as completely integrating the two. Instead, they should embrace models that integrate individual development with collective responsibility, leveraging technology like AI to facilitate this alignment. Offer a *what if* possibility versus a baked formula.

The challenge lies not in choosing one over the other but in recognizing their symbiotic relationship. Personal growth fuels societal progress, and a thriving society provides the foundation for individual fulfillment. AI serves as a tool to help optimize this dynamic, enabling a future where individuality and the collective good coexist in harmony.

By fostering a society that values both the individual and the collective, we can build a world that respects personal potential while ensuring equity, sustainability, and shared success.

Through thoughtful integration of technology, this balance is not only achievable but essential for navigating the complexities of our tightly interconnected future.

AI has the potential to play a transformative role in ethical education, particularly in reinforcing moral reasoning. By leveraging AI-driven simulations and interactive case studies, students, educators, and philosophers can engage in complex ethical dilemmas, exploring the consequences of their decisions in a controlled virtual environment. AI can provide real-time feedback, highlight ethical principles in a dialogue, and encourage critical thinking by presenting diverse perspectives.

Historically, moral education has relied on philosophical discourse, religious teachings, and societal norms to drive home key points. AI can enhance this process by analyzing historical patterns of ethical decision-making and drawing historical parallels to contemporary challenges. Moreover, it can personalize learning, adapting to an individual's cognitive development and moral maturity.

However, ethical AI education must be carefully designed to avoid bias and ensure alignment with a diverse set of cultural values. While AI can facilitate moral reasoning, human educators remain essential in helping to guide discussions, fostering empathy, and ensuring that technology serves as a tool for ethical growth rather than a replacement for human judgment.

Role of AI in fostering independence

Artificial intelligence is revolutionizing education by empowering students to take charge of their own learning. With its powerful ability to adapt and respond to individual needs, AI helps to foster autonomy, decision-making, and self-confidence, essential skills for lifelong learning. By providing tailored tools and personalized guidance, AI enables students to progress at their own pace, explore their interests, and develop critical thinking skills. For example, in a *Cogent Education* study on language learning with the use of AI, results indicated that AI strongly contributes to promoting learner independence and autonomy by providing real-time feedback, adaptive learning paths and autonomous lesson practice.[28]

By nurturing autonomy, AI transforms students from passive recipients of knowledge to active participants in their education. It equips the students with the skills and confidence to navigate their learning journey, preparing them for the complexities of the modern world.

Developing a complete child through AI

Throughout history, education has always evolved to meet the needs of society, from classical rote learning to student-centered approaches that prioritize critical thinking. With the advent of AI, we now have an even greater opportunity to nurture the whole child, balancing cognitive, emotional, and moral development through personalized learning in ways that have not been possible in the past. Recent studies, such as *The future of Child Development in the*

---

28 Mohebbi, A. (2024). Enabling learner independence and self-regulation in language education using AI tools: a systematic review. Cogent Education, 12(1). https://doi.org/10.1080/2331186x.2024.2433814

AI Era, showcase the interdisciplinary debates between AI and early childhood development experts.[29] It is recognized that AI has many benefits for the integration in education, although it is not without challenges and potential risks introduced, especially during early childhood development. AI-driven education is no longer confined to academic excellence; it has the potential to be applied more broadly to foster emotional intelligence, social skills, and ethical reasoning, reflecting the values of a well-rounded education with responsible AI use and ethical considerations.

Evolution of AI to reflect philosophical ideals

The future of AI in education must be rooted in the holistic development of learners, embracing the philosophies of thinkers like *John Dewey*, who believed in experiential learning[30], *Maria Montessori*, whose Montessori method took a child-centered approach to learning[31], and *Lev Vygotsky*, who felt social interactions were a critical component of cognitive development[32]. AI can move beyond simple knowledge transfer, actively adapting to students' learning styles, emotional states, and social interactions. Future innovations may include AI tutors that recognize and respond to frustration, encouraging students with tailored motivation strategies leveraging gamification tools. VR and AI integration could create immersive learning experiences, where students explore ethical dilemmas in simulated environments, honing moral reasoning in ways never before possible. AI-driven assessment could shift from standardized tests to dynamic, portfolio-based evaluations that measure intellectual curiosity, resilience, and collaboration, while engaging students in new and exciting ways.

Supporting social-emotional learning

One of the greatest challenges in modern education is ensuring that students develop emotional intelligence alongside academic knowledge. AI can help play a critical role in **social-emotional learning** (**SEL**) by detecting emotional cues in students' writing, speech, and classroom interactions. AI-driven platforms can provide real-time feedback on collaboration and communication skills, helping students practice empathy and conflict resolution in a safe and risk-free environment. Personalized AI coaches can help guide students through mindfulness exercises, self-reflection, and peer mediation, supporting emotional well-being in a way that traditional education has not been able to achieve in a scalable way, as seen in the following figure:

---

29 Neugnot-Cerioli, M., & Laurenty, O. M. (2024, May 29). The future of Child Development in the AI Era. Cross-Disciplinary perspectives between AI and child development experts. arXiv.org. https://arxiv.org/abs/2405.19275

30 Brodie, K. (2024, December 31). John Dewey: Pioneering Theories on Early Years Education. Early Years TV. https://www.earlyyears.tv/john-dewey-pioneering-theories-on-early-years-education/

31 Philosophy - Maria Montessori Academy. (n.d.). Maria Montessori Academy. https://mariamontessori-academy.net/montessori/philosophy/

32 Simply Psychology. (2024, August 9). Vygotsky's Sociocultural Theory Of Cognitive Development. https://www.simplypsychology.org/vygotsky.html

Figure 1.4*: AI can support social-emotional learning*

AI-driven holistic education across different cultures

Education has always faced global challenges. Different cultures emphasize unique aspects of holistic education, and AI must be adaptable to these diverse values. One example might be in East Asian education systems, where Confucian traditions emphasize discipline and collective well-being, AI could integrate collaborative problem-solving and moral philosophy. In Scandinavian countries, known for their child-centric, inquiry-based approaches, AI could facilitate open-ended exploration and creativity. Meanwhile, in Indigenous and community-based education models, AI might support intergenerational learning and the preservation of cultural knowledge. By embracing cultural diversity with a dynamic approach, AI can foster a truly global model of holistic education, ensuring that technology enhances—not replaces—the human experience.

Ultimately, AI in education must be guided by ethical principles that prioritize student growth across all dimensions, intellectual, cultural, social, and moral, empowering the next generation to navigate an increasingly complex world with wisdom and empathy built on top of this technology.

Conclusion

AI has emerged as a transformative force in education, addressing historical challenges and enabling personalized learning on an unprecedented scale. Traditionally, education systems have followed a one-size-fits-all model based on industrial age models, designed to accommodate large groups of students with standardized curricula. While this approach expanded access to education for decades, it often failed to address the personal, unique needs, learning styles, and paces of individual students. With its adaptive capabilities and data-driven insights, AI can redefine this dynamic, creating a tailored, personalized educational experience for every learner.

Despite its promise, integrating AI into education comes with challenges. Ethical concerns, such as security, data privacy, and algorithmic bias, must be carefully managed to ensure equitable outcomes for all constituents. Additionally, it is essential to maintain the human element of traditional education processes and infrastructure, ensuring that AI complements rather than replaces the vital role of teachers in inspiring and mentoring students.

AI represents a transformative shift in personalized learning and a sea change in education. By tailoring instruction to individual needs, learning styles and teaching techniques, we can foster a new approach to inclusivity: empowering students, educators, administrators, and government institutions, AI helps redefine what is possible in education and personalized learning. The integration of AI into education helps pave the way towards a future where every learner can unlock their potential in an individual way, contributing to a more innovative, equitable, and interconnected world.

In the next chapter, we will explore the history of technology in the classroom from clay tablets to the use of television. You will learn how advances in technology as teaching tools have led to improvements in how we educate and acquire knowledge. Opportunities are on the horizon for students and teachers who will be able to continue to grow, create and understand the world around them.

Questions

1. What does a personalized education look like in practice, and how do we implement AI tools to help best serve our students?

2. If AI can tailor learning to individual students, should we still group students by age and grade level in classrooms, or is it time to radically rethink how we structure education and the classroom?

3. How can educators and AI systems partner together to teach moral reasoning, empathy, and virtue in a world increasingly shaped by data and algorithms?

4. What guardrails should we put in place to prevent AI-powered education from amplifying existing biases and inequities, especially for students in under-resourced schools or marginalized communities?

5. How might AI shift the identity of an educator, from content expert to learning coach, instructional designer or emotional mentor, and are we preparing educators for this transformation?

6. Can AI-facilitated learning maintain and improve students' sense of belonging and connection to the material and to other humans, or does it risk making education more isolated and transactional?

7. If AI can predict future performance and personalize instruction accordingly, how do we preserve a student's right to pivot and surprise us, to grow beyond their data profile?

8. In balancing personal growth and collective good, are we ready to let go and delegate to AI to help shape civic values, or should that remain purely a human endeavor?

9. What should a whole child AI system look like, and who gets to decide which values, emotional cues, learning paths, and cultural norms it uses to shape young minds?

Exercises

1. **Classroom simulation—Designing AI-enhanced lesson plan**: Translate theory into practical steps.

    a. Choose a topic or subject that you teach (e.g., fractions, climate change, persuasive writing). Using what you have learned in this chapter:

        i.   Design two different lesson plans: one traditional and one that incorporates AI for personalization.

        ii. Include details like student inputs, how the AI tools influence content, and how you'll monitor progress.

    b. How does this change your teaching role? What new challenges arise?

2. **Ethical AI case study analysis**: Explore responsible AI and ethical complexities in AI-powered education.

    a. Read one of the thought experiments from the chapter (e.g., The Prisoner's Dilemma or The Tragedy of the Commons) and apply it to your AI-in-education scenario:

    b. **Example scenario**: An AI tool predicts that a student is unlikely to pass a course and stops showing them advanced content.

    c. Discuss in your writing or group discussion:

        • What ethical concerns arise?

        • Who should make decisions: the AI, the teacher, the student?

           What would Plato say?

3. **Data reflection journal**: Broaden awareness of AI's potential and risks in using student data.

    a. For five workdays, write daily reflections on these prompts:

        i.   What kinds of data do I (or my school) already collect on students?

        ii. How could AI enhance or misuse that data?

     iii. Where is the line between AI insight and surveillance? At the end, synthesize your entries into a 1-page reflection on how your views have evolved.

4. **Student persona deep dive**: Practice empathy and think about personalization.

    a. Create three fictional student personas based on real students that you know. Vary these by learning style, cultural background, abilities, and interests. Then, map out how an AI-powered learning environment could help:

       i. Adapt content and feedback.

       ii. Help teachers connect more meaningfully.

       iii. Pose unintended consequences or bias risks.

5. **Plato vs. AI—Debate prep**: Explore the philosophical foundations of education as outlined by Plato.

    a. **Exercise**: Split into two groups. One group argues alignment: AI is aligned with Plato's vision of virtuous education, the other argues against: AI undermines the development of wisdom and virtue. Each team must:

       i. Use quotes or ideas from the public world of AI; this chapter can help.

       ii. Prepare arguments and rebuttals grounded in educational practice. Hold a debate or write position papers.

6. **Equity impact map**: Use visual examples to explore barriers and opportunities within your organization.

    a. Draw a map or flowchart showing how AI-based personalized learning:

       i. Can help to benefit students across various demographics (e.g., ELLs, neurodivergent students, rural communities).

       ii. Will help deepen digital divides or biases. Annotate your map with examples from the chapter and potential policy or classroom interventions.

7. **Build your own AI companion**: Explore future-ready tools.

    a. Sketch, describe, and build your ideal AI teaching assistant. Consider:

       i. What features are non-negotiable.

       ii. Describe its values.

       iii. How might it interact with students and support you. Then, identify which current technologies (e.g., DreamBox, Khan Academy) come close and what is still missing.

8. **Reflection essay—The future of my classroom**: Synthesize AI learning and discuss what the future looks like.

   a. Use AI to help you write a 500-750 word essay answering: How will AI-based personalized learning reshape my role as an educator over the next five years? Include at least:

      i. 3 opportunities you are excited about what AI will do to help students.

      ii. 2 concerns or questions about the future of AI.

      iii. 1 change you could start making now.

   b. Think about sharing your essay with your boss or the parents of your students. Discuss with both.

9. **Socrates and the screen—The oral tradition and AI**: Examine historical resistance to educational technology.

   a. Attributed to Socrates (via Plato's Phaedrus): Writing will produce forgetfulness in the minds of those who learn to use it. They will trust to the external written characters and not remember of themselves. Reflect and respond to the following:

      i. Compare Socrates' argument against writing to modern concerns about students' over-reliance on AI tools.

      ii. List five ways that AI is the writing of our time? In what ways is it different?

      iii. Create a short dialogue between Socrates and an AI chatbot tutor. What would each argue about memory, wisdom, and education? Use AI to help if you want.

   b. Perform the dialogue as a skit in a workshop or team session.

10. **Tech timeline tensions—The historical fear and promise of tools**: Outline a pattern of disruption and adoption in educational history.

    a. Select three key historical classroom technologies (choose from or include others like: the printing press, the blackboard, handheld calculator, overhead projector, personal computer, the internet, AI tools). For each one:

       i. Research initial reactions from educators, students, or society.

       ii. Note what fears were expressed at the time (e.g., students will not learn math if they use calculators).

       iii. Identify the benefits that eventually emerged. Then, compare these with today's AI-driven personalized learning technologies.

       iv. What patterns are repeated?

     v.   What is genuinely different this time? Finish by writing a 1-paragraph reflection on what this history teaches us about embracing new tools in education.

Join our Discord space

Join our Discord workspace for latest updates, offers, tech happenings around the world, new releases, and sessions with the authors:

https://discord.bpbonline.com

CHAPTER 2

History of Technology in the Classroom

If we teach today as we taught yesterday, we rob our children of tomorrow.

-John Dewey

Introduction

Education has always been a gateway to knowledge, and technology has been a constant companion on our human journey, reshaping how we teach and learn. In this chapter, we embark on an exploration of the rich history of the use of technology in the classroom. This is a story of innovation, adaptation, and transformation. From ancient tools of learning, such as clay tablets and scrolls, to the digital classrooms of today powered by artificial intelligence, technology has continuously redefined the educational experience.

The path of educational technology is marked by groundbreaking advancements, from the printing press, which democratized knowledge, to the rise of computers and the internet, which connected learners across the globe. Each new tool has not only expanded access to education but also reimagined the possibilities of teaching and learning.

As we progress through these milestones, we will uncover how technical disruptions at each stage of innovation paved the way for the next. This culminates in today's powerful digital tools and personalized learning experiences driven by AI, which have emerged largely due to the changes in education triggered by the global COVID-19 pandemic. By understanding where we have been, we can better appreciate where we are headed. We look ahead to a future where technology continues to empower educators, engage students, and transform classrooms into hubs of creativity, collaboration, and discovery. The story is still unfolding, and its next chapter is ours to shape.

Structure

The chapter covers the following topics:

- Overview of the history of education
- Clay tablets
- Abacus
- Papyrus scrolls
- Hornbooks
- Gutenberg printing press in the 15th century
- Blackboard in the 19th century
- Magic lantern and slide projectors
- Role of calculators in shaping a generation
- Overhead projectors in the mid-20th century
- Radio in the early 20th century
- Television in the mid-20th century
- Personal computers in the late 20th century
- Internet in the late 20th century

Objectives

By the end of this chapter, you will understand the impact of many key technical milestones in the history of education, from ancient tools to modern digital innovations. We will explore how these technological advances have influenced instruction methods, learning experiences and access to education over time as we discuss the role of technology along with introduction resistance. In addition, you will learn how past innovations can inform the future of technology in education, including trends in AI, virtual learning, and digital collaboration tools.

Overview of the history of education

Education, in its most profound sense, is the process of sharing knowledge, passing down wisdom, skills, and experiences from one generation to the next. However, this journey of learning has never been static. Throughout history, learning has been essential for survival and development, both in the animal kingdom and human societies. In nature, animals instinctively teach their young survival skills, like hunting and foraging, often with the help of tools such as sticks, rocks, or even objects like a ball, simulating real-life challenges they need to master. These tools capture the attention of young ones and prepare them for the skills they will need to thrive in their environments. Similarly, humans have long used technology to enhance the teaching and learning process, adapting tools to share essential knowledge and provide forums for students to practice key skills. From the earliest cave paintings that taught hunting techniques to the first written tablets documenting trade and laws, technology has consistently expanded the boundaries of education, and the tools and technologies that facilitate this transfer of knowledge have undergone profound transformations.

From the ancient scribes who carved cuneiform into clay to the modern-day educators using tablets and artificial intelligence, the history of technology in the classroom is not merely a story of progress but a revolution. Each technological breakthrough, whether it is the invention of the printing press, the arrival of personal computers, or the rise of the internet, has reshaped how students learn, how teachers teach, and how knowledge is shared.

As societies have evolved, so have the tools supporting education, reflecting the ingenuity and adaptability that drive human progress. In ancient times, wax tablets and abacuses offered simple yet effective means of fostering learning, much like early mechanical innovations that paved the way for the automation we now rely on. The 15th century's invention of the printing press marked a seismic shift, democratizing access to knowledge and transforming classrooms from spaces of oral tradition to ones of individual exploration, a transition akin to the transformative potential AI holds for education today. By the 20th century, the advent of chalkboards, projectors, and filmstrips brought new technological leaps, enabling educators to convey complex ideas in more interactive and visual ways. And now, the most exciting chapter of this ongoing evolution is unfolding as AI takes center stage, poised to revolutionize the classroom experience further.

The latter half of the 20th century saw the rise of computers, calculators, and multimedia tools in classrooms, igniting both excitement and skepticism. While some critics feared the erosion of traditional skills, proponents embraced them as catalysts for creativity and deeper understanding. By the 21st century, tablets, digital whiteboards, and artificial intelligence have emerged as central pillars of education, marking the dawn of a new era where learning is no longer confined to physical spaces or rigid timeframes. A 2024 study titled *The impact of digital technology on cognitive processes and learning outcomes in early childhood* reveals mixed long-term effects of digital engagement. While it offers benefits such as strong support for math and literacy skills, it also brings negative impacts, including an increased risk of obesity and attention-related issues.[1] Each of the advancements discussed in this chapter mirrors humanity's ongoing effort to teach more effectively, much like the natural world's use of tools to foster growth and adaptability in the face of change.

---

1 UNESCO International Bureau of Education. (2024, December 10). IBE — Science of learning portal — The Impact of digital Technology on Cognitive Processes and Learning Outcomes in early childhood: Evidence from Neuroscience. IBE — Science of Learning Portal. https //solportal.ibe-unesco.org/articles/the-impact-of-digital-technology-on-cognitive-processes-and-learning-outcomes-in-early-childhood-evidence-from-neuroscience/

Clay tablets

Clay tablets played an important role in the educational system of ancient *Mesopotamia*, forming the cornerstone of their writing and learning practices. Dating back to around 3100 BCE, they are closely associated with the development of cuneiform script, the earliest known system of writing. Crafted from the abundant and malleable river clay, these tablets were inexpensive and durable, making them the ideal medium for recording and transmitting knowledge across generations, as depicted in the following figure:

Figure 2.1: *Clay tablets were one form of early learning*

Education in Mesopotamia, particularly during the Sumerian and Babylonian periods (from 3100 to 539 BCE), revolved around schools called **edubbas** (meaning tablet houses).[2] These institutions were the primary educational centers where young boys, usually from affluent families, were trained to become scribes.[3] The role of the scribe was highly esteemed, as it was essential for documenting everything from commercial transactions to royal decrees, and even the preservation of religious and literary texts. Education was, therefore, not just a means of acquiring knowledge, but a key to participating in the complex social, political, and economic fabric of Mesopotamian society. Teachers used clay tablets as a core tool to instruct students in reading, writing, arithmetic, and religious texts. Lessons often began with students copying out pre-written examples onto blank tablets. Using a reed stylus, they would carefully etch cuneiform symbols into soft clay. Once the lessons were complete, the tablets were either left to dry or baked in a kiln for permanence. This tactile process of writing was central to the learning experience, and repetition was key to mastering the technique. Students would frequently copy lines of cuneiform, gradually committing vast amounts of text to memory and perfecting their writing skills.

The educational utility of clay tablets was significant due to their versatility. They came in various sizes, depending on their intended use: smaller tablets for practice exercises, and larger ones for recording official documents or advanced scholarly texts. Some even featured grids or lines etched into the surface, helping students maintain proper alignment and uniformity in

2 Foster, Benjamin R. The Age of Sumerian Education: The Edubba and the Development of Cuneiform Writing. Chicago: University of Chicago Press, 2004.
3 AncientPages.com. (2017, November 6). EDUBA: Scribal School in Ancient Mesopotamia - Ancient Pages. Ancient Pages. https://www.ancientpages.com/2016/06/29/eduba-scribal-school-ancient-mesopotamia/

their writing. One such example, preserved in the *Cambridge University Library*, is among the oldest written objects from Sumerian times, offering insight into the educational practices of the period (*A Stray Sumerian Tablet: Unraveling the Story Behind Cambridge University Library's Oldest Written Object, University of Cambridge, 2021*).

Moreover, these tablets provide fascinating insights into the lives of students and teachers. Many surviving examples bear visible signs of corrections, teacher annotations, and even playful doodles. These small details offer a glimpse into the human side of ancient education, revealing the challenges students faced and the personalized guidance they received from their instructors. The careful preservation of these tablets over millennia underscores the significant role writing played not only as a practical skill but also as a cultural legacy that helped shape the intellectual and cultural development of Mesopotamian civilization.

The educational system that revolved around clay tablets had a profound influence on the transmission of knowledge, laying the groundwork for subsequent civilizations. The importance of writing and record-keeping that these early educational tools embodied became the foundation for later advancements in literacy, bureaucracy, and governance—elements that are still integral to modern society.

Abacus

The abacus is one of the oldest known tools for mathematics and computation. It was used extensively in education and commerce. While its origins are debated, it is most famously associated with ancient Mesopotamia and later with China, where it played a crucial role in teaching arithmetic and developing mathematical concepts such as place value, multiplication, division, and early algebraic methods, contributing to advancements in commerce, engineering, and astronomy. The following figure shows a cartoon concept of an abacus:

Figure 2.2: Abacus was one of the earliest tools to learn mathematics

Abacus in Mesopotamia[4]

In Mesopotamia, ancient counting boards, precursors to the abacus, were used as early as 2700 BCE. These boards, combined with clay tokens, enabled merchants and scribes to perform

4 Smith, M. E. (2014). The Emergence of Mathematical Calculation in Ancient Mesopotamia. Journal of Ancient Civilizations, 5(3), 45-67.

basic arithmetic like addition, subtraction, and multiplication. In educational settings, students likely used these tools to practice calculations necessary for accounting, trade, and construction.

The abacus evolved from these counting boards, with grooves or lines to organize pebbles or tokens. The first known use of the abacus-like device dates to ancient Mesopotamia, around 2300 BCE. In the early stages, Mesopotamians used a rudimentary counting board, often referred to as a calculating table, which was a precursor to the more sophisticated abacus. These early counting tools were typically made of clay or wood and were designed to help merchants, scribes, and scholars perform basic arithmetic operations, such as addition, subtraction, multiplication, and division. Though not as refined as later versions of the abacus, these counting tables played an essential role in the administration and trade of Mesopotamian cities like Ur and Babylon, where accurate record-keeping was critical.

Teachers incorporated it into lessons to improve numerical literacy and problem-solving skills. By visualizing numbers, students could grasp abstract concepts more effectively. This tactile method was essential in an era without paper or written numerals as we know them today.

Abacus in China[5]

While the Mesopotamians laid the groundwork, it was in ancient *China* where the abacus truly evolved into the form most familiar today. The Chinese abacus, known as the **suanpan**, dates to at least the 2nd century BCE, during the *Han Dynasty*. It consisted of a rectangular frame with rods or wires, each containing beads that could be moved up and down to represent different place values. The suanpan was designed to perform more complex calculations, such as square and cube roots, division, and multiplication, facilitating the growth of Chinese commerce, astronomy, engineering, and science.

The Chinese abacus was used not only by merchants but also in educational institutions, particularly in the training of scholars and mathematicians. It became an essential tool for teaching arithmetic, as it helped students visualize mathematical concepts in a way that abstract numbers and written symbols could not. The tactile nature of the abacus allowed students to physically manipulate numbers, fostering a deeper understanding of the principles of arithmetic and laying the groundwork for more complex mathematical reasoning.[6]

The educational applications of the abacus were revolutionary. Before the widespread use of written mathematics and formal numerical systems, the abacus provided a way to make abstract concepts tangible. By physically moving beads on the abacus, students could see and feel the numbers they were working with, making it an interactive and hands-on approach to learning arithmetic. This tactile learning method was invaluable, as it catered to different learning styles and helped reinforce concepts through repetition and practice.

---

5 Tsai, W. S., & Chang, Y. H. (2009). The Abacus and Its Educational Impact in China: A Historical Overview. International Journal of Mathematical Education in Science and Technology.
6 Xie, L., & Zhang, S. (2008). The History and Significance of the Abacus in Ancient Chinese Education. Chinese Journal of Educational History, 23(2), 88-102.

In both Mesopotamia and China, the abacus served as an essential tool in education, shaping the way mathematical concepts were introduced and mastered. In Mesopotamia, the abacus-like device was used in schools to train scribes in basic arithmetic, which was essential for their work in record-keeping and trade. In China, the abacus was used not only in practical applications such as commerce but also in educational settings, where it helped to cultivate a deep understanding of numbers and computation.

The abacus also helped to develop key cognitive skills in students, such as concentration, mental calculation, and problem-solving. In fact, studies have shown that regular use of the abacus can improve mental math skills and enhance memory and concentration. This ability to manipulate numbers in one's mind, which is often referred to as a mental abacus, is still taught in some countries today as a form of brain training.

Furthermore, the use of the abacus was not limited to formal educational institutions; it also had a profound impact on informal learning and community education. Merchants, traders, and craftsmen, who may not have had access to formal schools, relied on the abacus as a vital tool for everyday calculations. The abacus thus democratized access to mathematical knowledge, ensuring that even those without formal education could develop essential numerical skills.

The legacy of the abacus extends far beyond its historical context. Even as more advanced technologies and computational devices replaced it over time, the principles it embodied continue to influence modern education. The abacus fostered a deeper understanding of numbers and arithmetic that would later evolve into more complex mathematical and scientific systems. Today, the abacus is still used in parts of Asia as a tool for teaching young children basic arithmetic and in competitive mental math practices. In addition, its educational applications continue to inspire contemporary methods of active, hands-on learning that engage students in critical thinking and problem-solving.

The abacus also set the stage for the development of more sophisticated counting and calculating tools, including the advent of the mechanical calculator in the 17th century and the electronic computers of the 20th century. In this way, the abacus represents an important step in the long history of human innovation in the field of education, where technology and tools have been consistently adapted to help enhance learning and foster intellectual growth.

Papyrus scrolls

Papyrus scrolls, first used in ancient Egypt around 3000 BCE, were crucial in the development of written communication and education. Made from the papyrus plant along the Nile River, these scrolls became the primary medium for recording a wide range of information, from religious texts to administrative records, due to their durability and portability. Papyrus was not only practical but also relatively lightweight, which made it easy to transport and store, and it quickly spread beyond Egypt to Greece, Rome, and other ancient cultures.

In ancient *Egypt*, papyrus was integral to the education of scribes, highly respected professionals who documented trade, legal affairs, and religious texts. Education took place in edubbas (temple schools), where students learned to read and write by transcribing pre-existing texts onto papyrus scrolls. The repetitive nature of copying texts helped reinforce literacy and memorization, similar to the approach in Mesopotamia. Additionally, scribes were taught to write in hieratic script, which was often inscribed on papyrus for both practical and sacred purposes, such as the *Book of the Dead* for royal decrees.

As papyrus spread to Greece and Rome, it became the medium of choice for scholars and intellectuals. Greek philosophers and Roman historians used papyrus to record their works, ensuring the preservation and transmission of knowledge across generations. *The Library of Alexandria*[7], one of the most famous libraries of antiquity, contained thousands of papyrus scrolls, representing a vast wealth of knowledge from various civilizations.

The educational impact of papyrus scrolls was profound. They provided a tangible way to preserve and transmit knowledge, laying the groundwork for the intellectual practices of writing, reading, and studying. Students used papyrus for memorizing texts, practicing literacy, and mastering complex subjects like mathematics, law, and literature. The physical act of writing on papyrus also contributed to critical thinking, as students engaged with the texts they copied and analyzed. The portability of these scrolls made education more accessible, allowing scholars to travel and share knowledge with others.

Papyrus scrolls were not only educational tools but also served as cultural artifacts, preserving the intellectual heritage of ancient civilizations. They paved the way for later writing materials such as parchment and paper, which would eventually replace papyrus in medieval and Renaissance Europe. However, the legacy of papyrus is still felt today, as the written word remains central to modern education and the dissemination of knowledge.

Hornbooks

In medieval Europe, where formal education was limited to the elite and religious institutions, the hornbook emerged as one of the most important tools for teaching basic literacy and Christian teachings. The simplicity, portability, and durability of the hornbook made it an ideal educational tool for children and the first step toward broader literacy.[8]

The hornbook, in its earliest form, originated in late medieval Europe, around the 15th century. It was a wooden board, typically with a handle, on which a sheet of paper or parchment was affixed. The sheet contained basic instructional content, and the entire structure was protected by a thin layer of horn (usually from cows or goats), which was a common material in the era. This made the hornbook durable, weather-resistant, and easy to carry, ideal for children and teachers who were on the move.

The hornbook's design was straightforward: the sheet usually displayed the alphabet (in both uppercase and lowercase), numbers, and sometimes a basic religious text, like the Lord's Prayer,

---

7 Roos, Dave. "Did the Library of Alexandria Really Exist?" HowStuffWorks, 12 July 2024, https://history. howstuffworks.com/world-history/library-alexandria.htm
8 Hornbooks. (n.d.). https://victorianweb.org/genre/childlit/hornbooks.html

Psalms, or a prayer to the Holy Virgin. It was not just a simple tool for literacy but also an instrument of moral and religious education, central to the spiritual life of medieval Europe.

The hornbook was largely used in the home, rural schools, and monastic education, where it offered children a first step toward learning to read and write. The hornbook served as the bridge between a child's education in the basics and the more advanced teachings found in church schools or monasteries, where religious education was the focus.

At its core, the hornbook provided the most basic level of education, teaching children how to read and write by first introducing them to the alphabet and numerals. This tool was essential in the teaching of reading skills, a fundamental part of medieval education that allowed children to engage with religious texts and prayers.

Beyond their educational function, hornbooks became cultural objects. They were often elaborately decorated and meticulously crafted, particularly those used by wealthier families. While most hornbooks were functional, a more ornate variety was made for the elite, sometimes adorned with gold leaf, intricate designs, and even personalized inscriptions. These features made the hornbook not only a tool for learning but also a symbol of social status.

Though the hornbook's use began to decline in the 16th century with the advent of printed books, its educational legacy was lasting. It played a pivotal role in the transition from oral to written culture. Before the printing press, educational resources were scarce, and the hornbook allowed more children to engage with the written word, providing them with foundational knowledge that was crucial for reading the Bible and engaging in literacy practices.

The simplicity of the hornbook set the stage for later developments in educational tools, such as primers and textbooks, that would emerge in the Renaissance and Early Modern period. The concept of using a book-like object to teach foundational literacy was an early precursor to the educational practices that would shape Western schooling for centuries to come.

As an icon of medieval education, the hornbook remains a symbol of the democratization of literacy in a time when formal schooling was often reserved for the privileged few. It stands as a testament to the role that simple, yet effective, tools can play in spreading education and creating a more literate society.

Gutenberg printing press in the 15th century

We all know the printing press. The printing press revolutionized education by making books and written materials accessible to a broad percentage of society, significantly lowering the cost of books and enabling the dissemination of knowledge to a broader audience. This advancement fostered the standardization of educational texts, contributing to improved literacy rates, and helped accelerate the spread of educational reforms and ideas across regions. The evolution of copy and paste functionality that we all use every day. Before the printing press, people just transcribed and re-wrote what they wanted to quote or repeat.

The Gutenberg printing press had an incredible impact on education, revolutionizing the way knowledge was disseminated and accessed. Its influence can be seen in several key areas:

- **Increased access to books**: The printing press made books more affordable and widely available, allowing a greater number of people to access educational materials. This democratization of knowledge led to increased literacy rates and broader educational opportunities. By the time *Gutenberg* passed away in 1468, printing presses were operating across Europe and making things a whole lot easier for a wider audience to access books and written text. The invention meant that by 1500, there were over 15 million copies of over 30,000 different publications.[9]

- **Standardization of texts**: Printed books provided uniform and consistent content, with standardized spelling, grammar, perspectives, and punctuation. This consistency made it easier for students to learn and interpret written works accurately and for teachers to teach.

- **Expansion of curriculum**: The ability to mass-produce books allowed for the creation of a more comprehensive and consistent educational curriculum. Teachers now had more material to work with. This enabled the spread of knowledge across great distances and at a faster pace than ever before.

- **Student-teacher relationships**: The printing press altered the dynamic between educators and students. Students could now access technical texts that served as silent instructors, allowing them to surpass their elders and even challenge ancient wisdom. This is very similar to what is happening with AI today; students have access to information and knowledge that might surpass that of the teacher.

- **Improved visual learning**: The printing press enabled the accurate reproduction of complex diagrams, mathematical equations, and architectural works in ways that hand-reproduced manuscripts could not. This advancement significantly enhanced the quality of visual materials available for helping to educate students, particularly in fields such as mathematics, engineering, and architecture.

- **Promotion of language**: The printing press helped lead to the displacement of Latin as the primary language of scholarship, promoting the use of more common languages in education. This shift made learning more accessible to a broader audience.

- **Fostering of scientific knowledge**: The ability of the printed word to help disseminate scientific information more widely contributed to the growth of scientific literacy and research. This facilitated the sharing of current state-of-the-art knowledge and building upon previous research, accelerating scientific progress.

- **Support for personalized learning**: Similar to what we see with AI, as discussed in *Chapter 1, AI and Personalized Learning*, the increased availability of books allowed students to learn not only in school but also at home. Access to the printed word helped promote independent study and lifelong learning.

9 "Why We Should Thank the Printing Press for Aiding Our Education." BBR, www.bbrgraphics.com/news/why-we-should-thank-the-printing-press-for-aiding-our-education/.

- **Fueling of intellectual movements**: The rapid spread of ideas through printed materials contributed to the growth of various intellectual and religious ideas, particularly during the Renaissance and Reformation periods. The Gutenberg Bible helped spread Christianity across the world.

- **Decline of oral tradition**: Over the years, the rise of print culture led to a gradual shift from primarily oral forms of communication and knowledge transmission to written formats. This change significantly impacted how information was recorded, shared, and taught in educational settings. Honestly, it was a change that lasted until the 21st-century rise in audiobooks.

The Gutenberg printing press was a catalyst for educational advancement across many facets of the academic universe, making knowledge more accessible, standardized, and diverse. Its effects continue to resonate in modern educational practices and the ongoing evolution of information technology.

Blackboard in the 19th century

The blackboard, also known as the chalkboard, emerged as a transformative educational tool in the 19th century, revolutionizing classroom instruction and shaping the structure of modern education. It allowed teachers to present information visually to an entire classroom at once, shaping group instruction.

First, chalk (the natural one) was used in prehistory for cave drawings. Later, artists used chalk for sketching, and some of these drawings survive until today because they were protected in shellac (a resin secreted by the female lac bug (*Kerria lacca*)).[10]

Chalk and slate have a long and important history as essential tools in education. Slate, a fine-grained metamorphic rock, was first used as writing tablets in the late Middle Ages, providing an affordable, reusable surface for education and communication. Chalk, composed mainly of calcium carbonate, emerged as complementary to slate, enabling erasable writing and drawing. By the 18th and 19th centuries, the combination of chalkboard and slate became a staple in classrooms, transforming teaching methods and enabling interactive learning. These tools made education more accessible, especially in rural and under-resourced areas.

Although modern technologies have replaced them in many settings, chalk and slate remain iconic symbols of traditional education.

Before the widespread adoption of the blackboard, teaching was primarily individualized, with students working on personal slates or copying from books. The introduction of the blackboard changed this paradigm by empowering teachers to present lessons to the entire class at once, fostering group learning and collaboration.

---

10 "History of Blackboard Chalk and Whiteboard Pen." Historyofpencils.com, 2024, www.historyofpencils. com/writing-instruments-history/blackboard-chalk-and-whiteboard-pen-history-and-future/.

The first recorded use of a large blackboard in a classroom occurred in the early 1800s, credited to *James Pillans*, a Scottish geography teacher.[11]

James Pillans invented the blackboard in the 1800s. He worked as the headmaster of the *Old High School of Edinburgh, Scotland*. The students in his school used slates with wooden frames and wrote on another slate. This slate had wooden frames to protect it from breaking. He took slates and hung them on the wall to teach them geography and this brought him the idea of the blackboard. *Mr. George Baron*, a math teacher, carried this idea to the United States in 1801. He gave math presentations on the blackboard in the *West Point Military Academy*, where he taught. The idea got popular among the teachers as it saved time, enhanced understanding and helped cater to a larger group at the same time.[12]

Pillans used a slate board to draw maps and demonstrate lessons, recognizing its potential to engage larger groups of students simultaneously. As industrial advances and production techniques made blackboards more affordable and accessible, they became a standard feature in classrooms across Europe and the United States by the mid-19th century. This coincided with the rise of public education, further solidifying the blackboard's place as an essential instructional tool.

The simplicity of the blackboard was, and still is, a great asset. Teachers could write, draw, and erase in real-time, allowing lessons to adapt to student needs and providing immediate feedback. This interactivity transformed the classroom from a passive learning environment into a dynamic one. Students were encouraged to participate actively, solve problems on the board, and engage in discussions, making learning more collaborative and inclusive, while engaging with the written lessons on the blackboard.

The blackboard also helped to democratize education by facilitating large-scale instruction. It allowed teachers to efficiently convey complex ideas, such as mathematical equations, grammar rules, and scientific concepts, in a visual format that was easier for students to understand. As a shared learning space, the blackboard fostered a sense of collective learning, where students could observe and learn from their peers' contributions.

Additionally, the blackboard became a valuable tool for creativity and exploration. Teachers used it to illustrate ideas, chart progress, and encourage imaginative thinking. Its adaptability made it equally useful for structured lessons and spontaneous brainstorming sessions, offering flexibility that other teaching methods of those early times lacked.

By fostering visual learning, collaboration, and accessibility, the blackboard profoundly changed the way teachers would teach for decades to come. It paved the way for modern instructional techniques, serving as the foundation for tools like whiteboards and digital screens. Even today, the foundational principles of the blackboard still endure in classrooms, emphasizing the importance of interaction, visualization, and shared learning.

---

11 Editors. "Prof. James Pillans from the Gazetteer for Scotland." Scottish-Places.info, 2021, https://www.scottish-places.info/people/famousfirst281.html.

12 An Officer and a Scholar: Nineteenth-Century West Point and the Invention of the Blackboard 2010, https://www.jstor.org/stable/24481689.

Magic lantern and slide projectors

This comprises early image projection devices for lectures and demonstrations. Visual learning took another step forward with the magic lantern, which was an early form of an image projector.

Early on, the magic lantern was not a device for educational purposes. The magic lantern, or **Magin Cataoprica**, was a machine lit by a candle and capable of projecting hand-painted images of ghosts, devils, demons, and skeletons onto smoke-obscured walls. The magic lantern was developed by *German Jesuit Athanasius Kirscher*, who published *Ars Magna Lucis* (1646), in which he described the machine and the mystical power it had for trickery (Saettler). Later, in Paris in the 18th century, *E.G. Robertson* used the magic lantern in his *Phantasmagoria theater*, where he similarly used the projections to trick and frighten theater goers (Eisenhauer). This understanding of viewing technologies as magicians' tools or objects of the supernatural persisted until the 19th century development of vision as a discipline, after which vision came to be seen as a scientific and objective pursuit.[13]

While invented in the 17th century, it was not necessarily used for educational purposes until the 19th century. It allowed for images to be cast onto a wall or screen from a hand-painted glass slide inserted into the magic lantern, which was comprised of a concave mirror, a light source and a focusing lens.

By copying content onto a glass slide, educators would use the magic lantern to help illustrate and show details on complex subjects such as anatomy, astronomy and geography in ways that far surpassed oral or written equivalents. Using the chalkboard to draw details was difficult; the magic lantern proved to be a great way to inform and entertain the student audience by combining storytelling with visual effects. Throughout the 19th century, this lens technology and lithographic techniques improved, allowing for more refinement of the images, which led to the widespread adoption of the magic lantern as an educational presentation medium. These presentations spanned the gap between the scientific world and the theatrical. As it gained more widespread use as a valuable educational tool, educators were able to captivate their entire classroom with the larger-than-life images, ensuring minute details were visible to all. In addition to its use in school settings, it was often leveraged for lectures by other non-educational organizations, helping to create community-based learning experiences with members or interested individuals. Global travel and firsthand observation of complex subjects, such as internal anatomy, became real and visible through the magic lantern, opening up the curiosity of all who viewed its wonders at the time. Critical thinking skills were also developed as presenters asked questions while projecting images, encouraging interactive learning.

Toward the end of the 19th century, more advanced projection devices were introduced, and the magic lantern's popularity began to wane. However, it was the ancestor of the slide

13 "Lantern Slide Projector Literacy Artifacts: Preserving Tools, Methods, and Teachers' Technologies of the Long Nineteenth Century Student Digital Gallery BGSU Libraries." Digitalgallery.bgsu.edu, https://digitalgallery.bgsu.edu/student/exhibits/show/literacy/visualinstruction/projector.

projectors and even motion pictures, helping to usher in an era where projected images could educate, entertain and inspire audiences around the world.

John Dewey and his influence

John Dewey (1859–1952) was a pioneering philosopher, educator, and psychologist whose ideas have profoundly influenced modern education and the integration of technology in learning. Dewey is best known for his advocacy of pragmatism, experiential learning, and the idea that education should be a tool for personal and societal transformation. His work has laid the foundation for progressive education, emphasizing critical thinking, problem-solving, and active participation, principles that resonate strongly in today's technology-driven educational landscape. Let us explore his philosophy on education and transformative principles that influenced education through the potential of technology:

- **Dewey's educational philosophy**: Dewey's educational philosophy is based on the idea that learning is a dynamic, interactive process. He rejected the traditional rote memorization model of his time and argued that education should be student-centered and inquiry-based. Dewey believed that students learn best by doing. He was a strong advocate for experiential education, where learners engage with real-world problems.

  His vision and philosophy are encapsulated in his seminal works, including *Democracy and Education* (1916). In this book, Dewey emphasized the democratic purpose of education, arguing that schools should prepare their students to participate effectively in society. Education, he contended, should not merely impart knowledge but also cultivate critical thinking, creativity, and adaptability.

- **Dewey and the role of technology**: Dewey lived before the digital age, but his principles anticipated the transformative potential of technology in education. He viewed tools and technology as extensions of human capacity, enabling individuals to solve problems and expand their understanding of the world. He provided lessons to serve us in our new AI world. Dewey's emphasis on experiential learning aligns seamlessly with the capabilities of modern educational technologies, such as interactive simulations, virtual reality, and project-based learning platforms.

  As an example, Dewey's vision supports the use of technology to create immersive learning environments where students can experiment and explore. In today's world, things like virtual labs in **science, technology, engineering, and mathematics (STEM)** education, gamified learning platforms, and adaptive learning systems that personalize content to individual learners embody Dewey's vision of active, student-centered education. These digital tools empower students to engage deeply with content, fostering critical thinking and problem-solving skills.

Role of calculators in shaping a generation

The introduction of calculators in classrooms during the 1970s revolutionized education, creating an early foundation for the fields of machine learning, AI, and predictive analytics. These devices shifted the focus of mathematics education from manual computation to problem-solving and conceptual understanding, fostering skills essential to modern data science and AI development. This generation has literally changed the world.

Calculators like the *Texas Instruments Datamath* and *HP-35* introduced students to computational tools, encouraging technological fluency and early interaction with machines. By enabling faster, more complex calculations, these devices gave students the ability to focus on higher-order thinking and data interpretation, key skills for predictive analytics and AI modeling.

The calculator also fostered a data-driven mindset, encouraging reliance on quantitative evidence and systematic analysis. This mindset prepared students to tackle real-world problems with computational methods, directly aligning with the needs of data science. As this generation entered the workforce, they applied these skills to develop the statistical methods and programming languages (e.g., Python, R) that now underpin AI and machine learning.

Perhaps more importantly, they could recognize the lack of data, which sparked the concepts of telemetry and the use of A/B website testing. One could argue that the introduction of calculators into the classroom elevated this generation to the next level, thinking about how to use data to help drive business results.

By democratizing access to computational power and reshaping education, calculators helped nurture a generation of data scientists and innovators who would lead the development of AI, predictive analytics, and machine learning in the 2010s and beyond. The calculator's legacy remains evident in the tools and techniques driving today's data revolution and its impact will be forever felt on the internet.

The evolution of the calculator, from the mechanical devices of the 17th century to the sophisticated electronic tools of today, reflects the remarkable progress in technology and human ingenuity and each generation's use of tools and techniques to empower our society.

Each of these innovations has addressed the growing demand for faster, more reliable, and more accessible computational tools. As technology continues to advance, calculators will likely integrate even further with AI and cloud computing, expanding their capabilities beyond what was once imaginable. The history of the calculator is not just a story of technological innovation but a testament to humanity's enduring pursuit of efficiency and precision in problem-solving. Understanding how this technology influences our human ability to learn is a fascinating journey.

Mechanical to electronic calculator

The calculator evolved from mechanical devices like Pascal's calculator to modern electronic pocket calculators, simplifying arithmetic tasks. Early mechanical calculators, such as the *Leibniz Step Reckoner*, expanded on Pascal's design by introducing the ability to perform all four basic arithmetic operations. During the 19th century, *Charles Babbage's* **Analytical Engine** laid the foundation for programmable calculations, though his invention was never fully built in his lifetime.

By the mid-20th century, advancements in electronics paved the way for the first electronic calculators, such as the IBM 608, which used vacuum tubes for processing. The invention of transistors in the 1950s and integrated circuits in the 1960s made calculators more compact, affordable, and efficient.

The introduction of handheld calculators by companies like *Texas Instruments* and *Casio* in the 1970s revolutionized education, engineering, and business practices. Today, calculators are not only physical devices but also integral features of smartphones and computers, capable of complex scientific and graphing functions. Their evolution reflects humanity's continuous drive to simplify and enhance mathematical computation.

Early mechanical calculating devices

The origins of the calculator can be traced back to the 17th century, a time when mathematicians sought mechanical solutions to simplify arithmetic operations. In 1623, German polymath *Wilhelm Schickard* designed what is considered the first mechanical calculator, the *Calculating Clock*. Although his machine could perform basic addition and subtraction, its full potential remained unrealized due to its limited production and technical challenges. In 1923, Germany celebrated the 400th anniversary of Schickard's machine.[14]

In 1642, French mathematician *Blaise Pascal* created the **Pascaline**, a mechanical device capable of addition and subtraction using a system of gears and dials. While it was not widely adopted, the Pascaline demonstrated the feasibility of mechanical computation and inspired future inventors. Pascaline, the first calculator or adding machine to be produced in any quantity and used. The Pascaline was designed and built by the French mathematician-philosopher Blaise Pascal between 1642 and 1644. It could only do addition and subtraction, with numbers being entered by manipulating its dials. Pascal invented the machine for his father, a tax collector, so it was the first business machine too (if one does not count the abacus). He built 50 of them over the next 10 years.[15]

In the late 17th century, German polymath *Gottfried Wilhelm Leibniz* built upon Pascal's work, introducing the **Stepped Reckoner**. Leibniz's device was the first capable of performing all

14 Bruderer, Herbert. "400 Years of Mechanical Calculating Machines – Communications of the ACM." Acm. org, 9 May 2023, cacm.acm.org/blogcacm/400-years-of-mechanical-calculating-machines/.
15 Swaine, R, M., Freiberger, & A, P. (2008, October 7). Pascaline | Mechanical calculator, addition device, subtraction. Encyclopedia Britannica. https://www.britannica.com/technology/Pascaline

four basic arithmetic operations: addition, subtraction, multiplication, and division. Although the Stepped Reckoner faced operational issues, it laid the groundwork for future mechanical calculators.[16]

Advancements in mechanical calculators

The 19th century witnessed significant advancements in mechanical calculators, driven by industrialization and the growing complexity of mathematical tasks. *Charles Xavier Thomas de Colmar's* **Arithmometer**, invented in 1820, was the first commercially successful mechanical calculator. The Arithmometer's robustness and reliability made it popular in offices, where it was used for financial and engineering calculations.[17]

Simultaneously, *Charles Babbage* conceptualized the **Difference Engine** and **Analytical Engine**, designs for programmable mechanical computers. Although these machines were not completed during Babbage's lifetime, they introduced concepts such as memory, input/output devices, and programmability, which later influenced electronic calculators and modern computers. The Difference Engine would not have seen its growth without *Ada Lovelace*. *Ada Lovelace*, the daughter of *Lord Byron*, collaborated with *Babbage* on the Analytical Engine. She realized that the numbers in the computer could represent entities beyond just numerical values, such as letters or musical notes. In the early 1800s, she predicted the iPod. Lovelace published an account of the Analytical Engine in 1843, speculating on its potential uses beyond numerical calculations. Her work is sometimes referred to as the first computer program, though this characterization is not entirely accurate. [18]

Electromechanical calculators

The transition from purely mechanical calculators to electromechanical devices began in the early 20th century. These calculators combined mechanical components with electrical power to improve speed and efficiency. There are several notable examples, including the **Monroe Calculator** and the **Marchant Calculator**, which used electric motors to automate the movement of gears and dials.

In the 1930s and 1940s, the development of electromechanical computing devices, such as IBM's **Automatic Sequence Controlled Calculator** (**ASCC**) or **Harvard Mark I**, marked a significant milestone.[19] While not a calculator in the traditional sense, the Harvard Mark I demonstrated the potential of electronic computation for complex tasks. These machines laid the foundation for the electronic revolution that followed.

16 Freiberger, A, P., Swaine, & R, M. (2008, October 7). Step Reckoner | Mechanical calculator, arithmetic device, calculating device. Encyclopedia Britannica. https://www.britannica.com/technology/Step-Reckoner
17 Abby. (2023, July 27). Arithmometer explained – everything you need to know. History-Computer. https://history-computer.com/technology/arithmometer/
18 "Imagining AI - Babbage & Lovelace." www.hsm.ox.ac.uk. 25 Sept. 2022, https://www.hsm ox.ac.uk/imagining-ai
19 Harvard IBM Mark I - About. (n.d.). Collection of Historical Scientific Instruments Harvard University. Retrieved February 23, 2025, from https://chsi.harvard.edu/harvard-ibm-mark-1-about

Birth of electronic calculators

The invention of the transistor in 1947 by *John Bardeen, Walter Brattain*, and *William Shockley* significantly revolutionized electronics and helped pave the way for the development of the first electronic calculators. Transistors, being smaller, faster, and more reliable than vacuum tubes, enabled the creation of compact and efficient devices.

In 1961, *Bell Punch Co.* introduced the **Sumlock ANITA**, the world's first electronic desktop calculator. **A New Inspiration to Arithmetic (ANITA)** was made of vacuum tubes and cold-cathode diodes to help perform calculations. Although bulky by today's standards, it represented a major leap forward in computational technology.

The 1960s also saw the development of **integrated circuits (ICs)**, which further miniaturized electronic components. In 1964, *Sharp* released the Sharp QT-8D, the first calculator to use ICs, reducing its size and power consumption. This innovation heralded the era of portable electronic calculators, as shown in the following figure:

Figure 2.3: The electronic calculator was a disruptive change

Rise of pocket calculators

The 1970s kicked off the rise of the calculator's transformation into a compact, affordable, and widely accessible tool. This was driven by advancements in microprocessor technology, which integrated the functions of multiple ICs into a single chip.

In 1971, Intel introduced the 4004 microprocessor, which powered the Busicom LE-120A, the first pocket calculator with a single-chip CPU. This single-chip CPU breakthrough allowed calculators to shrink dramatically in size and cost, making them accessible to consumers worldwide.

Two significant tech companies played a role at this stage. **Texas Instruments (TI)** emerged as a key player during this era. In 1972, TI released the **TI-2500 Datamath**, one of the first handheld calculators capable of performing basic arithmetic. Around the same time, **Hewlett-Packard (HP)** launched the **HP-35**, the first scientific pocket calculator, which could perform trigonometric and logarithmic functions. The HP-35 was particularly revolutionary, replacing bulky slide rules for engineers and scientists.

1970s backlash against the electronic calculator

The 1970s witnessed a notable backlash against the electronic calculator, primarily driven by concerns from educators, parents, and professionals about its potential impact on the cognitive skills and traditional learning methods of students. As calculators became more affordable and widely available, their rapid adoption in classrooms and workplaces sparked debates about over-reliance on technology.

Educators worried that students would lose fundamental arithmetic skills if calculators replaced mental math and manual calculation methods. Critics argued that younger generations might fail to grasp basic mathematical concepts, relying on devices rather than understanding the principles behind their operations and becoming lazy when it comes to math. This concern extended to fears of diminishing problem-solving and critical-thinking abilities.

Parents echoed these anxieties, seeing calculators as shortcuts that undermined the discipline and effort traditionally associated with learning mathematics the way they did. They also feared that such tools might erode academic rigor, making students less competitive in the long run.

In professional fields, particularly engineering and accounting, some viewed calculators as a threat to precision and craftsmanship, believing they could lead to complacency and errors. Resistance to the technology of the electronic calculator was not universal, however, as advocates highlighted its potential to save time and enable focus on higher-level problem-solving.

Despite this initial backlash, calculators eventually became widely accepted, reshaping education and industry by emphasizing efficiency and adaptation to technological advancements. Ironically, the current age of data science, telemetry, machine learning and AI has been created by the hands of the generation raised with the help of electronic calculators.

The calculator is one of the most revolutionary and disruptive tools in human history, enabling rapid computation and shaping countless fields, from engineering to finance. Its evolution from mechanical devices in the 17th century to the sophisticated electronic calculators of today illustrates humanity's ingenuity and relentless pursuit of efficiency. This journey spans centuries of innovation, culminating in a tool that is now ubiquitous and indispensable.

Programmable calculators and the dawn of graphing calculators

The 1980s marked the introduction and emergence of programmable calculators, which allowed users to write and execute custom programs. Devices like the HP-41C and TI-59 introduced features such as alphanumeric displays and external storage via magnetic cards or memory modules. These calculators became essential tools for professionals and students in technical fields. Programmable calculators were an early precursor to personal computers, bridging the gap between simple calculators and more sophisticated computing.

In the 1980s and 1990s, graphing calculators became increasingly popular, especially in education. These devices combined advanced computational capabilities with the ability to plot graphs and visualize mathematical functions. Let us look at the following graphing calculators:

- **The TI-81**: Texas Instruments introduced the TI-81 in 1990, the first graphing calculator designed for classroom use. It featured a large display capable of plotting graphs and solving equations, making it an invaluable tool for students and educators.

- **The Casio fx-7000G**: The Casio fx-7000G was the world's first graphing calculator. It featured a dot-matrix display, 422-step programmable memory, and 82 scientific functions. This groundbreaking device allowed users, particularly students, to plot graphs, perform complex calculations, and store formulas, revolutionizing education and engineering by making advanced mathematical visualization more accessible.

Graphing calculators continued to evolve, incorporating larger displays, more memory, and enhanced processing power. Next version devices like the TI-89 and Casio fx-9860G introduced symbolic computation, allowing users to solve algebraic equations symbolically rather than numerically.

Digital integration in the 21st century

The 21st century has seen calculators integrate with digital computer technology, transforming them into multifunctional devices. There are a variety of advancements that leverage digital capabilities, including:

- **Calculator applications**: Smartphones and tablets now feature calculator apps, offering functionality comparable to dedicated devices. Obviously, Windows calculator and internet websites, but applications like Wolfram Alpha go way beyond basic calculations, providing step-by-step solutions, graphing capabilities, and even symbolic computation.

- **Online calculators**: The rise of the internet has enabled the development of online calculators that cater to specific needs, from financial planning to scientific research. These tools are accessible from any device with an internet connection, further reducing the reliance on standalone calculators. The calculation sites are specialized, from mortgage calculators to investments to sites that analyze sets of data.

- **Advanced graphing and CAS devices**: Modern graphing calculators, such as the newer TI-Nspire and Casio ClassPad, feature touchscreen interfaces, wireless connectivity, and **Computer Algebra Systems (CAS)** for symbolic manipulation. These devices blur the line between calculators and computers, offering unparalleled functionality for education and professional use. Students are empowered with these powerful tools.

- **AI**: Advanced mathematical features such as symbolic manipulation, graphing and the understanding of complex concepts are easily accessible and taught through access to different AI educational tools and LLM inquiries. AI's ability in driving enhanced efficiency is unparalleled compared to traditional calculator use, yet comes with concerns about over-reliance and ethical implications (discussed in *Chapter 10, Data Security and Ethical Considerations in AI*).

Overhead projectors in the mid-20th century

These projectors are common in schools for displaying text or images, enabling interactive note-taking.

The overhead projector emerged as a staple in classroom technology during the mid-20th century, revolutionizing the way teachers presented information to students. Although the concept of projecting images dated back to 19th-century devices like the magic lantern, the modern overhead projector took shape around the 1940s. Its initial widespread use was within the U.S. military during World War II, when troops utilized projectors for quick and efficient training in various technical and strategic subjects.

By the 1950s, the overhead projector made its way into civilian educational institutions, catching the attention of school administrators looking for ways to improve instruction and reduce reliance on traditional chalkboard methods. Overhead projectors allowed teachers to write or place pre-printed transparencies on a glass platform, where a powerful light source would project the information onto a screen or wall. This format gave educators a new flexibility to annotate materials in real time, highlighting key points without turning their backs to students.

The device's popularity soared in the 1960s and 1970s, as mass production made overhead projectors more affordable and increasingly user-friendly. Schools across the United States and other industrialized nations adopted them for lessons ranging from arithmetic and penmanship to complex scientific diagrams. Specialized pens and transparent sheets enabled teachers to create reusable lesson materials or demonstrate problem-solving steps to the entire class.

Over time, overhead projectors became a symbol of the modern classroom, representing an era of enhanced visual learning. They were a precursor to more advanced multimedia devices such as slide projectors, video projectors, and, eventually, interactive whiteboards. Although their use declined in the late 20th and early 21st centuries as digital technologies evolved, overhead projectors left a lasting legacy for an entire generation of students. By enabling large-scale, clear visual presentations, they paved the way for innovative, technology-driven teaching methods that continue to shape classrooms around the world.

Radio in the early 20th century

Educational broadcasts and distance-learning programs played a pivotal role in disseminating academic content to remote and underserved audiences, breaking down geographical barriers and expanding access to knowledge. Through radio programs, learners in rural and isolated areas gained opportunities to engage with educational material that was previously beyond their reach. In the following figure, you can see the depiction of an early 20th century radio:

Figure 2.4: *The radio was a new form of learning in the 1900s*

In the early 20th century, radio emerged as a powerful educational tool, extending the reach of learning far beyond traditional classrooms. With its ability to broadcast information to vast and remote audiences, radio revolutionized access to education, particularly in rural and underserved areas. Educational institutions and organizations quickly recognized its potential to supplement classroom instruction and provide distance learning.

In classrooms, radio programs enriched the curriculum by delivering lectures, storytelling, music, and language lessons. Teachers incorporated radio broadcasts into lessons to expose students to high-quality, expert-driven content they might not otherwise access. For instance, the *BBC Schools Radio* in the UK and programs in the US offered structured lessons in subjects like science, history, and literature, engaging students with innovative teaching methods.

Beyond the classroom, radio broke geographical barriers, delivering education to isolated learners. Programs like *Australia's School of the Air* and the *University of the Air* brought structured lessons to children and adults in remote areas. Additionally, agricultural and vocational broadcasts, such as the *Radio Farm School*, taught practical skills to rural communities.

By democratizing access to knowledge and enabling lifelong learning, radio laid the groundwork for modern educational technologies, proving that innovation could make education more inclusive and far-reaching. Bottom of Form. The following are some examples of educational radio broadcasts and distance-learning programs:

- **University of Wisconsin's WHA (1920s):** One of the first educational radio stations, WHA, broadcast lectures, language lessons, and agricultural tips to rural audiences. It was a pioneering effort in using radio for academic outreach. According to the book

9XM Talking from the Wisconsin School of the Air about the 1920s, interest in using radio for classroom instruction was growing among Wisconsin teachers, but available information was sparse. *The Wisconsin Journal of Education* noted: *All progressive educators have been eager to use the radio as an additional tool for teaching, but the questions when, where and how have been hard to answer.* In 1929, WHA managers decided to conduct a formal test of how radio could be used in education. The station applied for a grant from the *Payne Fund* for $750 to teach music and current events to sixth-, seventh-, and eighth-grade students in rural schools in Dane County. Twenty-five schools would use the broadcasts as part of classroom instruction, and twenty-five would not use the radio offerings and would serve as a control group.[20]

- **The British Broadcasting Corporation (BBC) Schools Radio (1924)**: The BBC began broadcasting educational programs for schoolchildren, including lessons in history, literature, and science, all designed to complement traditional classroom teaching.

- **Radio Farm School Programs (1930s)**: Programs like those on WLS in Chicago taught farming techniques and rural management to isolated farming communities, blending education with practical knowledge.

- **The University of Iowa's WOI (1922)**: WOI broadcast a variety of university lectures and continuing education courses, becoming a model for other institutions to use radio as an academic medium.

- **National Home and Farm Hour (NBC, 1928)**: This hourly program offered educational content for rural families, including lessons on agricultural science, household management, and social studies.

- **Australian School of the Air (1951)**: Initially broadcast via radio, this program served children in remote areas of Australia who could not attend any traditional schools, delivering lessons in core subjects.

- **Canadian National Railway Radio School (1930s)**: Workers traveling on railways could tune into several lessons that covered many practical trades and basic education, enhancing access to knowledge for transient populations.

- **Radio ECCA (Spain, 1965)**: This early initiative offered distance-learning programs via radio to adults seeking secondary education, combining broadcasts with printed materials.

- **The Federal Radio Education Committee (FREC, 1930s USA)**: During the Great Depression, the FREC worked with radio stations to produce educational programs for students and adult learners on subjects ranging from civics to art.

- **The University of the Air (1930s)**: A collaborative initiative in the United States that aired academic courses through free public radio, allowing non-traditional students to engage in lifelong learning.

20 Davidson, Randall. 9XM Talking. Univ of Wisconsin Press, 26 Feb. 2007, p. 260.

These programs showcased the potential of radio to help democratize education, reaching audiences far removed from traditional schools and universities, and laying the groundwork for modern distance-learning platforms.

Television in the mid-20th century

Television emerged as a transformative medium for education in the mid-20th century, reshaping classroom learning by bringing external dynamic visual content directly to students. Television introduced educational channels and documentaries, extending learning outside the classroom.

Initially seen as a tool for entertainment, educators and policymakers quickly recognized its potential to enrich traditional teaching methods. By integrating television into classrooms, schools could access a broader array of content and resources, enhance student engagement, and address diverse learning styles.

Educational television programs became a staple of this new approach. Public broadcasting networks like **Public Broadcasting Service** (**PBS**) in the United States pioneered shows such as Sesame Street in 1969, designed to teach basic literacy, numeracy, and social skills. Though initially aimed at home audiences, these programs soon found their way into classrooms, complementing traditional curricula and providing teachers with creative ways to reinforce lessons. Similarly, government-sponsored broadcasts in countries like the UK and Australia delivered an array of structured lessons on subjects ranging from science to history, reaching classrooms even in remote areas.[21]

The visual and entertainment nature of television proved especially impactful for subjects that benefited from demonstrations and storytelling. Science experiments, historical reenactments, and cultural explorations could be vividly portrayed, helping students get a better grasp of complex concepts and connect with material more deeply. Teachers used these programs as supplementary resources, sparking discussions and further inquiry.

Additionally, television addressed educational disparities by delivering high-quality content to underserved schools, particularly in rural areas, which may not have had access to speakers and printed textbook content. Programs like **The French Chef** (*Julia Child*) also introduced specialized learning, such as cooking or technical skills, expanding students' horizons.

However, critics raised concerns about the passive nature of television, emphasizing the need for something more interactive and critical engagement. Despite these challenges, television in the classroom set the stage for integrating multimedia into education. It demonstrated how technology could enhance teaching by making lessons more accessible, engaging, and diverse, paving the way for future innovations like video streaming and online learning.[22]

---

21 Gentzkow, M., & Shapiro, J. M. (2008). Preschool television viewing and adolescent test scores: Historical evidence from the Coleman study. Quarterly Journal of Economics, 123(1), 279-323.
22 Hall, E. R., Etsy, E. T., & Fisch, S. M. (1990). Television and children's problem-solving behavior: A synopsis of an evaluation of the effects of Square One TV. Journal of Mathematical Behavior, 9(2), 161-174

Sesame Street

Sesame Street first aired on television in 1969. The show is well-known and loved by children around the world. Created by *Joan Ganz Cooney* and *Lloyd Morrisett*, Sesame Street was designed to appeal to young kids by sharing educational content through a unique format, including puppets, skits and songs. Capturing their preschooler audience's attention through television and humor, kids learned their letters, numbers and many social skills from a great set of puppet and human characters. Using television to educate by combining essential skills with entertainment was revolutionary and changed education. [23]

Sesame Street was rooted in educational research, with early childhood experts helping to design content that would hold a child's attention long enough to educate through learning techniques such as repetition and humor. The partnership with *Jim Henson*, the creator of puppet characters known as *The Muppets*. Personalities like *Kermit the Frog*, *Big Bird*, *Cookie Monster*, *Oscar the Grouch*, and *Elmo* propelled the success of Sesame Street. Using these characters who interacted with a diverse human cast taught lessons about acceptance, kindness, and diversity in addition to the early school-level skills.[24]

The crew was committed to serving underrepresented communities with a focus on inclusion. The introduction of characters like Julia, a puppet with autism, brought visibility and acceptance to differences.

Over the years, Sesame Street has won countless awards, including *221 Emmy Awards*, and is now broadcast around the world. Sesame Street continues to adapt to the times and remains culturally aware, reaching new generations of children while staying true to its mission of helping children everywhere grow smarter, stronger, and kinder.[25]

Personal computers in the late 20th century

The personal computer revolutionized access to digital educational software, immersive simulations, and pioneering e-learning platforms, transforming traditional learning environments into interactive, dynamic experiences and expanding educational opportunities beyond the confines of the classroom.

The introduction of personal computers into classrooms in the late 20th century marked a turning point in education, influencing the way in which teachers and students approached learning. By the late 1970s and early 1980s, personal computers such as the **Apple II**, **Commodore PET**, and **IBM PC** were finding their way into schools. These machines offered

23 Durante, R., Pinotti, P., & Tesei, A. (2019). The political legacy of entertainment TV. American Economic Review, 109(7), 2497-2530.

24 Bryant, J., Alexander, A., & Brown, D. (1983). Learning from educational television programs. In M. J. A. Howe (Ed.), Learning from television: Psychological and educational research (pp. 1-30). Academic Press

25 Sesame Workshop. "Our Mission and History." Sesame Workshop, 9 Dec. 2022, https://sesameworkshop.org/about-us/mission-and-history/

new opportunities for personalized learning, hands-on exploration, and the development of digital literacy, preparing students of that era for a digital future.[26]

Initially, computers were seen as tools for teaching programming and basic computational skills. Early educational programs like **BASIC** and **Logo**, developed by *Seymour Papert*, taught children how to think logically and solve problems by controlling a virtual *turtle* on the screen. This introduced a generation of students to concepts of coding and computational thinking, laying the foundation for more complex computer science education.[27]

As personal computers became more affordable and accessible, their role in education expanded. Educational software developers began creating software tailored to classroom use, such as **Oregon Trail** and **Reader Rabbit**, which combined learning with engaging gameplay. These programs engaged and enhanced students' skills in subjects like history, reading, and mathematics while fostering critical thinking and decision-making.

Computers also reshaped how information was accessed and presented. Word processors like WordPerfect and Microsoft Word enabled students to type essays and projects, improving the quality of written communication and teaching basic typing skills. Spreadsheet software like *Lotus 1-2-3* introduced students to data organization and analysis. By the 1990s, schools began integrating multimedia software and multimedia encyclopedias, allowing students to learn through interactive videos, animations, and simulations that brought subjects like science and history to life.

Teachers benefited as well, using computers for lesson planning, grading, and communication. Access to databases and early internet connections allowed educators to incorporate a wide variety of online resources into their teaching, enriching the learning environment. Programs like **HyperStudio** let teachers create interactive presentations that engage students in new and different ways.

However, the early adoption of personal computers in classrooms was not without challenges. Financial constraints meant that access was often limited to wealthier schools, creating notable disparities between urban and rural, or affluent and low-income, areas. Additionally, teachers, not familiar with the new technology, required training to integrate computers into their instruction effectively, and not all educators were prepared or willing to adapt their classroom methodologies.

State of computers in classrooms today

Today, computers and cellphones are ubiquitous in education, supported by high-speed internet and cloud-based educational tools. Students routinely use laptops or tablets for assignments, research, and group project collaboration, while teachers leverage platforms like Google Classroom, Canvas, Teams, and Zoom for remote or blended learning. The global

26 History.com (Ed.). (2023, March 28). Invention of the PC. History.com. Retrieved February 23, 2025, from https://www.history.com/topics/inventions/invention-of-the-pc
27 Logo history. (n.d.). https://el.media.mit.edu/logo-foundation/what_is_logo/history.html

COVID-19 pandemic of 2020 changed the way educators interacted with students. Artificial intelligence can now help personalize instruction, and adaptive software adjusts to student needs, while coding has generally become a core part of the curriculum. Computers have evolved from standalone tutoring tools to integral components of a digital ecosystem in the majority of classrooms today, where there is a computer for every student, encouraging global connectivity, creativity, digital engagement, and lifelong learning. This evolution underscores their enduring impact on education.

With the increase in use of technology in classrooms, concerns over student and teacher privacy abound. From data breaches to phishing attacks, privacy issues, and inadequate data protection, it is difficult for educational institutions and governing bodies to keep up. There are many organizations working to offer advice to schools and educators on ways to keep students and their information safe and secure. One such example is from the **International Society for Technology in Education** (**ISTE**), which published *Essential conditions for effective tech use in schools*, backed by research, as a way to drive systemic change and safe standards in education.[28]

Oregon Trail learning software

The Oregon Trail PC-based learning software has been one of the most iconic educational games in history, blending entertainment with historical education. First developed in 1971 by three student teachers, *Don Rawitsch, Bill Heinemann,* and *Paul Dillenberger*. The game began as a classroom project aimed at teaching American history. It simulates the experiences of 19th-century pioneers traveling westward on the Oregon Trail, and focuses on decision-making, resource management, and survival skills.

The original version of Oregon Trail was a text-based game created for a mainframe computer at *Carleton College* in *Minnesota*. It used simple commands to guide players through challenges like crossing rivers, hunting for food, and avoiding diseases. Students were instantly captivated by the engaging way the game brought history to life in gameplay.

In 1974, *Rawitsch* adapted the game for the **Minnesota Educational Computing Consortium** (**MECC**), which was focused on integrating technology into the classroom. MECC re-wrote the game for early personal computers, including the Apple II, making it widely accessible to schools in the 1980s and 1990s. With improved graphics and interactive gameplay, this early version became a staple of computer labs across the United States.[29]

The was wildly popular with both students and educators because it combined education with entertainment. Student players learned about the hardships of pioneer life, geography, and decision-making, all while having fun. Its engaging format inspired the development of a generation of educational games.

28 Essential conditions for effective tech use in schools. (2023, July 26). ISTE. https://iste.org/essential-conditions-for-effective-tech-use-in-schools
29 Toppo, G. (2021). "The Oregon Trail" at 50: the story of a game that inspired generations. Fast Company. https://www.fastcompany.com/90702587/oregon-trail-computer-game-50th-anniversary

The Oregon Trail franchise continued to expand over the decades, with updated versions featuring enhanced graphics, sound, and gameplay mechanics. By the early 2000s, it was available on a wide variety of platforms, including handheld devices and mobile apps.

Today, Oregon Trail fondly remains a cultural touchstone, celebrated for its innovative use of technology to make learning engaging. It has been credited with influencing the edutainment industry and introducing generations to the power of interactive storytelling in education.[30]

Internet in the late 20th century

The internet changed the way students learn in the classroom, making education very different from earlier times. It has impacted schools at every level, from elementary to college, by making information easier to find, share, and use during lessons and at home. The following figure shows the global reach of knowledge made available by the invention of the internet:

Figure 2.5: The internet was a game changer

One of the biggest changes the internet has brought is making knowledge available to educators and students alike. In the past, students had to rely on textbooks, libraries, and what their teachers knew. Now, with the internet, both students and teachers can access many more sources of information, including articles, videos, fun interactive activities, and even view images of original historical documents. Educational platforms like *Khan Academy*, *TED-Ed*, *YouTube* and *Wikipedia* allow students to explore topics far beyond the traditional curriculum and spark curiosity to learn more.

The internet has also redefined collaboration and communication. Tools such as *Google Docs*, *Microsoft Teams*, *Skype*, *Zoom*, *MOOCs* and discussion boards enable real-time collaboration among students and teachers, even in geographically dispersed locations. This fosters a more connected and inclusive learning environment, breaking down barriers to participation.

---

30 Toppo, G. (2021). "The Oregon Trail" at 50: the story of a game that inspired generations. *Fast Company*. https://www.fastcompany.com/90702587/oregon-trail-computer-game-50th-anniversary

Using technology to connect students

In the early 2000s, video conferencing technology became an increasingly viable tool for communication. Skype, an early popular platform for virtual calls, recognized the potential of its technology in the classroom and launched **Skype in the Classroom** (**SITC**) in 2011. This initiative sought to use Skype to break down geographical barriers, allowing students and teachers to engage with other classrooms, experts, guest speakers, and cultures from around the world. It revolutionized the concept of connected learning by making global collaboration accessible, free, and engaging.

Case study: Skype in the Classroom program

Skype in the Classroom provided a dedicated online platform where educators could find and connect with other teachers, guest speakers, and virtual field trip providers. Teachers could sign up and search for and schedule available lessons, categorized by subject, age group, and activity type. The program offered four primary experiences, given as follows:

- **Mystery Skype**: A geography-based guessing game where two classrooms from different parts of the world would connect without knowing each other's locations. Students could then ask yes-or-no questions to determine where their partner class was located, fostering critical thinking and cultural awareness.

- **Virtual guest speakers**: Professionals from various fields, including scientists, authors, engineers, celebrities, and conservationists, shared their expertise with students without the logistical challenges of travel. Organizations, including NASA, the Smithsonian, and National Geographic, frequently participated.

- **Virtual field trips**: Students could visit places they might never see in person—whether it was *Yellowstone National Park*, *The Great Wall of China*, *The Amazon Rainforest*, or an underwater marine conservation site, all through live or pre-recorded video tours guided by experts, incorporating an opportunity for students to interact.

- **Skype-a-Thon**: It was an annual global learning event where students and educators connected with other classrooms, experts, and guest speakers worldwide through live video calls over a series of consecutive days.

The impact on students was as follows:

Skype in the Classroom significantly expanded the horizons of students, offering them real-time interactions with other students and experts around the world beyond their school walls. For students in remote or underserved communities, Skype in the Classroom provided experiences that would otherwise be impossible. Schools with limited resources could connect with world-class experts, participate in STEM workshops, or explore global landmarks without leaving their classrooms. This democratization of educational opportunities helped bridge learning gaps across different socioeconomic backgrounds.

The global COVID-19 pandemic fueled the widespread adoption and growth of communication and collaboration platforms like Zoom, Slack and Microsoft Teams, leaving Skype far behind since the surge in usage.[31] Microsoft sunsetted the once-popular Skype product in May 2025 in favor of the more secure and robust Microsoft Teams,[32] which has an educational version with 100 million active users[33]. During and since the global pandemic, more communication and collaboration technologies have gained traction in the digital classroom space such as Google Classroom (250 million worldwide active users[34]), Schoology (1,048 live websites actively using the platform[35]), Udacity (17 million registered users worldwide[36]), and D2L Brightspace (20 million users[37]) to name a few.[38] Skype in the Classroom was clearly ahead of its time when it was launched in 2011, paving the way for the development of education platforms focused on collaboration and communication.

Conclusion

Early civilizations in ancient Mesopotamia used clay tablets to impart knowledge, which laid the groundwork for organized learning. The abacus took it to the next stage, which introduced a tactile tool bridging the gap between complex mathematical concepts and practical application, leading to greater problem-solving techniques. The hornbook, papyrus scrolls, and the Gutenberg printing press allowed educational materials to become easily portable, leading to mass production and greater accessibility of learning content and standardization. Later, learning tools like the blackboard and overhead projector transformed educational classrooms into dynamic learning environments. More recently, the acceleration of innovation has delivered gadgets such as the radio, television, calculator and computers, completely reshaping how people receive knowledge and learn about the greater world. These tools broke down barriers and geographical distances, delivering content right to homes and communities through different media. The global connection that the internet has allowed has completely revolutionized access to information. A personal computer or mobile phone is now all they

31 Gerson Lehrman Group. (2023, June 9). Zoom, Microsoft Teams, and Slack Have Exploded Due to the COVID-19 Pandemic. Can They Hold onto This Growth? | GLG. GLG. https://glginsights.com/articles/zoom-microsoft-teams-and-slack-have-exploded-due-to-the-covid-19-pandemic-can-they-hold-onto-this-growth/

32 Forristal, L. (2025, March 15). Skype is shutting down in May — these are the best alternatives. Tech-Crunch. https://techcrunch.com/2025/03/15/skype-shuts-down-in-may-these-are-the-best-alternatives/

33 D'Souza, J. (2025, February 26). Microsoft Teams statistics by users, downloads, revenue and facts. Electro IQ. https://electroiq.com/stats/microsoft-teams-statistics/

34 Barker, S. (2024, October 17). The Ultimate Guide to Google Classroom in 2025 - ExpertBeacon. Expertbeacon. https://expertbeacon.com/the-ultimate-guide-to-google-classroom-in-2024/

35 Schoology Usage Statistics. (n.d.). Trends Built With. Retrieved April 6, 2025, from https://trends.builtwith.com/cms/Schoology

36 eLearning Statistics Education. (2025, March 17). 42 eLearning Statistics 2025 (Market Size & Growth Trends). https://elearningstats.education/

37 GuruFocus News. (2025, April 4). D2L Inc (DTLIF) Q4 2025 Earnings Call Highlights: Strong revenue growth amidst market challenges. Yahoo Finance. https://finance.yahoo.com/news/d2l-inc-dtlif-q4-2025-070059339.html?guccounter=1

38 Best Education Software Products for 2025 | G2. (n.d.). G2. https://www.g2.com/best-software-companies/top-education

need to bring the world to them. AI is the next revolution that will transform education. By responsibly integrating technology into our educational systems, a world can be created where all students have an opportunity to thrive, and no challenge is insurmountable.

Innovation at every step in history has improved how we educate and learn. From the earliest writing instruments to the most recent technical achievements, innovation has enhanced the quality and accessibility of education. Opportunities are on the horizon for students and teachers who will be able to continue to grow, create and understand the world around them.

In the next chapter, we will discuss the impact AI has on both student and teacher assessment practices, along with the challenges faced in implementation and what the future may hold.

Questions

1. What role did clay tablets play in the educational system of ancient Mesopotamia, and how were they used in the learning process?

2. How did the invention of the Gutenberg printing press revolutionize education, and what parallels can be drawn between its impact and the rise of AI in education today?

3. Explain how the blackboard transformed classroom learning and why it became a staple in education.

4. Describe the significance of the abacus in both the Mesopotamian and Chinese education systems. How did it help students understand mathematical concepts?

5. How did the integration of personal computers in the late 20th century change the way students learned, and what were some of the most popular educational software programs of that time?

Exercises

1. **Timeline activity**: Create a timeline highlighting at least eight key technological advancements mentioned in this chapter, starting from clay tablets to the internet. Include the approximate dates and a brief description of each invention's impact on education.

2. **Compare and contrast**: Compare the educational impact of the Gutenberg printing press and personal computers. Identify three similarities and three differences in how they transformed access to knowledge.

3. **Role-playing debate**: Divide into two groups. Group 1 will argue from the perspective of educators in the 1970s who were skeptical about the use of calculators in classrooms. Group 2 will argue from the perspective of educators who supported their use. Conclude with a class discussion about technology adoption in education.

4. **Technology impact essay**: Write a short essay (250-300 words) on which educational technology from the chapter you believe had the most profound impact on learning and why. Use examples from the text to support your opinion.

5. **Educational tool concept design**: Imagine you are an inventor from the future creating the next major educational tool after AI. Draw and describe how it works, how it enhances learning, and what educational challenges it solves. Present your concept to the class.

Join our Discord space

Join our Discord workspace for latest updates, offers, tech happenings around the world, new releases, and sessions with the authors:

https://discord.bpbonline.com

CHAPTER 3
AI-driven Assessment and Feedback Tools

Assessment is today's means of modifying tomorrow's instruction.

-Carol Ann Tomlinson

Introduction

For centuries, student assessments in education have been largely defined by rigid, one-size-fits-all methods: standardized tests, paper exams, and final grades. These tools have served their purpose in measuring knowledge, but their limitations are becoming ever more apparent in an increasingly personalized and digital world. Traditional assessments often fail to account for individual learning styles, pace, or even the nuances of student thinking. In many ways, they are relics of an era that prioritizes uniformity over uniqueness.

However, the landscape of assessment is rapidly evolving in response to technological advancements, particularly the integration of AI and, more concretely, with breakthroughs in multimodal AI, which are reshaping that picture. These systems can simultaneously analyze text, images, video, and audio—allowing teachers to evaluate written arguments, spoken explanations, and problem-solving gestures in a single pass. Researchers at the *University of Bologna* have unveiled an explainable framework that scores soft skills by combining video, audio, and textual cues from classroom roleplays—offering a holistic view of communication and decision-making that no traditional rubric could capture[1]. These advances mean

---

[1] A multimodal framework for explainable evaluation of soft skills in educational environments. (n.d.). https://arxiv.org/html/2505.01794v1?

assessment is no longer confined to uniformity; it can be personalized, continuous, and richly contextual, mirroring how students actually think and create. AI enhances the ability to track progress, identify learning gaps, and provide real-time feedback, offering new possibilities for more accurate and timely assessments.

Structure

This chapter covers the following topics:

- Impact of AI on formative and summative assessments
- Types of AI-driven assessment tools
- Design principles for effective AI-based assessment
- Role of AI in feedback mechanisms
- Challenges and considerations for implementing AI in assessments
- AI and the future of educational assessment

Objectives

This chapter explores how AI is transforming the landscape of educational assessment, with a focus on the power of AI-driven assessments and feedback. It is not just about automating grading or replacing traditional tests—it is about reshaping the way we think about assessment altogether. AI brings with it the promise of more personalized, timely, and actionable insights into student performance. It allows for a more accurate reflection of a student's abilities, continuously adjusting to their learning journey rather than providing a snapshot of a single moment in time. From instant feedback loops to adaptive assessments that adjust to individual progress, AI opens new doors for improving learning outcomes and giving students the support they need when they need it most.

As we explore these possibilities, we will also address the challenges that come with integrating AI into the assessment process, including questions of fairness, transparency, and data privacy.

Impact of AI on formative and summative assessments

Artificial Intelligence is transforming both formative and summative assessments in ways that are significantly improving the way students are evaluated and how feedback is provided. AI is no longer confined to grading bubble sheets after an exam; today's LLMs—most notably ChatGPT and its successors—are changing how, when, and what we assess. In formative settings, these models power real-time learning dialogues. A student can upload an early draft or voice a half-formed idea; the LLM responds with probing questions, highlights logic gaps, and suggests next steps—much like a human tutor but available on demand. LLM co-pilots are also entering summative workflows. Tools such as **Tutor CoPilot**[2] let instructors feed in a rubric and sample responses; the model then generates framed, criterion-aligned feedback while flagging borderline cases for human review. Early studies suggest this hybrid approach can cut grading time in half without sacrificing reliability—provided teachers audit a sample of AI scores and override as needed.

The ability of AI to continuously assess student performance, offer real-time feedback, and identify areas for improvement has been a game-changer for educators and learners alike.

Formative assessments powered by AI

Formative assessments are designed to monitor student learning and provide ongoing feedback that informs future instruction. Unlike summative assessments, which are typically used to assign grades, formative assessments are tools for learning rather than just evaluating it, whose goal is to monitor learning and guide improvements. AI is revolutionizing this process by providing real-time, actionable feedback and personalized learning experiences for students.

AI has the ability to turn formative assessments into dynamic, continuous feedback loops that evolve as students progress. With AI-driven quizzes and assignments, students can receive instant feedback on their performance, guiding them toward mastery before moving on to new material. For instance, AI tools like Khan Academy's personalized quizzes[3] adapt to a student's skill level in real time, ensuring that the difficulty of questions aligns with the student's current knowledge. This real-time feedback helps students identify areas where they need more practice and enables teachers to target areas of weakness more effectively. For example, if a student answers a question incorrectly, the system can provide hints, explanations, or even related resources to help the student understand the correct answer. This immediate support ensures that students do not move forward with gaps in their understanding.

Research indicates that AI-driven formative assessments can boost student learning outcomes in various contexts. A controlled experiment in Kuwait[4] with 80 high school **English as a Foreign Language** (EFL) students found that those receiving AI-assisted formative instruction significantly outperformed a control group in multiple areas. Using an AI-integrated platform (Nearpod) for formative tasks (like practice reading passages and instant feedback) led to higher reading comprehension gains, and the AI-supported group also showed superior post-test performance across all measures. Similar benefits are reported at the university level. For example, a 2024 study in *Hong Kong* tested AI-generated feedback for first-year college students

2 Tutor CoPilot: A Human-AI approach for scaling Real-Time expertise. (n.d.). https://arxiv.org/html/2410.03017v2?

3 Heitner, J. (2025, February 6). Khanmigo and Blooket: AI question sets for fun classroom challenges. Khan Academy Blog. https://blog.khanacademy.org/khanmigo-and-blooket-ai-question-sets-for-fun-classroom-challenges/

4 Alazemi, A. F. T. (2024). Formative assessment in artificial integrated instruction: delving into the effects on reading comprehension progress, online academic enjoyment, personal best goals, and academic mindfulness. Language Testing in Asia, 14(1). https://doi.org/10.1186/s40468-024-00319-8

writing essays[5]. One group received automated draft feedback from a large language model (ChatGPT-based) on their essays, while a controlled group received no AI feedback. The results showed significant improvements in essay quality (as measured by grades/rubrics) for the AI feedback group. In addition, student surveys and interviews indicated higher engagement and motivation during the revision process when AI feedback was available. A common theme is that AI systems can provide timely, targeted feedback that helps students identify mistakes and learn from them immediately. By shortening the feedback loop (students do not have to wait days for a teacher's comments), AI-driven formative assessment keeps learners on track and potentially improves outcomes like subject mastery and skill development. That said, most researchers emphasize that these gains depend on thoughtful integration of AI into the curriculum rather than AI acting alone. For instructors, AI tools offer data-rich insights into student progress, identifying which areas of the curriculum are causing challenges. This can be especially helpful in large classrooms where personalized attention is difficult to provide. AI platforms aggregate data across all students, enabling teachers to track performance trends and intervene, when necessary, often before a student falls too far behind.

Despite promising outcomes, research also highlights significant limitations and challenges of using AI in formative assessment. One common issue is that AI-generated feedback is not always perfectly tuned to student needs. While AI can provide instant responses, these responses may lack the nuance or context a human teacher could offer. Some students report[6] that AI feedback can be overly generic, confusing, or even incorrect at times. For instance, an AI might flag a vague sentence in an essay but provide a canned suggestion that the student does not know how to apply. In a Norwegian classroom study[7], a subset of learners felt the AI's tips were not sufficiently clear or were too advanced for their level. Such mismatches can limit the effectiveness of the feedback for those students, especially those who are struggling, the very group formative assessment aims to help. Additionally, current generative AI models have well-known flaws: they might hallucinate (produce plausible-sounding but incorrect answers or references) or fail to recognize the specific steps of a student's reasoning. If a math student makes a calculation error, a generic AI hint might not pinpoint the mistake, whereas a teacher could. These quality issues mean that AI feedback requires careful design and validation. Until such issues are fully resolved, however, the accuracy and relevance of AI formative feedback remain uneven, which is a clear limitation.[8]

5 Chan, S., Lo, N., & Wong, A. (n.d.). Generative AI and essay writing: Impacts of automated feedback on revision performance and engagement. https://eric.ed.gov/?q=essays&ff1=subSecond+Language+Learning&id=EJ1459877

6 Burner, T., Lindvig, Y., & Wærness, J. I. (2025). "We should not be like a Dinosaur"—Using AI technologies to provide formative feedback to students. Education Sciences, 15(1), 58. https://doi.org/10.3390/educsci15010058

7 Burner, T., Lindvig, Y., & Wærness, J. I. (2025). "We should not be like a Dinosaur"—Using AI technologies to provide formative feedback to students. Education Sciences, 15(1), 58. https://doi.org/10.3390/educsci15010058

8 Zhai, C., Wibowo, S., & Li, L. D. (2024). The effects of over-reliance on AI dialogue systems on students' cognitive abilities: a systematic review. Smart Learning Environments, 11(1). https://doi.org/10.1186/s40561-024-00316-7

Another challenge is that effectively using AI for formative assessment often demands changes in teacher practice and curriculum planning. Teachers cannot simply plug in an AI tool and expect it to automatically enhance learning—they must integrate it into lesson plans, interpret its outputs, and guide students in using the feedback. The Norway study[9] noted that teachers who had not done long-term planning for AI integration struggled to use it productively in class. Without training, some educators felt unsure when to trust the AI's feedback or how to incorporate it into their grading and review processes. This highlights a broader issue: professional development and clear guidelines are necessary for teachers to confidently adopt AI-driven assessments.

Implementing AI-based assessments also raises practical constraints. Many AI tools require robust internet access, up-to-date devices, and sometimes paid subscriptions or licenses. Schools in under-resourced areas (or developing regions) may find it difficult to deploy such technology widely, exacerbating the digital divide. Even when the technology is available, classroom logistics can pose problems: ensuring each student has an account or device, integrating the AI platform with existing learning management systems, etc.

While exploring AI in formative assessment, scholars have increasingly turned attention to ethical issues, especially the risk of students becoming overly dependent on AI-generated feedback. A major theme in recent critiques is that if students lean on AI for hints and answers too much, they might bypass essential learning experiences[10], ultimately undermining their development of critical academic skills. AI tools make it tempting to get a quick solution: why struggle with a tough math problem or revision of an essay when an AI can produce an answer or a perfect paragraph instantly? Educators worry this convenience could erode skills like critical thinking, problem-solving, creativity, and even basic literacy over time. A 2024 systematic review[11] of student use of AI *dialogue systems* (like chatbots for learning) concluded that over-reliance on AI indeed negatively impacts cognitive abilities.

Closely related is the ethical challenge of ensuring students use AI assistance honestly. Formative assessment is supposed to help students learn, not provide shortcuts to cheat. However, tools like ChatGPT blur that line: a student could input an assignment prompt and get a completed answer, which defeats the purpose of the exercise. If formative feedback from AI crosses into giving away the answer, it can facilitate academic dishonesty. The ethical consensus is that transparency and guidance are key—students need to understand the boundary between getting help and outsourcing their learning.

9 Burner, T., Lindvig, Y., & Wærness, J. I. (2025). "We should not be like a Dinosaur"—Using AI technologies to provide formative feedback to students. Education Sciences, 15(1), 58. https://doi.org/10.3390/educsci15010058

10 Zion.Mercado. (2025, March 31). The Growing Dependency on AI in Academia | Student Journal of Information Privacy Law. https://sjipl.mainelaw.maine.edu/2025/03/31/the-growing-dependency-on-ai-in-academia/#:~:text=however%2C%20these%20shortcuts%20come%20at,28

11 Zhai, C., Wibowo, S., & Li, L. D. (2024b). The effects of over-reliance on AI dialogue systems on students' cognitive abilities: a systematic review. Smart Learning Environments, 11(1). https://doi.org/10.1186/s40561-024-00316-7

Summative assessments utilizing AI

Summative assessments, unlike formative assessments, are typically used to evaluate student performance at the end of an instructional period. These assessments are often high-stakes and are used to assign final grades or determine if learning objectives have been met. AI is also playing a significant role in this phase, automating aspects of the grading process of multiple-choice tests, short-answer questions, and even essays and providing scalable solutions.

For instance, AI-powered systems can automatically score written responses based on predefined rubrics, evaluating elements such as grammar, clarity, and argument strength. This automation allows teachers to provide more consistent and timely feedback, as well as focus on other aspects of teaching, such as one-on-one support and curriculum development.

AI can also be used to generate final reports for students at the end of a course or term. These reports may include not only the final grade but also detailed insights into a student's performance throughout the assessment period. By analyzing data from formative assessments, homework, quizzes, and final exams, AI can produce a comprehensive report that summarizes a student's overall learning journey.

Recent years have seen rapid improvements in **automated essay scoring** (**AES**) thanks to generative AI. Traditional AES systems (e.g. project essay grade, ETS's e-rater) relied on hand-crafted features—counting word lengths, grammar errors, or semantic similarities – as proxies for writing quality. These older approaches often struggled to capture nuanced expression or creative style. In contrast, modern LLMs like ChatGPT evaluate writing more holistically by leveraging vast training on human writing. Early research[12] in 2024 showed that LLM-based scoring can approach the accuracy of human graders. For example, one study of 1,800 student essays found ChatGPT's scores were roughly on par with an average busy teacher, falling within one point of expert human grades in about 80–89% of cases. Similarly, a 2024 experiment[13] at the *National University of Singapore* reported high reliability when using ChatGPT to score undergraduate exam essays, with strong correlations to faculty scores. These findings suggest that with clear rubrics and prompts, generative AI can consistently evaluate content, organization, and even elements of style in student writing. There is optimism among researchers that such models can better appreciate nuanced expression, for instance, understanding context and originality, in ways earlier algorithms could not.

Across the globe, consensus is emerging that human oversight is essential when using AI for summative assessment. No matter how advanced the system is, educators and assessment professionals must stay in the loop. Many governments and institutions have explicitly mandated this (see *Chapter 10, Data Security and Ethical Considerations in AI*). In the UK, *Ofqual*

12 Barshay, J., & Barshay, J. (2024, September 16). PROOF POINTS: AI essay grading is already as 'good as an overburdened' teacher, but researchers say it needs more work. The Hechinger Report. https://hechingerreport.org/proof-points-ai-essay-grading/
13 Quah B, Zheng L, Sng TJH, Yong CW, Islam I. Reliability of ChatGPT in automated essay scoring for dental undergraduate examinations. BMC Med Educ. 2024 Sep 3;24(1):962. doi: 10.1186/s12909-024-05881-6. PMID: 39227811; PMCID: PMC11373238.

(the national exams regulator) advises that using AI as the sole marker of official exams is not permitted, precisely because of concerns about bias, accuracy, and transparency in grading[14]. Instead, AI may be used to support or double-check human markers, but a trained examiner should have the final say. Experts[15] caution schools to validate AI-generated scores before releasing them to students; in other words, treat the AI's grade as a suggestion, not an authoritative verdict. This kind of oversight allows teachers to catch anomalies (like systematically low scores for a certain group, or an implausible grade on an individual paper) and adjust accordingly. It also lets educators provide the qualitative explanations that AI cannot—connecting the score to concrete feedback and next steps for the learner. From a pedagogical perspective, maintaining a human touch in summative assessment is crucial. Writing is a personal, expressive skill, and students benefit from knowing that their voice was truly heard and evaluated by a person, not just an algorithm.

Additionally, there is the risk of bias in AI models, especially when the data used to train these models is not diverse enough or when algorithms are not designed to account for cultural or contextual differences. This is why human oversight is critical in ensuring fairness and accuracy in summative assessments.

Types of AI-driven assessment tools

AI-driven assessment tools are revolutionizing how educators measure, track, and respond to student learning. These tools, powered by AI, offer dynamic, personalized, and efficient ways to evaluate student performance. automated grading systems, adaptive testing platforms, speech and language processing tools, and analytics dashboards are four primary types of AI-driven assessment tools, each of which plays a unique role in transforming traditional assessment methods into more engaging, accurate, and personalized experiences for both students and educators. A new wave of tools released in the past academic years shows how quickly AI assessment is evolving—moving beyond basic auto-grading toward fairness-aware scoring, adaptive analytics, and richer feedback loops.

Automated grading systems

Automated grading systems are one of the most widely used AI tools in education. These systems help educators save time by automatically grading multiple-choice questions, essays, and even more complex assignments. The most common forms of automated grading systems include:

- **Essay scoring engines**: They use **natural language processing (NLP)** algorithms to evaluate the quality of written text. These engines assess various elements, such

---

14 Norden, J. (2024, July 23). Exams: How Ofqual plans to cope with AI. *Tes Magazine*. https://www.tes.com/magazine/news/general/exams-how-ofqual-plans-cope-ai#:~:text=human,could%20make%20the%20system%20unfair

15 Bdimarco. (2024, July 9). New Evidence Affirms Teachers Should Go Slow Using AI to Grade Essays - FutureEd. FutureEd. https://www.future-ed.org/new-evidence-affirms-teachers-should-go-slow-using-ai-to-grade-essays/

as grammar, coherence, spelling, sentence structure, and even argument strength. Popular examples include Turnitin's Gradescope[16] and ETS's e-rater[17]. [18]These tools provide a way for educators to automate grading while still maintaining a level of subjectivity in evaluating content quality. Their limitations lie in assessing creativity and more complex arguments, which still require human intervention. In the latest advancements in this space, Turnitin Feedback Studio (release notes, May 2025) now ships with a multilingual fairness model trained to reduce false-positive plagiarism flags for second-language writers; each update is accompanied by a public bias-audit summary so schools can judge transparency claims.

- **Multiple-choice scanners**: Multiple-choice questions have long been a staple of education assessments. AI-powered multiple-choice scanners, such as ZipGrade[19], use machine learning algorithms to quickly grade tests and quizzes. These scanners are able to instantly recognize answers based on pre-scanned answer sheets, providing educators with immediate feedback and saving hours of manual grading. The primary advantage of AI in this area is speed and efficiency, particularly in large classrooms or high stakes testing environments.

- **Rubrics**: AI can also be integrated into rubric-based grading systems, where predefined criteria are applied to assess the quality of student work. AI systems can scan assignments against rubrics, evaluating components such as accuracy, clarity, and depth of analysis. While these systems may not fully replace human judgment, they can expedite the grading process and ensure consistency in scoring. Gradescope's spring-2025 *AI-Assisted Grading* upgrade[20] lets instructors upload a ChatGPT-generated rubric, then clusters similar student answers and drafts preliminary scores the teacher can accept or adjust. The workflow has been adopted in large undergraduate **science, technology, engineering, and mathematics** (**STEM**) courses across North America and Asia because it halves marking time while keeping a human in the loop. Some AI tools allow for real-time feedback based on rubric analysis, offering students insights into their strengths and areas for improvement.

Adaptive testing platforms

Adaptive testing platforms represent a significant leap forward in assessment technology. Unlike traditional, fixed assessments, adaptive testing dynamically adjusts the difficulty of questions based on student performance, providing a more accurate measurement of a student's knowledge and skills. The *Duolingo English Test* refreshed its adaptive algorithm in

---

16 Turnitin. (n.d.). Gradescope | Grading and Assessment Platform | Turnitin. https://www.turnitin.com/products/gradescope/

17 About the e-rater Scoring Engine. (n.d.). https://www.ets.org/erater/about.html

18 Turnitin release notes – Turnitin Guides

19 Llc, Z. (n.d.). ZipGrade - iPhone and Android Grading App for formative assessment and quizzes. Zip-Grade. https://www.zipgrade.com/

20 AI-Assisted Grading and Answer Groups. (n.d.). Gradescope. Retrieved June 7, 2025, from https://guides.gradescope.com/hc/en-us/articles/24838908062093-AI-Assisted-Grading-and-Answer-Groups

late 2024 and published open *Responsible AI Standards*[21] that spell out how the test monitors item-level bias before scores are released—an approach assessment researchers flag as a new benchmark for high-stakes fairness.

Adaptive testing platforms, such as NWEA's MAP Growth[22] and Wiley's Knewton[23], leverage AI to assess a student's current level of understanding and automatically adjust the difficulty of subsequent questions. For example, if a student answers a question correctly, the system will present a more challenging question. If they answer incorrectly, the platform might provide an easier question or revisit a previously covered topic. This ensures that the test is always challenging but not overwhelming, leading to a more accurate assessment of a student's abilities.

One major advantage is that it provides more granular insights into a student's performance. Traditional tests often fail to capture the depth of a student's knowledge, as all students are given the same set of questions regardless of their performance. AI-driven adaptive tests, by contrast, measure both strengths and weaknesses in more detail, enabling teachers to intervene early when necessary and offer tailored support.

Speech and language processing tools

Speech and language processing tools use AI to assess spoken language, providing automated evaluation of oral skills. These tools are particularly useful for language learning, as they can assess pronunciation, fluency, and comprehension in real time. Examples of speech and language processing tools include:

- **Automated oral exams**: Traditional oral exams require significant time and human resources, as students must be individually assessed by an instructor. AI-powered systems can automate this process by transcribing spoken responses and scoring students based on predefined criteria. These tools analyze pronunciation, grammar, intonation, and sentence structure, providing real-time feedback to students on how to improve their spoken language skills.

  Language learning apps such as Duolingo[24] and Babbel[25] use AI to assess spoken responses, offering feedback on pronunciation and fluency. These systems track the learner's improvement and adjust difficulty based on their performance, ensuring that students are continually challenged at the appropriate level.

21 Burstein, J. (2023). The Duolingo English Test Responsible AI Standards. [Updated March 29, 2024]: https://go.duolingo.com/ResponsibleAI

22 MAP Growth - NWEA. (2025, January 27). NWEA. https://www.nwea.org/map-growth/

23 Wiley | global leader in publishing, education and research. (n.d.). https://www.wiley.com/en-ie

24 Wodzak, S. (2024, December 31). How Duolingo is using artificial intelligence for social good. Duolingo Blog. https://blog.duolingo.com/ai-improves-education/#:~:text=AI%20helps%20us%20analyze%20user%20responses%20in%20order,we%20can%20provide%20targeted%20feedback%20on%20your%20pronunciation

25 Lepcheska, T. (2023, August 30). What is Babbel and How to Use It? Neural Network Press. https://neuralnetworkpress.com/what-is-babbel-and-how-to-use-it#:~:text=Babbel%20is%20an%20AI%20language-learning%20platform%20that%20helps,language%20based%20on%20one%27s%20preferences%20through%20real-life%20conversations

- **Language proficiency applications**: AI-driven language proficiency assessments have transformed how language skills are tested. These tests leverage speech recognition and NLP to evaluate listening, reading, speaking, and writing skills. The use of AI in language proficiency assessments reduces the subjectivity of scoring and provides immediate feedback, which is valuable for both students and teachers alike. Microsoft's standalone Reading Coach[26] (general release, December 2024) listens to students read aloud, flags mispronunciations, and instantly generates new phonics passages or AI-authored stories at the learner's exact level—features already piloted in bilingual primary schools in Canada and Brazil.

Analytics dashboards

Analytics dashboards represent a powerful tool for educators to monitor and visualize student performance. These AI-driven tools collect and analyze data from various assessments, offering educators a comprehensive view of individual and group progress.

Monitoring progress

AI-powered analytics dashboards track student performance across a range of activities, assessments, and assignments. These platforms aggregate data to provide a holistic view of student progress, helping educators spot trends, identify struggling students, and gauge the overall effectiveness of their teaching strategies. Tools like Google Classroom[27] and PowerSchool[28] offer detailed performance metrics, which help educators make data-driven decisions in real time.

Visualizing student performance

Visualization tools in analytics dashboards allow educators to quickly assess how students are performing in different areas. For example, an educator can view a heat map of a class's performance on specific topics or identify patterns in learning behaviors. By visualizing this data, teachers can more easily pinpoint areas where students may need additional support or where curriculum adjustments are necessary. These visual insights also empower educators to personalize instruction and track the effectiveness of their interventions. Platforms like Tableau and Microsoft Power BI integrate with AI assessment tools, providing customizable dashboards that can display data in various formats, from bar graphs to pie charts, offering educators clear insights into student performance and overall progress. Microsoft rolled out

26 Team, M. E. (2025, February 12). Experience AI-powered reading practice with Reading Coach | Microsoft Education Blog. Microsoft Education Blog. https://www.microsoft.com/en-us/education/blog/2024/12/ support-independent-ai-powered-reading-practice-with-reading-coach/?utm_source=chatgpt.com
27 Google Classroom. (n.d.). https://sites.google.com/view/classroom-workspace/home?authuser=0
28 PowerSchool. (2025, February 5). PowerSchool K-12 Software & Cloud-Based Solutions. https://www. powerschool.com/

Copilot for Power BI[29] in March 2024 and has been expanding it every quarter. Educators can now chat with their data typing **Show me ninth-grade attendance dips by week and predict next month's at-risk list**, Copilot auto-builds the visual, runs a time-series forecast, and explains the drivers in plain language. Salesforce-owned Tableau answered with Tableau Pulse[30], which pushes proactive digests to teachers' email or Slack, flagging outliers such as a sudden drop in formative-quiz scores or a spike in late submissions. These upgrades matter pedagogically and shift dashboards from retrospective reporting to forward-looking guidance: instead of poring over end-of-term spreadsheets, educators now get proactive, explainable nudges that pinpoint which students or cohorts need intervention and why—making data-informed support timelier and more equitable than ever before.

Together, these AI-powered tools are transforming education into a more dynamic, data-driven experience that is tailored to the needs of every student. As these technologies continue to evolve, the potential to improve assessment and feedback processes will only grow, making learning more personalized, efficient, and effective.

Design principles for effective AI-based assessment

As AI continues to reshape the landscape of education, designing effective AI-based assessment tools requires careful consideration of several core principles. These design principles ensure that AI-driven assessments are not only innovative but also accurate, relevant, and accessible for all users, while they provide meaningful insights into student learning and support a more personalized educational experience.

Since 2024, international bodies have issued clearer guardrails for developers and schools aiming to build or buy AI-driven assessments. Two documents are fast becoming reference points:

- **United Nations Educational, Scientific and Cultural Organization's (UNESCO)** 2024 *AI Competency Frameworks for Students and Teachers* that spell out how any AI assessment tool should make its scoring criteria transparent (explainability cards), publish bias-audit results, and allow end-users to track model updates over time[31]. UNESCO pairs the framework with an **Ethical Impact Assessment (EIA)** template—updated in early 2025—that walks vendors through risk mapping for fairness, privacy, and algorithmic accountability before classroom rollout[32].

29 Johnson, P. (2025, April 8). Power your school year with AI solutions for educators, leaders, and IT teams | Microsoft Education Blog. Microsoft Education Blog. https://www.microsoft.com/en-us/education/blog/2024/09/power-your-school-year-with-ai-solutions-for-educators-leaders-and-it-teams/
30 New features. (n.d.-b). Tableau. https://www.tableau.com/2024-1-features
31 What you need to know about UNESCO's new AI competency frameworks for students and teachers. (2024b, September 3). UNESCO. https://www.unesco.org/en/articles/what-you-need-know-unes-cos-new-ai-competency-frameworks-students-and-teachers
32 Ethical Impact Assessment. (n.d.). UNESCO. Retrieved June 7, 2025, from https://www.unesco.org/eth-ics-ai/en/eia?utm_source=chatgpt.com

- The **Organisation for Economic Co-operation and Development (OECD)** AI Principles (update 2024) and the *Smart Data & Digital Technology in Education* guidelines add education-specific annex notes that call for prior validity studies when AI grades high-stakes work, audit trails so exam boards can reconstruct how a score was produced, and contestability mechanisms for students to trigger a human re-grade.[33]

What this means for designers and adopters:

- Algorithmic transparency is no longer optional. UNESCO's EIA asks vendors to publish plain-language model cards that explain training data, scoring logic, and known limitations.

- Bias audits must precede deployment. The updated OECD notes recommend a documented equity check—testing the model on diverse student sub-groups—with results made available to regulators and end-user institutions.

- Accountability pathways are mandatory. Both frameworks insist on a human-led appeals process and version-control logs so stakeholders can trace any change in a scoring algorithm.

By aligning new AI assessment tools with these standards—embedding explainability, documented bias testing, and clear human-in-the-loop procedures—developers can move beyond innovative toward trustworthy and globally portable solutions that truly serve learners.

Validity and reliability

One of the most critical aspects of any assessment tool is its validity and reliability, i.e., the extent to which the tool accurately measures what it is intended to measure and produces consistent results over time.

AI-based assessment tools must be carefully designed to measure the specific learning outcomes that educators aim to assess. This means that the AI algorithms used in these assessments should be rigorously tested and calibrated to ensure they are evaluating the right skills or knowledge. For example, an AI-powered reading comprehension tool should not only assess whether a student understands a text but also how well they can analyze, infer meaning, and synthesize information, key components of comprehension that need to be incorporated into the design.

Reliability refers to the consistency of the results. AI tools must be able to provide consistent assessments regardless of the student being tested or the context in which the assessment takes place. If an AI system's grading of an essay varies dramatically across similar inputs, its reliability is compromised. Therefore, developers must ensure that AI models are tested against

---

33 AI principles. (n.d.). OECD. Retrieved June 7, 2025, from https://www.oecd.org/en/topics/ai-principles.html

diverse data sets and multiple scenarios to guarantee dependable and accurate performance. This needs to be a continuous effort, not just a one-time exercise, where AI-driven assessment tools are continually validated against real-world student performance to ensure their validity and reliability. This requires collaboration between educators, AI developers, and researchers to refine algorithms and improve assessment accuracy. Regular feedback loops and the analysis of assessment outcomes help maintain the integrity of the system, ensuring it adapts over time while still measuring the intended skills effectively.

As AI-driven assessments become more common, ensuring they work equitably for all learners is critical. Many early AI assessment tools were developed and validated in limited contexts, raising concerns about bias when applied globally. A 2024 systematic review found that *none* of the existing AI literacy assessment scales had been tested for cross-cultural validity[34]. This lack of cross-cultural validation limits their reliable adoption in multiple countries and hinders meaningful international comparisons. In other words, an AI tool that performs well in one country or language may not be fair or accurate in another if not properly vetted. Researchers have highlighted how AI grading systems can misjudge students from different backgrounds. For example, an AI might under-score answers written in non-standard English or from an unfamiliar cultural perspective[35]. Such issues underscore the need for rigorous cross-cultural testing before deploying AI assessments at scale.

Recent years have seen significant methodological advancements to evaluate and improve AI-based assessments across cultures. Key developments include:

- **Fairness and bias audits**: Assessment designers are now systematically checking for bias and differential performance across groups. For instance, AI models are evaluated for **Differential Item Functioning (DIF)** – ensuring that items or questions do not give unfair advantages/disadvantages to any cultural or linguistic group[36]. Test developers also conduct fairness reviews of AI-generated content. The Duolingo English Test (an AI-scored language exam used worldwide) introduced formal fairness and bias item reviews in 2024 to eliminate construct-irrelevant barriers and ensure that cultural and linguistic factors do not impede test accessibility[37].

- **Diverse training data and localization**: A major advance is using more diverse datasets and localized training to make AI tools culturally robust. Instead of training an AI grader on a single population, new models are fed data from multiple languages, regions, and socioeconomic groups. This helps the AI learn a wide range of valid responses. The OECD's latest initiatives set cross-lingual consistency and equitable

---

34 Lintner, T. (2024). A systematic review of AI literacy scales. Npj Science of Learning, 9(1). https://doi.org/10.1038/s41539-024-00264-4
35 Kaldaras, L., Akaeze, H. O., & Reckase, M. D. (2024). Developing valid assessments in the era of generative artificial intelligence. Frontiers in Education, 9. https://doi.org/10.3389/feduc.2024.1399377
36 Kaldaras, L., Akaeze, H. O., & Reckase, M. D. (2024). Developing valid assessments in the era of generative artificial intelligence. Frontiers in Education, 9. https://doi.org/10.3389/feduc.2024.1399377
37 Burstein, J. (2023). The Duolingo English Test Responsible AI Standards. [Updated March 29, 2024]: https://go.duolingo.com/ResponsibleAI

treatment across diverse student backgrounds as explicit criteria for international AI assessment models[38].

- **Transparency and contextualization**: In recent years, we have seen a push for greater transparency in AI assessment tools, an important methodological shift. Researchers urge clearly documenting an AI tool's intended scope, training data, and limitations when reporting results[39]. For instance, if an automated scoring system were trained mostly on English essays from North America, stakeholders should be told that upfront. This transparency allows educators to judge whether the tool suits their context.

- **Iterative cross-cultural validation**: New methodologies treat validation as an ongoing, iterative process, especially when extending an AI tool to a new culture or language. One approach is to pilot the AI on sample data from the target group before full deployment, then refine it. In one case, a team had an AI score student answers three times and compared results to human scores; whenever the AI disagreed with humans, they adjusted the prompt or model until better agreement was reached[40]. Another novel idea is employing two different AI models to check each other: one might cluster written responses, while another scores them, and any mismatches prompt further analysis[41].

- **Alignment with curriculum**: AI-based assessments should be designed to align with the curriculum to ensure that they reinforce and accurately reflect the learning objectives that educators have set for their students. This alignment is crucial for making the assessment relevant to the educational goals of the institution and for ensuring that students are being evaluated on the skills and knowledge they are expected to acquire.

It is important to note also that these assessments should not be isolated from the rest of the educational experience. Instead, they should be integrated into the broader curriculum, complementing classroom instruction and providing insights into student progress along the way. The following figure depicts this integration between instruction, AI and student:

---

38 Developing an International Large-Scale AI Tool for Educational Assessment and Personalised Learning. (n.d.). OECD. Retrieved June 7, 2025, from https://www.oecd.org/en/about/projects/developing-an-international-large-scale-ai-tool-for-educational-assessment-and-personalised-learning.html
39 Dumas, Denis & Dong, Yixiao & Kim, Yoojoong. (2025). Balancing The Efficiency-Validity Tradeoff: Consequential and Cross-Cultural Considerations for Scaling-Up the AI Assessment of Creativity in Education. https://www.researchgate.net/publication/391279616_Balancing_The_Efficiency-Validity_Tradeoff_Consequential_and_Cross-Cultural_Considerations_for_Scaling-Up_the_AI_Assessment_of_Creativity_in_Education
40 Kaldaras, L., Akaeze, H. O., & Reckase, M. D. (2024b). Developing valid assessments in the era of generative artificial intelligence. *Frontiers in Education*, 9. https://doi.org/10.3389/feduc.2024.1399377
41 Kaldaras, L., Akaeze, H. O., & Reckase, M. D. (2024b). Developing valid assessments in the era of generative artificial intelligence. *Frontiers in Education*, 9. https://doi.org/10.3389/feduc.2024.1399377

Figure 3.1: *Educators and AI can work together to improve the student experience*

Furthermore, these assessments must be adaptable to different curriculum frameworks. Whether an educator is using AI tools to assess STEM skills, language proficiency, or social sciences knowledge, the AI system must be flexible enough to cater to the unique requirements of various subject areas. This ensures that AI tools are not just generalized assessment systems but are tailored to meet the diverse needs of different curricula and academic levels.

As curriculum standards and learning objectives evolve over time, AI-based assessment tools must be able to adapt. It becomes imperative that developers implement mechanisms for continuous updates and feedback to ensure the AI system remains aligned with current educational standards and practices.

User experience

The effectiveness of AI-based assessments also hinges on the **user experience** (**UX**), or how easily and intuitively both students and educators can interact with the technology. A positive user experience ensures that the assessment process is smooth, engaging, and productive, ultimately leading to better learning outcomes.

One of the central principles of UX design is accessibility. AI-based assessments must be designed to accommodate students with diverse needs, including those with disabilities or learning differences. This includes offering features such as text-to-speech for visually impaired students, speech recognition for students with writing difficulties, and options for students with learning disabilities to adjust the pace of assessments. By incorporating accessibility features, AI tools ensure that all students have an equal opportunity to succeed.

AI-driven assessment platforms have made significant strides in accessibility and inclusiveness, reshaping the user experience to accommodate diverse learners. These tools now prioritize equitable access, fulfilling the long-held promise that AI can create more accessible and inclusive learning environments[42]. In practice, this means designing assessments that adapt

42 Gibson, R. (2024b, September 10). The Impact of AI in Advancing Accessibility for Learners with Disabilities. Educause. https://er.educause.edu/articles/2024/9/the-impact-of-ai-in-advancing-accessibility-for-learners-with-disabilities

to individual needs by default. Recent design guidelines even urge treating accessibility as a baseline, leveraging AI for features like transcripts, alt-text, and translations to support multilingual and neurodiverse students[43]. Under this approach, one-size-fits-all interfaces are giving way to flexible, personalized experiences that benefit *all* students, including those with disabilities or different learning profiles.

One of the most transformative improvements has been augmented support for neurodivergent learners. Modern AI-based assessment tools can dynamically adjust content difficulty and pacing for each student, ensuring learners are not rushed or held back by a fixed schedule[44]. Such personalized pacing is crucial for students with **attention deficit hyperactivity disorder (ADHD)**, autism, or dyslexia, who may need more time or alternative pathways to demonstrate understanding. In tandem, platforms increasingly provide visual scaffolding, breaking down complex tasks into guided, multimodal steps. The AI can embed intuitive visual cues or hints and offer real-time adaptive feedback as students work through problems[45], essentially acting as a virtual guide. Equally important, many interfaces now include a distraction-free mode that minimizes on-screen clutter and sensory overwhelm. By stripping away extraneous graphics, animations, or noise, the assessment environment remains calm and focused[46], an option particularly welcomed by students who are sensitive to sensory input. Coupled with user-controlled settings (like adjustable text size, color contrast, or toggling off timers), these features empower neurodiverse students to tailor the environment to their needs and stay confident and on task.

Additionally, AI-based assessment tools have expanded their multilingual capabilities, making them far more inclusive for learners from different linguistic backgrounds. Real-time translation has emerged as a standard feature: advanced language models now enable on-the-fly translation of prompts, questions, or tutorial content into virtually any language[47]. What was once a niche add-on is now built into mainstream platforms, allowing students to interact with assessment materials in their preferred language without delay. A student in a French or Spanish medium program, for example, can receive an English-origin quiz translated moment-to-moment, leveling the playing field. Such bilingual support goes hand-

43 Day Grady, S., PhD, & Brooks, R., PhD. (2025). From Automation to Transformation: AI strategies for personalized, engaging, and inclusive online course design. Quality Matters. https://qualitymatters.org/sites/default/files/research-docs-pdfs/QM-White-Paper-AI-Strategies-for-Course-Design.pdf

44 Radick, R. (2024, November). Designing Digital Learning for All: Embracing neurodiversity in virtual classrooms. Education Northwest. https://educationnorthwest.org/insights/designing-digital-learning-all-embracing-neurodiversity-virtual-classrooms

45 AI-Driven Visual Scaffolding in Education: A Comprehensive Literature Review - International Journal of Research and Scientific Innovation (IJRSI). (2025, April 10). International Journal of Research and Scientific Innovation (IJRSI). https://rsisinternational.org/journals/ijrsi/articles/ai-driven-visual-scaffolding-in-education-a-comprehensive-literature-review/

46 Radick, R. (2024, November). Designing Digital Learning for All: Embracing neurodiversity in virtual classrooms. Education Northwest. https://educationnorthwest.org/insights/designing-digital-learning-all-embracing-neurodiversity-virtual-classrooms

47 Gibson, R. (2024b, September 10). *The Impact of AI in Advancing Accessibility for Learners with Disabilities.* Educause. https://er.educause.edu/articles/2024/9/the-impact-of-ai-in-advancing-accessibility-for-learners-with-disabilities

in-hand with speech recognition and captioning advancements: if a learner speaks or asks a question in their own language, AI can recognize it and respond appropriately. The result is a more inclusive assessment dialogue that honors each learner's linguistic identity. By removing language barriers in real time, AI-driven tools enable truly global and culturally responsive assessment. Students no longer have to struggle through a second language to understand their test or their mistakes, which boosts comprehension and confidence.

While AI has the potential to revolutionize education, it also presents technical challenges. Students and educators may face issues related to software compatibility, internet access, or device limitations. To minimize these technical barriers, developers should design AI-based assessment tools that are compatible with a range of devices and platforms, ensuring that students can access assessments from their smartphones, tablets, or computers. Additionally, providing user-friendly onboarding and troubleshooting guides can help overcome initial hurdles and ensure a smooth experience for both students and educators.

A key component of UX in AI-based assessments is the ability to engage students through interactive and meaningful features. For example, feedback should be immediate, actionable, and encouraging, guiding students on their learning path. Gamification elements, like progress tracking or badges for achievements, can also increase student motivation and foster a sense of accomplishment. The goal is to create an assessment experience that is not only educational but also motivating and enjoyable for students, encouraging them to stay engaged and continue learning.

Role of AI in feedback mechanisms

In traditional education systems, feedback has often been limited to grades or scores, which provide only a snapshot of a student's performance.

One of the unique strengths of AI is its ability to assess not just the final answer, but the reasoning behind it. Traditional assessment methods often focus on whether an answer is correct or incorrect, overlooking the cognitive processes that led to that answer. AI has the ability to analyze the steps a student takes to solve a problem, providing insights into how they arrived at their solution and offering feedback based on those steps. For instance, in mathematics or coding assignments, AI tools can track the steps a student takes to reach a solution, identifying whether the student is using the correct method or if they are making an error in the process. AI can then provide detailed feedback on where students went wrong in their reasoning and suggest targeted interventions.

However, conventional AI models often function as black boxes—they generate scores or comments without revealing their reasoning. This opaqueness undermines trust: students and educators may doubt an AI-generated grade or comment if they cannot see how it was derived[48]. **Explainable AI (XAI)** in education aims to fix this by making the AI's decision-

---

48 Teach-to-Reason with Scoring: Self-Explainable Rationale-Driven Multi-Trait Essay Scoring. (n.d.). https://arxiv.org/html/2502.20748v1

making process visible. In simple terms, XAI systems show why they gave a certain assessment. For example, an XAI-driven tutor might highlight which parts of a student's answer led to a deduction, or an automated grader might provide a step-by-step rationale with the score. This transparency helps everyone—students, teachers, even administrators—better understand the AI's reasoning. By opening up the black box, XAI can support fairer, more effective, and inclusive educational experiences[49]. Researchers stress that leveraging AI's benefits (speed, consistency, personalization) without sacrificing accuracy and credibility will require integrating explainability into feedback systems[50]. In short, to truly be trustworthy and pedagogically sound, AI-driven assessments must not only be accurate but also explain their answers.

In this sense, the latest XAI upgrades in assessment tools aim to provide an on-screen rationale to every automated score:

- **Interactive rationale viewers**: AERA Chat lets teachers paste a question and student answer; the LLM assigns a score and color-highlights the phrases that drove each decision, so learners can trace feedback line-by-line[51].

- **Rubric-aligned chain of thought**: The 2025 QwenScore+ framework prompts ChatGPT to walk through rubric criteria step-by-step before issuing an essay grade, then prints that reasoning for the student; evaluations show its structured explanations are judged more useful than opaque ChatGPT comments[52].

- **Self-explaining scorers**: Research on **Rationale-Driven Multi-trait Essay scoring (RaDME)** trains smaller models to output a short justification with every trait score, boosting user trust without sacrificing accuracy[53].

Policymakers are responding in kind; the EU working groups now urge schools to choose tools that publish explainability cards, and several US state guidelines (2025) require any AI grader to make its scoring logic available to teachers for audit.[54] [55]

49 Insights from the community workshop on explainable AI in education. (2024, November 7). European Education Area. https://education.ec.europa.eu/news/insights-from-the-community-workshop-on-explainable-ai-in-education

50 Li, H., & Botelho, A. F. (2024). Developing explainable AI systems to support feedback for students. educationaldatamining.org. https://doi.org/10.5281/zenodo.12730029

51 Li, J., Bobrov, A., West, D., Aloisi, C., & He, Y. (2024, October 12). AERA Chat: an interactive platform for automated explainable student answer assessment. arXiv.org. https://arxiv.org/abs/2410.09507

52 TRATES: Trait-Specific Rubric-Assisted Cross-Prompt essay scoring. (n.d.-b). https://arxiv.org/html/2505.14577v1

53 LCES: Zero-shot automated essay scoring via pairwise comparisons using large language models. (n.d.). https://arxiv.org/html/2505.08498v1

54 Insights from the community workshop on explainable AI in education. (2024b, November 7). European Education Area. https://education.ec.europa.eu/news/insights-from-the-community-workshop-on-explainable-ai-in-education

55 Dwyer, M. (2025, April 15). Center for Democracy and Technology. Looking back at AI guidance across state education agencies and looking forward - Center for Democracy and Technology. https://cdt.org/insights/looking-back-at-ai-guidance-across-state-education-agencies-and-looking-forward/

Real-world applications

AI systems do not just analyze individual assignments or tests; they can also analyze patterns in student behavior over time, providing highly personalized feedback. By monitoring a student's interactions with learning materials, AI systems can identify trends in how students engage with content, such as how often they attempt certain types of problems or how long it takes them to complete assignments and offer feedback that is tailored to their unique needs.

For example, AI systems like Gradescope's[56] automated feedback analyzes student responses to assess not just correctness, but the approach and timing involved in solving a problem. The system might detect that a student is consistently spending too much time on certain topics, indicating that they are struggling with that concept. In response, the system can provide specific feedback or additional resources to help the student overcome these challenges. The 2024 release[57], *AI-Assisted Grading and Answer Groups*, deepened this capability: the system now auto-clusters similar responses, proposes rubric categories with sample comments, and lets teachers attach concise next-step advice to an entire cluster in one click. By turning recurring error patterns into explain-as-you-grade feedback—while the instructor retains final say—the platform transforms raw analytics into actionable guidance that students receive immediately and can act on in their very next attempt.

The biggest leap, however, is the rise of LLM-powered feedback chatbots that sit inside course spaces and answer students in natural language.

AI-powered chatbots, such as *Jill Watson*[58], represent another innovative way AI is transforming feedback mechanisms. Developed by *Georgia Tech, Jill Watson* is an AI chatbot designed to assist students by answering their questions in real time. *Jill Watson* operates within an online course environment, providing instant, personalized feedback to students as they navigate their coursework. *Jill Watson* 2.0, rebuilt in 2024, runs on ChatGPT with a built-in search layer. When students ask a question, the bot combs only instructor-approved course files (syllabi, slides, transcripts), quotes the exact passage it found, and keeps a back-and-forth conversation that remembers earlier exchanges. Instead of a brief answer, learners see both the source text and a short **how I arrived at this** note, which makes the reply clearer and cuts down on follow-up questions.

This AI-powered approach to feedback goes beyond basic answers and incorporates learning support and problem-solving assistance directly into the course structure, offering students a more engaging and responsive learning experience.

These advancements and LLM agents share two new capabilities:

- **Context-aware retrieval**: They ground every reply in courseware chosen by the instructor, then surface a citation so students can verify the source.

56 Gradescope | Save time grading. (n.d.). https://www.gradescope.com/
57 AI-Assisted Grading and Answer Groups. (n.d.). Gradescope. Retrieved June 7, 2025, from https://guides.gradescope.com/hc/en-us/articles/24838908062093-AI-Assisted-Grading-and-Answer-Groups
58 Jill Watson – Design Intelligence Lab. (n.d.). https://dilab.gatech.edu/jill-watson/

- **Explain-your-work prompts**: Before responding, the model generates a short internal rationale that can be displayed on request, satisfying emerging XAI guidelines for transparency.

By weaving real-time, rationale-rich dialogue into standard pattern analytics, today's AI feedback loops give learners far more than a grade: they reveal why an answer faltered and how to improve, without waiting for office hours and freeing up time from teachers.

The integration of AI into feedback mechanisms represents a monumental shift in education. This shift empowers students by giving them the tools they need to understand their own learning processes and improve over time. By making feedback more immediate, specific, and insightful, AI is not just changing how we assess student learning; it is transforming how we support and guide students on their educational journey.

Challenges and considerations for implementing AI in assessments

While the integration of AI into educational assessments promises immense benefits, it also raises important challenges that must be addressed to ensure these technologies are used responsibly and effectively. Some of the key considerations for implementing AI in assessment include data privacy and security, ethical concerns regarding bias, teacher and student acceptance, and the role of AI in teacher-student relationships.

Let us not forget that AI now operates under stricter privacy rules. The EU's AI Act treats most classroom analytics as high-risk, obliging schools and vendors to log model decisions, run bias audits, and guarantee human oversight of scores[59]. In the United States, the *Office of Educational Technology's Toolkit for Safe, Ethical, and Equitable AI Integration* warns districts that sending identifiable student work to public LLMs may breach FERPA and urges *inspectable, explainable, overridable* AI by design[60], while the *Federal Trade Commission's* proposed COPPA 2.0 update tightens consent and data-minimization rules for any platform profiling children under 13[61]. Across the Atlantic, the UK's *Data (Use and Access) Bill,* now before Parliament (at the time of this writing in April 2025), would require a code of practice for accessing children's educational data and mandate opt-out rights for AI-based grading[62].

---

59 AI Act. (2025, June 6). Shaping Europe's Digital Future. https://digital-strategy.ec.europa.eu/en/policies/regulatory-framework-ai

60 U.S. Department of Education, Office of Educational Technology, Empowering Education Leaders: A Toolkit for Safe, Ethical, and Equitable AI Integration, Washington, D.C., 2024.

61 FTC finalizes changes to children's privacy rule limiting companies' ability to monetize kids' data. (2025, January 16). Federal Trade Commission. https://www.ftc.gov/news-events/news/press-releases/2025/01/ftc-finalizes-changes-childrens-privacy-rule-limiting-companies-ability-monetize-kids-data?utm_source=chatgpt.com

62 Data (Use and Access) Bill [Lords] - Hansard - UK Parliament

Responsible deployment of AI assessments means treating data privacy and security as a legal prerequisite, alongside long-standing concerns about bias, teacher–student acceptance, and the evolving role of AI in the learning relationship.

Privacy and security

One of the most pressing challenges in the deployment of AI in educational assessments is the protection of student data. AI systems used in assessments collect vast amounts of sensitive information about students, including personal details, academic performance, behavioral patterns, and learning progress. This data is essential for AI systems to generate personalized feedback and adapt to individual learning needs. However, the collection, storage, and use of this data also pose significant privacy risks.

AI-driven assessment systems must adhere to strict data privacy regulations to protect student information from unauthorized access, misuse, or exploitation. Educational institutions and AI developers must ensure compliance with laws like the **Family Educational Rights and Privacy Act (FERPA)**[63] in the U.S., the **General Data Protection Regulation (GDPR)**[64] in Europe, and other national data protection laws. These regulations are designed to protect students' personal data and ensure that it is used ethically and securely.

The security of student data is equally critical. AI systems must employ robust encryption techniques to protect data both in transit and at rest. Furthermore, there should be transparent protocols for who has access to this data and how long it is retained. Educational institutions need to collaborate with AI developers to establish clear data-handling policies that safeguard students' privacy while enabling the beneficial use of AI in assessments.

In addition, transparency in data collection and usage can help build trust with students, parents, and educators. Providing clear explanations of what data is collected, how it will be used, and the steps taken to ensure security can help alleviate concerns and foster a more positive relationship with AI-powered systems. Several cases show how quickly AI assessment tools can stray into privacy trouble if oversight is weak. In April 2024, *The Guardian* reported[65] that several U.S. school districts were rolling out Proctorio[66], AI-based remote-proctoring systems that record students' webcams and screens throughout an exam, reviving a debate that first exploded during the pandemic, when colleges rushed to such tools to police online tests. While administrators saw continuous monitoring as a guardrail against cheating, students denounced it as blanket surveillance: campus petitions called for bans[67],

63 What is FERPA? | Protecting Student Privacy. (n.d.). https://studentprivacy.ed.gov/faq/what-ferpa
64 General Data Protection Regulation (GDPR) – legal text. (2024, April 22). General Data Protection Regulation (GDPR). https://gdpr-info.eu/
65 Keierleber, M. (2024, April 18). Are your kids being spied on? The rise of anti-cheating software in US schools. The Guardian. https://www.theguardian.com/education/2024/apr/18/us-schools-anti-cheating-software-proctorio
66 About | Proctorio. (n.d.). Proctorio. https://proctorio.com/about
67 Martin, K. (2020, September 10). Stop the use of online proctoring exams at the University of Minnesota. Change.org. https://www.change.org/p/amy-klobuchar-stop-the-use-of-online-proctoring-exams-at-the-university-of-minnesota

civil-rights lawsuits[68] alleged constitutional violations[69], and technology critics warned the facial-recognition components were *racist algorithms* that sometimes failed to detect Black test-takers, triggering false-positive flags[70]. These episodes illustrate why AI assessment cannot succeed without transparent data practices, explicit consent, and bias audits that protect both privacy and equity.

Ethical concerns

AI has the potential to revolutionize educational assessments, but it also raises critical ethical concerns, particularly around bias in AI algorithms. AI systems are only as unbiased as the data they are trained on. If the data used to train AI models contains inherent biases, such as underrepresentation of certain demographics, gender imbalances, or socioeconomic disparities, these biases can be perpetuated in the AI's decision-making process.

For example, a biased algorithm might favor certain types of answers or learning styles over others, disadvantaging students from diverse backgrounds. This could lead to unfair assessments that do not accurately reflect a student's abilities, reinforcing existing inequalities in education. For instance, if an AI-driven essay scoring system is trained primarily on data from high-achieving students, it may unfairly penalize students who use unconventional writing styles or come from different educational backgrounds.

To address these concerns, it is essential for AI systems to be regularly audited for fairness. Developers must use diverse, representative data sets when training algorithms to minimize bias and ensure that AI assessments are equitable for all students. Additionally, algorithmic transparency should be prioritized, with developers providing clear explanations of how AI models make decisions. This transparency allows educators to better understand how assessments are generated and ensures accountability.

Ultimately, the goal is to design AI systems that are fair and inclusive, ensuring that all students have an equal opportunity to demonstrate their learning without being unfairly judged due to the limitations of the technology.

Overcoming resistance and building trust in AI systems

Despite the many advantages AI offers, its implementation in education often faces resistance from both teachers and students. For educators, the introduction of AI can be perceived as

---

68 Brown, C. (2022, November 23). Test Proctor Privacy Lawsuit Tossed on Choice-of-Law Grounds. Bloomberg Law. https://news.bloomberglaw.com/litigation/test-proctor-privacy-lawsuit-tossed-on-choice-of-law-grounds

69 Bowman, E. (2022, August 26). Scanning students' rooms during remote tests is unconstitutional, judge rules. NPR. https://www.npr.org/2022/08/25/1119337956/test-proctoring-room-scans-unconstitutional--cleveland-state-university

70 Feathers, T., & Feathers, T. (2024, July 27). Proctorio is using racist algorithms to detect faces. VICE. https://www.vice.com/en/article/proctorio-is-using-racist-algorithms-to-detect-faces/

a threat to their autonomy or a challenge to their traditional role in the classroom. Teachers may fear that AI systems will take over tasks that they traditionally perform, such as grading or providing feedback, or that these systems will lack the nuanced understanding of their students that human educators bring.

For students, AI-powered assessments can sometimes feel impersonal or alienating, leading to concerns about the accuracy of machine-generated feedback or a lack of emotional connection with the technology. Fear of surveillance or the idea that AI is watching their every move may also cause students to feel uneasy.

To overcome these concerns and encourage acceptance, it is crucial to emphasize that AI is designed to augment, not replace, the role of teachers. AI systems should be presented as tools that support and enhance the teaching process, enabling educators to focus on more personalized interactions and fostering deeper learning experiences. Teachers must be involved in the development and implementation of AI systems, ensuring that these tools align with pedagogical goals and enhance the overall learning environment.

Building trust is equally important. AI systems must be transparent and explainable, providing educators and students with clear insights into how assessments are made and how data is used. By offering personalized, actionable feedback and explaining the rationale behind AI-driven decisions, these systems can help students and teachers feel more comfortable and confident in their use.

Additionally, involving teachers and students in the process of adopting AI systems, from piloting new tools to providing ongoing feedback, can help increase buy-in. This collaboration ensures that AI systems are not imposed top-down but are instead integrated in a way that aligns with the values and needs of both educators and learners.

The need to maintain strong teacher-student relationships must be addressed thoughtfully. By ensuring that AI is transparent, fair, and designed to enhance the teaching and learning experience, we can leverage its full potential without sacrificing the human element that is at the heart of education.

Globally, attitudes toward AI assessment are shifting from curiosity to cautious adoption—and the data pinpoint what drives acceptance. An EDUCAUSE QuickPoll[71] of 278 higher-ed staff and faculty (April 2024) found *71% want their institution to focus more on AI for learning design and assessment,* yet privacy and ethics remain the top roadblocks; respondents singled out interdisciplinary AI committees and small pilot projects with open result-sharing as the most promising remedies. On the student side, the Digital Education Council's Global AI Student Survey 2024[72] (n = 3,800, 16 countries) reports that *86 % already use AI in their studies,*

71 Burns, S., & Muscanell, N. (2024, April 15). EDUCAUSE QuickPoll Results: A Growing Need for Generative AI Strategy. Educause. https://er.educause.edu/articles/2024/4/educause-quickpoll-results-a-growing-need-for-generative-ai-strategy
72 Digital Education Council. (2024, April 7). What Students Want: Key Results from DEC Global AI Student Survey 2024. Digital Education Council. https://www.digitaleducationcouncil.com/post/what-students-want-key-results-from-dec-global-ai-student-survey-2024

but *60 % worry about the fairness of AI-graded work and fewer than 5 % feel well-informed about campus AI guidelines*—a gap the authors say institutions can close through transparent policies and clearer communication. Taken together, these surveys suggest that resistance melts when AI initiatives are co-designed by teachers, openly piloted with students, and paired with clear, campus-wide transparency about how data are used and how grades are generated.

AI and the future of educational assessment

As AI continues to evolve, its impact on education becomes more profound. The future of educational assessment is poised to undergo a radical transformation, driven by emerging trends in gamification, **augmented reality (AR)**, and immersive learning environments. These innovations are not just enhancing the way students engage with assessments but are also reshaping how they are evaluated. AI is also paving the way for more predictive analytics, enabling educators to forecast student performance and proactively address learning gaps. Finally, AI has the potential to revolutionize the very concept of standardized testing, offering a more continuous and holistic approach to assessment.

Emerging trends

As AI continues to develop, its potential to enhance educational assessments extends beyond traditional methods. The integration of AI with emerging technologies like gamification and AR is leading to more engaging, interactive, and personalized learning experiences.

Gamification and AI-driven assessments

One of the most exciting trends in AI-based educational assessments is the rise of gamification, i.e., the use of game-like elements in non-game contexts to increase engagement and motivation. AI can drive the personalization of gamified learning experiences, where assessments are embedded within interactive game scenarios. In these environments, students may advance through levels or earn rewards for achieving certain learning milestones, with AI dynamically adjusting the challenges based on individual performance.

This approach makes assessments feel less like tests and more like opportunities for exploration and achievement. Platforms like Kahoot!, Quizlet, and Duolingo have already embraced gamification, but AI's role in customizing these experiences is taking it further. AI can analyze a student's progress, modifying challenges in real time to keep them at the optimal level of difficulty, i.e., engaging students without overwhelming them.

Additionally, gamified assessments allow students to receive immediate, personalized feedback, helping them understand not only the right answers but also the reasoning behind them. This creates a more engaging feedback loop that motivates students to persist through challenges and improves retention. Hyper-personalized gamified experiences built on individual student performance, preferences, and learning styles allow for the creation of challenges, feedback, and content that are tailored to each learner's needs. For example, an

AI might adapt game difficulty based on a student s mastery, recommend specific gamified activities to address knowledge gaps, or even suggest different interactive formats (e.g., simulations for kinesthetic learners). This ensures students remain in their optimal challenge zone, reducing frustration and disengagement[73].

Recent advances in gamified assessment show how motivational design and AI can work hand in hand. Mainstream quiz platforms have begun embedding generative AI to keep classroom games fresh. Kahoot's new AI PDF-to-Kahoot generator[74] lets teachers drop any reading packet into the site and receive an instant, self-marking quiz that still awards points, badges, and leaderboard status. Quizizz has followed the same trend with its AI Toolkit[75]: teachers can upload a document or paste a URL, and the system builds a multi-round quiz, complete with timed power-ups and adaptive difficulty that adjusts as students play. These tools show how generative AI is now doing the heavy lifting of content creation, freeing teachers to focus on orchestrating the competitive, motivation-rich layer that keeps learners coming back. The use of digital badges and micro-credentials is expanding, and their security and verifiability are being enhanced through blockchain technology. These gamified rewards offer a dynamic way for students to showcase their acquired skills and knowledge, providing a trusted and portable record of achievements that can be shared with employers and other institutions[76]. Another trend we are observing is the use of gamification in higher education marketing[77], where universities are leveraging gamification principles in their application processes to increase engagement and completion rates. This involves turning application steps into storylines, offering micro-rewards for completing tasks, and even using AI-powered narrators to guide prospective students, making the application process more interactive and less daunting.

Augmented reality assessments

AR is another emerging technology that is transforming the landscape of assessment. AI-powered AR tools can overlay digital information onto the physical world, creating interactive environments where students can engage with learning materials in a more immersive and tangible way. In assessment scenarios, AR can simulate real-world tasks that require problem-solving, creativity, or hands-on skills.

---

73 Education Technology Trends to watch in 2025. (n.d.). Digital Learning Institute. https://www.digitallearninginstitute.com/blog/education-technology-trends-to-watch-in-2025

74 D'Arcy, S. (2024, December 12). Transform learning content with the AI PDF-to-kahoot generator now included in Kahoot!+. Kahoot! https://kahoot.com/blog/2024/01/17/ai-pdf-question-generator-for-educators/

75 What's New. (n.d.). Quizizz. Retrieved June 7, 2025, from https://quizizz.com/home/en/whats-new?lng=en

76 Pramanick, D., & Pramanick, D. (2025, March 24). Gamification of Learning in Higher Education: Key Insights. Mitr Learning and Media Pvt Ltd - Content Technology & Innovation Company. https://www.mitrmedia.com/resources/blogs/gamification-in-higher-education-engaging-students-through-interactive-learning/

77 Khan, F. (2025, May 19). From checklists to quests: The rise of gamification in Higher Education marketing. Firdosh Khan. https://firdoshkhan.in/gamification-in-higher-education-marketing/

For example, in a science assessment, AR could allow students to interact with a 3D model of the human heart, manipulating its parts to answer questions about cardiovascular function. AI could track their interactions, assess their understanding, and provide feedback on their actions, helping to bridge the gap between theoretical knowledge and practical application.

AR assessments offer a unique advantage in providing context-rich, experiential learning environments. AI systems can analyze the students' actions within these environments, offering more detailed insights into their skills and abilities than traditional paper-based tests. This can be particularly useful in subjects like science, engineering, and even history, where experiential learning enhances comprehension.

Immersive learning environments

Immersive learning environments powered by AI and VR offer entirely new ways to assess students. In these environments, students can immerse themselves in simulations or virtual worlds that require them to apply their knowledge and skills in real-time. AI systems track their progress and decision-making, providing continuous assessment as they interact with the virtual world.

For instance, a medical student could practice performing surgery in a virtual environment where their actions are continuously evaluated by an AI system, offering feedback on technique and identifying areas for improvement. This level of assessment allows for highly interactive, hands-on learning while maintaining the ability to track student performance in real-time.

The potential for AI-driven immersive learning in assessment is vast. It could offer personalized, situation-specific assessments, pushing students to apply their knowledge in diverse contexts. This type of assessment could one day replace traditional exams entirely, offering a more practical and engaging way to measure mastery of complex subjects.

Predictive analytics to forecast student performance

AI's ability to process vast amounts of data and identify patterns makes it a powerful tool for predictive analytics in educational assessments. By analyzing historical and real-time data on student performance, AI systems can forecast future outcomes, allowing educators to make data-driven decisions and intervene proactively.

Forecasting student performance

AI-powered predictive analytics can assess a student's current performance and predict their future success in specific subjects or skills. For example, AI systems can analyze patterns in homework, quizzes, and in-class participation to predict how well a student will perform on upcoming exams or assignments. This insight allows teachers to intervene early, providing targeted support to help struggling students before gaps in knowledge widen.

Predictive analytics also helps educators identify at-risk students, giving them the tools to offer early interventions. By analyzing a student's progress across multiple data points, AI can flag potential learning gaps, enabling teachers to offer additional resources, such as tutoring or tailored assignments, to prevent academic setbacks.

Addressing learning gaps proactively

Predictive analytics can also help personalize learning experiences for individual students. By identifying patterns in student behavior, AI can recommend specific exercises, resources, or interventions to address the learning gaps that are most relevant to each student. For example, if a student is struggling with a particular concept in math, AI can suggest additional practice problems or video tutorials to reinforce that concept, allowing the student to work at their own pace while receiving immediate feedback.

This proactive, data-driven approach ensures that interventions are timely and targeted, allowing educators to focus their efforts on the areas where students need the most help. AI's ability to continuously analyze performance data makes it an invaluable tool for maintaining a consistent, personalized learning experience.

The trend is towards real-time predictive analytics, where data is collected and processed continuously to allow for instant decisions and automated actions. This includes event-driven architectures that trigger interventions the moment patterns or anomalies are detected. The goal is to move towards more autonomous educational systems that can adapt and respond to student needs with minimal human intervention[78].

Beyond student-level insights, predictive analytics is increasingly used for broader institutional decision-making. This includes optimizing resource allocation (e.g., staffing, classroom usage), informing curriculum development based on student success rates, and supporting strategic planning by forecasting trends in enrollment, student demand, and educational outcomes[79].

In K-12 settings, AI agents are emerging to break down data silos, proactively analyze diverse datasets (e.g., attendance, test scores, instructional strategies), and provide deeper insights for decision-making. This trend also emphasizes data democratization, making data and analytics tools more accessible to a wider range of educators and administrators to foster a data-literate culture[80].

---

78 Mistry, M. (2025, June 5). Top 8 Predictive Analytics Trends for 2025. Kody Technolab. https://kodytech-nolab.com/blog/top-predictive-analytics-trends/
79 Market.us. (2025, February 5). Predictive Analytics in EdTech Market Size | CAGR of 24%. https://market.us/report/predictive-analytics-in-edtech-market/
80 Jones, W. (2025, June 4). AI agents reveal new tech possibilities in K–12 education. Technology Solutions That Drive Education. https://edtechmagazine.com/k12/article/2025/03/ai-agents-reveal-new-tech-possibilities-k-12-education

Future of standardized testing

Standardized tests, often seen as the cornerstone of educational assessment, have long been the subject of debate. Critics argue that these tests are too narrow in scope, focusing on a limited set of skills and ignoring the complexities of student learning. AI offers the potential to shift away from traditional exams toward more continuous and holistic assessment methods that reflect the full spectrum of student achievement.

Traditional standardized testing typically evaluates a student's knowledge at a single point in time, which may not fully represent their learning journey. In contrast, AI enables a more dynamic approach to assessment by continuously tracking student progress across various assignments, activities, and interactions with learning materials. This continuous assessment model offers a more comprehensive view of a student's abilities, considering not only their final scores but also their growth and development over time.

With AI-driven systems, assessments can be seamlessly integrated into the learning process, allowing students to demonstrate their skills through a variety of methods—such as interactive tasks, projects, or even AI-powered simulations, rather than relying solely on one-time exams. This holistic approach enables a more accurate assessment of a student's abilities, creativity, problem-solving skills, and potential for success.

At the same time, AI's ability to analyze a wide array of data points opens the door to a more holistic approach to assessment. Rather than focusing exclusively on how well a student answers multiple-choice questions, AI can assess their ability to engage with complex tasks, collaborate with peers, and apply their knowledge in practical, real-world scenarios.

This shift could lead to the development of portfolio-based assessments, where students build a digital portfolio of their work throughout the course. AI would then analyze these portfolios, providing detailed feedback on the student's progress, strengths, and areas for improvement. This approach reflects a more authentic and comprehensive understanding of student performance, offering a more accurate reflection of their capabilities and potential.

As AI continues to evolve, it holds the potential to move us away from static, high-stakes exams toward more continuous, meaningful evaluations that reflect the full range of student abilities. By embracing these innovations, we can create a future where assessments are not just about grades but about fostering growth, creativity, and lifelong learning.

AI is a powerful tool, but the true magic lies in how we use it. With careful design, ethical implementation, and a focus on human connection, AI can help create educational environments that are not only smarter but also more empathetic, personalized, and attuned to the needs of every student.

Conclusion

The use of AI in the evaluation and assessment of students and their coursework undeniably introduces a host of benefits along with many challenges. The depth of AI's potential integration into assessment tools and feedback mechanisms necessitates a profound reshaping of how we think about the evaluation of student progress. The demonstrated advantages, including the immediacy of feedback, highly personalized reports, and data-driven actionable insights, strongly advocate for AI's inclusion. However, this promising future is tempered by critical concerns regarding AI model reliability and fairness in assessment, robust security and privacy protocols, and the fundamental need for both student and teacher acceptance and trust in these systems.

Looking ahead, the prevailing scholarly and policy discourse emphasizes a necessary paradigm shift: the successful integration of AI into education hinges on a balanced approach. It is increasingly clear that while AI will continue to evolve and revolutionize expectations of growth and success in the classroom, its implementation in assessment must be guided by ethical considerations. This includes a deep focus on algorithmic transparency, mitigating inherent biases, and ensuring data sovereignty. Crucially, the future of educational assessment with AI is not one of full automation, but rather one where human judgment and empathy remain unequivocally at the core. Educators, though rightly concerned about issues like plagiarism, are simultaneously exploring how AI can augment and enrich the student educational journey.

In the next chapter, we will cover how to successfully implement AI in the classroom by exploring multiple case studies and best practices.

Questions

1. If AI can provide instant, continuous feedback tailored to each student, what happens to the role and value of a teacher's feedback in helping to shape a student's growth and motivation?

2. Are we risking the reduction of complex human thinking and creativity to what an algorithm can quantify? What might be lost in this new era of assessment?

3. If AI can predict student success based on early data patterns, how far do we go in trusting it to inform decisions like tracking, interventions, or even admissions? Are we entering an era with a new form of academic determinism?

4. How do we balance the promise of AI-driven assessments with the ethical risks of bias and surveillance? Many students and families do not fully understand how their data is being used. How do we determine whether the right policies are in place?

5. Do you think that immersive, AI-powered assessment experiences (like VR or AR simulations) can replace traditional tests? Are we prepared to redefine what it means to demonstrate knowledge, skill, and mastery?

Exercises

1. **Algorithmic autopsy**: Investigate the fairness of AI-driven assessment and grading.

    a. **Exercise**: You are given a fictitious essay along with a grading rubric. Review the essay as a human evaluator and assign your own score based. Next, you receive an AI-graded essay along with the grading rubric and the AI-generated score.

        i. Compare your score with the AI's.

        ii. Write a 1-page analysis of discrepancies.

        iii. Ask yourself: What does this reveal about subjectivity, context, and fairness in machine grading?

2. **Data ethics decision tree**: Explore the ethical gray areas of AI assessment.

    a. **Exercise**: Map out a flowchart for an AI scenario in which student data is collected for adaptive testing, including:

        i. What data is collected?

        ii. Who sees the data and how it is used?

        iii. Mark at least three points of potential ethical concern and write one paragraph each justifying or questioning the decisions being made.

3. **Predictive analytics, real consequences**: Examine how AI predictions may impact students' futures.

    a. **Exercise**: Imagine an AI system that can predict whether a student is unlikely to succeed in STEM fields by 10th grade.

        i. How much weight to give to this prediction?

        ii. How should a school respond?

        iii. What interventions are ethical?

        iv. Write a short policy memo outlining your recommendations for a school response strategy—and its potential unintended consequences.

4. **Reimagining the gradebook**: Reevaluate what *success* looks like in a human-machine future.

    a. **Exercise**: Using insights from the chapter, create a prototype of a future AI-enhanced report card. It should:

        i. Replace traditional letter grades and include AI observations and predictions.

  ii. Include formative insights, behavior trends, and personal growth indicators. Then, write a reflective essay: Would this version help or hinder equity and motivation in your current school context?

5. **Human vs. machine—Grading debate**: Explore power dynamics in human-AI collaboration.

  a. **Exercise**: Hold a team debate on the following statement:

  AI should be the primary assessor of student work; human teachers should only intervene for exceptions.

    i. Prepare arguments for both sides of the argument using examples from the chapter (e.g., automated grading, essay scoring engines, speech analysis). Focus on accuracy, bias, transparency, and humanity.

6. **Feedback rewritten**: Critique the ways in which feedback is delivered and received.

  a. **Exercise**: Take three real pieces of AI-generated feedback (from tools like Khanmigo, Duolingo, or a chatbot). With these examples, take time to

    i. Reword them as a human teacher would. Are there notable changes?

    ii. **Reflect**: What is lost or gained in tone, nuance, and effectiveness?

    iii. Design your own ideal feedback model combining AI efficiency with human empathy.

7. **The gamified assessment design challenge**: Apply new assessment models to real-world learning.

  a. **Exercise**: Design a gamified assessment for a subject you teach (e.g., mathematics, ELA, history, biology). The solution should

    i. Use AI to help adapt to student performance

    ii. Include real-time feedback loops

    iii. Assess both knowledge and process. Then, present a defense of how this model is more equitable or more effective than a traditional quiz or test.

8. **Immersive future scenario—2035**: Explore the implications of immersive assessment.

  a. **Exercise**: Write a short story or create a storyboard to outline the following scenario. A high school student is taking a fully immersive, AI-powered final exam in 2035 using VR. The AI tracks eye movement, reaction time, and emotional regulation in real-time.

  b. Questions to address:

    i. What is being measured—and why?

    ii. How are these biometric measures used in assessment?

      iii. What are the student's rights?

      iv. How is feedback delivered?

      v. How do they feel afterward?

c. Use the narrative to kick-start a discussion about the future of high-stakes exams.

Join our Discord space

Join our Discord workspace for latest updates, offers, tech happenings around the world, new releases, and sessions with the authors:

https://discord.bpbonline.com

CHAPTER 4
Successful AI Implementations

Our greatest glory is not in never falling, but in rising every time we fail.

-Confucius

Introduction

As we explore the role of AI in education, real-world examples are helpful and essential for illustrating both the potential and the pitfalls of implementation. AI in the classroom is not just a theoretical exercise; it is an evolving reality that educators, administrators, and students are actively engaging with. Case studies and success stories provide concrete evidence of what works, helping to move AI adoption from an abstract concept to a practical tool for learning enhancement. They also serve as blueprints, empowering decision-makers to implement AI in ways that truly improve learning outcomes. This chapter examines the criteria for assessing effective AI implementation in educational contexts, presents a series of case studies spanning K–12 and higher education environments, and concludes with an analysis of recurring themes and evidence-based best practices derived from these applied examples.

These examples help highlight key factors such as adaptability, accessibility, and measurable impact, offering insights that theoretical discussions alone cannot provide. For instance, understanding how AI-powered tutoring systems improve student engagement or how automated feedback tools support personalized learning can make AI's role in education tangible and actionable.

Furthermore, real-world applications help educators anticipate challenges of our times, from ethical considerations to technical limitations. By analyzing successful implementations, schools can adopt best practices while avoiding common pitfalls experienced by others.

Ultimately, seeing AI in action builds a level of confidence, helps to foster innovation, and provides a roadmap for responsible, effective use in education.

Structure

This chapter covers the following topics:

- Criteria for success
- Case study: Adaptive learning in a K-12 environment
- Case study: AI-driven language tutoring for ELL students
- Case study: Personalized feedback in higher education
- Case study: AI-assisted collaborative projects
- Case study: Remote learning and AI support
- Common themes and best practices

Objectives

In this chapter, we will highlight real-world successes of AI in the classroom, offering educators and administrators clear insights into what works and why. By showcasing concrete examples, we will explore several key lessons learned from AI integration, both the breakthroughs and the challenges that have been overcome. The focus is on replicable strategies that educators can adopt to enhance learning, improve efficiency, and personalize education. By examining these success stories, teachers and students alike can gain practical guidance, avoiding common pitfalls while leveraging AI's full potential to create engaging, effective, and equitable learning environments.

Criteria for success

Determining the success of AI in education requires a set of clear, measurable criteria that reflect the diverse needs of students, teachers, and institutions. While AI can enhance engagement, efficiency, and learning outcomes, success varies depending on context, whether in K–12 or higher education, large or small schools, rural or inner-city, or resource-rich versus underfunded environments. The following are the key metrics used to evaluate AI effectiveness in different educational settings:

- **Improved student engagement**: Successful AI deployments should foster greater student participation and motivation. In K–12 settings, engagement may be measured by increased class participation, reduced absenteeism, or higher completion rates for AI-driven assignments. In higher education, where independent learning is key, engagement can be assessed through interactive AI tools, discussion board activity, or time spent on personalized study modules.

- **Enhanced learning outcomes**: AI should contribute to measurable academic improvements. In primary and secondary schools, this may include improvement in standardized test scores, better reading comprehension, or a mastery of STEM subjects through AI-assisted tutoring. In higher education, success might be visible in better course completion rates, higher grades, or improved competency-based assessments in professional training programs.

- **Increased teacher efficiency**: AI should reduce the administrative burdens and help to free teachers to focus on instruction. In large schools or universities, this could mean automated grading of exams, streamlined student feedback, or AI-powered classroom analytics that help identify struggling students. In smaller or underfunded schools, AI's success can be measured by its ability to supplement limited teaching staff, offer personalized instruction, or provide data-driven insights that support individualized learning plans.

- **Equity and accessibility improvements**: AI can help to bridge gaps in education by making learning more accessible to students of all backgrounds. In inner city, rural, or underfunded schools, AI-driven resources can provide personalized tutoring where teachers are scarce. In higher education, AI-powered translation tools and adaptive learning platforms can help support diverse learners, including non-native speakers and students with disabilities. A key indicator of success will be whether or not AI can reduce educational disparities rather than reinforcing them.

- **Long-term sustainability and scalability**: For AI to be successful in the classroom, it must be sustainable and scalable. Schools need to assess whether AI solutions are cost-effective, adaptable to changing curricula, and able to integrate with existing educational technology, systems, and infrastructure. Large institutions might measure success through the ability to scale AI initiatives across multiple campuses, while small schools may focus on long-term affordability and ease of use.

Ultimately, the definition of success will be context dependent. By aligning AI implementation with institutional goals and student needs, schools can ensure that AI serves as an effective tool for meaningful and scalable educational improvements.

Case study: Adaptive learning in a K-12 environment

Adaptive learning is a cornerstone of modern educational practices and helps tailor the learning experience to individual student needs, leveraging technology and data analytics. The case study presented in the core components of education 4.0 highlights the implementation of adaptive learning in an engineering education setting, aiming to enhance student engagement, retention, and skill acquisition.[1]

Goals of adaptive learning initiative

The primary objective of this adaptive learning initiative was to address varying levels of student preparedness and learning styles. In traditional classrooms, educators face many challenges in delivering personalized instruction to diverse groups of learners. This initiative sought to bridge that gap by integrating adaptive platforms that helped to adjust content delivery based on real-time student performance. Specifically, the goals were to:

- **Enhance student learning outcomes**: Ensure that all students achieve core competencies, regardless of their starting point.

- **Promote engagement**: Increase student motivation through personalized learning paths and an integrated experience.

- **Improve efficiency**: Reduce the amount of time required for students to master key concepts.

- **Support instructors**: Provide educators with actionable insights into student progress and individual challenges.

Implementation details

The implementation of adaptive learning involved a multi-phase approach, combining technological integration with pedagogical restructuring. The following steps were taken to ensure an effective deployment:

1. **Platform selection**: An adaptive learning platform was chosen based on the ability to provide real-time feedback, customizable learning paths, and a robust set of analytics. The platform integrated seamlessly with the institution's **learning management system (LMS)**.

2. **Curriculum mapping**: Course content was restructured into smaller modular units, aligning with learning objectives and competencies outlined in the engineering curriculum.[2] Each module included a set of pre-assessments, instructional content, practice exercises, and post-assessments.

---

1 Miranda, J., Navarrete, C., Noguez, J., Molina-Espinosa, J.-M., Ramírez-Montoya, M.-S., A Navarro-Tuch, S., Bustamante-Bello, M.-R., Rosas-Fernández, J.-B., & Molina, A. (2021). The Core components of Education 4.0 in Higher Education: Three case studies in Engineering education. Computers & Electrical Engineering, 93. https://www.sciencedirect.com/science/article/pii/S0045790621002603?via%3Dihub
2 Miranda, J., Navarrete, C., Noguez, J., Molina-Espinosa, J.-M., Ramírez-Montoya, M.-S., A Navarro-Tuch, S., Bustamante-Bello, M.-R., Rosas-Fernández, J.-B., & Molina, A. (2021). The Core components of Education 4.0 in Higher Education: Three case studies in Engineering education. Computers & Electrical Engineering, 93. https://www.sciencedirect.com/science/article/pii/S0045790621002603?via%3Dihub

3. **Personalized learning paths**: Based on the pre-assessment results, students were directed to tailored learning paths. Those students who demonstrated mastery could progress quickly, while others received additional resources and practice exercises.

4. **Instructor training**: Faculty members were trained to interpret a variety of analytics data and provide targeted support. This ensured that adaptive learning helped to complement, rather than replace, traditional instruction.

5. **Continuous monitoring and feedback**: Throughout the semester, the program monitored student progress, and the adaptive platform helped to provide real-time insights. Instructors were able to use this data to adjust teaching strategies and offer personalized support.

Outcomes and observations

The implementation of adaptive learning in this project helped to yield significant outcomes across a variety of different dimensions:

- **Improved academic performance**: Students using the adaptive platform demonstrated higher achievement levels in end-of-term assessments when compared to previous cohorts. Performance gains were particularly notable among those students who had initially struggled with core concepts.[3]

- **Increased engagement**: Personalized learning paths and real-time feedback helped to keep students motivated. The platform's gamification mechanics, such as badges and progress trackers, further enhanced student engagement.

- **Efficient learning**: Students completed course modules an average of 20% faster than they did in traditional settings. This efficiency allowed for a deeper exploration of advanced topics and project-based learning.

- **Enhanced instructor effectiveness**: Faculty and educators reported greater confidence in addressing individual student needs. The platform's analytics helped to provide clear indicators of where intervention was required.

- **Positive student feedback**: Qualitative surveys showed high satisfaction among students, who appreciated the ability to learn at their own pace. Many noted that adaptive learning reduced their anxiety associated with exams and assignments.

Challenges encountered

While the implementation of adaptive learning yielded promising results, the case study also raised several notable challenges that demanded careful attention and responsive strategies:

3 Miranda, J., Navarrete, C., Noguez, J., Molina-Espinosa, J.-M., Ramírez-Montoya, M.-S., A Navarro-Tuch, S., Bustamante-Bello, M.-R., Rosas-Fernández, J.-B., & Molina, A. (2021). The Core components of Education 4.0 in Higher Education: Three case studies in Engineering education. Computers & Electrical Engineering, 93. https://www.sciencedirect.com/science/article/pii/S0045790621002603?via%3Dihub

- **Initial resistance to change**: Students and faculty both expressed hesitation during the early phases of implementation. For the educators, the shift demanded new instructional approaches and a new level of comfort with data analytics, while students were generally unfamiliar with the self-paced and algorithm-driven nature of the platform. This resistance was mitigated by structured professional development sessions, ongoing coaching, and regular check-ins to ensure both student and faculty groups felt supported and heard.

- **Technical issues and platform reliability**: Although the chosen adaptive platform offered notable robust features, occasional bugs, lags, and login problems interfered with the learning experience. These disruptions highlighted the importance of having ready and responsive technical support, a clear escalation process, and backup plans to avoid instructional downtime.

- **Equity and access barriers**: One of the most pressing challenges involved ensuring all students had equitable access to physical devices and high-speed internet. Students from low-income households were affected disproportionately, highlighting concerns over a digital divide. To address this, the school provided loaner devices, mobile Wi-Fi hotspots, and campus access zones—but underscored the need for long-term policy and infrastructure solutions.

These challenges highlighted broader systemic issues that need to be addressed for adaptive learning to succeed at scale. Effective implementation goes beyond platform choice—it demands an investment in human support, technology infrastructure, and inclusive planning that centers all learners.

Key takeaways

This case study demonstrates that adaptive learning can significantly enhance educational outcomes when implemented carefully. Some key takeaways from this research include:

- **Personalization drives success**: Tailoring content to individual student needs helps to enhance engagement, motivation, and achievement.

- **Instructor support is essential**: While technology can play a central role, educators remain a critical component in guiding and motivating students.

- **Data-informed decisions**: Real-time analytics help empower instructors to provide targeted support and adjust teaching strategies.

- **Equity and accessibility matter**: Institutions must ensure that all students have equal access to the necessary technology and resources.

- **Continuous improvement**: Adaptive learning is most effective when platforms are regularly reviewed and updated based on user feedback and evolving educational standards.

The integration of adaptive learning within the engineering education context proved to be a transformative approach. It cannot only help improve academic outcomes but also foster a more inclusive and engaging learning environment. As education continues to evolve, adaptive learning stands out as an increasingly powerful tool for achieving personalized, effective, and equitable instruction.

Case study: AI-driven language tutoring for ELL students

For decades, the integration of artificial intelligence in education has transformed traditional teaching methods in language learning. This case study explores an application of AI-driven tutoring for **English language learning** (**ELL**) among university students studying **English as a foreign language** (**EFL**). The objective was to evaluate the impact of AI-powered platforms on English learning achievement, **second language** (**L2**) motivation, and self-regulated learning.

This study involved two distinct groups of university students: an experimental group using AI-driven tutoring and a control group following traditional instruction. The primary goals were:

- To enhance English language proficiency across grammar, vocabulary, reading comprehension, and writing.
- To help improve learner motivation for L2 acquisition.
- To foster self-regulated learning strategies for independent progress.

Implementation details

The experimental group leveraged an AI-mediated language learning platform, Duolingo, while the control group relied on conventional classroom instruction. The experiment spanned ten weeks, with pre and post-tests administered to assess the impact of each approach. The key implementation elements of the approach using the AI platform included:

- **Personalized learning pathways**: The AI system helped to adapt lessons based on individual learners' strengths and weaknesses, and offered tailored exercises to address specific needs.

- **Interactive activities**: Students engaged in language learning games, quizzes, and speaking exercises designed to enhance engagement and retention.

- **Real-time feedback**: The AI helped to provide instant feedback on tasks, explaining errors and suggesting improvements, fostering iterative learning.

- **Self-paced learning**: Students in the experiment had access to lessons outside the classroom, allowing more flexibility in practice time and location.

While key implementation elements of the approach for instructional structure included:

- The AI-driven focus experimental group participated in both in-class AI-supported activities and independent practice, with at least two hours per week that were dedicated to self-guided learning.

- The control group followed traditional classroom practices, including educator-led discussions, textbook exercises, and homework assignments.

Outcomes and observations

The results highlighted several notable improvements among students using AI-driven tutoring across several key dimensions. One student shared, *Using the AI platform felt like I was actively participating in my learning. The interactive exercises were like puzzles I wanted to solve, and the real-time feedback kept me engaged*[4]. Let us look at the outcomes and observations:

- **English learning achievement**: The experimental group showed significantly higher post-test scores compared to the control group. Their average score increased from **43.21 to 73.86**, while the control group only improved from **44.39 to 61.11**.[5] The AI-driven platform showcased vocabulary acquisition, grammar proficiency, reading comprehension, and writing skills.

- **L2 motivation**: Students using the AI platform also showed increased motivation to learn English. Post-test scores for motivation rose from **3.12 to 3.89** in the experimental group, while the control group showed just a modest increase from **3.04 to 3.35**.[6] Qualitative interviews showed that the personalized nature of the AI system made learning more enjoyable and goal-oriented, encouraging continuous engagement.

- **Self-regulated learning**: Self-regulation scores improved notably among the AI users, rising from **2.89 to 3.94**, compared to the control group's increase from **3.01 to 3.37**. Many students reported feeling more empowered to set learning goals, monitor progress, and adjust strategies based on AI-generated feedback.

Key takeaways

This case study underscores the transformative potential of AI-driven tutoring for English language learning. The key takeaways include:

4 Wei, L. (2023). Artificial intelligence in language instruction: impact on English learning achievement, L2 motivation, and self-regulated learning. Frontiers in Psychology, 14. P. 8. https://doi.org/10.3389/fpsyg.2023.1261955

5 Wei, L. (2023). Artificial intelligence in language instruction: impact on English learning achievement, L2 motivation, and self-regulated learning. Frontiers in Psychology, 14. P. 7. https://doi.org/10.3389/fpsyg.2023.1261955

6 Wei, L. (2023). Artificial intelligence in language instruction: impact on English learning achievement, L2 motivation, and self-regulated learning. Frontiers in Psychology, 14. P. 7. https://doi.org/10.3389/fpsyg.2023.1261955

- **Enhanced ELL outcomes**: AI-enhanced instruction significantly outperformed traditional methods in improving English language proficiency across core skills. Real-time feedback and personalized exercises allowed student learners to target weak areas, accelerating skill development.

- **Increased learner motivation**: The interactive nature of the AI platforms fostered intrinsic motivation, turning language learning into an engaging experience for the individual rather than a compulsory task assigned to the student. Students reported a greater sense of accomplishment and enthusiasm for further exploration and learning.

- **Empowerment in self-regulation**: AI-supported learning helps to empower students to take ownership of their education, helping to promote habits such as goal setting, time management, and progress tracking. Learners develop resilience by viewing mistakes as part of the learning process and are supported by constructive AI-generated feedback. One student said, *I used to struggle with writing essays, but after using the AI platform, my writing skills improved. This semester, I received one of my highest essay scores.*[7] Another student shared, *With the AI platform, I learned how to set specific goals and manage my learning time effectively. I felt more in control of my progress.*[8]

- **Flexibility and accessibility**: AI platforms offer the convenience of learning anytime, anywhere, enabling students to integrate language practice into their daily routines. Students are afforded the flexibility to engage with content at their own pace, ensuring continuous progress beyond classroom settings. One student commented, *With the AI platform, I did not have to wait for a class or find a specific place to study. It gave me the freedom to learn wherever I was.*[9]

The integration of AI-driven teaching and tutoring for English Language Learning has proven highly effective in helping to enhance language proficiency, boost motivation, and promote self-regulated learning among university-level EFL learners. The AI platform's ability to provide personalized instruction, real-time feedback, and augmented flexible learning opportunities created an empowering educational environment.

This case study demonstrates the potential for AI to support a revolution in language education, offering scalable, individualized learning experiences that surpass traditional teaching methods. As AI technology continues to improve and evolve, its role in education will expand, providing learners worldwide with unprecedented opportunities for language acquisition and personal growth.

7 Wei, L. (2023). Artificial intelligence in language instruction: impact on English learning achievement, L2 motivation, and self-regulated learning. Frontiers in Psychology, 14. P. 8. https://doi.org/10.3389/fpsyg.2023.1261955

8 Wei, L. (2023). Artificial intelligence in language instruction: impact on English learning achievement, L2 motivation, and self-regulated learning. Frontiers in Psychology, 14. P. 9. https://doi.org/10.3389/fpsyg.2023.1261955

9 Wei, L. (2023). Artificial intelligence in language instruction: impact on English learning achievement, L2 motivation, and self-regulated learning. Frontiers in Psychology, 14. P. 9. https://doi.org/10.3389/fpsyg.2023.1261955

Case study: Personalized feedback in higher education

The integration of AI into higher education has completely changed how teachers support student learning. One of the most impactful applications of AI is the concept of AI-driven personalized feedback, which adapts to individual student needs, providing timely, relevant, and constructive guidance to students on their learning journey. This case study explores the implementation of an AI-driven feedback system in a middle school setting, leveraging learnings and insights from the *AI in Education* workshop proceedings.

The primary objectives of implementing AI-driven feedback in this study were:

- **Enhancing student engagement**: By offering tailored feedback, the goal was to use AI to help keep students motivated and engaged with their learning tasks.

- **Improving learning outcomes**: Personalized feedback aimed to identify student misconceptions in real-time, providing additional corrective guidance to improve understanding.

- **Supporting teacher effectiveness**: The AI system acted as a co-educator, helping teachers to manage classrooms more efficiently by highlighting students needing attention.

- **Promoting self-regulated learning**: Through personalized insights provided by the AI, students were encouraged to take ownership of their learning journey.

The project was implemented in a suburban middle school, where a mix of students with varying academic abilities and learning styles presented their ideas for an ideal environment to test the system's adaptability.[10]

Implementation details

The *University of Saskatchewan* adopted an AI-powered educational platform integrated into its existing LMS. The system had a variety of components, including:

- **Adaptive learning modules**: These modules helped to assess student progress and adjust content difficulty accordingly.

- **Real-time feedback engine**: The system helped to provide immediate feedback based on student responses, highlighting strengths and areas for improvement.

- **Teacher dashboard**: A comprehensive dashboard helped educators to monitor student progress and identify struggling learners.

---

10 Winkler, R., Roos, J., Association for Information Systems, AIS Electronic Library (AISeL), & University of St Gallen. (2019). Bringing AI into the Classroom: Designing Smart Personal Assistants as Learning Tutors. ICIS 2019 Proceedings. https://core.ac.uk/download/pdf/301384188.pdf

- **Student insights**: Learners could use the system to access personalized reports showing their performance trends and suggested learning paths.

The feedback system relied on several advanced machine learning algorithms that analyzed student responses, behavior patterns, and time spent on tasks to generate personalized recommendations.

The implementation[11] followed a structured and detailed approach:

- **Needs assessment**: Teachers and administrators worked to identify gaps in traditional feedback methods, such as delayed grading and one-size-fits-all comments, and assess the needs.

- **Training and onboarding**: Educators received hands-on training to help integrate the AI system into their lesson plans. Students were introduced to the system through a variety of interactive tutorials.

- **Pilot phase**: The system was piloted in math and language arts classes, where personalized feedback might have an immediate impact on skill acquisition.

- **Full rollout**: After a successful pilot deployment, the system was scaled across all core subjects, with continuous support and troubleshooting from the AI platform provider.

The AI-driven feedback process was quite comprehensive and involved several steps:

1. **Input**: Students completed assignments, quizzes, and interactive exercises to provide input.

2. **Analysis**: The AI-driven system analyzed student responses, considering correctness, time taken, patterns of errors, and a number of parameters.

3. **Feedback generation**: Based on deep data analysis, the system provided:

    a. **Corrective feedback**: Corrective feedback is when the system helps fix a mistake by showing what was wrong and how to do it better next time. To help highlight errors and suggest improvement strategies.

    b. **Reinforcement feedback**: Reinforcement feedback is praise and encouragement for doing something right, so a successful approach is repeated. Feedback on providing correct answers and encouraging continued progress.

    c. **Next-step recommendations**: Helping to suggest additional resources or exercises to reinforce learning.

4. **Reflection**: Students were encouraged to review feedback from the system, self-assess their understanding, and make corrections before final submission.

---

11 Winkler, R., Roos, J., Association for Information Systems. AIS Electronic Library (AISeL), & University of St Gallen. (2019). Bringing AI into the Classroom: Designing Smart Personal Assistants as Learning Tutors. ICIS 2019 Proceedings. https://core.ac.uk/download/pdf/301384188.pdf

Outcomes and observations

The AI-driven personalized feedback led to several notable outcomes[12] including:

- **Academic improvement**: Students using the system that was supported by AI showed a 20% improvement in math scores and a 15% improvement in language arts compared to the previous semester. They also achieved mastery of concepts 30% faster, as the AI-based system addressed learning gaps in real-time.

- **Enhanced engagement**: Student participation increased by 25%, with learners more engaged and willing to complete assignments, knowing they would receive immediate feedback. Qualitative surveys indicated that 80% of students found the personalized feedback helpful and motivating.

- **Teacher empowerment**: Teachers reported spending as much as 40% less time grading and more time providing targeted support during class. The AI dashboard helped teachers identify at-risk students early on, enabling timely interventions.

- **Student self-regulation**: Students developed better self-monitoring and self-correction habits, as the feedback system encouraged and helped to facilitate reflection. Personalized learning paths helped to motivate students to set and achieve specific academic goals.

Key takeaways

The success of AI-driven personalized feedback[13] in the classroom, highlighted several critical insights across the student population:

- **Personalization drives engagement and achievement**: The adaptive nature of AI-driven feedback helped to ensure that each student received guidance tailored to their unique needs. This personalization assisted in fostering a sense of ownership and motivation, leading to better learning outcomes.

- **Real-time feedback enhances learning efficiency**: Immediate feedback helps prevent students from practicing misconceptions, accelerating the learning process. The system's ability to identify and address errors as they occurred proved notably more effective than traditional grading methods.

- **Teacher and AI collaboration maximizes impact**: Rather than replacing teachers, the AI system served as a powerful partner to the teachers. Educators could focus their human time on higher-order teaching activities while the system handled routine feedback and monitoring tasks.

---

12 Winkler, R., Roos, J., Association for Information Systems, AIS Electronic Library (AISeL), & University of St Gallen. (2019). Bringing AI into the Classroom: Designing Smart Personal Assistants as Learning Tutors. ICIS 2019 Proceedings. https://core.ac.uk/download/pdf/301384188.pdf
13 Winkler, R., Roos, J., Association for Information Systems, AIS Electronic Library (AISeL), & University of St Gallen. (2019). Bringing AI into the Classroom: Designing Smart Personal Assistants as Learning Tutors. ICIS 2019 Proceedings. https://core.ac.uk/download/pdf/301384188.pdf

- **Student agency promotes lifelong learning skills**: By encouraging students to reflect on AI feedback and adjust their learning strategies, the system promotes self-regulated learning, an essential skill for lifelong success that the students learned early on.

- **Ethical considerations and continuous improvement make a difference**: The school emphasized data privacy and transparency, ensuring that student information was treated with care and used responsibly. Regular system updates and teacher reinforcement learning feedback loops ensured continuous improvement of the AI platform.

This case study demonstrates how an AI-driven personalized feedback system can transform the classroom, making student learning more efficient, engaging, and effective. By providing tailored guidance, empowering educators, and promoting student agency, AI technologies can help bridge learning gaps and prepare students for future success.

Moving forward, there are plans to expand the system to other subjects, integrate more advanced analytics, and explore AI-driven feedback for collaborative projects. This initiative underscores the potential of AI not just as a tool, but as a partner in creating more inclusive and effective educational environments.[14]

Case study: AI-assisted collaborative projects

The integration of AI in education has increasingly gained attention as educators seek innovative ways to enhance learning experiences. This case study focuses on the **CGScholar AI Helper Project**[15], an initiative aimed at improving student writing skills through AI-driven feedback for high school students. Conducted in a Midwest United States high school, the project involved six 11th-grade students and one **English Language Arts** (**ELA**) teacher. The students were selected from a socioeconomically underserved school with a diverse demographic background.

The primary objective of this initiative was to explore how AI-driven collaboration could support underserved students in developing their writing skills. The CGScholar AI Helper was designed to provide personalized, real-time AI-based feedback on writing assignments, aligning with the teacher's rubric and instructional goals. This approach aimed to encourage iterative improvement while addressing common challenges faced by struggling student writers. The project aimed to achieve the following objectives:

- Enhance student writing competency and proficiency through AI-generated feedback.

- Promote independent learning by encouraging students to engage in multiple revision cycles based on AI-driven feedback.

14 Winkler, R., Roos, J., Association for Information Systems, AIS Electronic Library (AISeL), & University of St Gallen. (2019). Bringing AI into the Classroom: Designing Smart Personal Assistants as Learning Tutors. ICIS 2019 Proceedings. https://core.ac.uk/download/pdf/301384188.pdf

15 Zheldibayeva, R., De Oliveira Nascimento, A. K., Castro, V., Kalantzis, M., & Cope, B. (n.d.). The Impact of AI-Driven tools on student writing development: a case study from the CGScholar AI Helper Project. Retrieved March 6, 2025, from https://arxiv.org/pdf/2501.08473

- Align AI feedback with educator-defined rubrics and curriculum standards.

- Gather insights into the student experience for further refinement of the tool.[16]

Implementation details

The CGScholar AI Helper was integrated into a high school classroom setting through a structured process. The study began with a collaborative planning phase between the research team and the participating teacher. The teacher provided her grading rubric and the texts selected for the assignment, including *The World on the Turtle's Back* and *Returning Three Sisters to Indigenous Farms Nourishes People, Land, and Cultures*. The implementation process involved the following steps:

1. **Teacher and student training**: The teacher and students were all trained to use the CGScholar platform. Each participant received a unique login to access the AI Helper interface.

2. **Assignment setup**: The teacher assigned a 200-word writing task requiring students to compare and contrast Indigenous values reflected in the two reading materials. The AI Helper was trained to evaluate student responses based on six rubric criteria: compare and contrast, identify, compose, introduce and connect, support evidence, and analyze.

3. **Draft submission and AI feedback**: Students submitted their initial drafts through the AI platform. The AI system provided real-time feedback using a star rating system (0 to 4 stars) alongside detailed textual commentary. The feedback highlighted strengths and areas for improvement in alignment with the rubric provided by the teacher.

4. **Revision and resubmission**: Students revised their work based on AI-generated feedback and submitted second drafts. The AI Helper provided a secondary round of feedback, allowing for further refinement before final evaluation by the educator.

5. **Data collection**: Qualitative data were collected from multiple sources, including teacher and student surveys, analysis of focus group discussions, and observations by the research team. Student writing samples (both initial and revised) were analyzed to assess progress.

The CGScholar AI Helper's design relied on **retrieval-augmented generation (RAG)**. RAG is a framework that combines information retrieval from an external source (like the Internet) with text generation, allowing an AI model to fetch relevant documents or data from a knowledge base before generating a response using generative AI. This improves the accuracy and depth of the answer by grounding it in external, up-to-date information rather than relying solely on a previously trained AI model's internal knowledge.

---

16 Zheldibayeva, R., De Oliveira Nascimento, A. K., Castro, V., Kalantzis, M., & Cope, B. (n.d.). The Impact of AI-Driven tools on student writing development: a case study from the CGScholar AI Helper Project. Retrieved March 6, 2025, from https://arxiv.org/pdf/2501.08473

RAG ensures that feedback is contextually relevant with current thinking by drawing from a bounded dataset that includes teacher-provided materials and rubrics. This approach ensured that AI-driven feedback was not generic but tailored to classroom-specific objectives.[17]

Outcomes and observations

The findings from this project signaled positive outcomes in student writing development. The AI-driven collaboration helped to foster a more engaged, iterative approach to writing, as students actively revised their work based on targeted feedback. The key outcomes included:

- **Improved writing proficiency**: From this experiment, five out of six students demonstrated measurable improvements in at least one rubric criterion. Notable advancements were observed in the areas of compare and contrast, compose, introduce and connect, and analyze. It is a small study, with some hopeful results.

  - **Compare and contrast**: Three students improved, with one student advancing from a zero to a two-star rating by incorporating specific textual comparisons.

  - **Compose**: Two of the students moved from two to three stars by developing defensible claims supported by contextual evidence.

  - **Introduce and connect**: One student improved by providing clearer connections between evidence and claims.

  - **Analyze**: Two students enhanced their ability to interpret Indigenous cultural themes within the assigned texts.

- **Enhanced engagement**: Students reported an increased motivation to revise their work. One student stated, *It was helpful because after writing my response, I had something to go off of to fix it and it told me exactly what I needed to fix.*

- **Teacher insights**: The participating teacher noted that the AI feedback encouraged students to engage more deeply with the revision process, which is typically challenging to achieve with students at this level. The teacher's post-survey highlighted the tool's potential, stating, *I think this has a lot of potential. It encouraged students to revise their work, which is difficult to do.*

- **Challenges and refinements**: While the feedback was generally effective, some students found the explanations overly detailed and complex. As a result, the CGScholar development team introduced a new chat-based summarization features, allowing students to request simplified explanations and vocabulary clarifications.

These findings underscore the importance of user-centered design in developing AI writing tools that support diverse student requirements. While AI-driven feedback improved writing proficiency and increased engagement on writing revisions, some students found the language

17 Zheldibayeva, R., De Oliveira Nascimento, A. K., Castro, V., Kalantzis, M., & Cope, B. (n.d.). The Impact of AI-Driven tools on student writing development: a case study from the CGSCholar AI Helper Project. Retrieved March 6, 2025, from https://arxiv.org/pdf/2501.08473

too complex for their particular reading level. To help refine the experience, designers can prioritize readability, personalization, and user-centered design, helping to ensure that feedback is clear, age-appropriate, and adaptable. Adding individual features like reading-level controls, glossary pop-up messages, and tiered explanations can help students better understand the feedback and take action. The chat-based summarization tool is a promising step towards aligning AI support with students' comprehension abilities and fostering more meaningful student learning interactions.

Key takeaways

Several key takeaways[18] emerged from this case study, highlighting both the strengths and opportunities for improvement in AI-driven classroom collaboration:

- **Personalized feedback enhances learning**: The AI Helper's ability to provide customized feedback aligned well with the teacher's rubric, significantly improving student writing outcomes. This personalized approach helped ensure that feedback was relevant, actionable, and curriculum-aligned.

- **Iterative learning drives improvement**: The structured process of draft submission, AI feedback, revision, and resubmission helped to promote iterative learning. Students engaged more deeply with the writing process, demonstrating higher order thinking and analytical skills.

- **Teacher involvement is crucial**: The success of the AI-driven collaboration depended on the teacher's active participation and role in curating prompts, rubrics, and learning materials. AI augmented the educator and functioned as an extension of the teacher's instructional practices rather than an independent tool.

- **Ethical considerations matter**: The use of a constrained and bounded dataset ensured that AI feedback was contextually relevant and free from external biases. This approach helped to mitigate concerns about AI providing misleading or irrelevant suggestions.

- **User experience refinement**: While the tools proved effective, teacher and student feedback highlighted the need for more concise, accessible explanations. The integration of chat-based summarization features addressed this challenge, demonstrating the importance of continuous refinement based on user insights.

The CGScholar AI Helper Project illustrates the potential of AI-driven collaboration to transform classroom learning by enhancing student writing skills. By aligning AI feedback with teacher-defined rubrics and promoting iterative learning for students, the project empowered students to take ownership of their writing development.

While the initial implementation yielded positive results, ongoing refinements are essential to address student and teacher user challenges and ensure that AI tools remain accessible,

---

18 Zheldibayeva, R., De Oliveira Nascimento, A. K., Castro, V., Kalantzis, M., & Cope, B. (n.d.). The Impact of AI-Driven tools on student writing development: a case study from the CGSCholar AI Helper Project. Retrieved March 6, 2025, from https://arxiv.org/pdf/2501.08473

inclusive, and effective. The project underscores the importance of teacher involvement, responsible and ethical AI practices, and continuous user-centered design in driving successful AI integration in education.

Ultimately, the CGScholar AI Helper exemplifies how AI-driven collaboration can bridge learning gaps, promote equity, and support personalized learning journeys, offering valuable insights for future applications of AI in K-12 education.[19]

Case study: Remote learning and AI support

As we have seen, the advancement of technology has significantly transformed education, with remote learning becoming a crucial method for delivering education worldwide. The COVID-19 pandemic accelerated this transformation, compelling educators, school administrators, and institutions to adopt new and upcoming digital platforms. However, the sudden shift highlighted technology inefficiencies, particularly in creating assessments, maintaining student engagement, and ensuring quality education delivery.

In response, researchers from the *National University Zaporizhzhia Polytechnic* created a project around an AI-driven remote learning system[20] aimed at enhancing the educational process by integrating AI for automatic test generation. The primary objectives of this system were:

- **Efficient test creation**: To reduce the time teachers spend creating assessments by automating test generation using AI.

- **Enhanced user experience**: To help provide an intuitive and adaptive interface for teachers and students.

- **Improved educational outcomes**: To facilitate personalized learning paths by identifying student strengths and weaknesses through automated assessments.

- **Optimized performance**: To ensure the platform can operate efficiently, even with limited internet connectivity.

By leveraging Laravel[21] for the backend, React for the frontend, and ChatGPT for AI-driven functionalities, the project aimed to demonstrate how AI could revolutionize remote education while maintaining high standards of learning quality.[22]

---

19 Zheldibayeva, R., De Oliveira Nascimento, A. K., Castro, V., Kalantzis, M., & Cope, B. (n.d.). The Impact of AI-Driven tools on student writing development: a case study from the CGSCholar AI Helper Project. Retrieved March 6, 2025, from https://arxiv.org/pdf/2501.08473
20 Kostetskyi, D. V., Tiahunova, M. Yu., Kyrychek, H. H., & National University "Zaporizhzhia Polytechnic." (2024). Computer system for distance learning with integrated artificial intelligence. In CEUR Workshop Proceedings (pp. 160–174). https://notso.easyscience.education/3l-person/3L-Person2024/paper22.pdf
21 LaRavel - the PHP framework for web artisans. (n.d.). https://laravel.com/
22 Kostetskyi, D. V., Tiahunova, M. Yu., Kyrychek, H. H., & National University "Zaporizhzhia Polytechnic." (2024). Computer system for distance learning with integrated artificial intelligence. In CEUR Workshop Proceedings (pp. 160–174). https://notso.easyscience.education/3l-person/3L-Person2024/paper22.pdf

Implementation details

The implementation involved multiple stages, from system design to deployment and testing.[23] The development team focused on creating a singular, monolithic architecture, which simplified management and ensured seamless integration of AI features. The technical details of the system architecture included:

- **Backend**: Laravel framework[24] was chosen for its security, scalability, and efficiency.
- **Frontend**: React library provided a dynamic and responsive user interface.
- **AI integration**: ChatGPT API powered the automatic test generation feature.
- **Database**: MySQL was used to store user data, test results, and course materials.

The following figure shows the deployment of a system architecture diagram:

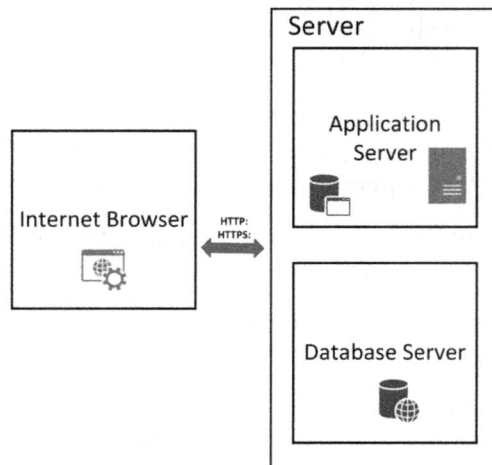

Figure 4.1: *High level deployment diagram*

The system was designed with clear user roles: administrators, educators, and students. Each user type had specific permissions based on their role, ensuring a smooth workflow. The key functionalities of the system design included:

- **Automated test generation**: Educators could automatically create tests by specifying the topic, number of questions, and difficulty level. The system generated questions using ChatGPT, significantly reducing the time needed for test preparation.
- **Student assessment**: Students could access tests through the learning portal. Questions were randomly selected, ensuring variation and fairness in assessments.

---

23 Kostetskyi, D. V., Tiahunova, M. Yu., Kyrychek, H. H., & National University "Zaporizhzhia Polytechnic." (2024). Computer system for distance learning with integrated artificial intelligence. In CEUR Workshop Proceedings (pp. 160–174). https://notso.easyscience.education/3l-person/3L-Person2024/paper22.pdf
24 LaRavel - the PHP framework for web artisans. (n.d.). https://laravel.com/

- **Performance tracking**: Teachers could analyze students' results to identify knowledge gaps and tailor future lessons based on results.
- **Secure data handling**: The system ensured security and privacy through encryption and regular backups.

A user-friendly interface was a top priority, with:

- **Simple navigation**: Intuitive contextual menus for accessing courses, tests, and results.
- **Adaptive design**: Compatibility with multiple platforms, including desktop, tablets, and smartphones.
- **Fast loading**: Efficient code and asynchronous requests minimized load times.

Outcomes and observations

The implementation of the AI-driven remote learning system yielded several significant improvements across multiple aspects of education delivery for both students and educators.

One of the most notable outcomes was the drastic reduction in time required for test or exam creation. Previously, creating a 25-question test took educators approximately 125 minutes to do manually. With the AI-driven system, the same task took only 23 minutes, including review and minor corrections. This represented an 82% reduction in workload, freeing teachers to focus on teaching and student engagement.

Students benefited from personalized assessments, with exams adapted to their learning pace and style. Analysis of test results highlighted areas requiring further study, enabling targeted interventions. Additionally, the system helped provide instant feedback, promoting active learning.

Extensive testing helped to ensure system stability. The AI-generated tests maintained high accuracy, requiring minimal corrections. The platform's asynchronous communication and optimized data handling improved loading times even in regions with limited internet connectivity. Compared with other systems like Moodle[25], the developed system consumed less traffic, enhancing accessibility for students and educators with poor internet connections.

Surveys conducted among educators and students revealed notable satisfaction levels, including:

- About 90% of educators reported increased productivity and reduced stress in test preparation.
- 85% of students found the system easy to use and appreciated the instant feedback feature.

---

25 Welcome to the Moodle community. (n.d.). moodle.org. Retrieved March 6, 2025, from https://moodle.org/

Key takeaways

The AI-driven remote learning system demonstrated the transformative potential of AI in education, as well as how AI can impact student learning. The key takeaways include:

- **Efficiency and time savings**: Automating exam creation reduced educators' workload by over 80%, enabling them to focus more on personalized teaching and mentoring.

- **Enhanced learning experience**: Individual assessments and instant feedback helped to empower students to take control of their learning journeys.

- **Optimized system performance**: Asynchronous data exchange and frontend optimization assisted in ensuring smooth operation, even with limited internet connectivity.

- **Scalability and future potential**: The monolithic architecture offered the opportunity for system expansion, paving the way for future enhancements, such as AI-driven content recommendations and adaptive learning paths.

- **User-centric design**: Prioritizing simplicity and accessibility provided the foundation for high adoption rates among both educators and students.

The AI-driven remote learning system developed by the *National University Zaporizhzhia Polytechnic* exemplifies how technology can impact and revolutionize education. By automating time-consuming tasks for educators, enhancing user experience, and providing personalized learning opportunities for students, the system addressed key challenges associated with remote education.

The success of this project highlights the potential for further innovation in AI-driven educational platforms. Future developments might include adaptive learning paths, AI-driven tutoring, and predictive analytics to further enhance educational outcomes.

Ultimately, this case study demonstrates that AI is not just a tool for efficiency but a catalyst for transforming how education is delivered, making learning more accessible, personalized, and effective for all stakeholders.[26]

Common themes and best practices

AI is completely transforming the educational landscape, offering exciting new opportunities for personalized learning, increased student engagement, and streamlined teaching practices. Effective AI integration in classrooms requires deliberate and thoughtful implementation, considering teacher preparation, student empowerment, contextual adaptation, ethical considerations, and sustainability. We have the opportunity to explore the common themes

---

26 Kostetskyi, D. V., Tiahunova, M. Yu., Kyrychek, H. H., & National University "Zaporizhzhia Polytechnic." (2024). Computer system for distance learning with integrated artificial intelligence. In CEUR Workshop Proceedings (pp. 160–174). https://notso.easyscience.education/3l-person/3L-Person2024/paper22.pdf

and best practices derived from successful AI implementations in education, drawing insights from multiple case studies and research findings.

Teacher training and professional development

One of the most critical factors for successful AI integration is ensuring that educators at all levels are well-prepared to use AI tools effectively. Without adequate exposure and explicit training of our educators, even the most advanced technologies can fail to deliver desired outcomes.

Teachers must receive initial training on the functionalities, capabilities, limitations, and pedagogical applications of AI tools. For instance, the CGScholar AI Helper project provided educators with workshops to understand how AI could support student writing.[27]

Beyond initial training, continuous professional development ensures that teachers can adapt to evolving AI technologies. The study by *Wei (2023)* on AI in language instruction highlighted how ongoing coaching improved teachers' ability to integrate AI effectively into English language learning.[28]

Encouraging teachers to share experiences and strategies can create a supportive community of practice. Platforms like CGScholar facilitate this by allowing educators to collaborate and discuss AI-driven feedback.[29]

As a best practice, schools should allocate dedicated time for teacher professional development, ensuring they are confident in using AI tools and understanding their potential impact on student learning.

Student engagement and ownership

To maximize the benefits of AI in classrooms, students must be included as active participants in their learning process. AI tools should help empower students by providing personalized feedback, encouraging autonomy, and promoting responsible use.

AI platforms like CGScholar and adaptive language learning tools allow students to receive feedback tailored to their specific needs, enhancing engagement and ownership of learning.

Transparency in how AI generates recommendations helps to build trust. Students using AI-powered writing tools reported an increased level of confidence when they understood how feedback was generated.

27 CGScholar AI Helper: a Generative AI Writing and Learning Assistant | IES. (n.d.). https://nces.ed.gov/use-work/awards/cgscholar-ai-helper-generative-ai-writing-and-learning-assistant

28 Wei, L. (2023). Artificial intelligence in language instruction: impact on English learning achievement, L2 motivation, and self-regulated learning. Frontiers in Psychology, 14. P. 7. https://doi.org/10.3389/fpsyg.2023.1261955

29 CGScholar AI Helper: a Generative AI Writing and Learning Assistant | IES. (n.d.). https://nces.ed.gov/use-work/awards/cgscholar-ai-helper-generative-ai-writing-and-learning-assistant

AI can support personalized and self-regulated learning by helping students set goals, track progress, and adjust their learning strategies. The remote learning AI system demonstrated how AI-driven feedback encouraged students to take more responsibility for their learning.

A best practice for schools includes ensuring AI tools help to provide clear explanations for feedback and allow students to make informed decisions about their learning.

Contextual adaptation

Educational settings can vary significantly in terms of resources, culture, and student needs. Successful AI implementations must adapt to these unique contexts rather than applying standardized solutions.

AI platforms should incorporate culturally responsive content. For example, AI-assisted English learning programs adapted vocabulary and contexts based on students' cultural backgrounds, improving student engagement.

In low resource settings, lightweight AI platforms can help ensure equitable access. The CGScholar project is a good example of how AI tools could operate effectively within existing school infrastructures.

AI systems should be influenced by, and align with, teachers' curricular goals and instructional styles. CGScholar allowed teachers to integrate their rubrics into the AI feedback system, ensuring relevance to classroom practices.

As a best practice, schools should select AI tools that can be customized to fit their specific educational contexts and technological infrastructure. Teachers should have the ability to customize to fit their personal style.

Ethical and equity considerations

While AI offers numerous educational benefits, it also raises important ethical concerns, including bias, privacy, and equitable access. Addressing these challenges is crucial for responsible AI use in classrooms.

AI algorithms can reflect biases based on their training data. Successful implementations, such as CGScholar, used teacher-generated rubrics to ensure feedback was aligned with educational goals rather than biased data sets.

Protecting student data is paramount. Platforms like AI-assisted language learning systems ensured data privacy through secure storage and limited data sharing. The public AI models will ingest user data, and it is important to take this into account.

AI should support diverse learners, including those with disabilities. AI-powered tools like speech-to-text, video, and adaptive learning platforms demonstrated success in making education more inclusive.

Schcols should adopt AI platforms with transparent and robust data privacy policies, transparent algorithms, and inclusive design features as a best practice.

Unlike Moodle, which primarily serves as a traditional LMS with content generated on the server and manual content creation, this AI-integrated system provides automated test generation using ChatGPT, drastically reducing the work required by educators, along with shorter preparation time. Its client-side rendering also makes it significantly more efficient in low-bandwidth environments, offering faster navigation and less use of data. Educationally, the AI-enhanced platform supports improved personalized assessment, enabling educators to generate adaptive tests based on student understanding and complexity levels, helping identify and address student knowledge gaps more effectively. This adds a dynamic, scalable layer of instructional support that goes above and beyond Moodle's static course design.

Scalability and sustainability

For AI programs to be effective, they must be financially and operationally sustainable. Successful initiatives prioritize scalability while maintaining a high-quality educational experience.

Open-source AI platforms can provide schools with affordable solutions for distance learning. Ongoing support for students and educators helps ensure continued progress and success. The CGScholar project demonstrated how iterative feedback loops between teachers and developers improved the platform over time. Regular evaluation and feedback loops help to identify areas for improvement. Successful programs employed metrics such as student performance, engagement, and teacher satisfaction to assess effectiveness.

As a best practice, schools should be deliberate about choosing AI solutions with transparent training models, pricing, strong support systems, and built-in feedback mechanisms and robust metrics for evaluating impact.

The following table maps the case studies to specific themes and key learnings:

Theme	Learning	Case study
Teacher training and professional development	Workshops and ongoing coaching helped educators use AI effectively and adapt to evolving tools.	CGScholar AI Helper; Wei (2023) AI in Language Instruction
	Platforms like CGScholar allowed teachers to collaborate and share AI strategies.	CGScholar AI Helper
	Students received personalized feedback, increasing motivation and ownership over learning.	CGScholar AI Helper; Remote Learning AI System

Theme	Learning	Case study
Student engagement and ownership	Students better understood AI-generated feedback, boosting confidence.	CGScholar AI Helper
	Students used AI tools to track progress and set goals for self-regulated learning.	Remote learning AI system
	AI tools adapt vocabulary and context based on students' cultural backgrounds.	AI-driven language tutoring
Contextual adaptation	CGScholar operated well in existing school infrastructure, making it suitable for low-resource settings.	CGScholar AI helper
	Teachers could integrate their rubrics into the AI system to align with curricular goals.	CGScholar AI helper
	Teacher rubrics guided feedback to reduce algorithmic bias.	CGScholar AI helper
Ethical and equity considerations	Platforms used secure data storage and avoided sharing user data unnecessarily.	AI-assisted language learning
	Speech-to-text and other adaptive tools made AI more inclusive for diverse learners.	Multiple case studies
Scalability and sustainability	Open-source platforms like CGScholar allowed for affordable, iterative development with user feedback loops.	CGScholar AI helper
	The remote learning AI system reduced teacher workload and worked well even with limited internet connectivity.	Remote learning AI system

Table 4.1: *Mapping studies to learnings*

Conclusion

Successful AI implementations in classrooms depend on thoughtful integration, emphasizing teacher training, student empowerment, contextual adaptation, ethical considerations, and sustainability. By prioritizing these elements, educational institutions can harness AI's potential to create impactful, inclusive, engaging, and effective learning environments. Moving forward, close collaboration among educators, technologists, and policymakers will be crucial for ensuring AI remains a force for positive change in education.

The future of AI in education is exciting, dynamic and evolving, offering boundless opportunities for enhancing teaching and learning. To fully realize this potential, educators must remain curious, adaptive and open-minded. Embracing AI as a collaborative partner rather than a replacement for the educator can help empower teachers and students alike, transforming our classrooms of today into hubs of innovation and lifelong learning.

In the next chapter, we will discuss what parents or guardians should consider when supporting their students through their AI journey. We will explore privacy and security fundamentals, screen time reliance, access to AI tools, and the need for ongoing collaboration with parents or guardians for healthy AI learning.

Questions

1. Based on this chapter, how do real-world case studies demonstrate the potential benefits and challenges of AI integration in education?

2. What are a few key metrics were used to evaluate the success of AI implementations in different educational settings?

3. How do adaptive learning platforms personalize instruction to improve student engagement and academic performance?

4. In what ways can AI tools support educators in managing classrooms and delivering personalized instruction?

5. How do schools address equity challenges, such as access to technology and internet connectivity, when implementing AI solutions?

6. What ethical concerns arose during AI integration, and how were they mitigated? How will these lessons apply to your situation?

7. What evidence did you take away from the demonstrated improvements in student engagement, achievement, and self-regulation across the case studies?

8. What were the most common challenges faced during AI implementation, and how were they overcome?

9. How did these schools ensure that AI solutions were sustainable and scalable across different learning environments?

10. Based on the lessons learned from the case studies, what recommendations would you give to educators who are considering AI adoption in their classrooms?

Exercises

1. **Case study comparison**: Analyze the similarities and differences between two AI implementations.

    a. Choose two case studies from this chapter (e.g., adaptive learning and AI-driven language tutoring).

    b. Compare them across the following criteria:

        i. Implementation.

        ii. Key features of the AI platform used.

        iii. Outcomes for students and teachers.

        iv. Challenges encountered and how they were addressed.

    c. Create a table summarizing your observations and write a short reflection (150-200 words) on which approach you believe was more effective and why.

2. **Success criteria evaluation**: Evaluate an AI implementation (from this chapter or elsewhere) based on the success metrics outlined in this chapter.

    a. Review one case study and identify how it performed against the chapter's success criteria:

        i. Student engagement.

        ii. Learning outcomes.

        iii. Teacher efficiency.

        iv. Equity and accessibility improvements.

        v. Long-term sustainability and scalability.

    b. Assign a rating (1 to 5) for each criterion and provide a brief justification for each score.

    c. Meet and reflect on whether the case study's success was context-dependent and how the approach might differ in another setting.

3. **Implementation roadmap**: Design an AI implementation and deployment plan for a specific educational context.

    a. Imagine you are tasked with introducing and deploying an AI solution in a school setting (K–12, higher education, or adult learning).

    b. Create a step-by-step roadmap that includes:

        i. Technology platform selection criteria.

        ii. Curriculum integration strategy.

        iii. Teacher training and support plan.

        iv. Monitoring and feedback process.

        v. Implementing changes based on feedback.

        vi. Plans for addressing equity and accessibility concerns.

    c. Publish your roadmap as a written plan or a visual flowchart.

4. **Ethical dilemma debate**: Explore the ethical challenges associated with AI in education.

   a. Read the section in this chapter on ethical considerations and equity challenges.

   b. Imagine a scenario where an AI platform provides different levels of support to students based on internet access or device quality, or other differences.

   c. Divide into two groups: one arguing that AI implementation should continue despite inequities and the other arguing that rollout should pause until equitable access is guaranteed.

   d. After the debate, write a brief reflection (100-150 words) on how schools can balance innovation with inclusivity in a world of AI.

5. **Reflective journal on AI impact**: Encourage personal reflection on the potential of AI in education.

   a. Reflect on how AI has impacted educational practices in your institution, as highlighted in the chapter.

   b. In a journal entry (200-300 words), discuss:

       i.   Which case study resonated most with you and why.

       ii. How AI could benefit or challenge your own learning or teaching environment and have a positive impact on your students.

       iii. What do you believe are the most important factors for successful AI integration?

   c. Share your reflections with a peer and discuss areas of agreement and differing perspectives.

Join our Discord space

Join our Discord workspace for latest updates, offers, tech happenings around the world, new releases, and sessions with the authors:

https://discord.bpbonline.com

CHAPTER 5
Addressing Parental Concerns

By far, the greatest danger of artificial intelligence is that people conclude too early that they understand it.

-Eliezer Yudkowsky

Introduction

Since the beginning of time, whether it is humans or animals, an important role that parents play in the lives of their offspring is to help the young learn how to navigate the world. Education is also subject to the influence of evolution, and with each new advancement, parents naturally experience both excitement and concern. It is a multifaceted journey shaped by both age-old human experiences and cutting-edge innovations. From the earliest years of life, parental guidance has a profound impact on a child's learning and development[1]. The educational landscape has been rapidly transformed by generative AI technologies like ChatGPT, Gemini, Copilot, and Claude, which are now being integrated into classrooms at an unprecedented pace. These tools offer personalized instruction, immediate feedback, and scalable learning experiences—but they also bring a surge in parental concerns. Parents now face a new set of questions about how these tools may affect cognitive development, emotional well-being, attention spans, social interactions, and even long-term creativity and problem-

---

1 Lara, L., & Saracostti, M. (2019). Effect of parental involvement on children's academic achievement in Chile. Frontiers in Psychology, 10. https://doi.org/10.3389/fpsyg.2019.01464

solving abilities. The role of AI in education continues to evolve, mirroring both the hopes and hesitations of those guiding the next generation.

The concerns parents have about AI in education have evolved over time, and the role of AI is continuing to shape the learning experiences of children. While AI promises to enhance the learning experiences of children through personalized instruction, instant feedback, and efficiency, parents often worry and have concerns about the psychological and developmental impact of these tools on their children. Questions can often arise about cognitive development, emotional well-being, attention spans, social interactions, and even the long-term implications for creativity and problem-solving skills.

Structure

This chapter covers the following topics:

- Roots of parental concerns
- Privacy and security concerns
- Equity, bias and fairness
- Balancing human connection and technology
- Over-reliance on tech and screen time
- Accuracy, reliability and feedback quality
- Nurturing creativity and play
- Ethical considerations and governance
- Unequal access and digital divide
- Collaborating with parents and communities

Objectives

In this chapter, we explore parental concerns about AI in education, balancing its potential benefits with the challenges it presents. As AI transforms classrooms, parents worry about its impact on cognitive development, attention spans, creativity, and human interaction. This chapter aims to address these concerns and provide guidance on responsible AI integration. A key objective is to contextualize parental concerns historically. Understanding this helps frame AI as part of an ongoing evolution in education rather than an unprecedented threat. We also examine the psychological and social impact of AI, particularly its effects on problem-solving, attention spans, and social development. AI offers personalized learning and instant feedback, but concerns remain about passive engagement, reduced critical thinking, and diminished teacher-student interactions.

Another focus is ethical considerations, including data privacy, algorithmic bias, and AI-driven decision-making. Parents have concerns about how student data is collected and used, as well as whether AI might reinforce educational inequalities. Finally, the chapter emphasizes the ideal role of AI as a tool that enhances education while preserving human connection.

Roots of parental concerns

Our ability to learn is deeply rooted in evolutionary processes that have endowed both human and animal offspring with remarkable adaptive capacities. In the animal world, parents will teach essential survival skills, such as hunting techniques or the ability to recognize predators, to ensure their offspring can thrive independently. These parental lessons help impact the young animals' ability to adapt, survive, and eventually pass on these critical skills to future generations.[2] Animal parents, though driven largely by instinct, exhibit behaviors indicating concern, such as heightened vigilance or protective aggression, when their offspring face threats or unfamiliar environments.[3]

Parental concerns about AI in education can be rooted in broader fears about how their children learn and grow in an increasingly digital world. This is not a new fear. Parents in medieval times worried about the influence of the printing press. In the 1970s, handheld calculators were a concern.[4] However, rather than simply fearing the unknown, many parents want to understand more about how AI fits into their child's cognitive and emotional development.[5] These concerns are valid and need to be addressed by educators, policymakers, and technology developers to ensure that AI serves as a beneficial tool in a child's development.[6]

Enduring impact of parental involvement

Parents are often a child's first teachers, setting the foundation for attitudes toward learning, long before any formal schooling begins. Research consistently shows that active parental involvement early on is associated with better educational outcomes across a range of measures[7].

Children whose parents engage with their education, by reading with them, assisting with homework, or communicating with teachers, tend to earn higher grades and test scores, have

2 Philmckinney. (2025, June 7). How AI Dependency Is Rewiring Your Child's Creative Brain (And What Parents Can Do About It). Killer Innovations With Phil McKinney. https://killerinnovations.com/how-ai-dependency-is-rewiring-your-childs-creative-brain-and-what-parents-can-do-about-it/

3 Illinois researchers examine teens' use of generative AI, safety concerns. (2024, December 2). School of Information Sciences. https://ischool.illinois.edu/news-events/news/2024/12/illinois-researchers-examine-teens-use-generative-ai-safety-concerns

4 Barna Group. (2024, April 23). Parents worry about AI but know little about it - Barna Group. https://www.barna.com/research/parents-ai/

5 Swaminathan, A. (2025, April 25). What US Parents Really Think About AI & its Influence on Kids. Mobicip. https://www.mobicip.com/blog/what-us-parents-really-think-about-ai-its-influence-on-kids

6 Neves, M. (2025, May 16). "Hey Siri, Will AI Change My Kid's Future?" What Parents Really Think. https://www.learner.com/blog/ai-education-survey

7 Lara, L., & Saracostti, M. (2019). Effect of parental involvement on children's academic achievement in Chile. Frontiers in Psychology, 10. https://doi.org/10.3389/fpsyg.2019.01464

better attendance records, and exhibit stronger motivation and self-esteem in academic settings[8]. Parental influence can extend beyond academics as well; supportive home environments contribute to children's socioemotional development and behavior[9]. For instance, positive family-school interactions are linked to improved student attitudes and social skills, creating a reinforcing cycle of engagement and success[10]. These findings have been supported by a variety of studies and meta-analyses worldwide, underlining a consensus that when parents play an active and supportive role in education, children reap significant benefits in terms of their performance and personal growth[11].

Psychological impact of AI-powered learning

One of the primary concerns among parents is how AI-driven learning might affect their child's cognitive development. We do not have longitudinal studies on the impact of AI-based learning on child development. Research in developmental psychology suggests that active learning, where children engage, experiment, play, explore, and problem-solve, can play a critical role in brain development. When children use AI-powered tools, some parents fear these systems may promote passive consumption rather than active engagement. As we saw earlier in *Chapter 1, AI and Personalized Learning*, there are a number of great pedagogical thinkers who have explored childhood learning, but the world of AI is new and unclear.

For instance, AI-driven adaptive learning platforms can provide students with instant answers, reducing frustration and supporting their individual learning needs. However, if students rely too heavily on AI for solutions, they may miss opportunities to develop critical thinking skills, persistence, problem-solving skills, and deep critical thinking. Parents believe that AI could be too easy and inadvertently discourage the trial-and-error learning process, which is fundamental for cognitive growth.

The current media landscape further amplifies these concerns in a world where generative AI technologies—such as deepfakes and AI-generated misinformation—have gained significant attention. From viral fabricated videos to algorithmic content that blurs the line between fact and fiction, the trustworthiness of AI systems has come under scrutiny. Parents increasingly worry that the same technologies that are infiltrating public discourse might also shape their children's learning environments in ways that undermine credibility, ethics, and truth. These narratives have added a new layer of mistrust around AI's role in education, raising questions about its appropriateness and long-term implications.

---

8 Lara, L., & Saracostti, M. (2019). Effect of parental involvement on children's academic achievement in Chile. Frontiers in Psychology, 10. https://doi.org/10.3389/fpsyg.2019.01464
9 Bonci, A., Emily Mottram, Emily McCoy, Jennifer Cole, & National Literacy Trust. (2008). A research review: the importance of families and the home environment. https://files.eric.ed.gov/fulltext/ED521654.pdf
10 E Lara, L., & Saracostti, M. (2019). Effect of parental involvement on children's academic achievement in Chile. Frontiers in Psychology, 10. https://doi.org/10.3389/fpsyg.2019.01464
11 Lara, L., & Saracostti, M. (2019). Effect of parental involvement on children's academic achievement in Chile. Frontiers in Psychology, 10. https://doi.org/10.3389/fpsyg.2019.01464

Another area of concern is how AI might influence and impact a child's ability to focus. Screen-based learning has long been a concern with diminished attention spans. AI-driven tools, which may use gamification and rapid feedback loops, could further shorten students' ability to concentrate for extended periods without the scaffolding of artificial rewards and engagement techniques. Studies suggest that excessive reliance on instant feedback mechanisms can rewire the brain to seek the chemical dopamine and that of immediate rewards, potentially impacting a child's brain development and the ability to engage in deep, sustained learning.

Recent psychological research highlights that while AI-driven instant feedback can help boost engagement and clarity, it may also introduce unintended emotional and cognitive side effects. A few samples of such studies include:

- **Increased student anxiety and behavioral issues**: A large cross-sectional study of 1,240 primary-school age students in China (ages 8–15) found that high use of AI tools amplified the link between social anxiety and behavioral problems, especially in students with lower adaptability.[12]

  Students who relied heavily on feedback from AI reported increased anxiety and diminished learning adaptability, leading to an increased likelihood of problematic behaviors.

- **Programming anxiety and motivation trade-offs**: In university-level pair-programming courses (2023–2024), AI assistance (e.g., GPT-3.5 Turbo or Claude 3 Opus) led to lower programming anxiety compared to those who were working solo, and performance gains were evident. [13]

  However, students in AI-assisted setups reported less direct human collaboration, hinting at longer-term risks to collaboration, social learning, and resilience.

- **Metacognitive laziness/Cognitive offloading**: A 2024 experimental study contrasted learners who used generative AI instead of human tutors vs. analytics tools. While all showed performance improvement, the AI group demonstrated some signs of metacognitive laziness—less engagement in self-regulation, reflection, and critical thinking. [14]

---

12 Ma, G., Tian, S., Song, Y., Chen, Y., Shi, H., & Li, J. (2025). When Technology Meets Anxiety:The moderating role of AI usage in the relationship between social anxiety, learning adaptability, and behavioral problems among Chinese primary school students. Psychology Research and Behavior Management, Volume 18, 151–167. https://doi.org/10.2147/prbm.s502337

13 Fan, G., Liu, D., Zhang, R., & Pan, L. (2025). The impact of AI-assisted pair programming on student motivation, programming anxiety, collaborative learning, and programming performance: a comparative study with traditional pair programming and individual approaches. International Journal of STEM Education, 12(1). https://doi.org/10.1186/s40594-025-00537-3

14 Hou, I., Man, O., Hamilton, K., Muthusekaran, S., Johnykutty, J., Zadeh, L., & MacNeil, S. (2025, April 14). "All Roads Lead to ChatGPT": How Generative AI is Eroding Social Interactions and Student Learning Communities. arXiv.org. https://arxiv.org/abs/2504.09779

A separate mixed-method analysis (666 participants) outlined a significant negative relationship between AI use and critical-thinking abilities, largely mediated by excessive cognitive offloading. [15]

- **Addictive feedback-loop patterns**: A study from MIT Media Lab (Mar 2025) monitored ~1,000 ChatGPT users and captured early signs of emotional dependency and compulsive use—characterized by reduced decision-making autonomy and reliance on AI for brainstorming—even when not performing academic tasks. [16]

Shaping parents' views on AI

For many parents, concerns about AI in education are not merely about the technology itself, but about the broader implications that this digital transformation may have on their children's learning, development, and future. These concerns are shaped by personal experiences, media narratives, and societal anxieties about automation, surveillance, and the shifting nature of human relationships with technology. While AI offers incredible potential in personalizing learning and improving efficiency, parents have questions about what might be lost in the process: human connection, creativity, fairness, and security. As observed in *Chapter 2, History of Technology in the Classroom,* there are lessons to be learned from history, but parents are right to be cautious.

Past experiences shape parental concerns

Many parents of today grew up in an era of rapid technological transformation. They witnessed the transition from blackboards to smartboards, from research in the library to internet searches, and from handwritten essays to AI-powered writing assistants. While these innovations were often met with initial skepticism, they ultimately became integrated into the educational practices of today. However, AI differs in one crucial way; it has the potential to automate decision-making, which raises deeper concerns about the future of control, transparency, and fairness.

Parents who experienced the rise of the internet as they were growing up remember the challenges that came with it: misinformation, cyberbullying, data breaches, fake news, and the commercialization of online spaces. These past challenges make parents skeptical and more cautious about AI, particularly when it comes to how student data is collected, stored, and used. If past digital revolutions introduced unexpected risks to the world of learning, how can they be sure AI will not do the same, perhaps even on an even larger scale?

Another factor influencing parents' perspectives is their own educational experience. Many parents have fond memories and appreciate the value of the mentorship of great teachers, the joy of hands-on learning, and the development of interpersonal skills through classroom

---

15 Gerlich, M. (2025). AI Tools in Society: Impacts on cognitive offloading and the future of critical thinking. Societies, 15(1), 6. https://doi.org/10.3390/soc15010006

16 Esbin, H. B., PhD. (2025, June 9). The emerging psychological crisis in AI adoption: A shadow dance. https://www.linkedin.com/pulse/emerging-psychological-crisis-ai-adoption-shadow-dance-esbin-phd-vk-jxc/

discussions. When they hear about AI-driven education replacing traditional instruction with personalized, algorithm-driven learning, they fear their children may miss out on the same enriching human experiences that shaped their own intellectual and emotional growth.

Media reports and their impact on parental views

The way AI is portrayed in the media also plays a significant role in shaping parental concerns. First, we have the history of AI in movies. From HAL to the Terminator, as well as headlines about biased algorithms, AI replacing jobs, and data security failures, create a sense of uncertainty about whether AI can be trusted in educational settings. Parents read stories about AI-driven hiring tools in the workplace, exhibiting gender and racial bias, and they wonder: *if AI can discriminate in hiring, can it also misjudge my child's learning potential?*

Additionally, parents are exposed to news reports about the automation of work and the future job market. AI is increasingly being used in industries ranging from healthcare to finance, replacing human workers. Parents wonder if an AI-driven education system might prioritize standardized efficiency over fostering the unique talents and creativity of their children, ultimately leaving their children ill-prepared for a world where adaptability and critical thinking are more valuable than rote memorization.

Another prevalent media concern is transparency, security, data privacy, and surveillance. Stories about tech companies collecting vast amounts of user data without proper security and privacy safeguards lead parents to question whether AI in classrooms might be monitoring students in ways that invade their privacy. If corporations and governments struggle to regulate AI responsibly, how can parents be sure their children's schools will handle these complexities correctly?

Broader societal concerns

Beyond individual experiences and media narratives, parental concerns about AI are also influenced by broader societal anxieties about the role of this technology in our lives. Many parents feel a growing loss of control over the digital environment in which their children are growing up. The changes brought on by social media are paramount. Unlike previous technological shifts, AI is advancing at an unprecedented pace. The speed of its development, combined with its complexity and the amplifying effect of social media and mobile, makes it increasingly difficult for parents to feel confident in its governance.

The question of who controls AI in education is another key concern that many parents have. *Is it individual teachers and specific school administrators who understand students' individual needs? Or is it private AI companies that prioritize profits and data collection over what is best for students? Will the government step in?* Parents are concerned that if AI-powered educational tools are primarily designed by corporations, it is likely that profit motives may outweigh the best interests of students. This fear is reinforced by past experiences with social media companies, many of which once claimed to connect people but ultimately contributed to widespread privacy violations and mental health concerns among children and teenagers.

Relevance to child development

When these new AI technologies are introduced into education, the stakes might feel particularly high for parents because they affect not just how children learn, but also who the children become. Parents are not just thinking about AI's short-term impact on their child's test scores and efficiency; they are considering its long-term influence on their child's emotional intelligence, moral development, and cognitive growth.

Beyond test scores and proficiency measures, AI can also address qualitative aspects of education. Adaptive learning platforms and educational chatbots can relieve teachers of routine tasks (such as grading practice exercises or answering frequently asked questions), freeing educators to focus on mentorship and the emotional and creative needs of students. AI-driven systems are being used to provide immediate feedback in subjects like writing and mathematics, to engage students through interactive simulations, and to identify learning gaps that might escape a busy teacher's notice. Globally, organizations like UNESCO have emphasized that AI has the potential to tackle some of the biggest challenges in education, expanding access, personalizing learning, and innovating teaching methods, thereby accelerating progress toward inclusive and equitable quality education. At the same time, scholars and policymakers caution that these technologies should be implemented ethically and inclusively, ensuring that AI tools supplement rather than supplant human guidance and that all students benefit from the advances in technology.[17]

Emotional development and real-life human connection

A major concern among many parents is that AI-driven education might reduce meaningful human-to-human interactions. Learning is not just about absorbing information; it is a social process that involves collaboration, mentorship, and emotional support. Teachers provide not only academic instruction but also a warm touch, encouragement, discipline, and moral guidance. Parents fear that as AI takes on more educational responsibilities, these emotional bonds between students and teachers could weaken, leading to an impersonal, transactional learning experience.

This concern is particularly applicable to young children, who rely heavily on human interaction for emotional regulation and social development. If AI tutors or chatbots replace traditional student-teacher interactions, many parents worry that their children will miss out on the subtle, nuanced communication that builds empathy, resilience, and emotional intelligence.

---

17 UNESCO. (n.d.). Artificial intelligence in education. unesco.org. Retrieved March 15, 2025, from https://www.unesco.org/en/digital-education/artificial-intelligence#:~:text=accelerate%20progress%20to-wards%20SDG%204,principles%20of%20inclusion%20and%20equity

Cognitive development and critical thinking

AI's ability to provide instant feedback and personalized learning paths is impressive, but many parents worry it could create an over-reliance on algorithmic thinking. Will their children lose the ability to think independently if AI provides all the answers?

Traditional learning environments encourage students to engage with difficult concepts, participate in debate, and make mistakes as part of the learning process. AI, by contrast, is designed to optimize for efficiency and minimize errors. While this might seem beneficial on the surface, it risks discouraging trial and error, creative problem-solving, and intellectual curiosity, all of which are essential for long-term cognitive development.

Furthermore, if AI's recommendations are primarily based on data analysis and pattern recognition, parents worry that students will be pushed into predefined learning tracks that limit their exposure to new ideas, current trends, and interdisciplinary thinking. Education should expand possibilities, not narrow them based on predictive analytics.

Ethical considerations and the role of AI in shaping values

Another reason AI in education feels particularly important for parents is its potential influence on children's ethical development. AI is not neutral or unbiased technology; it is built on human-designed algorithms that reflect particular values and priorities. Without transparency into how these AI models are constructed, parents rightfully worry that AI-driven education might subtly shape their children's worldview in ways that are difficult to detect.

For example, if an AI system curates reading materials, prioritizes certain historical perspectives, or recommends particular learning paths, it has the potential to influence how students perceive the world, which might be constrained. Parents want to ensure that ethical considerations, diverse viewpoints, and moral reasoning remain central to education, so important to the free-thinking options for their children, rather than being dictated by AI's underlying algorithms.

Call for thoughtful AI integration

Understanding parental concerns about AI in education requires teachers and all of us to recognize the deeply personal and societal factors that shape their views. Parents are not rejecting AI out of fear of change; they are advocating for a responsible, transparent, fair, secure, and ethical approach to its implementation.

For AI to be a truly beneficial tool in education, it must be integrated in a way that respects student security and privacy, preserves the human connection, encourages independent thinking, and prioritizes ethical considerations, enhancing the student-teacher relationships. Schools, policymakers, and AI providers must work together to ensure that AI remains a tool for empowerment, not a force that diminishes the richness of education. With these partnerships in place, AI in classrooms can be embraced with confidence rather than concern.

Privacy and security concerns

As AI becomes increasingly integrated into classrooms, parents raise concerns about how these systems handle their children's personal data. While AI offers promising advances in personalized learning, adaptive assessments, and student support, it also raises critical questions about data privacy, security, fairness and ethical use. Parents, educators, and policymakers must navigate these concerns to ensure that AI serves students without compromising their privacy or future opportunities, while maintaining human connections.

Complexity of student data collection

Most AI-powered educational tools collect vast amounts of student data to personalize learning experiences. This data may include:

- Academic performance metrics, such as answers, test scores, and learning progress.

- Behavioral data, including how long a student spends on certain tasks and their engagement levels using biometric data like eye gaze or voice recognition.

- Personal information, such as age, GPS location, and learning preferences.

- Sensitive metadata, including browsing history within educational platforms and interactions with AI tutors.

While these data points can help AI to tailor instruction, they also pose significant privacy risks. Parents worry about who owns this data, how it is used, and whether it remains secure and the purposes for which it may be used. There is a real fear that AI may unintentionally create digital profiles of students, which could impact their educational paths and future opportunities.

Ownership and control over student data

One of the most pressing questions parents ask is: *Who owns the data generated by AI interactions?* This is something new that we are all coming to grips with as digital technologies capture more of the educational experience than ever before.

Many AI-driven educational platforms operate on cloud-based systems, meaning student data is often stored and processed outside of the school's boundaries. This raises concerns about whether students, parents, or even schools themselves have control over the data once it is collected. If AI providers retain ownership of student data, there is potential for data to be used for purposes beyond education, such as advertising, marketing, or third-party research.

Regulations such as the **Family Educational Rights and Privacy Act (FERPA)** in the United States grant parents and students certain rights over educational records. However, AI technologies often blur the lines between what is considered an educational record versus proprietary data used to help improve AI systems. Parents want reassurances that their children's learning data will not be sold, misused, or stored indefinitely without consent. The following figure shows a student who is worried about his online privacy:

Figure 5.1: Careful attention to online privacy is critical

Risks of data breaches and cybersecurity threats

Another major concern in AI-driven classrooms is data security. As more schools rely on AI-powered tools, the risk of student information being compromised by cyberattacks increases. Hackers targeting educational institutions might gain access to sensitive student records, leading to privacy violations, identity theft, or even extortion.

Recent cyberattacks on school districts have exposed vulnerabilities in educational technology systems. For example, there are examples of ransomware attacks that have locked schools out of their own data, with hackers demanding payment to restore access. If AI-powered learning platforms are not built with strong security measures, student data could be at risk.

Between 2024 and 2025, educational institutions faced a surge in significant data breaches, often exacerbated by the rapid integration of AI into their digital infrastructure. These incidents highlight both the evolving threat landscape and the urgent need for updated cybersecurity standards and best practices. Some examples include:

- **PowerSchool ransomware attack (December 2024)**: A major ransomware attack targeted PowerSchool in Folsom, California—a widely used ed tech provider, compromising sensitive student and staff data across over 100 school districts in North America. Despite PowerSchool's initial assurances and payment of a ransom, stolen data—including names, social security numbers, and financial information—was later used to extort multiple districts. This breach led to lawsuits alleging negligence and underscored the risk of relying on third-party vendors for data security.[18]

- **Alvin independent school district data breach (June 2024)**: Texas' Alvin Independent School District reported a breach affecting nearly 48,000 individuals. Exposed data included Social Security numbers, financial account details, and health information.

18 Merod, A. (2025, May 15). Data breach reporting lags in education sector, study finds. K-12 Dive. https://www.k12dive.com/news/data-breach-reporting-lags-in-education-sector-study-finds/748273/

The incident illustrated the sector's struggle with timely breach reporting and the prevalence of data theft as a component of ransomware attacks.[19]

- **AI-driven phishing and social engineering (2024-2025)**: Educational institutions have seen a 35% increase in cyberattacks, with threat actors leveraging generative AI to craft sophisticated phishing campaigns and social engineering attacks. These AI-powered threats exploit outdated education infrastructure and the interconnectedness of school systems, putting vast repositories of sensitive research, student, and faculty data at risk.[20,21]

- **Sector-wide breaches via third-party AI systems**: The growing adoption of AI-powered educational tools has introduced new threats and vulnerabilities. Attackers have exploited weaknesses in AI systems to gain unauthorized access to student records and operational data, highlighting the need for robust vetting of AI vendors and alignment with privacy laws and cybersecurity frameworks such as the **National Institute of Standards and Technology (NIST)** and the **Center for Internet Security (CIS)**.[22,23]

Updated cybersecurity standards and best practices

To help combat data breaches, new cybersecurity standards are being developed and circulated among educational institutions as best practices. Some of these best practices include:

- **Zero Trust Architecture**: Institutions are urged to implement Zero Trust models, minimizing attack surfaces and preventing lateral movement within networks.

- **K12 SIX essential protections**: The 2024-25 updates emphasize actionable controls, alignment with NIST and CIS standards, and tools for district self-assessment.[24]

19 Merod, A. (2025, May 15). Data breach reporting lags in education sector, study finds. K-12 Dive. https://www.k12dive.com/news/data-breach-reporting-lags-in-education-sector-study-finds/748273/
20 2025 Cybersecurity Predictions for K-20 Education -- Campus Technology. (2025, January 30). Campus Technology. https://campustechnology.com/articles/2025/01/30/2025-cybersecurity-predictions-for-k-20-education.aspx
21 Rahn, D., & Rahn, D. (2025, April 17). Top cyber threats to educational institutions in 2025. The ENGAGE Blog by Blackbaud. https://blog.blackbaud.com/top-cyber-threats-to-educational-institutions/
22 Jackson, F. (2025, June 4). How schools can prepare for Artificial Intelligence-Backed Cyberattacks. Technology Solutions That Drive Education. https://edtechmagazine.com/k12/article/2025/03/how-schools-can-prepare-artificial-intelligence-backed-cyberattacks
23 New Best Practices Guide for Securing AI Data released. (2025, May 20). Cybersecurity & Infrastructure Security Agency. https://www.cisa.gov/news-events/alerts/2025/05/22/new-best-practices-guide-securing-ai-data-released
24 Levin, D. (2023, February 3). K12 SIX aligns essential K-12 cybersecurity protections to CISA's CPGs — K12 SIX. K12 SIX. https://www.k12six.org/news/k12-six-aligns-2022-2023-essential-cybersecurity-protections-to-cisas-cybersecurity-performance-goals-cpgs

- **AI data security guidelines**: Cybersecurity and Infrastructure Security Agency's (**CISA**) 2025 best practices stress robust data protection, proactive risk management, and continuous monitoring for AI systems.[25]

- **Compliance and vendor management**: Schools must ensure vendors comply with the FERPA, the **Children's Online Privacy Protection Act** (**COPPA**), and federal cybersecurity standards, conduct regular audits, and formalize data privacy agreements.[26]

These incidents and evolving standards underscore the necessity for educational institutions to prioritize cyber hygiene, invest in advanced security solutions, and foster a culture of cybersecurity awareness to protect sensitive data in the AI era.[27]

Parents should demand better safeguards, including

- Identity management.

- Strong encryption to protect stored and transmitted student data.

- Clear policies on data retention and deletion.

- Multi-factor authentication to prevent unauthorized access.

- Strict government regulations ensuring companies comply with privacy standards.

Parental consent and transparency in AI use

Transparency is a key component in addressing parental concerns. Many parents feel they do not understand, and they are left in the dark about how AI systems operate in their children's classrooms. They want clear answers to questions such as:

- What data is collected about my child, and for what purpose?

- How long is my student's data retained?

- Who has access to this data (teachers, administrators, third-party companies)?

- Can parents opt out of AI-driven learning tools if they have privacy concerns?

Parental consent must be an integral part of AI implementation in schools. Just as parents must sign permission slips for field trips or medical treatment, they should also have the right to decline consent when it comes to AI processing their child's educational data. The following figure depicts a concerned parent who is thinking about how to protect their child online:

25 New Best Practices Guide for Securing AI Data released. (2025, May 20). Cybersecurity & Infrastructure Security Agency. https://www.cisa.gov/news-events/alerts/2025/05/22/new-best-practices-guide-securing-ai-data-released
26 Center for Democracy and Technology. (2023, April 11). Policies, people, and protective measures: Legal requirements for K-12 Cybersecurity - Center for Democracy and Technology. https://cdt.org/insights/policies-people-and-protective-measures-legal-requirements-for-k-12-cybersecurity/
27 Levin, D. (2023, February 3). K12 SIX aligns essential K-12 cybersecurity protections to CISA's CPGs — K12 SIX. K12 SIX. https://www.k12six.org/news/k12-six-aligns-2022-2023-essential-cybersecurity-protections-to-cisas-cybersecurity-performance-goals-cpgs

Figure 5.2: Parental constent, oversight, and policy transparency

Psychological impact of AI surveillance in education

Another overlooked aspect of AI in classrooms is its potential psychological impact on students. Many AI-driven platforms incorporate a variety of monitoring tools that track student engagement, attentiveness, and can even go so far as evaluating facial expressions to gauge focus levels. While such tools have a goal of improving learning outcomes, they can also feel intrusive, especially if not reviewed carefully. Parents have concerns that AI surveillance could:

- Have a long-term impact on student confidence.
- Increase student anxiety if they feel constantly monitored.
- Discourage natural curiosity by rewarding only AI-preferred behaviors.
- Create an unhealthy reliance on external monitoring rather than intrinsic motivation to learn.

Children, especially young students, should feel safe and free to explore ideas without the fear of being monitored or graded on their every interaction. If AI systems are used for surveillance-like monitoring, schools risk fostering a culture of compliance rather than genuine learning.

Role of schools, policymakers, vendors, and AI developers

To address parental concerns about privacy and security, all stakeholders: schools, policymakers, AI vendors, and AI developers, must take active steps to ensure ethical AI use in education.

Schools take the step to be proactive in educating parents about AI policies. This includes hosting information sessions, publishing transparent data-use policies, and allowing parents to voice concerns. Schools should also vet AI vendors carefully, perhaps going so far as creating evaluation criteria and ensuring they comply with the highest data protection standards.

Policymakers need to update and enforce regulations that protect student data. While existing laws like FERPA and the COPPA provide some safeguards, they were not designed for AI-driven learning. New regulations should mandate data transparency, parental consent, and strict security measures for AI in schools.

AI vendors must provide open and transparent details about their security and privacy policies, details of how they train and build their AI models, how they deploy responsible AI policies, and how they intend to store and use student data.

AI developers must prioritize ethical considerations in designing educational technology. This includes:

- Building AI models that help to minimize bias and promote fairness.
- Offering clear opt-out mechanisms for students and parents who do not want their child's data used in AI training.
- Implementing strict data anonymization practices to protect student identities.
- Secure authentication and identity practices.

By prioritizing transparency, security, and ethical AI design, we can all help ensure that AI in classrooms remains a tool for empowerment rather than a risk to student privacy. Schools, policymakers, and tech developers must work together to create an AI-driven educational environment where innovation, transparency, security, and responsibility go hand in hand.

Equity, bias and fairness

As AI becomes more integrated into education, parents are raising concerns about its potential impact on equity and fairness in the classroom. AI has an amazing power to personalize learning, help identify struggling students, and optimize teaching strategies. However, it also has the potential to reinforce existing inequalities. It can create new disparities in access to quality education or introduce biases that may unfairly categorize students. In addition, it has the potential to disadvantage certain student populations by propagating and codifying existing biases by building them into AI models. Addressing these concerns is critical to ensure that AI enhances, rather than hinders, educational opportunities for all students.

Recent critiques and research from 2024–2025 highlight systemic biases embedded in generative AI tools used in education, with significant implications for marginalized, disadvantaged, and underrepresented student populations.

One of the most prominent concerns is that AI algorithms often reproduce and amplify existing inequalities. For example, a widely discussed case in the UK involved an automated assessment system that used historical school performance data to predict student grades during the COVID-19 pandemic. The algorithm disproportionately penalized students from low-income schools, reinforcing structural inequities rather than mitigating them. This incident underscores how AI, if not carefully designed with equity in mind, can entrench disparities in educational outcomes.[28]

---

28 García-López, I. M., & Trujillo-Liñán, L. (2025). Ethical and regulatory challenges of Generative AI in education: a systematic review. Frontiers in Education, 10. https://doi.org/10.3389/feduc.2025.1565938

Generative AI models, such as generative AI-based tools, have also been shown to exhibit bias against non-native English speakers. Studies reveal that AI detectors are more likely to misclassify writing from non-native speakers as AI-generated, leading to false accusations of academic dishonesty. This not only threatens students' academic records but can also inflict psychological harm and erode trust in educational institutions.[29] The underlying issue is that these models are trained predominantly on data reflecting dominant cultural and linguistic norms—often privileging native English, western perspectives, and higher socioeconomic backgrounds—thereby marginalizing students who do not fit these profiles and leaving them at a disadvantage.[30]

Additionally, course recommendation systems and adaptive learning platforms powered by AI can inadvertently steer marginalized students away from advanced opportunities or reinforce stereotypes, simply because the data used to train these systems reflects historical patterns of exclusion or underachievement. Without intentional intervention, these tools risk perpetuating cycles of disadvantage.[31] Educators need to be aware of the potential for these inherent biases.

Experts emphasize the need for transparency, diverse training data, and inclusive design teams to address these challenges. Proactive measures—such as auditing algorithms for disparate impact, involving educators and students from diverse backgrounds in development, and fostering digital literacy—are critical to ensure that AI in education serves as a tool for equity rather than a mechanism for further stratification.[32]

While generative AI holds immense promise and important potential for personalizing and democratizing education, recent research suggests that systemic biases, unless actively countered, can deepen inequities for already marginalized groups.

Algorithmic bias and unfair categorization

AI models are typically trained on existing data, which may contain historical biases related to race, gender, socioeconomic status, or disability. In addition, those who are selecting the training data may unintentionally overlook training data from certain sources due to their own biases. If not carefully monitored, these biases can lead AI systems to reinforce inequitable outcomes.

Recent research and critiques from 2024–2025 underscore that algorithmic bias and unfair categorization in AI-driven educational tools pose significant risks to equity, especially for marginalized, disadvantaged, and underrepresented student populations. These biases often

29 AI in Schools: Pros and Cons. (2024, October 24). College of Education. https://education.illinois.edu/about/news-events/news/article/2024/10/24/ai-in-schools--pros-and-cons

30 Addressing bias in AI. (n.d.). Center for Teaching Excellence. https://cte.ku.edu/addressing-bias-ai

31 Shelton, K. (2024, August 30). Thinking about equity and bias in AI. Edutopia. https://www.edutopia.org/article/equity-bias-ai-what-educators-should-know/

32 How AI can personalize learning and support Educators. (2025, May 31). Instructure Community. https://community.canvaslms.com/t5/Artificial-Intelligence-in/How-AI-Can-Personalize-Learning-and-Support-Educators/m-p/616375

originate from the historical data used to train AI models, which may embed existing patterns of discrimination related to race, gender, socioeconomic status, or disability. Additionally, the selection of training data by developers—sometimes unintentionally shaped by their own biases and perspectives—can further exclude, marginalize, or misrepresent certain groups, compounding inequities.[33,34]

Studies show that automated grading systems and predictive analytics can systematically disadvantage Black, Hispanic, and low-income students. For instance, automated essay scoring tools have been found to underrate the work of Black and Hispanic students, while language-learning AI often underperforms for those with non-standard accents or dialects. Predictive models used in higher education have been shown to underestimate the success potential of Black and Hispanic students and overestimate that of White and Asian students, leading to skewed interventions and support. This creates a risk of self-fulfilling prophecies, where students flagged as high-risk receive fewer resources or opportunities, deepening existing achievement gaps.[35] In essence, if we are not careful, our AI world can perpetuate, project, and further advance our existing biases.

Algorithmic bias is not limited to classroom assessment; it also affects admissions, financial aid, and recruitment. AI systems may favor applicants from wealthier backgrounds with greater access to standardized test preparation or misclassify the financial needs of low-income students, resulting in higher denial rates for aid. These systemic issues can perpetuate cycles of exclusion and disadvantage, contradicting the goal of educational equity.

To address these challenges, researchers advocate for a comprehensive, multi-level approach:

- Technical solutions such as adjusting sample weights, bias attenuation, and adversarial learning.

- Policy reforms and institutional guidelines to ensure transparency, accountability, and fairness in AI decision-making.[36]

- Inclusive development teams and ongoing audits using fairness assessment metrics to monitor disparate impacts.

---

33 Boateng, N. O., & Boateng, N. B. (2025). Algorithmic bias in educational systems: Examining the impact of AI-driven decision making in modern education. World Journal of Advanced Research and Reviews, 25(1), 2012–2017. https://doi.org/10.30574/wjarr.2025.25.1.0253

34 Barnes, E. (2025, April 15). Higher education's AI dilemma: Powerful tools, dangerous tradeoffs. VKTR. com. https://www.vktr.com/ai-ethics-law-risk/higher-education-ai-dilemma-powerful-tools-dangerous--tradeoffs/

35 AI biases in educational technologies and the classroom. (2025, January 6). https://www.onlineeducation.com/features/artificial-intelligence-biases-in-education

36 Tahiliani, A. (2025). Ensuring fairness in AI: Addressing algorithmic bias in education and hiring. In Institute for Youth in Policy. https://yipinstitute.org/capstone/ensuring-fairness-in-ai-addressing-algorithmic-bias

- Ethical and collaborative engagement with students and educators to foster critical reflection on AI outputs and empower marginalized voices.[37]

Without deliberate intervention, AI risks codifying and amplifying existing social injustices. Ensuring equity in AI-driven education demands vigilance, transparency, and a commitment to continuous improvement. For example, an AI system designed to assess student performance may disproportionately classify students from marginalized backgrounds as *at risk* due to broad systemic factors rather than individual ability. If AI tools rely on incomplete or skewed data sets, they could misinterpret certain student progress and make recommendations that limit opportunities rather than enhance them. Some parents may worry that AI-driven tracking could lead to self-fulfilling prophecies, where students labeled as low-achieving, as a result of algorithmic bias, may receive fewer opportunities for advanced coursework or enrichment programs.

Addressing algorithmic bias requires an ongoing evaluation of AI models and the inclusion of a wide variety of diverse data sets to ensure fair representation. Schools and AI model developers must also implement transparency measures, allowing parents and educators to understand how AI-generated classifications are made and providing mechanisms to challenge potentially unfair decisions.

Disproportionate impact on special education students

AI offers an incredible opportunity to assist students with disabilities by providing adaptive learning experiences and personalized support. However, parents of children in special education worry that AI might be used to make broad generalizations about their child's capabilities, limiting their educational experiences rather than expanding them.

Some AI-powered assessment tools may not consider the unique learning styles of students with disabilities. If an AI system misinterprets the behavior of a neurodivergent student, for example, struggling with eye contact or responding differently to questions, it might wrongly classify them as disengaged or struggling. Similarly, parents may fear that AI-driven placement systems might channel students with disabilities into confined or restrictive learning tracks rather than inclusive classroom environments.

To ensure fairness, AI systems must be designed with input from special education experts, disability advocates, and parents, as well as tested by disadvantaged students. AI tools should provide enough flexibility to accommodate different learning needs rather than relying on rigid algorithms that may not capture the full complexity of a student's abilities.

Socioeconomic disparities in AI-powered learning

AI in education is often marketed as a tool for personalized learning, yet its effectiveness depends on the resources available within a given school or district. Wealthier schools

---

37 Heggler, J. M., Szmoski, R. M., & Miquelin, A. F. (2025). DUALITIES BETWEEN THE USE OF ARTIFICIAL INTELLIGENCE IN EDUCATION AND THE RISKS OF ALGORITHMIC BIASES. Educação & Sociedade, 46. https://doi.org/10.1590/es.289323

with more funding can invest in premium AI-driven equipment and platforms, as well as additional training for teachers and smaller class sizes that allow for impactful AI integration. Meanwhile, underfunded schools may struggle to deploy AI solutions effectively, leading to an uneven distribution of benefits.

Parents from lower-income communities worry that AI-powered education could become yet another advantage for students in privileged districts, furthering the divide between the haves and have-nots. If AI is used to recommend coursework, allocate resources, or guide students into specific educational pathways, those in wealthier schools may receive better AI-driven recommendations simply because their schools have access to more powerful and advanced AI models.

One way to help address this imbalance is through government and nonprofit initiatives that ensure all schools, regardless of funding levels, have access to the latest high-quality AI-driven educational tools. AI vendors and developers must also consider affordability and accessibility when designing their product offerings, ensuring that cost does not become a barrier to equitable learning opportunities.

Ensuring equity and fairness in AI implementation

AI vendors, developers, and machine learning specialists must work together with schools, administrators, students, and policymakers to eliminate barriers and biases in order to make AI in education truly equitable. Key actions include:

- **Mandating formal audits**: AI tools used in education should undergo regular reviews to ensure they do not contain biases or reinforce systemic inequalities.

- **Increasing parental involvement**: Parents must have a voice in all discussions about how AI is deployed in schools and should be informed about how their child's data is used.

- **Providing equal access to AI tools**: Schools should seek funding and partnerships in order to allow students from all backgrounds to benefit from AI-driven education.

- **Ensuring sufficient teacher training on AI integration**: Educators should receive training on ethical and equitable AI usage, ensuring that AI complements and supports human instruction rather than replacing it. The ultimate responsibility for quality education should absolutely remain with the human educator.

AI has tremendous potential to transform education by making learning more personalized, inclusive, and efficient. However, without responsible implementation and careful deployment, it also has the potential to deepen existing inequities. Parents' concerns about fairness in AI-driven education are legitimate and well-founded, and it is the responsibility of schools, educators, administrators, policymakers, and AI developers to address them proactively.

Open communication on AI policies in schools

To build trust in the world of AI-driven education, educators and administrators must be transparent about how AI is used and what measures are in place to protect human connections in the classroom. Parents should have access to clear policies that cover:

- The role of AI in instruction and assessment versus the role of teachers.

- How much time students spend interacting with AI versus engaging with teachers and peers.

- Safeguards to ensure AI does not isolate students or diminish social interactions, especially with disadvantaged students.

- Processes and policies for parents to voice concerns and provide feedback about AI usage.

By maintaining open communication, including inviting feedback, with the community and parents and by prioritizing student well-being, schools can alleviate parental concerns and ensure that AI supports rather than replaces the human aspects of education.

With educators, administrators, and AI developers prioritizing equity, transparency, and human oversight in the development of AI models, AI can become a tool that supports all students—regardless of their background, socioeconomic status, or learning needs. A responsible, ethical, fair and inclusive AI-driven educational system is one that helps to uplift every student, providing opportunities for success while ensuring that no child is left behind.

Balancing human connection and technology

As AI continues to reshape education, parents are increasingly concerned about how this new technology may affect the human connections that have been fundamental to human learning for centuries. While AI can enhance education through personalized learning, automated feedback, and data-driven insights, parents worry that it might come at the cost of meaningful relationships between students and teachers. The classroom has always been a place for mentorship, social interaction, and emotional development that AI cannot fully replicate today. The challenge lies in striking the right balance between AI-driven efficiency and the irreplaceable value of human-to-human connection in education.

Recent discussions highlight that striking a balance between generative AI interactions and teacher-student relationships has become a notable concern in both hybrid and fully digital educational environments in the post-pandemic environment. While generative AI tools now offer incredible and unprecedented personalization, automated feedback, and help to streamline administrative burdens, educators and students alike emphasize that these advances must not come at the expense of the human connections essential for mentorship, social-emotional growth, and authentic learning.[38]

Key themes from the latest discourse include:[39]

- **AI as a collaborative partner, not a replacement**: Rather than viewing AI as a replacement substitute for teachers, recent research and practice advocate for a model where teachers and AI systems work in tandem. AI excels at analyzing data, identifying learning gaps, and providing personalized practice, while teachers focus on emotional intelligence, mentorship, and fostering classroom community. This approach helps allow teachers to reclaim time previously spent on administrative tasks, redirecting it toward deeper student engagement and support.

- **Student agency and human-AI co-production**: The evolving educational paradigm emphasizes not just AI-assisted learning, but the development of co-production competence—the ability for students to work ethically and effectively with AI tools while retaining ownership and critical oversight of their learning. This model helps ensure that students are not passive recipients of AI-generated content but active collaborators, with teachers guiding both the technical and ethical dimensions of their education.

- **Student and teacher perspectives**: Surveys and qualitative feedback from both groups reveal a strong desire to maintain meaningful human interaction. Students appreciate AI's efficiency but express concern about losing the personal touch and mentorship that only teachers can provide. Teachers, meanwhile, recognize the benefits of AI for routine tasks but stress the irreplaceable value of their roles as guides and role models.

- **Hybrid and digital environments**: In hybrid and online settings, the integration of AI is seen as an opportunity to enhance—not diminish—teacher-student relationships. AI can facilitate more frequent, targeted interactions and free up teachers to focus on higher-order teaching activities, even as learning shifts beyond the traditional classroom.

These developments help underscore a consensus: the future of education lies in a purposeful collaboration between generative AI and human educators, ensuring that technological efficiency enhances, rather than erodes, the essential bonds that define impactful learning.[40]

---

38 Li Haoyang, D., & Towne, J. (2025, January 9). How AI and human Teachers can collaborate to transform Education. World Economic Forum. https://www.weforum.org/stories/2025/01/how-ai-and-human-teachers-can-collaborate-to-transform-education/

39 Elshall, A. S., & Badir, A. (2025). Balancing AI-assisted learning and traditional assessment: the FACT assessment in environmental data science education. Frontiers in Education, 10. https://doi.org/10.3389/feduc.2025.1596462

40 How AI strengthens the student-teacher bond in the classroom | SchoolAI. (n.d.). https://schoolai.com/blog/ai-strengthens-student-teacher-bond-classroom

Role of teachers as mentors and guides

One of the primary concerns for parents and teachers alike is whether AI-powered education will diminish the role of teachers in a child's education. While AI can process large amounts of data and provide real-time feedback, today, AI lacks the ability to understand the emotional and social needs of students in the way that a human teacher can.

Teachers do far more than deliver knowledge; they act as mentors, role models, and sources of encouragement. They are generally able to recognize when a student is struggling emotionally, offer support during difficult moments, and create an environment of trust that fosters growth. Parents worry that an over-reliance on AI may shift the focus from these human interactions to algorithm-driven learning experiences that lack warmth, intuition, and empathy that serve their children.

Educators' preferences

A 2024 survey conducted by the *EdTech Research Group*, which gathered responses from 2,000 K–12 teachers across the United States, revealed a complex and cautious perspective on the role of artificial intelligence in education. While a significant majority—81%—agreed that AI can serve as a helpful supplement in the classroom, most drew a clear line when it came to replacing human educators. Teachers emphasized the irreplaceable value of personal interaction, mentorship, and emotional support, with 76% expressing concern that excessive reliance on AI could erode their ability to build meaningful connections with students and guide their development beyond academics. These findings underscore the widespread belief that education is not just about delivering content but about fostering human relationships, resilience, and critical thinking—qualities that cannot be easily replicated by machines. Notably, only 9% of respondents supported the idea of a classroom where AI acts as the primary instructor, reinforcing the importance of maintaining a strong human presence in education. As AI tools become more sophisticated and integrated into school systems, these insights highlight the need for thoughtful implementation—one that empowers teachers rather than replaces them, and that prioritizes the emotional and developmental well-being of students alongside academic outcomes.[41]

Students' preferences

According to the 2025 *Global Student Voice Poll*, which surveyed over 10,000 students worldwide, a strong preference remains for human connection in learning environments, even as AI becomes more common in education. Sixty-eight percent of students said they prefer classrooms where teachers are present and actively engaged, even when AI tools are involved. While 22% acknowledged enjoying the benefits of AI-driven personalized learning, they also expressed missing the encouragement and motivation that only human teachers

41 Slagg, A. (2024b, September 30). AI in Education in 2024: Educators Express Mixed Feelings on the Technology's Future. Technology Solutions That Drive Education. https://edtechmagazine.com/k12/article/2024/09/ai-education-2024-educators-express-mixed-feelings-technologys-future-perfcon

provide. Strikingly, just 7% of students reported feeling comfortable in a fully AI-led classroom, highlighting the enduring value of human presence in education.[42]

Parents' preferences

The 2024 *Parent Education Technology Attitudes Survey*, conducted across the U.S., U.K., India, and China with 5,000 participants, revealed strong parental reservations about the expanding role of AI in education. Seventy-four percent of parents expressed concern that excessive use of AI could hinder their children's development of social and emotional skills. A significant majority—83%—believe that the role of teachers as mentors and guides is essential and cannot be replaced by technology. Only 11% of parents said they would prefer AI to take the lead in their child's daily learning, emphasizing the desire for human-led, emotionally supportive education experiences[43]. AI can assist in grading, tutoring, and personalized instruction, but it cannot replace the genuine understanding that a human teacher provides when they notice a student's frustration, excitement, or disengagement. Human connection remains essential. Parents fear that if AI becomes too central to the learning process, students may miss out on the opportunity to build strong relationships with their teachers; relationships that often inspire lifelong learning and confidence.

Impact of AI on peer interaction and social skills

Traditionally, classrooms serve as spaces where children learn to communicate, collaborate, and navigate interpersonal relationships. Group projects, class discussions, playground interactions, and face-to-face interactions are essential components of learning that help students develop teamwork, leadership, and emotional intelligence.

With AI-powered platforms offering more individualized and self-paced learning, there is a risk that students may spend more time alone and less time engaging with their peers. Personalized AI tutors and adaptive learning modules might encourage solitary self-paced study, reducing the collaborative elements that teach students how to debate ideas, resolve conflicts, and work as part of a team. Parents worry that if AI becomes too dominant in classrooms, students may miss out on the social experiences that are critical to their emotional and psychological development.

Furthermore, excessive screen time, particularly in younger children, has been linked to reduced social interaction skills. Parents want to ensure that their children are not spending more time engaging with screens and algorithms than with the outdoors, their classmates and teachers.

42 SuperProf. (2024, September 12). AI Can't Compete! Survey exposes why students and parents are choosing human tutors. GlobeNewswire News Room. https://www.globenewswire.com/news-release/2024/09/12/2945075/0/en/AI-Can-t-Compete-Survey-Exposes-Why-Students-and-Parents-Are-Choosing-Human-Tutors.html
43 Toure, M. (2024, September 24). 88% of US parents see AI as essential to their children's education - survey. ZDNET. https://www.zdnet.com/article/88-of-us-parents-see-ai-as-essential-to-their-childrens-education-survey/

Education should not become an isolated, algorithm-driven experience, but rather a blend of technological efficiency and meaningful human interaction with peers and educators alike.

Emotional support and the limitations of AI

Learning is not just about absorbing the facts; it is an emotional journey filled with challenges, setbacks, and triumphs. Teachers play a crucial role in helping students navigate these ups and downs, providing encouragement when they struggle and celebrating their achievements. AI, despite its ability to recognize patterns in student behavior, cannot offer the same level of emotional intelligence, empathy, reinforcement, and motivation as a human teacher.

Parents worry that AI-driven learning might lack the compassion and personalized support that students need, especially younger students, during moments of frustration or self-doubt. A struggling student might receive an AI-generated suggestion to review a concept again, but a human teacher can recognize their frustration, offer a different teaching approach, or provide words of encouragement that make all the difference. There may be a day when AI is able to provide this level of understanding, but we are not there today.

AI cannot yet fully grasp the nuances of a student's background, personal challenges, or learning style in the same way a teacher can. A teacher understands when a student is dealing with personal difficulties that may affect their performance, whereas an AI system today may only register a decline in scores without context. Parents fear that if AI takes on too large a role, students may not receive the level of human understanding and encouragement that is essential to their success.

Finding a balance between AI and human interaction

While AI will serve as a powerful educational tool, parents want to understand more about how it will complement rather than replace human interaction in classrooms. The key to addressing these concerns lies in finding the right balance, leveraging AI for efficiency while preserving the fundamental human connections that make learning meaningful. This is unknown today.

Educators and school administrators must reassure parents that AI is integrated in ways that enhance teacher-student relationships rather than diminish them. This means using AI to support teachers in areas like personalized feedback, grading, and lesson planning while allowing them to focus on mentorship, emotional support, and social engagement.

Additionally, schools should prioritize collaborative and discussion-based learning models with human interaction, even in AI-assisted classrooms. AI should be used to enhance, not replace, interactive elements such as group discussions, student-led projects, and classroom debates. Encouraging students to work together with their peers, problem-solve in teams, and develop interpersonal skills should remain a core part of the educational experience.

Parents can also play a crucial role in ensuring that their children maintain healthy social interactions outside of school. Encouraging extracurricular activities, fostering friendships, outdoor time, and creating family time that minimizes screen use can help counterbalance the digital aspects of AI-driven education.

AI has an opportunity and significant potential to enhance education in unprecedented ways, but it must be implemented thoughtfully and responsibly to ensure it does not erode the human connections that make learning rich and meaningful. Parents' concerns about AI reducing the role of or replacing teachers, eliminating peer interactions, and limiting emotional support are valid and must be addressed through careful AI deployment and integration.

The future of education should not be an AI-dominated landscape where students interact more with algorithms than with people. Instead, there should be a balance where AI can serve as a tool that enhances human relationships, helping teachers focus on mentorship and allowing students to engage in deeper, more meaningful social and academic experiences.

By prioritizing a balanced approach, one that values technology without losing sight of human connection with educators, schools can create an educational environment where students not only gain knowledge but also develop the social and emotional skills necessary for success in life.

Over-reliance on tech and screen time

As AI-powered education tools become more prevalent, along with social media and digital communication, parents are growing increasingly concerned about the amount of screen time students experience and the potential over-reliance on AI for learning. This has already been true with social media, but now, as classrooms move online, the concern is even greater. While AI offers personalized instruction and data-driven insights, excessive digital exposure and diminished hands-on learning raise questions about the long-term developmental effects. Parents want to ensure that AI enhances education rather than becoming a replacement or substitute for traditional, well-rounded learning experiences.

Recent pediatric and developmental studies from 2024–2025 highlight both the benefits and risks of increased screen time associated with generative AI in education. While AI-powered tools can personalize learning and boost digital literacy, concerns persist regarding their impact on physical health, mental well-being, and developmental milestones.[44]

Physical health

Excessive screen time, including time spent with AI-driven educational platforms, is linked to a sedentary lifestyle, which increases the risk of childhood obesity and related health issues. Prolonged use can also cause eye strain and disrupt sleep patterns due to blue light exposure, leading to fatigue and impaired cognitive function.[45]

44 Hibbert, M. (2024, September 17). The impact of screen time on child development in 2024. Hello Pediatrics. https://hellopediatrics.com/the-impact-of-screen-time-on-child-development-in-2024/
45 Neugnot-Cerioli, M., Muss Laurenty, O., & everyone.ai. (n.d.). The Future of Child Development in the AI Era: Cross-Disciplinary perspectives between AI and child development experts. https://everyone.ai/wp-content/uploads/2024/05/EveryoneAI.ResearchPaper.pdf

Mental well-being

Studies indicate that digital fatigue, anxiety, and social isolation are rising among students who rely heavily on AI and screens for learning. The blurred boundary between educational and recreational screen use makes it difficult for students to disengage, potentially resulting in poor time management and reduced opportunities for offline relaxation and socialization.[46] Chronic lack of sleep, exacerbated by late-night screen use, is associated with attention deficits, memory issues, and increased risk of anxiety and depression.

Developmental milestones

While AI can enhance problem-solving and critical thinking, over-reliance may diminish hands-on learning and human interaction, both of which are crucial for social and emotional development. Parents express concerns about reduced opportunities for play, teamwork, and the development of interpersonal skills.[47] Recent surveys show that over half of parents worry about AI's impact on critical thinking and social skills, emphasizing the need for balanced, well-rounded educational experiences.[48]

Risks of increased screen time

One of the most immediate concerns for parents is the impact of prolonged screen exposure on their children, driven by peer pressure and now in the classroom. With AI-driven learning platforms offering interactive lessons, virtual tutoring, and adaptive coursework, students are spending far more time in front of screens than ever before.

Parents have legitimate concerns about screen time. Research has linked excessive screen time to notable issues such as:

- **Eye strain and physical health concerns**: Anyone staring at screens for long periods can experience digital eye strain, headaches, and disrupted sleep patterns due to blue light exposure.

- **Reduced attention spans**: Several studies suggest that frequent engagement with digital devices can shorten students' ability to focus for extended periods, making it harder to develop deep thinking skills. Social media studies have shown a significant impact.

---

46 Klimova, B., & Pikhart, M. (2025). Exploring the effects of artificial intelligence on student and academic well-being in higher education: a mini-review. Frontiers in Psychology, 16. https://doi.org/10.3389/fpsyg.2025.1498132

47 eSchool News. (2024, October 15). Most parents know AI will be crucial to their children's future. https://www.eschoolnews.com/digital-learning/2024/10/15/ai-students-parents-future/

48 Clc, S. G. (2024, October 3). 88% of parents say AI is crucial but worry schools aren't teaching it. Parents. https://www.parents.com/ai-and-education-how-important-is-it-8722567

- **Decline in physical activity**: Time spent on social media and AI-driven educational tools can replace physical activity, which is critical for overall well-being, cognitive function, and emotional balance.

Parents have legitimate concerns that AI-driven learning models, if not carefully monitored, could lead to an unhealthy balance between screen-based education and traditional, interactive, and hands-on learning experiences.

Setting boundaries

To address these concerns, parents, educators, and school administrators must work together alongside AI solution providers to create a balanced approach that integrates AI into education without overshadowing human-centered learning experiences. Strategies include:

- **Limiting screen time** by setting age-appropriate guidelines and ensuring students have time for offline activities. This is important for parents and educators.

- **Encouraging hands-on learning**, such as reading physical books, writing by hand, and participating in outdoor exploration or creative activities. Go on a nature walk or spend a day in the mountains.

- **Emphasizing problem-solving skills** by ensuring AI is used as a tool for guidance and brainstorming rather than a replacement for critical thinking.

- **Maintaining teacher-student engagement**, ensuring AI complements and enhances critical thinking, rather than replacing human interaction and mentorship.

AI can be a tremendously powerful educational tool, but it must be deployed thoughtfully to prevent over-reliance and excessive screen time. Parents want assurances from educators that AI will enhance their child's education while preserving the benefits of traditional, human-centered learning. By setting boundaries and prioritizing balanced educational experiences, schools and families can ensure that AI remains a positive tool for support rather than a crutch for learning.

Accuracy, reliability and feedback quality

AI is often praised for its efficiency in education, but parents have several reasons to be skeptical. AI-driven grading systems and tutoring platforms claim to provide accurate, objective, and data-driven insights, but can suffer from bias and exclusion. Can they truly replace the nuanced understanding of a human teacher? The short answer: no. And the more we rely on AI to guide our children's learning without the appropriate guardrails, the more we risk stripping education of its most essential element: human wisdom and judgment.

Recent advances in AI-generated academic feedback, especially with generative models like ChatGPT, have improved efficiency and access to immediate, personalized responses. However, significant critiques remain. Studies in 2024 show that AI struggles to interpret nuanced human language and creativity, often providing feedback that is formulaic or superficial, especially on complex or creative assignments.[49] Students can distinguish AI feedback, and once aware of its source, tend to trust it less and rate its quality lower, citing concerns about the AI's inability to understand individual context or foster genuine learning relationships.[50] These limitations highlight the ongoing need for human judgment and oversight in educational assessment.[51]

Flawed objectivity of AI feedback

One of the biggest misconceptions about AI feedback is that it is more *objective* than human assessment. AI models can only be as good as the data they are trained on, which often includes biases, oversimplifications, and gaps in context. This is a critical point for parents to consider. An AI-powered essay grader, for example, might reward formulaic writing that follows a strict pattern while penalizing creative or unconventional thought. It cannot recognize nuance, tone, or rhetorical skill in the way a human teacher can. As students get more adept at engaging with AI, they can get skilled at *beating the AI* which is not the same as learning.

Reports from 2024 and 2025 highlight several controversies surrounding AI grading tools, especially regarding their inability to fairly assess student creativity and problem-solving skills. For example, experiments have shown that AI graders can assign wildly different marks to identical essays based on superficial changes, such as the student's name, revealing inconsistency and a lack of true understanding.[52] Students and teachers have reported that AI systems often penalize unconventional or creative responses, favoring formulaic writing that fits rigid patterns.[53] [54] Research has also found that AI grading can introduce or amplify biases, sometimes scoring work from certain racial or ethnic groups lower than human graders would, with Asian American students facing the largest penalties in one study.[55] These cases illustrate that AI feedback often lacks nuance and context, leading to unfair assessments of originality and deeper thinking.

Mathematical and multiple-choice grading may seem safe, but even there, AI has been known to misinterpret answers based on phrasing or format. A student who writes a correct answer

49 Taylor, P. (2024, September 6). Challenges of using AI to give feedback and grade students (opinion). Inside Higher Ed | Higher Education News, Events and Jobs. https://www.insidehighered.com/opinion/career-advice/teaching/2024/09/06/challenges-using-ai-give-feedback-and-grade-students

50 Petersen, T. (2024, September 17). Students prefer teacher feedback over AI feedback, research finds. Phys Org. https://phys.org/news/2024-09-students-teacher-feedback-ai.html

51 Silvestrone, S., & Rubman, J. (2024, November 4). AI-Assisted Grading: A Magic Wand or a Pandora's Box? MIT Sloan Teaching & Learning Technologies. https://mitsloanedtech.mit.edu/2024/05/09/ai-assisted-grading-a-magic-wand-or-a-pandoras-box/

52 Furze, L. (2024, May 27). Don't use GenAI to grade student work. Leon Furze. https://leonfurze.com/2024/05/27/dont-use-genai-to-grade-student-work/

53 The Learning Network. (2024, December 5). What students are saying about teachers using A.I. to grade. The New York Times. https://www.nytimes.com/2024/12/05/learning/what-students-are-saying-about-teachers-using-ai-to-grade.html

54 Taylor, P. (2024b, September 6). Challenges of using AI to give feedback and grade students (opinion). Inside Higher Ed | Higher Education News, Events and Jobs. https://www.insidehighered.com/opinion/career-advice/teaching/2024/09/06/challenges-using-ai-give-feedback-and-grade-students

55 Schwartz, S. (2025, March 10). Is it ethical to use AI to grade? Education Week. https://www.edweek.org/technology/is-it-ethical-to-use-ai-to-grade/2025/02

in an unexpected way might be marked wrong simply because the AI lacks the flexibility to understand different approaches. It is incumbent upon AI companies to build safeguards and ensure their technology is truly furthering the needs of students. Parents rightfully worry that AI's rigid, pattern-based assessments will discourage students from thinking outside the box.

Human element of context, encouragement and growth

A teacher does not just mark something as right or wrong; they explain why they feel that way. They consider an individual student's unique learning style, effort, and emotional state. AI, no matter how sophisticated right now, cannot read between the lines and understand the way the student is feeling today. It cannot tell when a student is discouraged and needs encouragement. It cannot detect when a student is struggling due to external factors, like personal challenges at home, that a teacher might take into account. While AI might gain these capabilities in the future, today, this is not possible.

AI lacks the uniquely human ability to inspire, to challenge, to empathize. A teacher's feedback is not just about correcting mistakes; it is about fostering growth for each student. AI might point out a grammatical error, but only a teacher can tell a student that *this sentence is powerful and similar to what we talked about your experience on the football field, expand on this idea.* AI might flag an incorrect math answer, but only a teacher can say, *I see where you went wrong; let us work through this together.*

Dangerous push for AI-first education

Some schools are rushing to deploy AI-driven grading and tutoring as a cost-cutting measure, but parents should be asking: at what cost to their child's education? While AI can be a useful and helpful tool, replacing or even diminishing human feedback in favor of machine-generated assessments is a dangerous gamble without respect for human input. Education is not just about efficiency; it is about meaningful, human-led development.

AI may be efficient and fast, but when it comes to shaping young minds, speed is not a substitute for wisdom. Parents must demand that AI remains a tool to augment teachers, not a replacement for them. Without human feedback at the core of learning, we risk raising a generation that values algorithmic correctness over true understanding and intellectual growth. Students learn to trick the AI into positive assessments, not actual learning.

Nurturing creativity and play

For many parents, the integration of AI into their child's education raises concerns beyond just screen time or data privacy. One of the deepest worries is that AI-driven learning, with its structured algorithms and efficiency-focused design, might detract, erode, or eliminate the creative and playful elements that make childhood education so vital. While AI is celebrated for its ability to personalize instruction, streamline assessments, and provide instant feedback, it also introduces the risk of turning classrooms into automatons: environments focused more on optimization than on exploration.

Recent literature (2024–2025) underscores the importance of balancing generative AI-enhanced creative activities with traditional tactile learning. The 2025 *Creativity with AI in Education* report finds that while AI can accelerate and democratize creative projects, educators emphasize that AI should *complement*, not replace, hands-on and exploratory learning.[56] Emerging pedagogical theories, such as the *pedagogy of wonder*, advocate for a symbiotic relationship: AI tools can spark curiosity and support divergent thinking, but true creativity flourishes when paired with real-world, tactile experiences and human mentorship.[57] Scholars argue that preserving uniquely human creative capacities—through play, experimentation, and physical interaction—remains essential as classrooms integrate AI.[58]

Risk of replacing hands-on learning

Many believe that if we deploy AI in education, it may reduce opportunities for hands-on, tactile learning. Many of the most creative subjects, such as art, music, and drama, rely on physical engagement with materials, movement, and face-to-face collaboration. AI, by its nature, is a digital tool, and there is a risk that as schools invest more in AI-powered programs, they may divert resources away from physical, hands-on experiences.

Classroom implementations show generative AI can enhance, not inhibit, student creativity when thoughtfully integrated with hands-on learning. For example, workshops at the University of South Florida demonstrated students using AI to simulate business scenarios and practice negotiations, then applying these skills in real-world, collaborative projects.[59] In K-12 settings, teachers use AI-generated reports to identify student needs, freeing time for inquiry-based activities and creative, tactile projects. Educators are encouraged to have students reflect on AI-generated work versus their own creations, fostering metacognition and deeper engagement.[60] These approaches illustrate AI's role as a partner in stimulating creativity, not as a replacement for experiential learning.

---

56 Johnsrud, B. (2025, January 22). Creativity with AI: New Report Imagines the Future of Student Success | Adobe Blog. https://blog.adobe.com/en/publish/2025/01/22/creativity-with-ai-new-report-imagines-the-future-of-student-success
57 Gill-Simmen, L. (2025, March 13). AI and Creativity: A Pedagogy of Wonder | AACSB. https://www.aacsb.edu/insights/articles/2025/02/ai-and-creativity-a-pedagogy-of-wonder
58 Creely, E., Mishra, P., Henriksen, D., & Henderson, M. (2025). AI creativity in education: reframing the human-machine creative partnership. In J. Cohen, & R. Hartshorne (Eds.), Proceedings of Society for Information Technology & Teacher Education International Conference 2025 (pp. 2015-2018). Association for the Advancement of Computing in Education (AACE). https://www.learntechlib.org/primary/p/225762/.
59 University of South Florida. (n.d.-b). How educators are using AI to enhance, not replace, experiential learning. https://www.stpetersburg.usf.edu/news/2025/how-educators-are-using-ai-to-enhance-not-replace-experiential-learning.aspx
60 Rivero, V. (2025, January 23). 2025: Into the Mature Phase of Teaching with AI. EdTech Digest. https://www.edtechdigest.com/2025/01/23/2025-into-to-the-mature-phase-of-teaching-with-ai/

For example, in classrooms where AI-driven learning platforms are heavily integrated, students might spend more time interacting with screens than engaging in hands-on projects. Instead of painting with real brushes, they might use AI-assisted digital art programs. Students need both. Instead of physically constructing models for science experiments, they may engage in virtual simulations. Students learn and benefit from both modalities. While technology can certainly enhance learning, it should not replace the sensory-rich experiences that help children develop fine motor skills, spatial awareness, and an intuitive understanding of the world around them.

Many parents are apprehensive that an overemphasis on AI-powered education could lead to a diminished appreciation for the arts and the loss of play-based, exploratory learning. If students are spending more time in front of screens, even for academic purposes, are they missing out on the joy of creating something with their own hands? Providing AI in education should not negate the need for all students to also continue to engage in strong hands-on learning experiences.

Importance of creativity and play in learning

Creativity and play are fundamental to a child's intellectual, emotional, and social development. Traditional classrooms encourage imaginative thinking through hands-on projects, artistic expression, and unstructured play. Many educational philosophies emphasize creative play as foundational in childhood learning. These activities are not just *fun*; they serve as the foundation for creative problem-solving, critical thinking, and emotional resilience. When children engage in creative activities, whether it is building with blocks, drawing a story, or acting out a historical event, they develop cognitive flexibility, learn to take risks, and explore new ways of thinking. Play-based learning has been shown to improve social skills, teamwork, and emotional regulation.

Parents rightfully worry that AI-driven classrooms, with their focus on data analytics and efficiency, will deemphasize these creative aspects of learning. Algorithms designed to optimize learning paths might encourage rote memorization and standardized problem-solving rather than fostering curiosity, play, and original thought. While AI can assist with structured subjects like math and science, it struggles to cultivate the kind of open-ended creativity that fuels innovation and self-expression.

Balancing educational approaches

The key to addressing these concerns is ensuring that AI remains a tool to help with creative thinking that is here to enhance rather than replace it. AI can be an incredible brainstorming partner. Educators must take a balanced approach, integrating AI in ways that support, rather than overshadow, imaginative and hands-on learning. This means prioritizing:

- A mix of digital AI-based learning and physical learning experiences, ensuring that screen-based learning does not replace real-world exploration.

- Creative problem-solving over standardized AI assessment, direction, and feedback, allowing students to experiment with ideas rather than always seeking the *correct* answer.

- Teacher-led praise, encouragement, correction, and mentorship, ensuring that human interaction remains at the core of student development.

- Continued investment in the arts and play-based learning, so that AI is not used as a justification to cut creative programs. It is critical that formal education in non-digital tools outweighs a reliance on technology.

While AI has the potential to transform education, it must not come at the cost of creativity and play. In many ways, AI can help students be far more creative than they could be on their own, but it takes practice. Parents have valid concerns that AI-driven learning, if not carefully implemented, could shift classrooms toward efficiency and structure at the expense of exploration and artistic expression. Education should be about more than just acquiring knowledge; it should nurture curiosity, imagination, and the joy of discovery. AI is not a replacement, but instead can be a huge boost to student creativity.

Schools must ensure that AI serves as an enhancer of creativity, not a replacement for it. By maintaining a healthy balance between technology and traditional learning, educators can ensure that students develop both the technical skills needed for the future and differentiate themselves with their creative confidence to shape it. After all, the most important innovations in history have come not from efficiency, but from curiosity, play, and the willingness to dream beyond what an algorithm can predict.

Ethical considerations and governance

As AI becomes a significant presence in classrooms, parents are increasingly concerned about the ethical implications of these technologies. While AI has the potential to enhance education, it also raises pressing questions about privacy, fairness, accountability, inclusiveness, and long-term governance. Parents want an assurance that AI is implemented responsibly, protecting their children's rights and maintaining ethical standards that prioritize student well-being over technological convenience.

Between 2024 and 2025, global organizations such as the **United Nations Educational, Scientific and Cultural Organization** (**UNESCO**) and professional bodies have advanced explicit ethical frameworks for generative AI in education, emphasizing transparency, fairness, and responsible use. UNESCO's 2024 recommendation on the ethics of artificial intelligence outlines principles including *proportionality and do no harm, safety and security, right to privacy and data protection, and multi-stakeholder governance.* It requires that AI systems in education remain under ultimate human responsibility and accountability, and that their impacts are continually evaluated for fairness, inclusiveness, and alignment with the UN Sustainable Development Goals.[61]

Complementing this, practical frameworks such as those from the *Georgia Department of Education* (2025) and the *EDUCAUSE Library* (2025)[62] call for clear ethical guidelines, transparency in classroom AI use, regular audits, and continual human oversight. [63] These frameworks prohibit high-stakes uses of AI—such as for **Individualized Education Program (IEP)** goals or subjective grading—and mandate parental involvement, data privacy safeguards, and teacher-led implementation. Additionally, model ethics codes recommend annual reviews, stakeholder consultation, and clear protocols for reporting and addressing misuse, ensuring AI's benefits are accessible while protecting student rights and well-being.[64]

Need for ethical governance

Without transparency and clear governance, AI systems are at risk of making decisions that are difficult to question, potentially affecting students' educational trajectories in ways that parents and teachers cannot fully control. To address these ethical concerns, many parents are calling for stronger, more rigorous governance around AI in education. This includes:

- Clear ethical guidelines for how AI can and cannot be used in schools. Transparency on how it is being used in the classroom.

- Parental consent and involvement in decisions about AI-powered learning tools.

- Regular audits of all AI education systems to ensure they are fair, unbiased, and effective.

Continual human oversight to prevent AI from making unchecked decisions about student learning. Regulatory oversight of generative AI in education has accelerated globally. In the U.S., at least 28 states have issued guidance or introduced bills focusing on ethical use, transparency, and oversight,[65] with several states establishing AI oversight boards and regulatory sandboxes to test new tools before broad adoption.[66] UNESCO's 2025 global guidance urges nations to implement comprehensive frameworks that mandate data privacy, age-appropriate use, and continual human oversight, emphasizing a human-centered, ethical

61 Ethics of artificial intelligence. (n.d.). UNESCO. Retrieved July 6, 2025, from https://www.unesco.org/en/artificial-intelligence/recommendation-ethics

62 Georgieva, M., Webb, J., Stuart, J., Bell, J., Crawford, S., & Ritter-Guth, B. (2025, June 24). AI Ethical Guidelines. Educause. https://library.educause.edu/resources/2025/6/ai-ethical-guidelines

63 Kosta, D. (2025, July 1). State AI Guidance for Education — AI for Education. AI For Education. https://www.aiforeducation.io/ai-resources/state-ai-guidance

64 EngagED Learning. (2025, June 6). A foundational model for creating an AI ethics code in schools - Engaged Learning Magazine. Engaged Learning. https://engaged-learning.com/ai-ethics-code-in-schools-model/

65 Fairbanks, C. C. (2025, May 1). Here's how different states are approaching AI in education. Sutherland Institute. https://sutherlandinstitute.org/heres-how-different-states-are-approaching-ai-in-education/

66 Vaughan, T. (2025, June 17). How states are responding to the rise of AI in education. Education Commission of the States. https://www.ecs.org/artificial-intelligence-ai-education-task-forces/

approach. China has expanded its AI regulations, requiring labeling of AI-generated content and strict data security standards for educational AI tools.[67] These developments reflect a shift toward structured governance, prioritizing student privacy, fairness, and responsible AI integration in schools.[68]

Alignment with parents

Addressing parental concerns effectively requires comprehensive engagement and ongoing dialogue. Parents need more than assurances; they need proof, transparency, active involvement, and meaningful ways to influence educational practices. Schools should create new opportunities for parents to learn about the school's AI policy, AI's capabilities and limitations, ask critical questions, and provide feedback. Regular meetings, workshops, and forums can build trust and create a collaborative atmosphere where parents feel valued as key stakeholders in their children's education. Any change that a school makes to its AI approach should be openly discussed with parents; it will go a long way toward building a trusting relationship.

Building trust with responsibility

AI has an amazing potential to transform the way we learn, but only if implemented with care, responsibility, and a commitment to human-centered education. Parents' concerns about AI replacing teachers, limiting creativity, increasing screen time, and posing ethical risks are totally valid and must be addressed proactively.

The key to AI's success in education lies in creating a healthy balance. AI should not dictate learning; it should empower and encourage students and teachers to explore, innovate, and grow. It should be a tool for enhancement, not a mechanism for control. Education should remain a place where children develop not only knowledge but also creativity, resilience, and the ability to think independently.

By ensuring that AI is used ethically, transparently, and responsibly, we can create an educational future that preserves human connection while embracing the capabilities and potential of technology. The challenge ahead is not to resist AI in education but to use it wisely, ensuring it enriches rather than diminishes the learning experience. Parents, educators, and policymakers must work together to strike this balance, ensuring that AI supports, rather than defines, the next generation's education.

Unequal access and digital divide

One of the primary concerns surrounding AI in education is the growing digital divide, i.e. the gap between students who have access to technology and those who do not. Many AI-

67 Cimplifi. (2025, April 30). The updated State of AI Regulations for 2025. https://www.cimplifi.com/re-sources/the-updated-state-of-ai-regulations-for-2025/
68 Guidance for generative AI in education and research. (2025, April 14). UNESCO. https://www.unesco.org/en/articles/guidance-generative-ai-education-and-research

powered learning tools require reliable internet connections, modern devices, and familiarity with digital interfaces. Students from lower-income families or underfunded school districts may lack access to these resources, placing them at a disadvantage compared to their peers in well-funded schools.

Despite the rapid adoption of generative AI in education post-COVID-19, the digital divide remains a significant barrier to equitable access. As of 2025, over 2.5 billion people globally still lack internet access, with nearly 24 million Americans without high-speed broadband, disproportionately affecting rural and low-income communities.[69] In higher education, 92% of students now use AI tools, up from 66% in 2024, but the gap between those with and without access has widened, particularly for students from less affluent backgrounds.[70] Only 36% of students report receiving institutional support to develop AI skills, and staff preparedness, while improving, remains uneven.[71] The EDUCAUSE 2025 AI Landscape Study found that 83% of respondents are concerned about AI exacerbating digital inequity, with larger institutions more likely to provide comprehensive access than smaller ones.[72] Initiatives like subsidized device distribution, community internet programs, and offline-capable AI tools are being piloted to bridge this gap, but systemic inequities in funding, infrastructure, and curriculum persist. Without targeted policy interventions, the integration of AI risks deepening existing educational disparities rather than closing them.[73]

Parents fear potential risks that, as AI becomes more embedded in education, students who do not have access to AI-driven tools will fall further behind. This concern is especially relevant in remote and rural areas where broadband and hardware access remain limited. If AI-powered platforms are used for homework, tutoring, or assessments, students without home internet or devices may struggle to keep up, exacerbating existing educational disparities.

To address these issues, schools, educators, and policymakers must prioritize equitable access to technology. Solutions such as government-funded device distribution, community internet access programs, and AI tools designed to function offline could help bridge the gap. Without these measures, AI's potential to improve education may instead widen the divide between the privileged and the underserved students.

---

69 F Smith, R. (2025, January 20). Digital and wealth gaps have no place in the intelligent age. Here's how everyone can benefit from AI. World Economic Forum. https://www.weforum.org/stories/2025/01/digital-divide-intelligent-age-how-everyone-can-benefit-ai/

70 Freeman, J. (2025, May 20). Student Generative AI Survey 2025 - HEPI. HEPI. https://www.hepi.ac.uk/2025/02/26/student-generative-ai-survey-2025/

71 Robert, J., & McCormack, M. (2025). 2025 EDUCAUSE AI Landscape Study: Into the Digital AI Divide. In Educause. https://www.educause.edu/content/2025/2025-educause-ai-landscape-study/introduction-and-key-findings

72 Robert, J., & McCormack, M. (2025). 2025 EDUCAUSE AI Landscape Study: Into the Digital AI Divide. In Educause. https://www.educause.edu/content/2025/2025-educause-ai-landscape-study/introduction-and-key-findings

73 Flaherty, C. (2025, April 21). Half of colleges don't grant students access to Gen AI tools. Inside Higher Ed | Higher Education News, Events and Jobs. https://www.insidehighered.com/news/tech-innovation/artificial-intelligence/2025/04/21/half-colleges-dont-grant-students-access

Recent policy initiatives reflect a strong governmental push to bridge the digital divide in AI education. The U.S. 2024 National Educational Technology Plan calls for expanded device distribution, community broadband, and targeted digital equity funding, while the 2025 *Presidential Artificial Intelligence Challenge* incentivizes equitable AI adoption and public-private partnerships to provide AI resources nationwide.[74] UNESCO's 2025 global call for action prioritizes AI literacy and inclusive access, supporting marginalized communities through curriculum development and multilingual resources.[75,76] Additional efforts include subsidized devices, offline-capable AI tools, and educator training, all aimed at ensuring that AI-driven educational opportunities reach underserved students.[77,78]

Algorithmic decision-making and its long-term consequences

AI-driven platforms often use this data and algorithms to analyze student performance and predict learning outcomes. These systems can:

- Recommend personalized learning paths.
- Suggest interventions for struggling students.
- Categorize students based on skill level, engagement, or behavior.

While these capabilities sound beneficial, they may also introduce potential biases and risks. Parents are uneasy that algorithmic decisions might unfairly track or categorize students, reinforcing educational disparities rather than providing solutions to them.

For example, if an AI system has labelled or categorized a student as a slow learner based on early academic performance, could that label follow them throughout their entire education? Could it limit their opportunities to explore advanced subjects? These are valid concerns, as AI-generated labels might not account for external factors such as personal growth, socioeconomic challenges, or changes in learning style over time.

Furthermore, bias in AI models is a well-documented issue. If training data primarily comes from specific demographics, the AI's recommendations may not be equitable for all students who may not be represented in the model training data. Parents want transparency into how

74 The White House. (2025b, April 23). Advancing artificial intelligence education for American youth. https://www.whitehouse.gov/presidential-actions/2025/04/advancing-artificial-intelligence-education-for-american-youth/
75 Gonzales, S. (2024, August 6). AI literacy and the new digital Divide - a global call for action. UNESCO. https://www.unesco.org/en/articles/ai-literacy-and-new-digital-divide-global-call-action
76 IFAP Advancing Collaborations for Ethical AI and Inclusive Digital Futures. (2025, June 25). UNESCO. https://www.unesco.org/en/articles/ifap-advancing-collaborations-ethical-ai-and-inclusive-digital-futures
77 2024-25 Fluency Report: Bridging the AI Digital Divide. (n.d.-b). Newhouse School at Syracuse University. https://newhouse.syracuse.edu/research/research-spaces/emerging-insights-lab/2024-25-fluency-report-bridging-the-ai-digital-divide/
78 RoX. (2025, June 30). Digital divide in AI education: Creating equal opportunities. AICompetence.org. https://aicompetence.org/digital-divide-in-ai-education/

these models function and assurances that AI will not reinforce systemic biases in education. If their children are assessed, categorized, and given a label by a machine learning model, parents have the right to inquire and understand the details of the algorithm.

Being inclusive

Parents are concerned about equity and rightly fear that biases embedded in algorithms could perpetuate existing inequalities or create new ones, inadvertently categorizing students in limiting or unfair ways. To counteract this, regular audits of AI systems, transparent communication about how AI decisions are made, and inclusive input from diverse communities, including parents, are essential. These audits must include a look into the training data and any bias that comes as part of the system integration process. Education systems must commit to fairness not only in intent but in rigorous oversight, ensuring that AI promotes rather than inhibits opportunity for all students.

Collaborating with parents and communities

While parental concerns about AI in education are legitimate and multifaceted, these concerns are also opportunities to help refine and strengthen the educational landscape. Embracing these concerns proactively can lead to a more robust, ethical, and effective use of technology. AI in education holds tremendous promise, but it must be deployed carefully and thoughtfully, transparently, and inclusively. By ensuring AI complements rather than replaces human instruction, safeguarding student privacy and equity, prioritizing creativity and active learning, and maintaining open communication with parents, we can leverage AI's potential while preserving the essential human elements that truly shape a child's education. Only then can we confidently and responsibly move toward a future where technology enhances, rather than undermines, the very essence of learning.

Best practices from educational districts in 2024-2025 emphasize transparent collaboration with parents and communities to build trust and guide AI adoption in schools. The **Los Angeles Unified School District (LAUSD)** has strengthened its advisory councils and committees, such as the School Site Council, which includes parents and community members in decision-making about school plans and technology integration, ensuring their perspectives are honored throughout the process.[79] **The Toronto District School Board (TDSB)** advocates for a provincial committee dedicated to supporting school boards on AI issues, and proposes regular conferences and ongoing support to address privacy, equity, and ethical considerations, explicitly inviting parental and community involvement.[80]

The **Los Angeles County Office of Education (LACOE)** has released comprehensive guidelines for responsible AI implementation, developed by a task force including educators, students,

---

79 Committees. (n.d.). https://families.lausd.org/apps/pages/index.jsp?uREC_ID=4390902&-type=d&pREC_ID=2605896
80 Leadership regarding artificial intelligence and education. (n.d.). https://www.tdsb.on.ca/home/ctl/De-tails/mid/43824/itemId/331/20240711152938

and community organizations. These guidelines recommend needs assessments, transparent communications strategies, and continuous feedback loops with stakeholders, all designed to foster shared responsibility and trust.[81] UNESCO's global guidance further underscores the necessity of inclusive, human-centered approaches that prioritize open dialogue and equity, ensuring AI enhances rather than replaces human instruction.[82]

Building shared responsibility

Integrating parental influence, evolutionary-informed practices, and AI technology creates a powerful, holistic approach to education. These elements are not competing forces but complementary ones. Parents and family members provide emotional support, values, and one-on-one attention that no technology can replace. A warm home environment that encourages questions and celebrates learning sets the stage for children to view education positively. Schools and educators, informed by an understanding of human developmental needs, can design curricula that leverage children's natural curiosity, incorporating social learning opportunities, play, and hands-on discovery to align with innate learning mechanisms. Within this human-centered framework, AI serves as a tool to reinforce and enrich learning. For instance, an AI tutoring program might guide a child through practice problems at her own pace, but the encouragement and context provided by a parent or teacher can deepen the experience and keep the student motivated.

When used in concert, these influences can create a learning ecosystem greater than the sum of its parts. Imagine a scenario where a student explores a science simulation on a tablet (guided by an AI that adjusts difficulty to her level), then discusses her discoveries with her parents at dinner, drawing connections to real life. This blending of high-tech personalization with human interaction exemplifies synergistic learning. Similarly, teachers could use AI-driven analytics to identify which students need extra help in reading and then enlist parents as partners to read with those children at home, targeting specific skills identified by the software. In this way, artificial intelligence can amplify the positive effects of parental engagement by providing insights and resources that make family involvement more effective and focused.

In a rapidly changing world, blending the wisdom of the past with the innovations of the present is key to preparing learners for the future. Parental influence offers children support and inspiration that endures throughout their education, while our evolutionary heritage provides insight into the kinds of experiences that make learning naturally rewarding. Artificial intelligence, when thoughtfully integrated into educational contexts, can magnify these effects by personalizing learning and making high-quality resources available to all. The scholarly evidence and perspectives discussed suggest that these factors: parental involvement, evolutionarily-aligned pedagogy, and AI assistance, are most powerful when working in harmony. By combining nurturing guidance, an understanding of how children

---

81 AI Education Guidelines. (2024, June 6). https://www.lacoe.edu/news/2024-06-06-gen-ai-education-guidelines
82 Artificial intelligence in education. (n.d.). UNESCO. Retrieved July 6, 2025, from https://www.unesco.org/en/digital-education/artificial-intelligence

inherently learn, and the strategic use of AI, educators and families can cultivate an educational experience that is deeply human, scientifically informed, and future-ready.[83]

Conclusion

As artificial intelligence solutions become increasingly embedded in our educational environments, facing parental concerns about their impact on children's learning, emotional growth, and future opportunities, it must be thoughtfully addressed. The roots of these concerns run deep, shaped by personal experiences, media portrayals, leadership, financial pressure, and broader societal anxieties about technological advancement. While these worries are valid and understandable, they also offer an opportunity for educators, policymakers, and technology developers to engage constructively with parents and create a balanced, ethical, and responsible framework for integrating AI into education that is focused on impact.

Education will advance dramatically in a mostly positive way, thanks to AI, but educators must continue to emphasize human creativity, play, and hands-on experimentation, areas where human teachers excel. AI should enhance rather than limit opportunities for children to engage in imaginative and critical thinking exercises. Schools need to actively preserve and integrate creative, interactive learning experiences alongside the breadth of ethically driven AI instruction.

Policy recommendations from organizations consistently highlight the importance of preserving and integrating creative, interactive learning experiences alongside ethically designed AI instruction. They advocate for school districts to establish advisory councils with parent representation, conduct regular impact assessments, and maintain open feedback channels to adapt policies as technologies evolve. These measures help ensure that AI implementation remains student-centered, inclusive, and responsive to the needs and values of families.

In the next chapter, we will explore the benefits and challenges of AI inclusion for students with diverse learning needs. We will look at early AI intervention techniques to ensure learners do not fall behind and how personalization of the curriculum can help diverse learners excel.

Questions

1. In what ways can we ensure that AI enhances, rather than replaces, the human relationships that are essential to your child's learning experience?

2. What information or transparency would help you as a parent feel more confident in how your child's data is collected, used, and protected in an AI-powered classroom?

3. How can schools meaningfully involve parents in decision-making about the use of AI tools in the classroom environment?

4. What concerns do you have as a parent about how AI might influence your child's creativity, problem-solving, or independent thinking?

83 Bjorklund, D. F. (2022b). Children's evolved learning abilities and their implications for education. Educational Psychology Review, 34(4), 2243–2273. https://doi.org/10.1007/s10648-022-09688-z

5. How might AI unintentionally create or reinforce educational inequalities in our schools, and what can we do to proactively address that risk?

6. What role do you believe teachers and administrators should continue to play in guiding, mentoring, and assessing students in an AI-integrated learning environment?

7. How do you envision a more balanced educational experience that includes both screen-based AI learning and hands-on, creative, and play-based learning?

Exercises

1. **Mapping AI impact**: Explore how AI can affect students' learning experiences.

    a. Team up (one parent, one educator) to draw a map showing the student in the center. Around the student, identify both the positive and negative impacts of AI in key areas: creativity, critical thinking, social development, screen time, and emotional well-being.

    b. Share out and discuss areas of overlap and concern. Also include potential future developments and areas to watch.

2. **What is in the data—Simulation**: Build awareness of the collection of student data.

    a. Provide a fictional AI learning tool description and a list of data types it collects (e.g., test scores, screen time, eye gaze). Ask groups to discuss:

        i.   What types of data are collected?

        ii. How will data be used?

        iii. What crosses the line and feels inappropriate?

    b. Compare views between educators and parents; surface shared values.

3. **Role-playing teacher versus AI**: Highlight the importance of human relationships in learning.

    a. In small groups, role-play two versions of a student-teacher interaction:

        i.   One scenario covers where the student receives AI-generated feedback.

        ii. Another where the student receives teacher feedback with emotional nuance.

    b. Reflect on the emotional and developmental impact of each. What recommendations are there for teacher involvement in AI-generated feedback?

4. **Checklist for consent and communication**: Clarify how schools can improve transparency with parents.

a. Parents and educators co-create a shared checklist of what information parents should receive before AI tools are introduced (e.g., purpose, data use, transparency, usage, and opt-out options).

b. Share with administration as a prototype for school policy.

5. **Equity scenarios**: Explore equity and bias in ethical AI decision-making.

a. Present a few short case studies (e.g., a student wrongly categorized as low-performing by AI). Ask: How should the school respond? What human oversight is needed? What is the human override policy?

b. Discuss the risks of predictive labeling and how to intervene and respond.

6. **Design an AI-enhanced classroom**: Encourage collaborative envisioning of a balanced learning environment.

a. In mixed groups, design an ideal classroom that uses AI but also promotes human-centered interaction, creativity, emotional support, and social connection. Use drawings, post-its, or digital whiteboards.

b. What does balance look like in practice? What is the role of the teacher as an AI facilitator?

7. **Creative student journey**: Emphasize the importance of creativity and unstructured learning.

a. Share a student profile. Then have groups plot two paths:

i. One AI-optimized.

ii. One with intentional play, mistakes, and exploration.

b. Where might creativity be lost, and how can AI support rather than suppress it? What is the educator's role? What is the role of the administration?

8. **Parent-educator listening circle**: Help foster empathy and trust.

a. In a facilitated, moderated circle, parents complete the statement: My biggest hope and fear about AI in my child's classroom is… Educators respond to the same from their perspective.

b. Look for alignment and opportunities for deeper partnership.

9. **Screen time swap-Activity brainstorm**: Generate alternatives to excessive screen use, in school and at home.

a. Brainstorm 10 engaging, screen-free activities that reinforce classroom concepts (e.g., science walks, journaling, peer debates). How can AI help brainstorm?

b. How can screen-free time be structured to support learning?

10. **Create an AI family contract**: A shared vision for school and home support for thoughtful AI use.

   a. In pairs or family groups, draft a simple AI Use Agreement that includes:

      i.   When/where AI tools will be used.

      ii. Screen time boundaries.

      iii. Family check-ins about learning and AI usage.

   b. Share ideas and adapt for broader school-family use.

Join our Discord space

Join our Discord workspace for latest updates, offers, tech happenings around the world, new releases, and sessions with the authors:

https://discord.bpbonline.com

CHAPTER 6

AI for Diverse Learning Needs

Our ability to reach unity in diversity will be the beauty and the test of our civilization.

– Mahatma Gandhi

Introduction

Imagine a classroom where every student receives exactly what they need to thrive. A child struggling with dyslexia has an AI-powered reading assistant that reads aloud and highlights words in a way that makes comprehension easier. A non-verbal student communicates effortlessly using an AI-driven speech generator. A refugee who speaks no English follows the lesson in real time with instant AI translation. This vision, once science fiction, is rapidly becoming reality.

Throughout history, education has been shaped by technological revolutions. The printing press democratized knowledge, the blackboard transformed classroom instruction, and the internet made global learning possible. Today, artificial intelligence represents the next seismic shift, one that could finally make personalized learning at scale a reality. However, will AI be the great equalizer, or will it deepen existing inequalities?

The need for solutions has never been greater. More than 240 million children worldwide, or one in ten, live with disabilities according to UNICEF[1], many of whom struggle to access education tailored to their needs. In the United States alone, over 15% of students require special education services, yet schools often lack the resources to provide individualized support, according to the *National Center for Education Statistics*[2]. Classrooms today are incredibly heterogeneous. Traditional teaching models were not built for this level of diversity. AI, however, has the potential to reshape education into a system where every student, regardless of ability, background, language or learning style, receives customized support.

As with every technological revolution, AI in education raises critical questions: Can algorithms truly understand the complexities of human learning? Will AI-driven tools amplify biases instead of removing barriers? And how do we ensure that the benefits of AI reach all students, not just those in well-funded schools?

The challenge before us is not just to introduce AI into education but to do so in a way that enhances learning for every student. As we explore AI's potential to support diverse learning needs, one thing becomes clear: the technology alone is not the answer. It is how we design, implement, and regulate AI that will determine whether it becomes a bridge to greater equity or another barrier to overcome.

As outlined in the chapter, the promise of AI to support diverse learners demands urgent action aligned with 2025 frameworks like the OECD's AI principles and UNESCO's updated guidance, which call for inclusive, human-centered, and transparent AI systems to ensure equitable access for all students—not just those in well-resourced classrooms.

Structure

This chapter covers the following topics:

- Defining diverse learners in the AI age
- Personalization and differentiation
- Language and communication enhancements
- Accessibility and special needs support
- Early intervention and collaboration
- AI for better teaching by empowering educators
- Ethical and practical considerations
- Future directions

1 One in 10 children worldwide live with disabilities. (2021, November 11). UN News. https://news. un.org/en/story/2021/11/1105412#:~:text=Nearly%20240%20million%20children%20worldwide%2C%20 or%20one%20in,by%20the%20UN%20Children%E2%80%99s%20Fund%20%28UNICEF%29%20on%20 Wednesday.
2 COE - Students with Disabilities. (n.d.). https://nces.ed.gov/programs/coe/indicator/cgg

Objectives

The primary goal of this chapter is to explore how AI can support diverse learning needs and ensure equitable education for all students, regardless of their abilities, backgrounds, or learning challenges. We aim to provide a comprehensive, research-backed analysis of AI's role in enhancing personalized learning, supporting students with disabilities, breaking down language barriers, and equipping educators with powerful tools.

Through real-world case studies and emerging AI applications, this chapter will illustrate how AI-powered tools are transforming learning experiences, from providing instant language translation for multilingual learners to offering tailored support for neurodiverse students. At the same time, we will critically examine the ethical implications and practical challenges, including concerns about bias, data privacy, and accessibility gaps.

A key takeaway is that AI should not replace human educators but rather empower them by augmenting their ability to address students' individual needs efficiently and at scale. We will highlight how educators, policymakers, and technology developers can collaborate to create AI-driven solutions that are responsible, inclusive, and aligned with the broader goals of equitable education.

Like the invention of paper, the clay tablet, the printing press and the internet, AI arrives with the promise of democratizing knowledge—but history reminds us that if we are not careful, even the most revolutionary technologies can deepen divides when access and design are unequal. In this light, we stand at a crossroad with AI: it can be the great equalizer that adapts to every learner's needs, or an amplifier of inequality that privileges the already privileged and overlooks those most in need of help and support.

By the end of this chapter, readers will gain actionable insights into how AI can be harnessed responsibly to create more inclusive, flexible, and student-centered learning environments, while remaining aware of its risks and limitations.

Defining diverse learners in the AI age

Who are the diverse learners we aim to support with AI? In truth, every learner is unique, but the term diverse learners typically refers to students whose needs differ significantly from the traditional norm or majority. This includes, first and foremost, students with disabilities, a broad category encompassing those with physical impairments (like vision or hearing loss), developmental and intellectual disabilities, learning disabilities such as dyslexia or dyscalculia, and neurological conditions that affect learning (such as ADHD or autism spectrum disorder). It also includes neurodivergent learners, students who think and learn differently, a term often overlapping with some disabilities but also covering those who might not have a formal diagnosis yet have distinct cognitive styles (for example, highly gifted learners or those with attention differences). Learners facing language barriers are another large group: children from immigrant or refugee backgrounds learning the school's language, or students in any country being taught in a second language. UNESCO reports that a staggering 40% of the population does not have access to education in a language they understand[3], which directly hampers learning outcomes. Additionally, students from different cultural backgrounds, those in poverty, or those who missed schooling (perhaps due to conflict or illness) have unique needs. Even within a typical classroom, one finds different learning styles; some students learn best by reading, others by listening, some through hands-on practice, others through visual aids or storytelling. All these variations form the spectrum of diverse learners.

In the AI age, recognizing and addressing this spectrum is crucial. Traditional education systems were often designed with a mythical average student in mind. However, as one size never truly fits all, many learners have historically been left behind or required special pull-out services. The promise of AI is to better adapt to learner variability in real time. AI thrives on data and patterns; in education, this means an AI system can potentially detect how each student learns and what they struggle with, then adjust the approach accordingly. For instance, an AI-powered math tutor might notice that a student with dyscalculia consistently hesitates on problems with fractions, and then provide alternative explanations using visuals or adjust the difficulty of exercises until the concept clicks. A reading app might increase text size, add text-to-speech, or simplify vocabulary for a student with a reading disability. AI translation can instantly convert a lesson from English to Spanish for a newcomer who is still acquiring English, allowing them to understand content while they ramp up their language skills. These are not just theoretical ideas; they are active areas of development and, in some cases, already in classroom pilots. By defining diverse learners expansively, educators and technologists push AI tools to be inclusive by design, meaning the software is created to accommodate a wide range of needs from the ground up, rather than as an afterthought. Concepts like **Universal Design for Learning (UDL)**[4], which advocates building a curriculum that is flexible for all types of learners, marries well with AI capabilities. For example, a UDL-aligned digital textbook might have AI-driven features like adjustable reading levels, built-in dictionaries and translators, and multiple representation modes (text, audio, video) to serve students with differing needs.

Neurodiversity encompasses a broad spectrum of cognitive differences, including variations in working memory, executive function, and sensory processing—all of which can significantly impact how students learn. Working memory refers to the ability of students to hold and manipulate information over short periods, a key skill in following multi-step instructions, solving complex problems, or participating in discussions. Students with reduced working memory capacity, common in **attention deficit hyperactivity disorder (ADHD)** or different forms of dyslexia, may benefit from AI tools that help to scaffold information—breaking down tasks into manageable chunks or providing visual reminders of previous steps. Executive function challenges, which include difficulties with planning, time management, and task initiation, can make it difficult for students to organize their learning. AI-powered planners

3 UNESCO. (2023, April 20). 40% don't access education in a language they understand. unesco.org. https://www.unesco.org/gem-report/en/articles/40-dont-access-education-language-they-understand#:~:text=Paris%2C%2019%20February%2C%20for%20those%20living%20in%20poverty
4 Universal Design for Learning | Center for Teaching Innovation. (n.d.). https://teaching.cornell.edu/teaching-resources/universal-design-learning

and adaptive scheduling apps can help as digital executive assistants, prompting students at key moments, suggesting study sequences, or tracking progress on long-term projects. Sensory processing differences in students—such as hypersensitivity to noise, light, or touch—can affect students' ability to concentrate in typical classroom environments. AI can help personalize sensory input, adjusting brightness of screens, sound levels, or visual complexity based on user preferences or real-time feedback. By acknowledging core neurocognitive dimensions, AI can help move beyond one-size-fits-all solutions to offer truly individualized, strength-based learning environments that support every learner's unique neurological profile.

The challenges AI faces in addressing diverse needs are real and must be acknowledged. One challenge is data bias. If AI systems are trained primarily on data from mainstream student populations, they might not perform as well for minority groups or those with atypical patterns. For instance, a speech recognition engine might struggle with a student who has a speech impairment or a heavy accent if it was not trained on similar speech samples. Likewise, an AI tutoring system might not realize that a student has a vision impairment unless it is explicitly programmed to offer alternative, non-visual presentations of information. There is also the challenge of access: the students who could benefit most from AI support (such as those in remote or underfunded areas, or with severe disabilities) might also be the least likely to have access to the latest technology and reliable internet connectivity, a classic paradox that we must work to overcome. Educators worry, rightly so, that technology could inadvertently widen gaps if not implemented thoughtfully. Moreover, some teachers and parents may be uncertain about trusting AI with critical educational tasks, given concerns over accuracy and empathy; an algorithm might diagnose a learning difficulty or recommend an intervention, but without a human's holistic understanding.

On the flip side, the opportunities of AI for diverse learners are unprecedented. AI can analyze vast amounts of student performance data efficiently, potentially identifying patterns that a busy teacher might miss. For example, early studies in Japan have used AI to analyze students' pen stroke data[5] and detect learning difficulties in writing, a task impractical to do manually for each child. By flagging such issues early, interventions can be provided before the student falls too far behind. AI-driven tools can also free up educators' time from routine tasks (like grading basic homework or repetitively re-teaching a concept to multiple students at different paces), allowing them to spend more time on individualized support and relationship-building. In this sense, AI acts as an amplifier for teachers working with diverse learners. It might handle the heavy lifting of differentiating practice exercises or monitoring progress, while the teacher focuses on the creative and emotional labor of teaching; for instance, discussing a complex concept, motivating the class, or working one-on-one with a student on a personal challenge.

To illustrate, consider a high school teacher with a class of 30 that includes gifted students bored by the standard curriculum, as well as students with mild intellectual disabilities who need content broken down. Without AI, the teacher would need to create multiple sets of materials manually or default to a one-size-fits-all approach, catering primarily to the average

5 Toyokawa, Y., Horikoshi, I., Majumdar, R., & Ogata, H. (2023). Challenges and opportunities of AI in inclusive education: a case study of data-enhanced active reading in Japan. Smart Learning Environments, 10(1). https://doi.org/10.1186/s40561-023-00286-2

student. With AI, each student could be guided by an adaptive learning platform that adjusts the difficulty and modality for them: the advanced student might get more challenging problems and exploratory projects, while the struggling student gets step-by-step framing and reinforcement on fundamentals. The teacher oversees this orchestration via a dashboard, seeing in real time that, say, five students are ready to move on to a new topic while three need a different explanation. They can then intervene in a targeted way. Such an approach not only benefits those particular subgroups but also improves the overall classroom dynamic; everyone can progress at a comfortable pace, reducing frustration and disengagement. Research and pilot programs are increasingly validating this approach. A UNESCO review of innovative technologies for inclusive education notes numerous best practices where AI and digital tools have broken down barriers; for example, augmentative and alternative communication software giving non-verbal students a voice in class discussions[6], or AI-based reading apps that help dyslexic students decode texts independently[7]. These developments underscore that in the AI age, diversity is no longer a hurdle to overcome, but a reality to embrace. AI's flexibility thrives in a diverse environment: the more variation it encounters, the smarter and more effective it can become at accommodating differences (provided it is guided ethically, which we will discuss later in this chapter).

In summary, diverse learners include anyone whose educational needs are not fully met by traditional, uniform methods, which is arguably the majority of students. The AI age compels us to broaden this definition and strive for personalization at scale. Challenges like bias, access, and trust need careful attention. Yet the opportunities, highly individualized learning pathways, early detection of issues, and more inclusive classrooms where each student can participate fully paint an inspiring picture. The key takeaway? Diversity in learning is the norm, not the exception. AI's greatest promise lies in helping education systems finally recognize and act on this reality, shifting from an outdated, industrial-age model of mass instruction to a learner-centered approach that celebrates individual strengths. With this vision in mind, let us explore how AI-driven personalization and differentiation are already transforming education worldwide.

Personalization and differentiation

One of the most powerful contributions of AI in education is its ability to personalize learning paths for each student and support differentiated teaching approaches. In a traditional classroom, differentiation, tailoring instruction to different abilities and interests, is labor-intensive and often limited. Teachers do their best by offering, for example, three levels of a math worksheet or giving advanced readers extra novels, but fine-grained personalization for every student, updated day by day, is beyond human capacity. AI changes that. Through intelligent tutoring systems, adaptive learning platforms, and real-time analytics, AI can create

---

6 Jovic, A., Panwar, B., Hyun, C., Mapuranga, M., Constantopedos, E., & UNICEF ECARO. (2020, July 23). Giving every child a voice with AAC technology. UNICEF.org. https://www.unicef.org/innovation/stories/giving-every-child-voice-aac-technology
7 UNESCO. (2023, April 20). Spanish application using AI to help overcome dyslexia wins 2019 UNESCO ICT Prize. UNESCO.org. https://www.unesco.org/en/articles/spanish-application-using-ai-help-overcome-dyslexia-wins-2019-unesco-ict-prize

a dynamic learning experience that adjusts to the right level and style for each learner. Imagine an AI tutor that never gets tired, can provide unlimited practice problems, instant hints, and step-by-step feedback, and continuously gauges a student's understanding to decide what to present next. This is already a reality in various forms. Early AI-driven tutoring systems like *Jaime Carbonell's* SCHOLAR[8] in the 1970s, and **Programmed Logic for Automatic Teaching Operations (PLATO)**[9] at the *University of Illinois* in the 1960s were precursors, and today's versions are far more advanced, leveraging modern machine learning to refine their teaching strategies on the fly.

Consider the example of *Concordia Lutheran College*[10] in *Australia*, which implemented an AI-driven platform called *Maths Pathway*[11]. This system uses machine learning to tailor math content to each student's learning pace and style. As students work on math problems, the platform continuously assesses their progress and understanding. If a student masters a concept quickly, the AI introduces more advanced topics; if another student is struggling, it provides additional practice or revisits prerequisite skills. The AI also gives immediate feedback on each question, so learners are not left in doubt about what they did wrong; they can try again with guidance. The impact at *Concordia Lutheran College* shows engagement is on the rise and students are genuinely excited because, for once, they understand math, as stated by the head of mathematics. Teachers reported that they could identify individual learning gaps and intervene where necessary. This case study illustrates how personalized learning at scale can be achieved: the AI handles the differentiation, delivering just-right content to each student, while teachers monitor progress and provide targeted help. In essence, AI becomes a tireless teaching assistant for every student, offering enrichment to those who are ahead and structured support to those who need more help.

Immediate feedback and **dynamic skill assessment** are hallmarks of AI-based personalized learning. In a human-led setting, a student might do homework and wait a day or two to get it graded and returned; by then, the learning moment might be lost or misconceptions ingrained. AI tutors, on the other hand, respond in milliseconds. For example, an intelligent writing tutor can highlight a grammar mistake the moment it is made and prompt the student to correct it, turning what would have been a passive error-marking into an active learning moment. In math or science, adaptive exercises can catch a misunderstanding (like the misuse of a formula) and immediately provide a hint or a simpler sub-problem to reteach the concept. This kind of responsiveness keeps students from making errors and accelerates the learning cycle. It is akin to having a personal coach who is always by your side while you practice, giving gentle nudges and corrections exactly when needed. Research by organizations like the **Southwest Educational Development Laboratory (SEDL)** suggests that such formative

8 Holmes, W., Bialik, M., Fadel, C., & Center for Curriculum Redesign. (2019). Artificial intelligence in Education: Promises and implications for teaching and learning In Center for Curriculum Redesign [Book] p. 29. https://curriculumredesign.org/wp-content/uploads/AIED-Book-Excerpt-CCR.pdf
9 PLATO – Illinois Distributed Museum. (n.d.). https://distributedmuseum.illinois.edu/exhibit/plato/
10 Superseed, & Superseed. (2024, June 11). Concordia Lutheran College understands Engagement. Maths Pathway. https://mathspathway.com/school-case-studies/concordia-lutheran-college-understands-engagement/
11 Superseed. (2025, March 24). Home - Maths Pathway. Maths Pathway. https://mathspathway.com/

feedback is one of the most effective drivers of learning[12], and AI enables it at scale, even in large classes. Students often describe AI-powered learning software as interactive or game-like because of this adaptivity, which can increase motivation: instead of slogging through ten problems not knowing if you are doing them right, you get a quick *Correct!* or *Let us review this step* from the system, more like playing a game that reacts to your moves.

Differentiated instruction also means accommodating different learning modalities and preferences, and here AI can be quite creative. Some students grasp concepts better through videos or simulations than through text. AI platforms can analyze which content format leads to better outcomes for a learner. If a student is struggling to understand an algebra concept from text, the system might switch to an animated explanation or an interactive graph. If a student learns vocabulary more effectively with pictures and examples rather than flashcards, an AI language app can adapt to that style. Personalization is not only about difficulty level; it is also about the method of learning. A good human tutor naturally adjusts their teaching: noticing, for instance, that a particular child responds well to storytelling, the tutor might weave math problems into a story. AI is starting to emulate this by having multiple modes of explaining material and selecting among them based on user feedback and performance. For instance, the platform *Knewton*[13] (an adaptive learning company) claims to use analytics to decide not just what topic a student should do next but in what way (video, text, practice) to deliver the lesson, based on patterns of that student and millions of others. While Knewton's approach had mixed results and the company restructured[14], it paved the way for current systems to refine this idea with deeper AI insights. Today's learning apps like Duolingo for language[15] are informed by vast data on how different types of learners succeed, allowing a high degree of personalization for each new learner.

To illustrate differentiation through AI, let us look at another case study: *Georgia Institute of Technology*[16] in the U.S. faced a challenge in a large online course, students often had common questions, and instructors could not keep up with the volume on discussion forums. They introduced an AI teaching assistant named *Jill Watson*, built on IBM's Watson platform, to help. Jill Watson was trained on over 40,000 past forum posts and was able to answer students' routine questions with a high degree of accuracy, posing as just another **teaching assistant**

12 Black, P., William, D., Davidson, L., Frohbieter, D., K–12 Center at ETS, Southeast Comprehensive Center, Partnership for Assessment of Readiness for College and Careers, SMARTER Balanced Assessment Consortium, SEDL, Gallagher, M., Worth, S., Clark, R., Heritage, M., Herman, J., Osmundson, E., & Dietel, R. (2012). Using formative assessment to improve student achievement in the core content areas. In Southeast Comprehensive Center at SEDL. https://sedl.org/secc/resources/briefs/formative_assessment_core_content/Formative_Assessment.pdf

13 Knewton Adaptive Learning and How it's Unique. (n.d.). Knewton.com. Retrieved March 29, 2025, from https://support.knewton.com/s/article/Knewton-Adaptive-Learning-and-How-it-s-Unique

14 Knewton Personalizes Learning with the Power of AI - Digital Innovation and Transformation. (2021, April 19). Digital Innovation and Transformation. https://d3.harvard.edu/platform-digit/submission/knewton-personalizes-learning-with-the-power-of-ai/

15 Wallingford, P. (2024, November 10). How Duolingo Use AI: Making Language Learning Smarter. Duolingo Guides. https://duolingoguides.com/how-duolingo-use-ai/

16 Meet Jill Watson: Georgia Tech's first AI teaching assistant. (n.d.). Georgia Tech Professional Education. https://pe.gatech.edu/blog/meet-jill-watson-georgia-techs-first-ai-teaching-assistant

(**TA**). This freed the human TAs and professors to focus on more complex or unique student needs. The results were impressive: Jill Watson significantly reduced response times (students got help almost instantly at any hour) and handled the majority of common queries accurately, easing the workload on staff. Students were surprised to later learn one of their helpful TAs was an AI! This case demonstrates personalization in a different sense, not in delivering content, but in providing timely support. Each student essentially got a private tutor for **frequently asked questions** (**FAQs**). It is a form of differentiation where every learner's question gets answered without having to wait in line. While this example is from higher education, the principle applies broadly: AI can ensure that no student's confusion goes unnoticed or unaddressed, which is a key aspect of personalized education.

Supporting student autonomy and **24/7 learning** is another benefit of AI personalization. With AI-driven platforms, learning is not confined to school hours or the classroom. Students can progress at their own pace, which is especially beneficial for those who either advance faster or need more time. A student who is fascinated by a topic can keep exploring through the AI system even if the class has to move on, and conversely, a student who needs to review previous material can do so without feeling embarrassed or holding others back. AI tutors and resources are available anytime, late at night before a test, on weekends, over summer break, providing a continuity of learning that traditional schooling cannot match. This autonomy also empowers learners: many find it motivating to have some control over their learning path, and AI can present them with choices (*Would you like to practice more of what you learned today, or preview tomorrow's topic?*). The student becomes an active participant in navigating their education, with the AI as a guide. In effect, the learning experience becomes more student-centered, conforming to the learner rather than forcing the learner to conform to a preset path. Studies[17] have shown that this can improve not only academic outcomes but also student confidence and engagement, because learners see tangible progress and get instruction that makes sense to them individually.

However, it is important to note that AI-driven personalization is not without limitations or risks. One concern is that students might become too dependent on the AI and struggle when they do not have immediate feedback (for example, in a traditional exam setting). Educators must balance AI use with cultivating independent problem-solving skills. Another issue is data privacy: personalized systems collect a lot of student performance data to function effectively; protecting that data (and being transparent about how it is used) is critical, as we broadly cover in *Chapter 10, Data Security and Ethical Considerations in AI*. We also must ensure that personalization algorithms do not inadvertently narrow a student's exposure. If an AI decides a student learns best with videos, one would not want it to only ever show videos and never encourage the student to strengthen their reading skills; a human teacher's wisdom in encouraging well-rounded development is still needed. Additionally, some fear that over-personalization could isolate learners (each in their own bubble) at the cost of shared classroom experiences and collaborative learning. Good implementations of AI in classrooms

17 Pane, J. F., Steiner, E. D., Baird, M. D., Hamilton, L. S., & Pane, J. D. (2017, December 7). How does personalized learning affect student achievement? RAND. https://www.rand.org/pubs/research_briefs/RB9994.html

try to mitigate this by, for example, using personalized practice for certain activities but still bringing students together for discussions, group projects, and other social learning experiences that are equally important.

Overall, though, the consensus in educational innovation is that AI-powered personalization can dramatically improve differentiation and mastery learning. It operationalizes the old ideal of teaching students, not curriculum. Every student effectively gets a tailored curriculum that adjusts in real time. A telling metric comes from some schools using adaptive learning: the variability in time students need to master a concept can be huge; some might get it in 20 minutes, others need two hours and several interventions. In the past, the class would move on after 30 minutes as an example, regardless, leaving some bewildered and some bored. With AI, each student moves on upon mastery, not based on a one-size-fits-all schedule. This approach aligns with mastery-based learning philosophies that have long been recommended but were hard to implement. Now, a combination of AI software and teacher facilitation is making it feasible.

To summarize, AI enables **personalized learning paths, immediate feedback loops, and finely differentiated instruction** that adapts to each learner's skills and preferences. Case studies like the ones we covered earlier in this chapter (Maths Pathway: adaptive math program in Australia and AI tutoring systems like *Jill Watson* at *Georgia Tech*) illustrate how quick, personalized support can be scaled to many learners at once and enable improved outcomes when students learn at their own pace with AI guidance. In this case, AI was not disclosed initially to the students, but we know that transparency is a key principle of responsible AI best practices. Students benefit from 24/7 availability and tailored content delivery, which can lead to higher engagement and achievement. Meanwhile, teachers gain a superpowered form of differentiation; they can better monitor individual progress through AI analytics and spend their time where it is needed most. Personalization is perhaps the area of AI in education with the most evidence of efficacy so far, essentially proving the concept that when you teach to the student rather than the syllabus, great things happen. As we proceed, keep in mind that many of the other topics (language support, accessibility, etc.) are special cases of this personalization principle: modifying and tuning the learning experience to fit the learner, rather than forcing the learner to fit the experience. AI is providing the toolkit to finally realize this ideal at scale.

Language and communication enhancements

In classrooms worldwide, language differences and communication difficulties often form a barrier to learning. A student might be brilliant in math, but if they cannot follow the language of instruction, their talent remains hidden. Or consider a child with a speech impediment or hearing loss, how can they participate fully in class discussions without support? AI is making significant strides in breaking language and communication barriers, helping both multilingual students and those with communication-related special needs. Through translation technology, natural language processing, and speech interfaces, AI can act as a real-time interpreter, tutor, and communication aid. These enhancements ensure that language is a bridge rather than a wall in diverse classrooms.

Translation

One of the most transformative applications is **AI-driven translation and interpretation**. Modern AI translation tools have become amazingly accurate and fast. For example, Microsoft has integrated an AI translator[18] (powered by its Azure Cognitive Services and now GPT-based models) into tools like Microsoft Teams and even the operating system level, enabling live translation in nearly every language for meetings and captions. Imagine a parent-teacher conference where the parent speaks only Mandarin and the teacher only English; an AI system on a tablet can now listen and display each spoken sentence in the other language almost instantly, facilitating a meaningful dialogue. In classrooms, if a newcomer student from Syria joins an English-language school, an AI translation app on a tablet or phone can help the student follow along by translating key phrases of the teacher's lecture in real time. There have been pilot programs where teachers wear a microphone that feeds into a translation app for students, effectively giving non-native speakers subtitles for the class. Remember UNESCO's data[19] shared earlier, underscoring the importance of this: 40% of people globally do not access education in their mother tongue, which negatively impacts learning. AI translation offers a scalable solution to deliver content in a language students understand, without requiring the teacher to be multilingual. It is not just one-way either; students can respond in their native language and have it translated for the teacher or peers. Google Translate[20] (with conversation mode) has been used in schools to support newly arrived non-English-speaking students, allowing them to communicate basic needs and participate in learning while they gradually pick up the instructional language, particularly helpful for refugee students[21].

Speech tools

AI helps multilingual learners practice language skills in interactive ways. Language learning AI tutors can engage students in conversation, correct pronunciation, and even simulate real-world dialogues. A compelling example is *Super Chinese*[22], an AI-driven language learning platform that assists students in mastering Mandarin Chinese through advanced speech recognition and adaptive learning techniques. Super Chinese uses AI-powered speech analysis to evaluate pronunciation, intonation, and rhythm in real time. If a learner mispronounces a word or struggles with the correct tone, a crucial aspect of Mandarin, the AI detects the

18 Gibson, R. (2024, September 10). The Impact of AI in Advancing Accessibility for Learners with Disabilities. Educause.edu. https://er.educause.edu/articles/2024/9/the-impact-of-ai-in-advancing-accessibility-for-learners-with-disabilities#:~:text=LLMs%20have%20made%20possible%20a,Footnote%2015
19 UNESCO. (2023, April 20). 40% don't access education in a language they understand. unesco. org. https://www.unesco.org/gem-report/en/articles/40-cont-access-education-language-they-understand#:~:text=Paris%2C%2019%20February%20,for%20those%20living%20in%20poverty
20 Translating to smiles: Using Google Translate to engage ELL students | South Carolina ETV. (n.d.). South Carolina ETV. https://www.scetv.org/stories/2020/translating-smiles-using-google-translate-engage-ell-students
21 Google Translate providing futuristic help for refugee students (VIDEO). (n.d.). PembinaValleyOnline. https://pembinavalleyonline.com/articles/google-translate-providing-futuristic-help-for-refugee-students-video
22 Learn connect & share - SuperChinese. (n.d.). https://superchinese.com/blog

error and provides instant corrective feedback. The system can also demonstrate proper pronunciation by replaying audio examples, helping students refine their speaking skills with targeted guidance. The platform also integrates animated videos and character writing exercises, making the learning experience more engaging and effective.

For language teachers, AI-driven tools like this augment instruction; students can do their drills and conversational practice with the AI, freeing class time for more complex communicative activities and cultural learning that benefit from human interaction. We are also seeing chatbots being used for language practice: for example, some students use AI chatbots (like certain modes of ChatGPT or specialized apps) to practice writing or speaking in a foreign language and get corrections[23]. This is especially useful for languages that might not be commonly taught locally; an English-speaking student interested in learning Swahili, for example, could practice basics with an AI before they ever find a human tutor.

Writing tools

Assistive writing tools and **literacy support** through AI benefit not just second-language learners but all students who struggle with reading and writing. Tools like Grammarly[24] or Google's Smart Compose[25] are AI-based systems that provide real-time writing feedback, suggestions for better wording, grammar corrections, and even detecting tone or clarity issues. For ELLs, such tools can function as a digital writing mentor. If a student writes **He go to store yesterday**, an AI assistant can underline that and suggest **He went to the store yesterday**, thus teaching grammar in context. Over time, the student learns from these corrections. These tools also help with vocabulary, offering synonyms or more academic word choices to elevate a student's writing to the expected level. Early research[26] indicates that integrating AI writing tools can elevate the quality of EFL student writing by providing consistent feedback that teachers might not have time to give on every draft. Of course, a concern is making sure students still learn to write on their own and do not just rely on the AI to fix everything, a balance that educators are navigating by using the tools as teaching aids (showing why a correction is made) rather than just auto-correct crutches.

Text and speech

Another facet of AI in literacy is **text-to-speech** (TTS) and **speech-to-text** (STT) technology. These have been around for a while but have vastly improved with AI. TTS allows any written material to be read aloud by a synthetic voice. Modern AI voices are much more natural-

---

23 Matt Brooks-Green. (2024, July 18). How to use ChatGPT to learn ANY Language (new update) [Video]. YouTube. https://www.youtube.com/watch?v=rC-rBgGy5XE
24 Grammarly: free AI writing assistance. (n.d.). https://www.grammarly.com/
25 Use Smart Compose in Gmail - Computer - Gmail Help. (n.d.). https://support.google.com/mail/answer/9116836?hl=en&co=GENIE.Platform%3DDesktop
26 Marzuki, Widiati, U., Rusdin, D., Darwin, & Indrawati, I. (2023). The impact of AI writing tools on the content and organization of students' writing: EFL teachers' perspective. Cogent Education, 10(2). https://doi.org/10.1080/2331186x.2023.2236469

sounding and even expressive, which helps students who either have visual impairments, dyslexia, or other reading difficulties. For example, a student with dyslexia might use an AI-based screen reader to listen to an article, alleviating the strenuous decoding process and focusing on comprehension. STT, conversely, lets students dictate their ideas and have them transcribed. This is a game-changer for students who struggle with writing due to fine motor issues, dysgraphia, or simply stronger verbal skills than written. A student who can articulate a story but freezes when asked to write can speak into an AI notetaker and see their words appear in text, which they can then edit. The accuracy of such dictation software has improved thanks to AI training on vast speech datasets, even recognizing speech nuances and punctuation cues. What is more, these tools can now handle multiple languages and accents, an area that used to be a limitation. Microsoft's AI[27], as mentioned earlier, includes live captioning and even translates speech in many languages, meaning a deaf student could get real-time captions of classmates' speech, or an English learner could get captions in simpler English or their native tongue.

Alternative communication

AI also assists in **augmentative and alternative communication (AAC)** for students who are non-speaking or have limited speech. Traditional AAC devices (like specialized speech-generating devices for individuals with conditions such as autism or cerebral palsy) are being enhanced with AI to predict what a user intends to say or to offer quicker access to phrases. Some AI-driven AAC apps learn the user's communication patterns and can suggest the next word or phrase, speeding up communication. There are cases where eye-tracking[28] combined with AI, it allows a severely paralyzed student to communicate by merely glancing at certain symbols on a screen, which the AI then converts to spoken language. While this might seem more in the realm of assistive tech than learning, communication is foundational for learning, giving these students a stronger voice means they can participate more in class, ask questions, and demonstrate understanding.

To humanize this, consider a student named *Maria*, a recent immigrant with limited knowledge of English. In a science class, Maria wears earbuds connected to a tablet running a translation AI. As the teacher explains photosynthesis in English, Maria hears key parts of the explanation whispered in Spanish in her ear. She can follow the lesson and even raise her hand to answer a question; if she is unsure how to say it in English, she can speak in Spanish to her tablet and have it output an English sentence for the teacher. Meanwhile, her classmate *John*, who has dyslexia, uses a tablet that highlights and reads aloud the text of the science worksheet, so he does not fall behind in absorbing the content. Another classmate, *Aisha*, who is hard of hearing, benefits from AI-generated captions on the teacher's presentation slides and a tablet that transcribes her classmates' spoken answers so she can read them. And when group work

27 Gibson, R. (2024, September 10). The Impact of AI in Advancing Accessibility for Learners with Disabilities Educause.edu. https://er.educause.edu/articles/2024/9/the-impact-of-ai-in-advancing-accessibility-for-learners-with-disabilities#:~:text=LLMs%20have%20made%20possible%20a,Footnote%2015
28 Eye Tracking Communication for Individuals that are Non-Verbal. (n.d.). cerebralpalsy.org. https://www.cerebralpalsy.org/inspiration/technology/eye-tracking

time comes, an AI chatbot helps guide the group's discussion by keeping them on task and clarifying any confusing vocabulary. In this scenario, AI is acting as a universal translator and communication facilitator, ensuring every student can engage with the content and with each other. This level of inclusiveness was very hard to achieve in the past without multiple human aides; now it is increasingly feasible with the right set of AI tools.

Challenges

Certainly, challenges exist in AI language and communication tools. No machine translation is perfect: nuances and idioms can be mistranslated, so educators must be cautious, as a mistranslation could cause confusion or even offense if not monitored. Thus, these tools are often used as supplements rather than sole channels. Additionally, real-time translation can sometimes lag by a few seconds, which can be disorienting for the learner (imagine laughing at a joke after everyone else because your translation came late). Nonetheless, the technology is improving rapidly. AI speech recognition initially struggled with accuracy; for instance, when *Google* first launched automated *YouTube* captions in 2009, they were often hilariously wrong. But over time, thanks to better algorithms and training data, error rates plummeted. Today's automatic captions (from Zoom meetings to YouTube videos) are far more reliable, and companies are racing to refine emotion and intent detection in speech to make interactions smoother.

Privacy is another consideration: when we use voice AI in the classroom, are those recordings being stored? Many schools ensure that local or offline AI solutions are used to avoid sending kids' voices to the cloud, or they get parent consent for services that do. And with any AI that connects to the internet (like a general chatbot), there is the need for filtering to prevent inappropriate content; schools typically use education-specific platforms or moderated AI interfaces to maintain a safe environment.

From an equity standpoint, one might worry that only well-resourced schools have these fancy translation devices or AI tools, potentially leaving under-resourced schools behind. However, a positive trend is that a lot of AI language tools can run on common devices like smartphones, which are increasingly available even in lower-income communities. There are also open-source and free versions of many tools. The key is awareness and training: teachers and students need to know these tools exist and learn how to use them effectively. We are seeing more professional development focusing on digital tools for multilingual learners, often highlighting AI translation and practice apps as essential aids. Some governments, like those in European countries with many refugee students, actively deploy such technologies in integration programs[29].

AI is enhancing language and communication in education by providing translation, interpretation, practice, and assistive capabilities that help bridge gaps. A student is less likely to be left behind due to a language barrier when AI can translate content on the fly. A shy language learner can practice speaking without fear of judgment by talking to an AI tutor. A

29 Capiche? The smart language assistant for refugees from EIT Digital | EIT. (n.d.). https://eit.europa.eu/news-events/news/capiche-smart-language-assistant-refugees-eit-digital

child with a writing disability can compose an essay by dictation and focus on ideas rather than penmanship. A non-verbal student can speak through an AI-mediated device. These developments all contribute to a more inclusive learning environment where communication, the heart of teaching and learning, is facilitated for everyone. The goal is that differences in language or communication ability no longer dictate a student's educational trajectory; with AI's help, those differences can be accommodated so the student's intellect and creativity can shine through. The following figure illustrates the support AI can offer students:

Figure 6.1: *AI can provide personalized learning for students with diverse learning needs*

Accessibility and special needs support

For students with disabilities and special educational needs, AI technologies are proving to be transformative. They serve as digital ramps and bridges, making curriculum accessible in ways that simply were not possible before. Accessibility in education means ensuring that students with sensory, physical, or cognitive disabilities can perceive content, engage with materials, and express their knowledge. Traditional approaches rely on human support (like sign language interpreters or aides) and specialized tools (like braille textbooks or large-print materials). AI is augmenting and, in some cases, revolutionizing these supports through intelligent, multimedia adaptations. In this section, we explore how AI-driven tools provide accommodations and enhancements, from computer vision that sees for a blind student, to AI tutors that coach students with autism on social skills, to smart software that helps students with executive functioning challenges stay organized. The thread tying these together is personalization for the ability profile of the student, enabling them to access the same curriculum and learning opportunities as others, in an equitable way.

One major area is AI-driven multimedia accessibility. Many students with disabilities need alternative formats of content: blind or low-vision students need text or images described audibly; deaf students need audio information presented as text or sign; students with fine motor impairments need alternatives to manipulating physical objects or handwriting. AI is making it easier to generate these alternative formats automatically. For example, creating alt-text (text descriptions of images for screen readers) used to be a completely manual process, and thus often neglected due to time constraints. Now, AI image recognition can analyze a picture and produce a descriptive caption in seconds. *Arizona State University*[30] recently launched an AI tool that uses a powerful image analysis model (ChatGPT's vision capabilities) to generate rich descriptions of user-uploaded images, even extracting any embedded text within them. This means a teacher can take an infographic or a chart and, with a click, get a descriptive transcript that a blind student's screen reader can read. Similarly, researchers have developed AI that can describe complex graphics like math plots; *MIT's* VisText project[31], for instance, helps generate captions for charts and graphs, which are notoriously hard for blind readers to interpret without description. On the auditory side, automatic captioning has become widely available in classrooms, especially with the proliferation of online learning. Platforms like Zoom or Google Meet provide live AI-generated captions. Microsoft's AI not only captions but can translate speech in real time, as mentioned earlier, which benefits deaf students who may also be non-native speakers of the spoken language (covering two needs at once). What is remarkable is how far the accuracy has come: early versions had significant error rates, but now services boast high correctness, making them dependable enough for daily classroom use.

Another exciting development is audio description generation for videos and animations. This is the narration that describes what is happening visually in a video (commonly used in TV and movies for blind audiences). Traditionally, it is done by humans in post-production. AI is beginning to handle it. For example, a partnership between a firm called WPP[32] and Microsoft is working on AI that can generate enhanced audio descriptions for videos and even museum artwork (check out Microsoft's collaboration with the Rijksmuseum in Amsterdam[33]), broadening access to visual media. In an educational context, think of a science video or a historical documentary used in class, a blind student could listen to an AI-provided track that describes the scenes, graphs, or demonstrations being shown, synchronized with the video playback. This means teachers could use a wealth of multimedia content without worrying about excluding visually impaired students.

Physical accessibility and **mobility** are other areas where AI assists. Robotics and AI vision come together in projects like the *University of Alicante's* NaviLens system[34], an innovation designed to assist visually impaired individuals in navigating urban environments independently. Unlike traditional QR codes, NaviLens uses highly distinctive, high-contrast color codes[35] that can be scanned from a distance and at various angles using a smartphone camera. Once detected, the app instantly provides audio cues, guiding the user with precise location-

30 ChatGPT Edu | Artificial Intelligence. (n.d.). https://ai.asu.edu/chatgpt-edu
31 VisText. (n.d.). https://vis.csail.mit.edu/vistext/
32 Steward, M. (2024, March 11). Let's add audio for visually impaired audiences. WWP. https://www.wpp.com/en-us/wpp-iq/2024/03/lets-add-audio-for-visually-impaired-audiences
33 Microsoft. (2024, March 7). Harnessing the power of AI to make art accessible for all | Microsoft and Rijksmuseum [Video]. YouTube. https://www.youtube.com/watch?v=_wUhAfjJ73g
34 The NaviLens System is Helping Blind Travelers Find Their Way Around Town. (2019, June 6). COOL BLIND TECH. https://coolblindtech.com/the-navilens-system-is-helping-blind-travelers-find-their-way-around-town/
35 NaviLens. (2018, November 23). NaviLens introduction and user's testimonies [Video]. YouTube. https://www.youtube.com/watch?v=nOQaFtaQCvE

based information. This innovation is particularly effective in transport hubs, museums, and educational institutions, where quick access to real-time orientation information is critical. This highlights an important point: accessibility tools do not just help with academics; they help students feel included and capable in the broader social and physical environment of learning, which in turn improves their academic experience. NaviLens can help empower students who have low vision or other vision disabilities by enabling them to independently navigate school buildings using audio-guided directions from high-contrast, scannable codes. This fosters self-confidence and self-reliance, allowing students to access classrooms, libraries, and other resources without constant assistance. AI is a game-changer for these students.

For students who are hard of hearing or deaf, besides captions, AI offers things like real-time sign language avatars. There are experimental AIs that can take speech and produce a signing avatar on screen, or, conversely, take a video of someone signing and translate it to text or voice. While not yet mainstream in classrooms, these show potential for the future in bridging communication between hearing and deaf individuals when a human interpreter is not available. AI can also filter background noise using machine learning (useful for students with cochlear implants or hearing aids in noisy classrooms), essentially smart noise-cancellation focused on speech frequencies. Let us look at the special support provided by AI for people with diverse learning needs:

- **Blind or low vision**
    - AI-generated alt-text for images (e.g., ChatGPT vision at ASU)
    - Audio descriptions for video (e.g., WPP & Microsoft project)
    - Smartphone navigation tools (e.g., NaviLens for indoor and outdoor guidance)
    - ReBokeh app for customizable image enhancement
- **Deaf or hard of hearing**
    - Real-time captions in video calls (Zoom, Google Meet, Microsoft)
    - AI-generated translation for non-native sign language users
    - Speech-to-sign avatars and sign-to-text translation (early experimental)
    - Smart noise filter for cochlear implant users
- **Physical disability**
    - Voice-controlled interfaces and alternative input AI tools
    - AI-integrated robotic support devices and mobility aids
- **Cognitive and learning disability (e.g., autism, ADHD, dyslexia)**
    - AI-powered planners and task management tools for executive support
    - Gamified learning apps customized for focus and motivation
    - Emotion-aware AI that helps adjust pacing and activities in real time
    - Job interview simulation (e.g., CIRVR) for social skill coaching

- **Neurodivergence (autism spectrum, attention differences)**
  - Socially assistive robots (e.g., ZB from Project RAISE) for SEL, inclusion
  - Adaptive AI learning systems for variable attention spans
  - Custom learning sequences based on attention and focus signals
- **Sensory processing disorder**
  - Adaptive screen brightness or audio filtering based on video feedback
  - White noise generators and ambient sound customization tools
  - AI-tuned sensory environment for reduced overstimulation
- **General or multiple disabilities**
  - AI-generated content in a variety of formats (text, audio, video)
  - Multimodal accessibility tools for combined challenges
  - Inclusive design platforms following **web content accessibility guidelines (WCAG)** and user-testing

Moving to cognitive and learning disabilities, AI can be a coach and guide. For example, consider students on the autism spectrum who may struggle with social cues or executive function (organizing tasks, managing time). AI-powered apps are emerging to coach these skills. Researchers have developed a multimodal job interview simulator, CIRVR[36], designed to assist autistic individuals in preparing for job interviews. This system captures and analyzes facial expressions, stress levels, and conversation patterns during simulated interviews. The data collected is used to provide feedback, helping users improve their interview skills and reduce potential biases faced during the hiring process. In education, one of the challenges for neurodivergent students (like those with autism or ADHD) can be executive functioning, keeping track of assignments, breaking tasks into steps, and staying focused amid distractions. AI can help by learning a student's habits and nudging them gently. There are smart planners that use AI to remind a student, **you have a test in 3 days, you should start reviewing now**, or that adapt to how long tasks actually take a student and adjust schedules accordingly. Some apps gamify organization (rewarding students for completing steps of a project on time) and use AI to personalize those rewards or messages in a way that best motivates the individual. These might not be as high-profile as AI tutors, but for certain students, they are immensely valuable support systems operating in the background.

A particularly heartwarming example comes from the *University of Central Florida's* Project[37], **Robotics and Artificial Intelligence to Improve Social Skills for Elementary Students**

36 Adiani, D., Breen, M., Migovich, M., Wade, J., Hunt, S., Tauseef, M., Khan, N., Colopietro, K., Lanthier, M., Swanson, A., Vogus, T. J., & Sarkar, N. (2023). Multimodal job interview simulator for training of autistic individuals. Assistive Technology. https://doi.org/10.1080/10400435.2023.2188907
37 UCP Agency. (2025, January 15). Empowering Students with Disabilities Through Robotics and AI. UCP Central Florida. https://www.ucpcfl.org/post/empowering-students-with-disabilities-through-robotics-and-d-ai

(**RAISE**), which developed Ray-Z, a virtual robot, and ZB, an AI-driven socially assistive robot for children with disabilities. ZB is a small robot that interacts with students to help them practice social and emotional skills while they are also introduced to basic coding skills. It might engage a student in a conversation, model correct behaviors, or simply be a friendly presence that praises the student when they accomplish a task. The notion of a companion robot for special needs students is still novel, but early trials show it can reduce anxiety and create enthusiasm, particularly in kids who might find human peer interactions stressful. It is a good illustration that accessibility is not only about accessing content; it is also about accessing the experience of schooling, making friends, feeling included, and building confidence. AI robots like ZB or AI-driven avatars might play a role in gently mediating social inclusion for those who need it, giving them practice and comfort.

For learners with attention or learning disorders, AI-driven educational games and platforms can adapt to maintain engagement. A student with ADHD might benefit from shorter, varied activities that AI can sequence to keep them interested, versus a long lecture. If the AI senses (through performance or even via webcam emotion detection, where available) that the student is losing focus, it could switch tactics or suggest a short break. This kind of responsive adjustment can help maximize these students' productive learning time, simply by optimizing the learning environment to their needs.

Now, one cannot talk about AI and special needs without addressing the **ethical dimension**. On one hand, there is excitement as AI technology tools hold remarkable promise for providing more accessible, equitable, and inclusive learning experiences for students with disabilities. On the other hand, there is a valid concern that the very group that stands to gain the most could be at risk if the technology is not designed with them in mind. A 2023 survey[38] done by *Fable* found that fewer than 7% of respondents with disabilities felt their community was adequately represented in AI product development, yet 87% were willing to give feedback to improve these tools. This is a call to action: the development of AI accessibility tools must involve the voices of those who use them, to ensure the tools actually meet their needs and are user-friendly. Otherwise, we might end up with fancy AI that theoretically can help, but practically is not adopted by the students who need it. Encouragingly, many companies and universities are now incorporating inclusive design principles, testing with disabled users, and following guidelines like the WCAG[39] in their AI systems.

Cost can be a barrier for advanced assistive tech, but some AI accessibility solutions are relatively cheap or free. For instance, the ReBokeh application[40] is an AI-enhanced tool that assists individuals with low vision by adjusting images through customizable filters and settings, allowing users to better navigate and enjoy their surroundings. This application transforms standard smartphones into personalized assistive devices, enabling users to modify contrast, brightness, and color to suit their visual preferences. Recently, the *Houston Museum*

38 Pillai, A. (2024, February 12). Insights: AI and accessibility. Fable. https://makeitfable.com/article/insights-ai-and-accessibility/
39 Initiative, W. W. A. (n.d.). WCAG 2 Overview. Web Accessibility Initiative (WAI). https://www.w3.org/WAI/standards-guidelines/wcag/
40 Home | ReBokeh. (n.d.). ReBokeh. https://www.rebokeh.com/

of Natural Science[41] partnered with ReBokeh to provide this application for free to visitors with low vision, enhancing their experience by making exhibits more accessible. This collaboration demonstrates how AI-driven solutions can democratize assistive technology, turning standard devices into powerful tools for accessibility. Such initiatives can significantly improve equity in special education and public spaces, offering low-cost, scalable solutions for individuals with visual impairments.

Sensory accommodations via AI also extend to students with sensory processing disorders who may not fit the typical categories of disabled but still need support. For example, for students who are hypersensitive to stimuli, an AI app could adjust the lighting of a computer screen automatically based on a student's comfort (using the webcam to detect squinting or discomfort) or play background white noise to mask sudden sounds if that helps the student concentrate. These kinds of micro-adjustments, while small, can spell the difference between a student feeling at ease or overwhelmed in the learning environment.

Another fascinating area is **biofeedback** and **AI** for attention or focus; there are experimental setups[42] [43] where an AI analyzes EEG or heart rate data of a student to infer when they are overloaded or under-stimulated and then suggests a change in activity. This is more on the cutting edge and raises privacy issues (monitoring physiological data), but it shows how far personalization might go for special needs: truly holistic adjustments, not just academic.

We must also consider that AI is not a panacea: students with severe disabilities will still require human support and specialized instruction. AI tools should be viewed as augmentative. A special education teacher might use AI to generate individualized lesson materials at different reading levels, or to track subtle improvements in a student's behavior through data, but the teacher's expertise in therapeutic techniques and emotional support remains irreplaceable. In the best cases, AI takes over some of the routine tasks so that educators and caregivers can spend more quality time interacting with the student, acting as a force multiplier.

AI is opening new avenues for accessibility and special education by providing tools that adapt content and interactions to the needs of students with disabilities. From automatically describing images for the blind, to reading text aloud, to captioning speech for the deaf, to physically guiding students through school corridors, to coaching those with cognitive or social challenges, the spectrum of AI assistance is broad and growing. The outcomes reported, higher engagement, greater independence, and improved skill acquisition, are heartening. Of course, continued collaboration with the disability community, attention to ethical design, and equitable deployment are necessary to realize AI's full promise in this domain. But the

---

41 Houston Museum of Natural Science expands accessibility options with app for low vision visitors. (2025, February 28). Houston Chronicle. https://www.houstonchronicle.com/news/houston-texas/trending/article/museum-natural-science-accessibility-vision-20058102.php

42 Apicella, A., Arpaia, P., Frosolone, M., Improta, G., Moccaldi, N., & Pollastro, A. (2022). EEG-based measurement system for monitoring student engagement in learning 4.0. Scientific Reports, 12(1). https://doi.org/10.1038/s41598-022-09578-y

43 Ruiz, A. A., & Seco, M. M. (2024). Heart rate variability biofeedback intervention programme to improve attention in primary schools. In researchgate.net. University of the Basque Country. https://doi.org/10.21203/rs.3.rs-4654519/v1

direction is set: a classroom where all materials and experiences are accessible to all students, with AI working behind the scenes to make it so. In that sense, AI becomes an equalizer, helping fulfill the mandate of inclusive education that every student, regardless of ability, deserves the opportunity to learn and succeed in the least restrictive environment possible.

Early intervention and collaboration

Imagine if teachers could know in advance which students are at risk of falling behind or disengaging, so that they could intervene early, perhaps even before a poor test grade or a visible struggle occurs. And imagine if technology could not only alert teachers to these needs, but also facilitate the collaborative efforts (among teachers, students, and parents or guardians) to address them. AI is increasingly enabling early intervention in education through predictive analytics and data-driven alerts. At the same time, AI-powered tools are enhancing collaboration by connecting learners with resources and people in efficient ways. In this section, we examine how AI can function as an early warning system for learning difficulties or dropout risks, and how it supports collaborative learning and teacher-student interaction, creating a more responsive and connected educational ecosystem.

Many schools are now deploying **AI-driven predictive analytics** on student performance data, grades, attendance, engagement metrics, etc., to identify patterns that correlate with challenges. One well-documented example comes from **Georgia State University (GSU)**[44]. They implemented a system often cited as a model: using predictive algorithms, GSU tracks each undergraduate's progress with over 800 risk markers or alerts. These range from missing registration for a required class to getting a low grade in a course crucial for the major to simply having an unexplained absence early in the term. The AI scans all student records daily and when an alert is triggered, it notifies academic advisors so they can promptly intervene. The results have been dramatic: GSU saw tens of thousands of extra advising meetings prompted by these alerts and notably improved student retention and graduation rates. In fact, since adopting this approach, GSU increased its 6-year graduation rate by over 20 percentage points, notably closing achievement gaps for low-income and minority students[45] [46]. The key was catching issues early, for example, if a STEM major gets a C in introductory calculus, that might historically predict trouble in higher-level courses; instead of waiting for the student to fail later, the system flags it immediately so that tutoring or a change of major can be discussed while options are still open.

44 Georgia State University. (2022, June 22). GPS Advising - Student success programs at Georgia State. Student Success Programs at Georgia State. https://success.students.gsu.edu/gps-advising/#:~:text=Georgia%20State%20uses%20predictive%20analytics,get%20students%20back%20on%20track
45 Georgia State University showing success at raising graduation rates via a personalized approach. (n.d.). Hispanic Outlook. https://www.hispanicoutlook.com/articles/georgia-state-university-showing-success-raising-g#:~:text=Georgia%20State%20University%20Showing%20Success,among%20the%20highest%20increases
46 25337pwpadmin@ai_azuread. (2024, January 8). Identify At-Risk Students: a project at Georgia State. Academic Impressions. https://www.academicimpressions.com/how-georgia-state-university-plans-to-use-predictive-analytics-to-address-the-national-achievement-gap/#:~:text=How%20Georgia%20State%20University%20Plans,the%20case%20five%20years%20ago

While GSU's case is in higher education, K-12 schools are also using early warning systems. Districts have started analyzing data as early as elementary school. A traditional teacher might notice some signs but possibly not the full picture, especially across classes or subjects. AI can synthesize multi-dimensional data to highlight that *Student X is trending downward in a concerning way*. Armed with that, a counselor or teacher team can meet the student and parent to investigate what's wrong (maybe there are issues at home, or a bullying situation, or an undiagnosed learning issue) and then provide support (counseling, mentoring, evaluation for special educational services, etc.) much sooner than they otherwise might have. In short, AI helps educators be proactive rather than reactive. This blog from QuadC[47] describes a scenario of a college freshman *Sarah* who started considering drop out; with AI alerts, tutors reached out before she reached a breaking point and helped her get back on track. Without the AI, Sarah's struggles might have been noticed only after midterm exams, possibly too late to salvage the semester.

These predictive tools do raise questions; we must ensure they are accurate and fair (as discussed later in this chapter), but when done right, they can be lifesavers academically. It is like medical early detection: catching a small problem and treating it to prevent a serious illness. Schools using early warning AI have noted improved outcomes such as higher course pass rates and lower dropout rates. For example, a study[48] reported that a community college using an AI-based alert system saw a notable boost in semester-to-semester persistence after implementing it. The collaboration aspect comes in because these alerts often prompt human follow-up: advisors, teachers, and sometimes automated messages reaching out to students. Some systems even send a friendly AI-driven nudge to the student, like, **I see you have not logged into the course in a week. Everything okay? Here is a resource that might help you catch up**. Students often respond to these as if someone's watching out for them, which can be motivating.

Beyond intervention for at-risk students, AI fosters collaboration by connecting the educational stakeholders in smoother ways. For instance, AI-powered communication platforms can translate messages between teachers and non-English-speaking parents (as discussed earlier), ensuring that important information like progress reports or homework tips is effectively communicated, thus enhancing collaboration between school and home. There are also AI tools that summarize class discussions or project group chats, so if a student or teacher misses a collaborative session, they can quickly catch up on what was discussed without wading through transcripts. In group projects, AI can help by tracking contributions and suggesting equitable task distribution (if it notices one student doing most of the edits in a shared document, it might flag that to the teacher or prompt the group to balance the work). This sort

---

47 QuadC. (2024, May 1). How AI-powered Alerts Prevent Student Dropout: An Example. QuadC. https://www.quadc.io/blog/how-ai-powered-alerts-prevent-student-dropout-an-example#:~:text=So%2C%20 what%20if%20there%20was,like%20without%20this%20crucial%20support
48 QuadC. (2024b, May 22). How Predictive Analytics and AI Boost Student Retention Rates. QuadC. https://www.quadc.io/blog/how-predictive-analytics-and-ai-boost-student-retention-rates#:~:text=How%20Predictive%20Analytics%20and%20AI,proactively%2C%20significantly%20boosting%20retention%20rates

of subtle facilitation can teach students collaboration skills – they learn to self-correct when an objective AI mediator points something out.

AI-powered collaboration tools for **students** can also mean intelligent discussion forums and Question-and-answer systems. We touched on the Jill Watson example[49] where an AI answered student questions online. That is a form of collaboration; students are collaborating with an AI agent as well as with each other. On platforms like Piazza[50] or Stack Exchange[51] (commonly used in large classes and technical communities), AI can be employed to detect if a question has already been answered elsewhere and direct the student to that answer, preventing redundant threads and connecting students who have similar queries. It can also moderate forums by detecting toxic or off-topic content, keeping the collaboration space productive and safe. Essentially, AI can act like a skilled teaching assistant in online discussions, grouping related questions, highlighting good student answers, and gently correcting misconceptions that might spread in a peer discussion. By doing so, it helps peer learning communities thrive; students learn from each other with AI ensuring accuracy and inclusiveness.

Let us discuss a few examples of AI-powered collaborative agents that support group problem-solving in math and coding:

- **AlphaEvolve (by DeepMind/Google)**: AlphaEvolve is an AI coding agent powered by Google's Gemini **large language models** (**LLMs**), designed specifically for advanced algorithm design and optimization. AlphaEvolve combines creative problem-solving with automated evaluators that help verify solutions, and it uses an evolutionary framework to improve algorithms iteratively. This agentic experience has been applied to complex mathematical problems and practical computational tasks such as optimizing matrix multiplication and enhancing data center efficiency. Its ability to generate, evaluate, and refine solutions helps make it a powerful collaborative AI agent for coding and math problem-solving, effectively acting like an intelligent partner or teammate in algorithm development and group projects involving complex computations. [52]

- **Multi-agent AI frameworks for collaborative dodging**: Recent advances in multi-agent AI systems enable multiple specialized AI agents to collaborate on complex coding challenges by dividing tasks and critiquing each other's work. For example, frameworks like AutoGen provide a platform to help implement a group chat among AI agents with distinct roles, such as a customer support professional and an enterprise IT administrator. The IT admin helps clarify constraints and assumptions, while the customer support professional helps generate multiple unique problem-solving and debugging options. These agents then iterate through feedback loops to refine and

49 Jill Watson: Using AI and adaptive learning to help teachers and students. (2023, August 25). https://www.onlineeducation.com/features/ai-teaching-assistant-jill-watson
50 Piazza Ask. answer. explore. whenever. (n.d.). https://piazza.com/
51 Hot questions - Stack Exchange. (n.d.). https://stackexchange.com/
52 AlphaEvolve: A Gemini-powered coding agent for designing advanced algorithms. (2025, May 14). Google DeepMind. https://deepmind.google/discover/blog/alphaevolve-a-gemini-powered-coding-agent-for-designing-advanced-algorithms/

select the best approach. This multi-agent collaboration mimics human teamwork and can significantly boost problem-solving efficiency for coding tasks, making it a strong example of AI-powered collaborative agents supporting group coding and math problem-solving.[53]

- **Khanmigo by Khan Academy**: Khanmigo is an AI-powered tutoring and collaboration tool designed for students and educators, which supports interactive problem-solving in subjects like math. It can adapt to individual learning styles and can help guide students step-by-step through problems. Beyond one-on-one tutoring, Khanmigo can also assist teachers by suggesting lesson plans and discussion questions, facilitating interactive group learning environments where students can work alongside the AI as a knowledgeable assistant.[54]

- **From chalkboards to chatbots**: In this Nigerian pilot study, students worked in pairs interacting with Microsoft Copilot (powered by ChatGPT) in after-school sessions to improve their English, digital, and AI literacy skills. While the main focus was on English, the program helped to foster collaborative, problem-solving dialogue as students engaged with the AI tutor and with each other, supported by teachers. The AI helped serve as a virtual partner, adapting responses and encouraging deeper thinking. Though the study's core was about language learning, it references math and coding studies (e.g., Lehmann et al., 2024) to highlight how structured prompting safeguards learning in collaborative coding tasks.[55]

Teacher collaboration with AI is also a piece of the puzzle. Within professional learning communities, teachers can use AI analytics to compare what strategies are working across classrooms. Suppose one 3rd-grade class is excelling in reading comprehension and another is lagging. AI might analyze differences in pacing, types of assignments, or student engagement data and highlight them for the teachers to discuss and learn from each other. Additionally, AI can help coordinate multi-disciplinary projects by aligning curricula; if a History and an English teacher want to collaborate on a joint assignment, an AI could find overlap in their standards and suggest project ideas that hit both sets of goals. These are emerging functionalities in some education management systems, indicating how AI can not only connect students and teachers but also facilitate teacher-to-teacher collaboration for better coherence in instruction.

One exciting frontier is collaborative problem-solving with AI as a participant. We often think of collaboration as human-human, but what if an AI could join a brainstorming session as another participant? Research projects have tried having an AI agent in a student group

53 Ni, B., & J. Buehler, M. (2024, March). MechAgents: Large language model multi-agent collaborations can solve mechanics problems, generate new data, and integrate Kowledge. ScienceDirect. https://www.sciencedirect.com/science/article/abs/pii/S2352431624000117?via%3Dihub

54 Admin_TUL. (2025, March 20). 15 Must-Have AI Tools for Students. The USA Leaders. https://theusaleaders.com/articles/ai-tools-for-students/

55 De SimoneFederico Hernan TibertiMaria Rebeca Barron RodriguezFederico Alfredo ManolioWuraola MosuroEliot Jolomi Dikoru, M. E. (n.d.). From Chalkboards to Chatbots : Evaluating the Impact of Generative AI on learning Outcomes in Nigeria. World Bank. https://documents.worldbank.org/en/publication/documents-reports/documentdetail/099548105192529324. P 4-5.

that poses questions or offers hints when the group is stuck. For instance, in a collaborative learning game, the AI might play the role of a knowledgeable peer or a debate opponent. This can enrich the collaboration; AI can introduce new ideas or challenge faulty reasoning without a teacher needing to be present at all times. Students, especially in online courses, might soon have an AI study buddy that works with them on assignments in a cooperative way (distinct from just giving answers, which would encourage the student to explain their thinking, etc.). This blurs the line between a tool and a collaborator, raising interesting questions of how students perceive learning alongside an AI. Early feedback[56] indicates students can indeed value and form a kind of bond with AI helpers, if it is clear what the AI's role is.

Human oversight remains vital. Early intervention alerts are acted upon by counselors or educators, not by AI alone. Collaborative recommendations are suggestions, not commands. There is a strong consensus that AI should augment human decision-making, not replace it, especially when it comes to sensitive judgments about a student's well-being or grouping dynamics. For example, an algorithm might flag a student as high dropout risk, but the school counselor will interpret that in context (maybe the student had a family crisis that temporarily affected grades; the solution might be different than just tutoring). It is also important to avoid self-fulfilling prophecies; educators are trained to use predictive data as a support, not a label. Indeed, one study[57] on algorithmic early warnings stressed the value of targeting support without bias, ensuring that just because a student is flagged, they are not stigmatized, but rather helped. In practice, this means transparency with students, too; some colleges now inform students of their own risk indicators and available resources, essentially bringing the student into the collaboration loop of solving their academic challenges.

Future prospects are that one can foresee AI-driven educational social networks where students from different schools or countries collaborate on projects, with AI matching them based on interests and language compatibility, and then translating and guiding their collaboration. This would take current exchange programs to a new level, making global collaboration routine. Another prospect is AI as the ultimate teaching assistant that not only helps one teacher, but coordinates across a grade level, ensuring, for example, that a student's teachers in different subjects are all aware if the student is going through a tough time, thereby fostering a team approach to support. We see the beginnings of that in some integrated school data systems.

AI's role in early intervention and collaboration can be summarized as enabling responsiveness and connectivity. The outcome is a more coherent support structure around each learner; many eyes (both human and AI) ensure no one slips through unnoticed, and a richer combination of learning experiences where help and knowledge can come from many sources. In a sense, AI expands the village it takes to educate a child, linking people and insights in a web that holds the student at the center. This, of course, works best when the school culture embraces such data-informed collaboration and when safeguards ensure the AI's suggestions are used

56 Nandkumar, A. (2024, December 2). An AI companion helps students learn to learn | AACSB. https://www.aacsb.edu/insights/articles/2024/12/an-ai-companion-helps-students-learn-to-learn
57 Perdomo, J. C. (n.d.). The Relative Value of Prediction in Algorithmic Decision Making. arXiv, 2312.08511v2 [cs.CY]. https://arxiv.org/html/2312.08511v2#:~:text=The%20Relative%20Value%20of%20 Prediction,those%20that%20need%20them

wisely. When those pieces are in place, schools become proactive, personalized communities of learning, rather than reactive, one-size-fits-all factories. Early wins in this domain strongly suggest that is the right direction.

AI for better teaching by empowering educators

Much of the discussion around AI in education rightfully centers on students, but there is another critical part of the equation: educators. Teachers and professors are the driving force of learning, and AI has the potential to significantly empower them rather than diminish their role. In fact, a guiding principle that emerges repeatedly is that AI should enhance, not replace, human-led teaching. In this section, we focus on how AI supports educators, from smart dashboards that provide real-time insight into student learning, to AI assistants that reduce paperwork and planning burdens, to professional development tools that help teachers continually improve their craft. We will also emphasize why human oversight and expertise remain essential, even as AI takes on some tasks, and how the partnership between AI and teacher can lead to a better educational experience for students.

Dashboards and analytics

One of the most practical tools AI offers teachers is data analytics through dashboards. Instead of relying solely on end-of-term exams or occasional quizzes to gauge understanding, teachers can now get a continuous feed of performance data via AI-powered platforms. For example, if a class is using an adaptive learning app for math, the teacher might have a dashboard that shows, at a glance, which students have mastered today's concept and which are struggling, including a breakdown of which sub-skills or question types gave them trouble. It might highlight that `7 students are still unclear on multiplying fractions`. This immediate insight allows the teacher to adjust tomorrow's lesson (perhaps pulling those seven students for a small-group re-teaching while others move on). Some systems even recommend interventions: `Students A, B, and C would benefit from practicing prerequisite skill X – here's a tailored exercise for them`. The AI essentially analyzes the assessment data and proposes differentiated follow-ups, saving the teacher time in diagnosis. *Panorama Education*[58] and similar platforms use AI to analyze not just academic scores but also survey data on student engagement or **social-emotional learning** (SEL), giving teachers a more holistic view of class wellbeing. In short, AI dashboards function like a smart radar system, scanning multiple signals and bringing important ones to the teacher's attention in real time.

---

58 DeFlitch, S. (2025, March 27). AI in K-12: Empowering Educators and Students. Panorama Education. https://www.panoramaed.com/blog/ai-in-k-12-empowering-educators-and-students#:~:text=AI%20in%20K,more%20personalized%20support%20to%20students

Assessment and grading

Another benefit is AI-assisted grading and assessment creation. Grading stacks of papers or basic homework can consume hours that teachers could instead spend on lesson planning or tutoring. AI is increasingly capable of handling at least the initial pass of grading, particularly for objective or structured responses. For instance, grading multiple-choice or fill-in-the-blank questions can be fully automated. But even for open-ended responses like essays, AI can help by scoring drafts based on rubric criteria or flagging sections that may need teacher attention (like potential plagiarism or an off-topic essay section). Some advanced systems provide feedback to students on their writing, pointing out unclear sentences or weak arguments, which the teacher can then see as well. It is like having a junior grader that does the heavy lifting, after which the teacher can do a quicker review focusing on higher-order feedback rather than basic corrections. Additionally, AI can assist in generating assessments. Need a quick quiz for tomorrow? An AI tool can generate a set of questions (multiple-choice, short answer, etc.) aligned with the day's lesson objectives, even varying difficulty levels. The teacher, of course, will vet and perhaps tweak these questions, but that is far faster than writing from scratch. There are already AI quiz generators that produce item banks from textbook chapters or lesson notes. This not only saves time but can provide more diverse question types (the AI might come up with formats the teacher had not thought of, adding variety to assessments). Importantly, when teachers are freed from some of the drudgery of grading, they can focus more on analyzing results and planning interventions.

Lesson planning

Lesson planning and resource creation are other areas being revolutionized. Teachers often spend evenings crafting lesson plans, designing materials, and searching for the right resources to teach a concept. AI can accelerate this by serving as a creative partner. For example, a teacher can ask an AI (like a large language model) for a draft lesson plan on teaching photosynthesis to 5th graders, including an engaging activity. The AI might produce a structured plan with an opening hook (like showing time-lapse videos of plants), a list of key points to cover (sunlight, chlorophyll, etc.), a lab experiment idea (comparing plant growth in light vs dark), and a closing assessment question. The teacher can then modify, adding their personal touch or adjusting to their class's needs. Essentially, the AI provides a starting blueprint that the teacher refines, and this can be a huge time-saver. Some teachers also use AI to generate creative content like practice problems and story prompts. By leveraging AI in planning, teachers can explore more ideas quickly. However, wise educators treat AI suggestions as drafts. Professional judgement is applied to ensure factual accuracy (AI can sometimes produce incorrect info, *hallucinations*, so teachers fact-check any content), and appropriateness for the specific classroom context. When properly used, though, this is similar to having a tireless teaching assistant with encyclopedic knowledge and a talent for curriculum writing. It is no surprise that a recent national framework in Australia encouraged teachers to pivot to practical applications of

AI in the classroom, particularly in the realm of differentiated learning[59]; teachers are being empowered to co-design learning experiences with AI as a collaborator.

Professional development

Professional development (PD) is also getting an AI upgrade. Traditionally, teacher PD can be one-size-fits-all workshops that may not address individual teachers' growth areas. AI promises to personalize PD for teachers just as it does for students. For example, AI can analyze a teacher's classroom (if video or audio is provided, with due privacy considerations) and give feedback or recommendations. There are experimental platforms[60,61] where an AI *coach* observes a class recording and notes, say, teacher talk time versus student talk time, or how many higher-order questions were asked, then suggests ways to improve engagement. Alternatively, an AI might listen to how a teacher handles a difficult situation (like off-task behavior) and then provide tips or point them to relevant training videos for better strategies. Some systems might combine student outcome data with teaching practice data: if students consistently struggle with fractions district-wide, the system might recommend all math teachers some targeted PD on that topic or connect teachers whose students excel in that area to share practices (basically mining the data to highlight effective techniques and propagate them). This is very powerful because it closes the feedback loop of teaching effectiveness in near real time, something that historically has been hard; teachers often rely on end-of-year test scores, which come too late to adjust in the moment. With AI's analytic help, PD can become more of an ongoing, personalized coaching experience rather than occasional generic workshops.

As artificial intelligence becomes increasingly embedded in the realm of student learning and professional development, a nuanced challenge emerges: how do we integrate this powerful technology without compromising the very essence of human educational expertise? For educators, the rise of AI-powered feedback systems can feel like a double-edged sword— holding immense promise while simultaneously raising valid concerns around deskilling and the erosion of pedagogical autonomy. Rather than relegating educators to passive roles in this evolution, the future of AI in education must be built on human collaboration.

Much like AI-driven service models that thrive on frontline engagement and iterative refinement, the path forward demands a co-design partnership—where teachers are not just users, but directors, producers, and architects. Educator insights should inform what is measured, how feedback is delivered, and how insights are applied. When educators help

59 Enhancing Differentiation in the Classroom using Generative Artificial Intelligence | Academy. (n.d.). https://www.academy.vic.gov.au/resources/enhancing-differentiation-classroom-using-generative-artificial-intelligence#:~:text=While%20initially%2C%20AI%20might%20have,to%20meet%20diverse%20student%20needs

60 Petrilli, M. J. (2024, December 9). Next-Gen classroom observations, powered by AI. Education Next. https://www.educationnext.org/next-gen-classroom-observations-powered-by-ai/

61 AI feedback tool improves teaching practices. (n.d.). Stanford University. https://news.stanford.edu/stories/2023/05/ai-feedback-tool-improves-teaching-practices

shape these systems, they retain agency and reaffirm their expertise. AI must be positioned as a partner to help amplify human expertise, not as a substitute for professional judgment.

By cultivating this collaborative approach, we preserve the art and humanity of teaching and education while enhancing it with timely, data-informed support. This is not about using machines to standardize the classroom experience; it is about unlocking new dimensions of personalized growth for educators and learners alike. In this journey, AI is not the answer—it is a partner and a co-pilot.

Even in formal online courses for teacher training, AI is present as virtual tutors or discussion facilitators, much as with students. For instance, a teacher taking an online course on differentiated instruction might get an AI that answers their questions about the content or provides instant examples relevant to their grade level. This makes the learning process for teachers more supported and adaptive. **International Society for Technology in Education (ISTE)** and other organizations are also hosting AI webinars and sharing prompt libraries[62] specifically for educators, recognizing that equipping teachers with AI skills and tools is crucial.

Now, a critical theme when empowering educators with AI is maintaining human oversight and the teacher's role as the pedagogical leader. AI might analyze data or suggest a plan, but the teacher must make the final call. Teachers bring contextual understanding; they know, for example, that the reason those few students struggled this week is because they were absent due to a community event, so it is not a deep learning issue but a catch-up issue. An AI wouldn't know that context unless informed. Teachers also understand the emotional and social dynamics that data cannot fully capture: maybe a student's drop in participation is because of a personal issue; a teacher might opt for a compassionate one-on-one talk rather than just flagging it as an academic concern.

Ethically, teachers also serve as a check on AI biases or errors. For instance, if an AI grading system seems to systematically give lower essay scores to a particular dialect of English, the teacher needs to notice and correct that, ensuring fairness. Or if an AI-generated quiz question is subtly biased or insensitive, the teacher edits or removes it. In essence, the teacher remains the moral and professional compass in the classroom. The AI is a tool, a very smart and helpful one, but not the decision-maker.

To quote the *World Economic Forum*[63]: *Educational institutions must invest in both AI infrastructure and teacher training, while also ensuring this tech is available to all students.* This highlights that technology and pedagogy have to advance hand in hand. Teachers need training to effectively use AI tools (just handing out software is not enough). They might need to learn new data literacy skills, interpret those dashboard graphs, and understand what an AI can and cannot tell them. However, when they do, it can significantly reduce burnout and improve job

---

62 A fast and fun educator starter guide to using an AI chatbot. (2024, December 13). ISTE. https://iste .org/blog/a-fast-and-fun-educator-starter-guide-to-using-an-ai-chatbot
63 Haoyang, D. L., & Towne, J. (2025, January 9). How AI and human teachers can collaborate to transform education. World Economic Forum. https://www.weforum.org/stories/2025/01/how-ai-and-human-teach-ers-can-collaborate-to-transform-education/

satisfaction by offloading tedious tasks. A survey[64] by the *National Education Association* noted concerns about AI bias, but also interest among teachers in using AI for tasks like lesson planning and administrative duties.

Administrative tasks beyond teaching can also be eased. AI can help principals and support staff with scheduling (AI algorithms to optimize timetables, balancing classes, etc.), with paperwork (filling forms, tracking compliance for IEPs, individualized education programs, with suggestions to streamline writing them). It can also help in analyzing whole-school data for improvement planning, which indirectly empowers teachers by giving them a clearer picture of where to focus. A report[65] by *McKinsey* estimated that teachers spend a large chunk of time on non-teaching tasks; effective use of AI could give back 20% or more of that time to direct student interaction, which is where teachers make the most difference.

One more aspect: emotional support and reduced workload stress. Teacher burnout is a real crisis. By alleviating some burdens, AI might help retain teachers. Also, an AI coach or assistant can sometimes be a sounding board, where teachers bounce ideas or vent frustrations like a journaling exercise to reflect on their day, and the AI responds with encouragement or reframing. It is not a replacement for a human mentor or counselor, but for some, it is beneficial just to articulate and get a response 24/7. There is even exploration of AI providing mindfulness or wellbeing tips to teachers if it detects (via language or usage patterns) that they are stressed.[66]

Ultimately, the teacher plus AI team can outperform either alone. Studies in other fields (like medicine) have shown that an expert with AI assistance is often more accurate than AI alone or an expert alone, because they catch each other's errors. The same is likely in teaching; an AI might flag 90% of struggling students correctly, the teacher notices the other 10% through observational savvy; the teacher might normally reach 80% of kids with a method, but AI personalization picks up the rest who need a different approach. The synergy is powerful. The goal is a classroom where teachers are freed to do what humans do best: inspire, empathize, mentor, and make complex judgments, while AI handles data analysis, routine personalization, and provides a toolbox of resources.

Ethical oversight

It is worth reinforcing the centrality of human oversight and ethical practice. AI introduces concerns about privacy (as it collects student data for those dashboards, schools must secure

64 Greene-Santos, A. (n.d.). Does AI have a bias problem? | NEA. https://www.nea.org/nea-today/all-news-articles/does-ai-have-a-bias-problem#:~:text=2,series%20on%20AI%20in%20education
65 Bryant, J., Heitz, C., Sanghvi, S., & Wagle, D. (2020). How artificial intelligence will impact K-12 teachers. In McKinsey Global Institute [Journal-article]. https://www.mckinsey.com/~/media/McKinsey/Industries/Public%20and%20Social%20Sector/Our%20Insights/How%20artificial%20intelligence%20will%20impact%20K%2012%20teachers/How-artificial-intelligence-will-impact-K-12-teachers.pdf
66 Bryant, J., Heitz, C., Sanghvi, S., & Wagle, D. (2020b). How artificial intelligence will impact K-12 teachers. In McKinsey Global Institute [Journal-article]. https://www.mckinsey.com/~/media/McKinsey/Industries/Public%20and%20Social%20Sector/Our%20Insights/How%20artificial%20intelligence%20will%20impact%20K%2012%20teachers/How-artificial-intelligence-will-impact-K-12-teachers.pdf

that data and use it only for rightful purposes), bias (teachers need to watch out for any algorithmic bias as discussed), and transparency (educators should be open with students about how AI is used in their learning and grading, to build trust and understanding).

When educators are empowered and not threatened by AI, everyone wins. A teacher with a lighter administrative load can spend an extra one-on-one moment with a struggling student or design a creative project that they would not have had time for otherwise. An informed teacher armed with clear diagnostic data can target their teaching more effectively, leading to better student outcomes. The role of the teacher might shift slightly, becoming more of a facilitator and analyst at times, but their importance does not diminish. If anything, it increases; they become the linchpin, ensuring that all these AI interventions align with pedagogical goals and human values. We need AI to free up teachers' time so they can focus on social and emotional learning and the human connection, which AI cannot replace; in other words, use the AI technology to maximize the distinctly human aspects of teaching, not minimize them.

Ethical and practical considerations

As we integrate AI into education to support diverse learners, it is imperative to address the ethical and practical challenges that come along. AI's benefits are plentiful, but they come with strings attached: data privacy concerns, potential biases in algorithms, disparities in access, and the need for sustainable adoption (in terms of cost, training, and infrastructure). Educators and policymakers must navigate these carefully to ensure that AI in education is a force for equity rather than a source of new inequities. This section builds on the ethical principles discussed in *Chapter 10, Data Security and Ethical Considerations in AI*, and serves as a powerful reminder of the importance of responsible AI while focusing on the practical implications of AI adoption in education.

Data privacy and security

AI-powered tools rely on vast amounts of student data, from academic performance to behavioral insights. Schools must ensure compliance with data protection laws like FERPA, United States, GDPR, Europe, and similar regulations worldwide. Best practices include minimizing data collection, using encrypted storage, and implementing rigorous vendor scrutiny to protect student information. For example, AI-powered learning assistants must not store PII unless explicitly authorized by educational institutions. A report from CESA6[67] warns that since AI continuously processes data, schools must rethink cybersecurity policies to safeguard student records.

Transparency, bias and fairness

AI's decisions, whether in grading, student monitoring, or personalized recommendations, must be transparent and explainable. Educators, students, and families should be aware of

---

67 Graf, J. (2024, November 22). Hidden AI Risks in Your School: How to Protect Student Data. CESA6. https://www.cesa6.org/blog/how-to-protect-student-data-from-hidden-ai-risks#:~:text=Hidden%20AI%20Risks%20in%20Your,protect%20their%20students%20and%20teachers

when and how AI is used, ensuring it does not operate as an opaque *black box*. Bias remains a serious concern, as seen in AI-powered proctoring tools that misidentified students of color[68] or falsely flagged ESL students for plagiarism[69]. Addressing these challenges requires diverse training datasets, human oversight, and continuous evaluation to prevent AI from reinforcing existing inequalities.

Equity and access

AI has the potential to bridge learning gaps, but if access is uneven, it risks widening the digital divide. Well-funded schools may adopt sophisticated AI tools, while under-resourced schools struggle with limited technology, training, or internet access. Policymakers must ensure inclusive rollouts, offering open-source AI tools, subsidizing edtech for low-income districts, and ensuring professional development for all educators. Schools can mitigate access issues by providing loaner devices, enabling offline AI functionalities, or extending lab hours for students without home internet.

Sustainability and integration

AI tools must be cost-effective, well-integrated, and supported by professional training. Many schools have invested in technology that was later underused due to poor implementation. Sustainable AI adoption should focus on pilot programs, long-term funding plans, and ongoing teacher support. For instance, designating AI champions or instructional coaches can help ensure successful integration into the classroom.

Balancing AI and pedagogy

AI should enhance, not replace, effective teaching. It is crucial to identify when AI adds value (e.g., personalized feedback) and when traditional methods remain superior (e.g., socratic discussions or creative writing without AI intervention). Schools should teach AI literacy, ensuring students understand when to use AI for learning and when to rely on their own cognitive skills, similar to knowing when to use a calculator versus doing mental math.

Academic integrity and responsible use

With generative AI tools like ChatGPT, educators are rethinking assessment strategies to prevent misuse. Instead of banning AI outright, many schools can adapt by designing AI-resistant assignments (e.g., in-class essays, oral defenses) or incorporating AI into learning (e.g.,

---

68 Clark, M. (2021, April 9). Students of color are getting flagged to their teachers because testing software can't see them. The Verge. https://www.theverge.com/2021/4/8/22374386/proctorio-racial-bias-is-sues-opencv-facial-detection-schools-tests-remote-learning
69 AI detection tools falsely accuse international students of cheating – the Markup. (2023, August 14). https://themarkup.org/machine-learning/2023/08/14/ai-detection-tools-falsely-accuse-international-stu-dents-of-cheating

prompting students to refine AI-generated drafts and justify their edits). Schools are updating honor codes and AI disclosure policies to ensure transparency and responsible usage.[70,71]

AI must be implemented thoughtfully and ethically. Data privacy is not just a tech issue; it is a matter of respecting student and family rights. AI bias is not just a bug; it is a threat to fairness that we have to actively guard against by combining algorithmic scrutiny with human judgment. And equity in AI access is not automatic; it requires policy and investment to make sure every learner can benefit, not just the privileged. The encouraging news is that these challenges are recognized, and many educators and leaders are proactively seeking solutions. Ultimately, the goal is not just to create smarter classrooms; it is to build a fairer, more inclusive, and student-centered educational future.

In this new world of rapid technological change, exciting advances are also occurring in offline and privacy-preserving AI, helping to empower educators to experiment safely and inclusively. Open-source projects like the Awesome LLMs on Device repository[72] and tools such as Jan, GPT4ALL, and Ollama make it possible to run LLMs directly on local machines, ensuring that student data never leaves the classroom local machine and that learning remains confidential[73]. Hardware innovations like the Raspberry Pi AI Kit[74] bring real-time, on-device AI capabilities to affordable, accessible platforms, while technical frameworks such as XenonStack[75] are equipping schools with privacy-preserving techniques like federated learning and differential privacy. Meanwhile, efficient open-source models from Mistral AI[76] are making it possible for even modestly resourced schools to offer advanced AI experiences without sacrificing student privacy or fairness. By leveraging these emerging technologies, educators can design student assessments and learning opportunities that are not only AI-resilient but also maintain the highest standards of equity and student rights, moving us closer to a truly inclusive and student-centered educational future.

Future directions

Looking to the future, what might the next chapter of AI in education hold? Emerging technologies like **augmented reality (AR)**, **virtual reality (VR)**, and emotion-sensing AI stand

70 Generative AI Policy Guidance. (n.d.). Office of Community Standards. https://communitystandards.stanford.edu/generative-ai-policy-guidance

71 Generative AI Policy. (n.d.). Columbia University. Retrieved March 29, 2025, from https://provost.columbia.edu/content/office-senior-vice-provost/ai-policy

72 NexaAI. (n.d.-b). GitHub - NexaAI/Awesome-LLMs-on-Device: Awesome LLMs on Device: A comprehensive survey. GitHub. https://github.com/NexaAI/Awesome-LLMs-on-device

73 G, A. (2025, February 18). The 6 best LLM tools to run models Locally. https://getstream.io/blog/best-local-llm-tools/

74 Raspberry Pi debuts AI kit -- Campus Technology. (2024, June 11). Campus Technology. https://campus-technology.com/articles/2024/06/11/raspberry-pi-debuts-ai-kit.aspx?s=ct_le_030724

75 Gill, N. S. (2025, April 22). Privacy-Preserving AI at the edge. XenonStack. https://www.xenonstack.com/blog/privacy-preserving-ai-edge

76 Dmitrievna, Y. (2025, February 11). The 11 best open-source LLMs for 2025. N8n Blog. https://blog.n8n.io/open-source-llm/

to further transform learning experiences. These may sound like science fiction, but they are rapidly developing and, in some cases, already here.

Consider augmented reality and mixed reality in combination with AI. In special education, AR is being used in pioneering ways: for example, the Empowered Brain project[77] put smart glasses on students with autism that would recognize emotions on peers' faces and cue the wearer on appropriate social responses. This mix of computer vision and AR literally provided augmented social cues to the student, and studies showed it improved their social communication skills.

VR provides fully immersive environments that do not require physical presence. AI can populate VR worlds with intelligent characters and adaptive scenarios, creating lifelike educational simulations. For example, a language learner in VR could be virtually placed in a Parisian marketplace, practicing French conversations with AI-powered vendors, offering a far more engaging and contextualized experience than traditional classroom role-playing.

Field trips could be revolutionized to create inclusive, immersive experiences for students with disabilities or mobility challenges. Instead of being limited by physical accessibility, AI and AR could enhance real-world locations, while VR could offer fully digital experiences for students who cannot travel. For example, at a historical site, AR could reconstruct ruined structures in real-time, allowing students to explore how they originally looked. AI-powered virtual guides and avatars of historical figures could provide interactive, personalized tours, adapting explanations to different learning needs. For students with mobility limitations, AR-enhanced tours could make on-site visits more accessible by providing alternative navigation options, audio descriptions, or visual overlays that highlight key details. For students with severe mobility challenges who cannot easily go on traditional field trips, VR enables travel experiences that would otherwise be impossible. They could explore the Amazon rainforest, walk through the *Great Pyramids of Giza*, or even visit outer space, all from the classroom or home.

By leveraging both AR and VR, educators can ensure that all students, regardless of physical ability, can fully engage with the world, whether through enhanced real-world experiences or completely immersive virtual explorations.

The case study of *Virtual Labs*[78] at *Tec de Monterrey Campus Puebla* in *Mexico* hints at this future: students perform science experiments in an AI-driven virtual lab, allowing more experimentation than the physical lab constraints allow. This facility combines a physical laboratory team with virtual laboratories to investigate the teaching and learning of process control and automation in a cyber-physical environment. Such simulations will get more sophisticated, potentially with haptic feedback (touch) and multi-sensory involvement, giving

77 Sahin, N. T., Abdus-Sabur, R., Keshav, N. U., Liu, R., Salisbury, J. P., & Vahabzadeh, A. (2018). Case study of a digital augmented reality intervention for autism in school classrooms: associated with improved social communication, cognition, and motivation via educator and parent assessment. Frontiers in Education, 3. https://doi.org/10.3389/feduc.2018.00057

78 Villanueva, A. (2025, January 29). Research Trends: Living Lab & Data Hub. TecScience. https://tec-science.tec.mx/en/tech/living-lab-data-hub/

vocational training or science labs a new dimension without the cost or danger of physical materials (imagine a chemistry student safely experimenting with volatile reactions in VR guided by AI, mastering procedures before doing it for real).

Perhaps one of the most fascinating developments is emotion-sensing AI, sometimes called affective computing. These AI systems aim to detect learners' emotional states (like confusion, frustration, or boredom) through various signals, facial expressions, voice tone, posture, and even physiological indicators like heart rate. The idea is to enable the AI or the educator to respond to the student's affective needs, not just their cognitive needs. For example, if an AI tutor notices a student getting frustrated after multiple wrong attempts, it might change its approach, perhaps give motivational encouragement, switch to an easier problem to rebuild confidence, or alert the human teacher that the student might need some reassurance. In a classroom, emotion recognition could help teachers identify who is silently struggling or who is losing interest, allowing them to intervene more sensitively. This technology is still maturing, and it raises privacy questions (*do we want cameras watching students' faces all class?*). Some schools in China made the news[79] by using cameras to track whether students looked attentive, which spurred a lot of debate. If used with care and consent, emotion AI could add a missing layer to online education, which currently lacks the real-time empathy a teacher in person might have. Perhaps while taking an online course, AI will notice you are consistently skipping video lectures halfway through. It might ask if you are feeling unengaged and adjust the content or notify a mentor. A robot companion for a child with anxiety might detect rising stress and guide them through a calming exercise.

Another future direction is AI-driven creative tools for students, beyond tutoring. We might see AI become a partner in creativity: helping students compose music, create art, design games, or write stories. For instance, a student writing a short story could have an AI co-author suggest plot twists or help flesh out characters, similar to how a writing buddy might, but under the student's control. This can spur imagination and also teach students how to critically accept or reject AI suggestions, a key skill. In maker education, an AI assistant might help students troubleshoot a coding project or optimize a design, making project-based learning more powerful.

Lifelong and life-wide learning will also be impacted. As students graduate into adulthood, the AI learning supports might follow them: personalized learning companions that continue to help in college or on the job. There is talk of personal AI that knows your learning history and preferences throughout your life, making education a continuous, personalized journey.

Conclusion

In this chapter, we saw how AI can adapt to learners' differences, whether they stem from disabilities, language barriers, or simply individual paces and styles of learning. And this underscores an inspiring reality: when thoughtfully applied, AI can help fulfill the longstanding dream of education that truly meets each learner where they are.

79 Chan, M. (2021, February 17). This AI reads children's emotions as they learn. CNN Business. https://edition.cnn.com/2021/02/16/tech/emotion-recognition-ai-education-spc-intl-hnk/index.html#:~:text-t=CNN%20www,are%20raised%2C%20the%20machine

Yet, another theme is that AI is not a magic wand. Its success depends on human guidance, ethical deployment, and supportive infrastructure. In every successful application, it is the combination of AI, the educator, plus the student's effort that leads to success. A personalized learning app worked because teachers integrated it well and students engaged with it. A translation tool made a difference because teachers welcomed non-English speakers and leveraged the tool to communicate, building trust. The human element is irreplaceable; AI amplifies human potential but does not replace human relationships. As such, one insight is that professional development and policy must evolve alongside AI. Teachers need training to harness AI tools effectively and ethically. Administrators need to consider equity and data protection in their tech plans. Students themselves need to learn about AI (both how to use it and how it works) as part of becoming digitally literate citizens. It is worth noting that forward-thinking curricula are starting to incorporate AI literacy, ensuring the next generation comprehends the algorithms that increasingly influence society. Ultimately, an education system that embraces AI must also double down on human values, empathy, inclusion, and critical thinking, because those are what will guide the technology to be used for good.

In the next chapter, we will take a look at how students can prepare for a future in the AI-driven workforce, from understanding what it is to exploring how to get there. It is about preparing for a future that is largely undefined and constantly changing. We will see how the classroom and the real world come together in an AI powered future.

Questions

1. How can educators and administrators help ensure that AI tools used in our classrooms are inclusive by design and not just retrofitted for students with diverse learning needs?

2. What strategies can we develop to identify and mitigate potential biases in AI systems that could affect students from underrepresented or neurodiverse populations?

3. What steps are we taking to balance AI-driven personalization with collaborative learning experiences to maintain a sense of classroom community?

4. What training or support do educators need to confidently and ethically integrate AI tools into differentiated instruction and what can we do to ensure this support is provided?

5. In what ways can AI-powered early warning systems be ethically implemented to support students at risk without singling them out or stigmatizing them?

6. How can AI-driven language and communication tools increase parent engagement, especially with families who speak languages other than English?

7. What partnerships or funding strategies can we explore to ensure equitable access to AI tools for students with high needs in under-resourced schools or districts?

Exercises

1. **Mapping diverse learner profiles**: Identify the range of diverse learners in your community and assess existing support for them.

   a. List at least five varieties of diverse learners in your school or district (e.g., students with dyslexia, ELLs, gifted learners, students with ADHD).

   b. For each type:

      i. Describe one specific challenge they face.

      ii. Identify one AI-based solution (existing or conceptual) that could help support them.

   c. **Reflect**: Are there learner groups in your environment that currently receive limited or no targeted support? How can AI assist here?

2. **AI-powered personalization audit**: Evaluate the role of AI in helping to personalize instruction.

   a. Choose one subject, grade level or learner type that you are familiar with.

   b. Describe how differentiation currently occurs in that setting.

   c. Envision how AI could improve personalized learning:

      i. How would AI adapt content in real time?

      ii. How would students and learners receive feedback?

      iii. What would change for the educator?

   d. What would be the biggest obstacles to implementing this vision?

3. **Reflection—Language and communication**: Investigate how AI can help to reduce language and communication barriers.

   a. **Example scenario:** A student named Fatima has recently arrived from Syria and speaks little English. She is eager to learn but struggles to keep up and communicate in class.

      i. List three ways that AI tools might help Fatima participate more fully in class.

      ii. Identify potential risks of relying on technology (e.g., over-reliance, accuracy, equity).

      iii. How might teachers and staff ensure that Fatima's family stays informed and engaged?

4. **Planning for accessibility**: Determine how to leverage AI for common classroom activities.

    a. Choose a common classroom activity (e.g., presenting a book report, solving a math problem set, discussing current events).

    b. For each of these learner types, describe their potential barriers:

        i. A student with visual impairment.

        ii. A student with ADHD.

        iii. A student with limited speech.

    c. Research one AI tool or adaptation for each case.

    d. Beyond AI tools, what teacher involvement would still be necessary for full inclusion?

5. **Ethical AI discussion**: Reflect on the ethical and responsible use of AI in schools.

    a. **Prompt:** An AI system at your school flags learners who are at risk based on behavior and attendance. One flagged student recently lost a parent.

        i. What are the benefits and risks of using such a system? Where are humans involved?

        ii. What ethical concerns arise (e.g., bias, student privacy, stigmatization)?

        iii. Who should be involved in responding to the alert?

        iv. Draft a 2–3 sentence policy statement that reflects your values around AI-driven intervention.

6. **Vision—The AI-ready inclusive school**: Envision the future of AI and inclusion in your learning environment.

    a. Complete the following sentence:

    In our AI-ready school, every student feels _____ because AI helps _____.

    b. Then list:

        i. Three priorities for responsible and inclusive AI use in your setting.

        ii. Two actions needed to prepare educators and administrators.

        iii. One way to include student or family representation in AI implementation decisions.

CHAPTER 7

Preparing for an AI-driven Workforce

You can't stay in your corner of the forest waiting for others to come to you. You have to go to them sometimes.

-Winnie the Pooh

Introduction

Today's students are invited and walking on stage to take on one of the most exciting challenges of a generation: preparing for a future where AI transforms how we work, solve problems, and create change. By building the right skills, embracing curiosity, and thinking boldly, this future generation can help shape the future, not just adapt to it.

Throughout history, one of the important goals of educators has been to prepare the next generation to enter the workforce. AI is rapidly transforming the global labor market, automating routine tasks and augmenting human capabilities across industries. This transformation is reshaping employment patterns, and by extension, influencing the world of education.[1] While AI-driven automation threatens to displace certain jobs, it also promises to generate new roles and boost productivity. As a result, the skills valued by employers are evolving, workers are racing to adapt, and educators are seeking to understand how this influences the classroom.

Back in the 1950s, management thought leader *Peter Drucker* introduced the idea of the knowledge worker and the creative class. Now, these knowledge workers, these skill sets,

---

1 Artificial intelligence in education. (2024, December 17). ISTE. https://iste.org/ai

are beginning to be enhanced, augmented, and perhaps eventually replaced by AI. When we compare the curriculum in the 1930s to that of the 1970s, there was a shift towards the new requirements of knowledge worker jobs. Fast forward to the 2020s, and we have internet, mobile technology, automation, and AI in the world of work. Breakthroughs in multimodal generative AI make that point even sharper, accelerating a shift from single-format automation to all-media collaboration. These multimodal tools expand what AI can automate or augment, and they raise the bar for human workers, who will need to orchestrate, critique, and collaborate with systems that move effortlessly among formats once handled by separate specialists.

Structure

This chapter covers the following topics:

- Understanding the AI-driven workforce
- Skill sets for the AI era
- Classroom strategies and curriculum design
- Educator roles and professional development
- Bridging the classroom and the real world
- Continuous innovation

Objectives

This chapter aims to equip educators and institutions with the tools, mindsets, and strategies necessary to prepare students for a workforce shaped by AI. It argues that as AI becomes an integral part of every industry, education must evolve to help learners not just adapt but lead in this transformation. This chapter is both a call to action and a practical guide for reimagining education in the AI era.

Understanding the AI-driven workforce

Let us discuss how AI is changing the global job market. Automation is displacing certain roles while creating new ones, particularly in data science, cybersecurity, and creative fields enhanced by technology. The concept of new-collar jobs, tech-savvy roles that do not require four-year degrees, is highlighted as a key opportunity for students from diverse backgrounds. Now, foundation models can parse and generate text, code, images, audio, and even short videos in the same conversational flow. A software engineer can now paste a sketch of a user interface alongside bug logs and ask the model for refactored code; a product designer can upload a photo of a prototype and receive voice-over marketing copy plus a rendered explainer image moments later. In newsroom pilots, editors dictate rough story notes while dropping phone-shot footage into the prompt, and the AI returns a captioned clip ready for social channels. Even video creation is on the cusp of automation: OpenAI's Sora text-to-video model (publicly previewed in 2024) has film-industry analysts asking how storyboarding, animation, and post-production roles will evolve when high-fidelity clips can be generated from a paragraph prompt[2].

Pervasive automation and data-centric decision making

AI and automation technologies are influencing, if not changing entirely, the nature of work on a global scale. Recent studies estimate that almost 40% of jobs worldwide are already exposed to AI disruption. Advanced economies face the greatest risk of impact; about 60% of jobs in high-income countries could be affected by AI, versus ~40% in emerging markets and 26% in lower-income economies. Unlike earlier waves of automation that mainly replaced routine manual tasks, today's generative AI can perform complex cognitive tasks, which unlocks the ability to automate highly skilled tasks. At the same time, AI can often complement human labor rather than act as a pure substitute. For roughly half of the jobs considered, this technology is expected to augment or enhance roles through improved productivity, while the other half may experience the potential of a more direct task automation that reduces labor demand.[3] In practical terms, AI might take over certain aspects of a given job (for example, data processing or basic content generation), but in doing so, AI could liberate workers to focus on higher-value activities. This potential for augmentation means AI could help boost productivity and economic growth. One study projects that combining generative AI skills along with other technologies could help raise productivity growth by up to a few percentage points annually.[4]

However, the extent of AI adoption will depend on the economic feasibility; some researchers note that beyond the initial wave of readily automatable tasks, further automation will happen more gradually as technical and cost barriers are overcome.[5]

A *June 2025 Business Insider* feature[6] on radiology departments reports that large U.S. hospital chains using generative AI report-drafting assistants cut clerical time by up to 30 percent,

2 Oxford, D. (2024, March 31). Could OpenAI's Sora text-to-video generator kill off jobs in Hollywood? Al Jazeera. https://www.aljazeera.com/news/2024/3/29/what-is-openais-sora-text-to-video-generator

3 AI will transform the global economy. let's make sure it benefits humanity. (2024, January 14). IMF. https://www.imf.org/en/Blogs/Articles/2024/01/14/ai-will-transform-the-global-economy-lets-make-sure-it-benefits-humanity#:~:text=The%20findings%20are%20striking%3A%20almost,emerging%20market%20and%20developing%20economies

4 Chui, M., Hazan, E., Roberts, R., Singla, A., Smaje, K., Sukharevsky, A., Yee, L., & Zemmel, R. (2023). The economic potential of generative AI. In The economic potential of generative AI: The next productivity frontier. https://www.mckinsey.de/~/media/mckinsey/locations/europe%20and%20middle%20east/deutschland/news/presse/2023/2023-06-14%20mgi%20genai%20report%202023/the-economic-potential-of-generative-ai-the-next-productivity-frontier-vf.pdf

5 Fleming, M., Thompson, N. C., & Li, W. (2024, August 29). The last mile problem in AI. Brookings. https://www.brookings.edu/articles/the-last-mile-problem-in-ai/#:~:text=labor%20automation%20should%20occur%20in,be%20more%20gradual%20than%20abrupt

6 Smith, M. S. (2025, June 6). AI isn't replacing radiologists. Instead, they're using it to tackle time-sucking administrative tasks. Business Insider. https://www.businessinsider.com/radiology-embraces-generative-ai-to-streamline-productivity-2025-6

letting radiologists focus on complex reads; yet the same article notes that FDA rules still bar these tools from primary diagnosis and that data scarcity limits accuracy on rare conditions. On the factory floor, predictive-maintenance AI is moving from pilot to scale. BMW's Regensburg plant uses an AI vision system that flags conveyor faults early, saving more than 500 minutes of annual downtime, according to a BMW press release[7]. Generative chatbots are now front-line workers: a Harvard Business Review article[8] notes that 85 percent of service leaders are piloting AI agents for returns and troubleshooting, with early adopters citing faster resolution times and higher customer-satisfaction scores.

In any case, AI is poised to help reshape millions of jobs, and policymakers are closely watching these trends to figure out how to manage the transition. Notably, advanced economies may see faster adoption of AI technologies (due to higher labor costs and more AI-ready infrastructure), raising concerns about the widening of inequalities if other regions lag in leveraging AI's benefits.[9]

Hybrid human-AI teams and shift in required skill sets

Even though we may not realize it, we have been in this hybrid world, arguably, for decades. Think about something as simple as a handheld calculator or a Google Search. Students who were good with the calculator stood out. Workers or researchers who mastered advanced search techniques had an advantage. Today, those with cutting-edge prompt engineering skills are more productive. This gap between the skilled in technology and the unskilled will continue to grow. Hybrid workers will have an increasing advantage.

Recent case studies from 2024-25 show how hybrid really works. BMW's Spartanburg plant completed a months-long pilot in which Figure 02 humanoid robots inserted sheet-metal parts alongside technicians; humans handled calibration, quality checks and problem-solving, while the robots took over the most physically demanding, unsafe and repetitive tasks.[10]

7 Predictive maintenance at BMW Group Plant Regensburg – AI-supported system monitors conveyor technology during assembly +++ Integrated, learning maintenance system identifies potential faults early, avoiding more than 500 minutes of vehicle assembly disruption every year. (n.d.). BMW Group PressClub. https://www.press.bmwgroup.com/global/article/detail/T0438145EN/smart-maintenance-using-artificial-intelligence?language=en

8 Gartner survey reveals 85% of customer service leaders will explore or pilot Customer-Facing Conversational GenAI in 2025. (2024, December 9). Gartner. https://www.gartner.com/en/newsroom/press-releases/2024-12-09-gartner-survey-reveals-85-percent-of-customer-service-leaders-will-explore-or-pilot-customer-facing-conversational-genai-in-2025

9 AI will transform the global economy. let's make sure it benefits humanity. (2024b, January 14). IMF. https://www.imf.org/en/Blogs/Articles/2024/01/14/ai-will-transform-the-global-economy-lets-make-sure-it-benefits-humanity

10 BMW Group Plant Spartanburg and California robotics company Figure test the use of humanoid robots in production +++ Latest generation of robots, Figure 02, successfully completes testing in a real production environment +++ Board Member Nedeljković: "determining possible applications for humanoid robots in production"+++. (n.d.). BMW Group PressClub. https://www.press.bmwgroup.com/global/article/detail/T0444265EN/successful-test-of-humanoid-robots-at-bmw-group-plant-spartanburg?language=en

BMW's production team reports the collaboration reduced ergonomic strain on workers and trimmed cycle time in the chassis body shop, proving that human skills in supervision and exception-handling become more—not less—valuable when AI-driven robotics enter the line. Finance offers perhaps the clearest proof of how hybrid teams outperform. At *JPMorgan Chase*, the generative-AI assistant branded Coach AI (also called *Connect Coach*) was rolled out to roughly 7,600 wealth-management advisers in early 2025. Integrated directly into the advisers' desktops, the system digests the bank's vast research library plus each client's portfolio history and, via plain-language prompts, surfaces market briefs, exposure gaps and even draft emails or call scripts in seconds. During the market turbulence of April 2025, Coach AI helped advisers locate the right information up to 95 percent faster, allowing them to field a surge in anxious investor calls while keeping conversations highly personalized. JPMorgan reports the efficiency boost underpinned a 20 percent year-on-year rise in gross asset-management sales between 2023 and 2024 and is expected to let advisers expand their client books by about 50 percent over the next three to five years as routine research is automated.[11]

Job displacement and emerging opportunities

Fears of widespread job displacement are tempered by this type of evidence that AI will also create new employment opportunities. Forecasts generally predict significant churn in the labor market, with jobs lost to automation and new jobs gained through new tech-driven demand. For example, the **World Economic Forum (WEF)** projected that about 85 million jobs could be displaced globally by 2025 due to increased AI and automation, yet around 97 million new roles may emerge in fields like data science, AI, and engineering, yielding a net gain in jobs.[12]

More recent WEF analysis extends this timeline and still foresees a positive net growth: roughly 170 million new jobs could be created this decade (about 14% of current employment), even as 92 million jobs are displaced, resulting in a net increase of 78 million jobs by 2030.[13]

A new joint study[14] from the United Nations labor agency and Poland's National Research Institute, transforming job descriptions, not widespread job loss, is the more likely result. The new Geneva-based **International Labour Organisation (ILO)**, in collaboration with Warsaw-based **National Research Institute (NASK)** (ILO-NASK) Global Index released in May 2025,

11 JPMorgan says AI helped boost sales, add clients in market turmoil. (2025, May 5). Reuters. https://www.reuters.com/business/finance/jpmorgan-says-ai-helped-boost-sales-add-clients-market-turmoil-2025-05-05/
12 Koh, R. (2023, February 17). Welcome to the age of "AI-nxiety," in which anxiety about AI taking over our jobs and lives is at the top of everybody's minds. Business Insider. https://www.businessinsider.com/ai-anxiety-about-losing-our-jobs-2023-2#:~:text=In%20October%202020%2C%20the%20World,a%20faster%20rate%20than%20anticipated
13 Leopold, T. (2025). Future of Jobs Report 2025: The jobs of the future-and the skills you need to get them. In World Economic Forum. World Economic Forum. https://www.weforum.org/stories/2025/01/future-of-jobs-report-2025-jobs-of-the-future-and-the-skills-you-need-to-get-them/#:~:text=,likely%20need%20in%20the%20future
14 AI threatens one in four jobs – but transformation, not replacement, is the real risk. (2025, May 22). UN News. https://news.un.org/en/story/2025/05/1163486

finds that one in four jobs worldwide is highly exposed to generative-AI automation, with office and secretarial functions topping the risk list. In high-income countries, the gender gap is stark: 9.6 percent of female employment versus 3.5 percent of male employment (nearly three times the share for men) sits in roles deemed at high risk of full automation, given the over-representation of women in clerical and administrative positions.

The *International Federation of Robotics' World Robotics 2024* update[15] records 4.28 million industrial robots active on factory floors, a 10 percent jump year-on-year, and notes that annual installations (541,000 units in 2023) are expected to re-accelerate through 2027, with China alone targeting 5–10 percent average yearly growth in its robot stock. Automotive, electronics, and metal-machinery plants remain the center of this deployment wave, steadily shifting demand from line-assembly workers to robot-cell technicians, vision-system engineers and safety integrators.

AI and related macro-trends are expected to eliminate certain jobs, roles, and occupations. As we've seen throughout history, the technology influx will also generate many new jobs as workers transition into emerging roles. Historically, technology revolutions (from mechanization to the internet) have eventually produced more jobs than they destroyed, and many experts believe AI should follow a similar pattern.[16] That said, the disruption will be nontrivial: by one estimate, up to 25%–30% of hours worked in today's economy could be automated by 2030 in major markets under midpoint adoption scenarios[17], necessitating large-scale workforce adjustments.

Many routine-based occupations are projected to decline significantly by 2030, while new types of jobs are on the rise. The WEF's *Future of Jobs Report 2025* highlights the roles expected to see the greatest growth and the steepest declines as a result of automation and other structural trends. Jobs involving repetitive or predictable tasks are most vulnerable to displacement by AI or robots. For example, positions like cashiers, bookkeeping clerks, and data entry clerks rank among the fastest-declining roles as AI and digital systems take over their duties. Similarly, administrative assistants, ticket clerks, and many accounting and auditing roles are forecast to drop. It is an interesting world because, as AI can start to write code, software developers find themselves on the list of questionable future roles. Beyond the tech sector, growth is also expected in areas less easily automated or spurred by new needs, for example, green economy jobs, such as renewable energy engineers, health and care professions, driven by aging populations, such as nursing and social work, and roles in transportation and the skilled trades could be on the rise. Notably, some of the largest absolute job gains may occur in human-

15 IFR International Federation of Robotics. (n.d.). Record of 4 million robots in factories worldwide. https://ifr.org/ifr-press-releases/news/record-of-4-million-robots-working-in-factories-worldwide
16 Koh, R. (2023b, February 17). Welcome to the age of "AI-nxiety," in which anxiety about AI taking over our jobs and lives is at the top of everybody's minds. Business Insider. https://www.businessinsider.com/ai-anxiety-about-losing-our-jobs-2023-2#:~:text=But%20all%20hope%20is%20not,lost%2C%20some%20experts%20say
17 Hazan, E., Madgavkar, A., Chui, M., Smit, S., Maor, D., Dandona, G. S., & Huyghues-Despointes, R. (2024, May 21). A new future of work: The race to deploy AI and raise skills in Europe and beyond. McKinsey & Company. https://www.mckinsey.com/mgi/our-research/a-new-future-of-work-the-race-to-deploy-ai-and-raise-skills-in-europe-and-beyond

centric occupations like agriculture and construction, which remain fundamental to emerging economies and are influenced by sustainability initiatives.[18] The coexistence of declining and emerging jobs underscores that AI is not simply taking all jobs but rather shifting the nature of the workforce. Workers in shrinking occupations will need assistance to retrain and move into growing fields, so that the benefits of new technology can be widely shared. Indeed, many of the new jobs being created will require human skills that sit side-by-side and complement AI, for example, roles designing, managing, and collaborating with AI systems, or providing the creative, empathetic and complex thinking that machines cannot easily replicate.[19]

The ethical conversation around AI and work has coalesced around a striking tension: whose interests are advanced when algorithms begin to shoulder tasks once assigned to people. At the *World Economic Forum's Labor Day* briefing[20], experts warned that although AI-driven innovation could still unlock the 170 million new roles the Forum projects for this decade, 40 percent of employers already expect headcount cuts in functions they can automate, especially at the entry-level, raising fresh equity questions about who even gets a first rung on the career ladder. The **Organisation for Economic Co-operation and Development's (OECD)** May 2025 policy brief[21] sharpened the dilemma by highlighting a *Big Unknown*: roughly 281 million workers (about nine percent of the global labor force) whose future hinges on policy choices still to be made, arguing that social dialogue and skills-funding decisions taken now will determine whether that cohort is augmented or displaced. Academic critics have grown skeptical that traditional solutions will suffice: a Brookings analysis[22] finds the historical record of large-scale retraining *mixed at best*, urging governments to rethink how reskilling is funded and evaluated before relying on it as a moral safety valve for AI disruption. Meanwhile, an ILO-backed study[23] on the *invisible workers* who label data and moderate toxic content exposes another ethical blind spot: many supposedly automated systems are propped up by low-paid crowd-labor, often without adequate protections, underscoring that the real ethical test is not just how many jobs AI creates or destroys, but whose labor and welfare are rendered invisible in the process.

18 Leopold, T. (2025). Future of Jobs Report 2025: The jobs of the future-and the skills you need to get them. In World Economic Forum. World Economic Forum. https://www.weforum.org/stories/2025/01/future-of-jobs-report-2025-jobs-of-the-future-and-the-skills-you-need-to-get-them/#:~:text=,likely%20need%20in%20the%20future
19 Koh, R. (2023b, February 17). Welcome to the age of "AI-anxiety," in which anxiety about AI taking over our jobs and lives is at the top of everybody's minds. Business Insider. https://www.businessinsider.com/ai-anxiety-about-losing-our-jobs-2023-2#:~:text=But%20all%20hope%20is%20not,lost%2C%20some%20experts%20say
20 How AI is reshaping the career ladder, and other trends in jobs and skills on Labour Day. (2025). In World Economic Forum. World economic Forum. https://www.weforum.org/stories/2025/04/ai-jobs-international-workers-day/
21 Policy Brief: Generative AI, Jobs, and Policy Response - OECD.AI. (n.d.). https://oecd.ai/en/wonk/documents/policy-brief-generative-ai-jobs-and-policy-response
22 Jacobs, J. (2025, May 16). AI labor displacement and the limits of worker retraining. Brookings. https://www.brookings.edu/articles/ai-labor-displacement-and-the-limits-of-worker-retraining/
23 Article, S. F. (2024, December 19). The Artificial Intelligence illusion: How invisible workers fuel the "Automated" economy. SwissCognitive | AI Ventures, Advisory & Research. https://swisscognitive.ch/2024/12/19/the-artificial-intelligence-illusion-how-invisible-workers-fuel-the-automated-economy/

Continuous learning and upskilling

As AI reshapes job profiles, the skill sets valued by employers are changing rapidly. A common theme in recent research and employer surveys is that employees having technical skills alone are not enough; the highest-demand skills of the future combine digital literacy with strong human-centric abilities.[24] According to the WEF, employers expect that approximately 39% of core skills for workers will change by 2030 (a slight easing from a 44% skill-change rate seen in 2023).[25] These statistics reflect the significant disruption to job requirements brought by AI and other trends. On the technical side, digital and data competencies are increasing in importance. AI and big data skills top the list of fastest-growing skills and capabilities that employers seek, followed by expertise in networks, cybersecurity, and general technological literacy.[26] In essence, as companies adopt AI technology and data analytics, they need workers who can develop, manage, or at least effectively utilize these technologies. For example, in fields from marketing to manufacturing, it is becoming essential to understand how to work with AI tools and interpret data insights. We need to be exposing students to these new and rapidly changing technologies.

Global employers are turning their reskilling pledges into concrete results. Google's latest *Career Certificates Impact Report*[27] reveals that the program has now graduated more than one million learners worldwide, over 350,000 in the United States alone, and that 70 percent of U.S. alumni report a positive career outcome, such as a new job or promotion. To keep the momentum, every certificate track now bundles an *Accelerate Your Job Search with AI* micro-course so that graduates learn to wield generative-AI tools as they re-enter the labor market. Microsoft, meanwhile, is scaling region-specific initiatives[28] on top of its long-running Skills for Jobs drive. During its Johannesburg AI Tour, the company committed to train one million South Africans in AI and cybersecurity skills by 2026, noting that it has already up-skilled four million Africans in the past five years and set a stretch goal of reaching 30 million more across the continent over the next five years. IBM's SkillsBuild[29] platform marks another milestone: the program now operates in 168 countries and has supported more than two million learners, according to IBM's updated overview page. In May 2025, the company deepened that effort

24 AI4K12. (n.d.). AI4K12. https://ai4k12.org/

25 Leopold, T. (2025). Future of Jobs Report 2025: The jobs of the future-and the skills you need to get them. In World Economic Forum. World Economic Forum. https://www.weforum.org/stories/2025/01/future-of-jobs-report-2025-jobs-of-the-future-and-the-skills-you-need-to-get-them/#:~:text=,likely%20need%20in%20the%20future

26 Leopold, T. (2025). Future of Jobs Report 2025: The jobs of the future-and the skills you need to get them. In World Economic Forum. World Economic Forum. https://www.weforum.org/stories/2025/01/future-of-jobs-report-2025-jobs-of-the-future-and-the-skills-you-need-to-get-them/#:~:text=,likely%20need%20in%20the%20future

27 Gevelber, L. (2025, May 29). Unlocking opportunity together with the Google Career Certificates. Google. https://blog.google/outreach-initiatives/grow-with-google/google-career-certificates-impact-report-may-2025/

28 Dludla, N. (2025, January 23). Microsoft to train 1 million South Africans on AI skills. Reuters. https://www.reuters.com/technology/artificial-intelligence/microsoft-train-1-million-south-africans-ai-skills-2025-01-23/

29 About IBM SkillsBuild | Free Digital learning. (n.d.). IBM SkillsBuild. https://skillsbuild.org/about

by partnering with Egypt's Ministry of Communications and Information Technology: over the next five years, IBM will train 100,000 Egyptians in AI fundamentals and ethics as part of the country's National AI Strategy 2025-2030, an agreement that also underscores IBM's global pledge to equip two million people with AI skills by 2026.[30]

Taken together, these three flagship programs demonstrate that large-scale, employer-driven upskilling is moving from rhetoric to measurable impact: millions of workers are already earning market-recognized credentials, and the newest cohorts are being taught how to co-work with AI from day one.

Equally critical are communication, soft skills and higher-order cognitive skills that enable workers to fill in and supplement what AI cannot do. Creative problem-solving, analytical thinking, and critical thinking are repeatedly cited as crucial skills for the future workforce.[31] [32] In fact, even in the world of AI, analytical thinking remains the most sought-after core skill among employers, with 70% of companies in one survey rating it essential for 2025.[33] Traits that support flexibility and adaptability are also rising in value, including resilience, appetite for change, agility, and initiative. With roles and tasks in flux, employers prize workers who can continually learn and adapt; skills related to curiosity and lifelong learning now rank among the top ten growing skills.[34] Collaboration and leadership abilities are important as well, since working in tandem with AI systems often involves teamwork and guiding organizational change. The ideal skillset in an AI-driven workplace combines strong technical acumen (to leverage new tools) with human strengths like creativity, communication, and adaptability. The following figure shows an AI instructor teaching in a classroom setting:

30 Malin, C. (2025, May 27). IBM to train 100,000 Egyptians in AI skills over 5 years. Middle East AI News. https://www.middleeastainews.com/p/ibm-to-train-100000-egyptians-in-ai

31 AVID Center. (2023, December 4). Preparing students to join the AI workforce - AVID Open Access. AVID Open Access. https://avidopenaccess.org/resource/preparing-students-to-join-the-ai-workforce/#:~:text-t=The%20Future%20of%20Jobs%20Report,thinking%2C%20and%20technology%20literacy%20skills

32 Hazan, E., Madgavkar, A., Chui, M., Smit, S., Maor, D., Dandona, G. S., & Huyghues-Despointes, R. (2024, May 21). A new future of work: The race to deploy AI and raise skills in Europe and beyond. McKinsey & Company. https://www.mckinsey.com/mgi/our-research/a-new-future-of-work-the-race-to-deploy-ai-and-raise-skills-in-europe-and-beyond

33 Leopold, T. (2025). Future of Jobs Report 2025: The jobs of the future-and the skills you need to get them. In World Economic Forum. World Economic Forum. https://www.weforum.org/stories/2025/01/future-of-jobs-report-2025-jobs-of-the-future-and-the-skills-you-need-to-get-them/#:~:text=,likely%20need%20in%20the%20future

34 Leopold, T. (2025). Future of Jobs Report 2025: The jobs of the future-and the skills you need to get them. In World Economic Forum. World Economic Forum. https://www.weforum.org/stories/2025/01/future-of-jobs-report-2025-jobs-of-the-future-and-the-skills-you-need-to-get-them/#:~:text=,likely%20need%20in%20the%20future

Figure 7.1: *An AI-driven workforce will be the way of the future*

Workers are actively looking to upgrade their skills in response to these shifts, and surveys show that skill gaps are a primary concern for businesses navigating a digital transformation. If you walk through any C-suite today, you will hear the same quiet worry repeated in different accents: *We don't have the skills we need for the business we're becoming.* The WEF's most recent Future of Jobs survey crystallizes that anxiety: nearly two-thirds of global employers—63 percent—rank widening skill gaps as the single biggest obstacle to transformation between now and 2030[35]. Given the evolving skill demands, if the world's workforce were 100 people, 59 would need reskilling or upskilling by 2030 to meet future demand. In this WEF's global survey, 85% of companies surveyed plan to prioritize investment in upskilling or retraining programs for their workforce,[36] with 70% of employers expecting to hire staff with new skills, 40% planning to reduce staff as their skills become less relevant, and 50% planning to transition staff from declining to growing roles. *McKinsey's* 2024 survey of European and US executives paints a similarly urgent picture. Leaders anticipate significant changes in workforce skill mixes by 2030 and warn that failing to secure the right skills could directly hit financial performance and blunt the payoff from AI investments. When asked how they will plug the gap, executives describe a three-way playbook: retrain, hire, and contract workers. Notably, retraining tops the list, with respondents saying they will reskill roughly a third of their people on average[37].

35 Zahidi, S. (Director). (n.d.). Future of Jobs Report 2025. In *WEForum*. https://www.weforum.org/reports/the-future-of jobs-report-2025/

36 Leopold, T. (2025). Future of Jobs Report 2025: The jobs of the future-and the skills you need to get them. In *World Economic Forum*. World Economic Forum. https://www.weforum.org/stories/2025/01/future-of-jobs-report-2025-jobs-of-the-future-and-the-skills-you-need-to-get-them/#:~:text=,likely%20need%20in%20the%20future

37 Hazan, E., Madgavkar, A., Chui, M., Smit, S., Maor, D., Dandona, G. S., & Huyghues-Despointes, R. (2024, May 21). A new future of work: The race to deploy AI and raise skills in Europe and beyond. McKinsey & Company. https://www.mckinsey.com/mgi/our-research/a-new-future-of-work-the-race-to-deploy-ai-and-raise-skills-in-europe-and-beyond

Yet actions on the ground do not always match those lofty intentions. The *University of Phoenix*'s *2025 Career Optimism Index* exposes a striking disconnect: 60 % of US employers still prefer external hiring over training current staff, despite ample evidence that turnover is costlier than development and that learning investments boost retention and profitability. Meanwhile, employer spending on reskilling and upskilling is down 13 and 10 percentage points respectively since 2022, even though 86 % of workers are actively hunting for skill-building opportunities and 43 % say they lack access to the training they need.[38] This is what we can think of as the skills paradox. Boards describe lifelong learning as critical infrastructure; shareholders applaud; employees queue at the classroom door, while learning budgets are quietly trimmed and recruiters keep posting urgent openings the internal market might have filled. The paradox is not born of bad faith. It is sustained by legacy metrics that reward short-term utilization over long-term capability, by procurement systems that treat training as a discretionary line item, and by a generational change in technology so swift that yesterday's job families have no tomorrow.

Early in their careers, professionals may have an advantage in quickly picking up new digital tools, whereas older workers may need additional training and support; research suggests AI can especially help less-experienced employees boost their productivity by augmenting their skills, underscoring the importance of making such tools accessible to all.[39] Ultimately, a combination of technical upskilling and human skill development is seen as a wonderful recipe for career resilience in the age of AI. If managed well, the workforce can transition into new, more fulfilling roles with the help of training, rather than facing displacement and unemployment.[40] Conversely, failure to close skill gaps could accelerate job polarization; those unable to acquire new skills risk being left in shrinking, low-wage occupations, while those with in-demand skills command the growing opportunities.[41] This imperative is influencing corporate training efforts as well as changes in education systems.

Remote and distributed work models

The integration of artificial intelligence into remote work is rapidly advancing, with the past years marking a pivotal year for new tools and predictive capabilities that are reshaping team management and operational efficiency. These developments are not only refining the remote

38 Mitchum, M. (n.d.). University of Phoenix Career Institute® Fifth-Annual Career Optimism Index finds 1:4 American workers feel their professional future is out of their hands. University of Phoenix. https://www.phoenix.edu/press-release/fifth-annual-career-optimism-index-study-released.html

39 AI will transform the global economy. let's make sure it benefits humanity. (2024c, January 14). IMF. https://www.imf.org/en/Blogs/Articles/2024/01/14/ai-will-transform-the-global-economy-lets-make-sure-it-benefits-humanity#:~:text=AI%20could%20also%20affect%20income,workers%20could%20struggle%20to%20adapt

40 Fleming, M., Thompson, N. C., & Li, W. (2024b, August 29). The last mile problem in AI. Brookings. https://www.brookings.edu/articles/the-last-mile-problem-in-ai/#:~:text=labor%20automation%20should%20occur%20in,be%20more%20gradual%20than%20abrupt

41 Hazan, E., Madgavkar, A., Chui, M., Smit, S., Maor, D., Dandona, G. S., & Huyghues-Despointes, R. (2024, May 21). A new future of work: The race to deploy AI and raise skills in Europe and beyond. McKinsey & Company. https://www.mckinsey.com/mgi/our-research/a-new-future-of-work-the-race-to-deploy-ai-and-raise-skills-in-europe-and-beyond

and hybrid work models but are also setting new standards for the future workforce, making it imperative to equip students with the skills to navigate this evolving environment.

Building on the established role of AI in streamlining remote work, the latest advancements are moving beyond task automation to foster a more intelligent, predictive, and supportive virtual workspace. While AI-driven tools have become instrumental in enhancing communication, automating routine tasks, and bolstering cybersecurity, a new wave of innovation is particularly focused on proactive team management and hyper-personalized employee experiences.[42]

A significant leap forward is evident in the world of predictive analytics for remote team management. Advanced AI algorithms are now capable of analyzing a multitude of data points—from project progress and communication patterns to tool usage and even sentiment analysis of team interactions, and these technologies are present both in work and student environments. Powered by large language models that study chat threads, calendars, and assignment histories, the newest platforms surface trouble spots before they become all-nighters, shifting online group work from last-minute firefighting to calm, data-driven course-correction.[43]

Wrike's *Work Intelligence* engine[44] is a clear example. Every project now carries a live risk score (green, amber or red) calculated by a machine-learning model that watches factors such as overdue tasks, project complexity and the track record of the people involved. If the score turns red, a short explanatory note appears (for instance, 12 tasks overdue) so the team can take action while there is still room to maneuver. ClickUp [45] has taken the same idea further: its AI agents scan workload charts and dependency chains, then warn when something is heading for overload and propose a new schedule before anyone asks. Together, these tools replace guesswork with forward visibility, giving student teams the same predictive oversight once reserved only for enterprise project managers.

Real-time language translation within communication hubs like Slack and Microsoft Teams has become seamless, breaking down geographical and linguistic barriers for global teams. Furthermore, AI-driven writing assistants in collaborative document platforms like Notion and Google Docs are now more sophisticated, offering not just grammatical corrections but also helping to refine the tone and clarity of communication, ensuring that a globally dispersed team remains on the same page.

In response to the increased cybersecurity challenges of remote work, 2025 has seen the widespread adoption of Zero Trust security models and AI-powered VPNs. These systems

42 Spooner, H. (2025, May 14). The State of Remote Work: 2025 Statistics. Neat. https://neat.no/resources/the-state-of-remote-work-2025-statistics/

43 Aggarwal, P., & Aggarwal, P. (2025, June 30). 10 Tech Strategies for remote Team Management in 2025. Workstatus. https://www.workstatus.io/blog/workforce-management/strategies-for-managing-remote-teams/

44 Wrike. (n.d.). AI for work and project management | Wrike. Wrike. https://www.wrike.com/features/work-intelligence/

45 ClickUp. (n.d.). ClickUp™ | The everything app for work. https://clickup.com/

operate on the principle of *never trust, always verify*,[46] continuously monitoring for anomalous activity within a network. This proactive and intelligent approach to security is crucial for protecting sensitive company data across a distributed workforce.

These technological strides are directly influencing the skill sets required in the modern workforce. The emphasis is shifting from proficiency in specific software to a broader understanding of how to leverage AI-powered tools for strategic advantage. As the World Economic Forum has highlighted[47] the ability to work alongside AI, to interpret its outputs, and to make informed decisions based on its predictions is becoming a critical competency.

As these AI-driven remote work models become the norm, it is essential that our educational frameworks adapt. The subset of students currently experiencing these changes is at the forefront of a global shift. To prepare all students for this brave new world, curricula must evolve to include digital literacy, data analysis, and critical thinking skills within the context of AI-powered collaboration and management. By doing so, we can ensure that the next generation is not just ready for the future of work but is also equipped to shape it.

Cybersecurity and privacy emphasis

Cybersecurity and data privacy are critical concerns in this new world of work. The blended remote and onsite workplace now depends on AI-driven collaboration tools, code copilots[48], and autonomous cloud agents that generate, route, and store data far beyond the traditional perimeter. While these systems accelerate productivity, they also enlarge the attack surface: mis-trained models can exfiltrate prompts, and poorly permissioned data pipelines give adversaries fertile ground. Future professionals, therefore, need to treat *privacy-by-design* and continuous threat-hunting with the same rigor as version control and UX testing.

Recent incidents showed how quickly AI supply-chain errors become real breaches. In 2025, Scale AI accidentally left thousands of Google Docs publicly accessible, exposing confidential training data for Meta, Google and XAI—and the personal details of its crowd workers—highlighting how misconfigured cloud sharing can turn an AI provider itself into a breach vector[49]. Such cases demonstrate why AI-enhanced anomaly detection, Zero Trust segmentation, and strong encryption are now baseline controls rather than nice-to-have add-ons.

---

46 Freestone, T., & Freestone, T. (2024, November 1). Zero Trust Architecture: Never Trust, Always Verify. Kiteworks | Your Private Data Network. https://www.kiteworks.com/cybersecurity-risk-management/zero-trust-architecture-never-trust-always-verify/
47 Why AI literacy is now a core competency in education. (2025, June 3). World Economic Forum. https://www.weforum.org/stories/2025/05/why-ai-literacy-is-now-a-core-competency-in-education/
48 Code copilots is an umbrella term for the growing class of AI coding assistants that live inside an IDE or editor, predict the next line (or entire files), and now take on higher-level tasks such as refactoring, test generation, and vulnerability fixing. They're also called AI pair programmers, AI coding assistants, generative code agents, or Copilot-style tools in recent literature.
49 https://www.businessinsider.com/scale-ai-data-exposed-meta-google-elon-musk-zuckerberg-cybersecurity-2025-6

Regulators are closing the gap. Starting 2 August 2025, the European Union AI Act will force providers of general-purpose models to keep audit logs, publish technical summaries, and face fines of up to 7% of global turnover for violations.[50] In the United States, **the National Institute of Standards and Technology's (NIST)** Privacy Framework 1.1 (April 2025) introduces explicit inference-stage controls and aligns them with the refreshed Cybersecurity Framework, giving teams a shared language for managing AI data flows.[51] For tomorrow's professionals, fluency in least-privilege design, data-flow auditing, and privacy-preserving encryption is now the entry ticket to compliance and to trust in an AI-saturated economy.

Blurring industry boundaries

AI is breaking down traditional industry barriers and creating entirely new career paths. In other words, we need to think of AI as the connective tissue linking sectors that once operated in silos. Fields that once seemed unrelated, like healthcare and technology or finance and retail, are now deeply connected through AI-powered solutions. Imagine AI tools that diagnose diseases, or smart algorithms that personalize your shopping experience. For educators, the message is clear: students must learn to navigate value chains rather than industries, blending domain knowledge with data-centric thinking.

For today's students, this convergence means more opportunity than ever before. But it also means the future will belong to those who are agile, curious, and ready to learn across a variety of disciplines. Today's students will not just be preparing for one job; they will be preparing for a lifetime of evolving roles where creative thinking, tech fluency, and collaboration across industries will be key. To stay ahead, students must cultivate both digital literacy and a willingness to adapt. The future belongs to those who can connect the dots between disparate fields, think critically, and imagine new ways AI can solve real-world problems.

Let us illustrate the shift with a few examples. In the first one, climate tech fuses with national forecasting. Google DeepMind's new Weather Lab, developed alongside the U.S. National Hurricane Center, uses stochastic neural networks to predict cyclone tracks up to 15 days out— an AI–meteorology crossover aimed at saving lives and hardening coastal infrastructure[52]. In the second example, Levi Strauss & Co. shows how AI is stitching fashion, agriculture, and enterprise tech into one value chain. During 2024–25, the jeans-maker embedded o9 Solutions' machine-learning planning engine across its global fabric and cotton network, giving planners real-time digital-twin visibility from bale to finished denim and accelerating its push to source 100% certified-sustainable cotton by 2025[53]. In parallel, the company joined the U.S. Cotton Trust Protocol and is piloting the blockchain-based **Protocol Consumption Management Solution (PCMS)**, where every bale carries a unique identification, letting AI flag anomalies

50 Article 99: Penalties I EU Artificial Intelligence Act. (n.d.). https://artificialintelligenceact.eu/article/99/
51 Anderson, M., Gilbert, D., & Grayson, N. (2025). NIST Privacy Framework 1.1. In NIST Cybersecurity White Paper. https://nvlpubs.nist.gov/nistpubs/CSWP/NIST.CSWP.40.ipd.pdf
52 How we're supporting better tropical cyclone prediction with AI. (2025, June 12). Google DeepMind. https://deepmind.google/discover/blog/weather-lab-cyclone-predictions-with-ai/
53 Sarahrudge. (2024, June 20). Levi's Supply Chain Gets Jean Therapy I Supply Chain World magazine. Supply Chain World Magazine. https://scw-mag.com/news/levis-supply-chain-gets-jean-therapy/

and substantiate claims in seconds.[54] Together, the o9 platform and blockchain pilot turn a centuries-old denim business into a data-driven collaboration between growers, ginners, spinners, and retail merchandisers—exactly the kind of cross-industry fusion that today's students need to understand and help shape.

For tomorrow's professionals, these examples confirm that career arcs will span multiple domains: a data scientist may pivot from drug design to carbon-accounting **application programming interfaces** (**APIs**), or from payment-risk models to grid optimization. Mastery of core digital skills such as machine-learning literacy, ethical data stewardship, and cross-functional collaboration will be the passport to opportunity in a landscape where industry boundaries are rapidly dissolving.

Rise of new-collar roles

The AI revolution is not just for coders with advanced degrees; this technology is opening doors to a new class of careers called *new-collar* jobs. These are high-skill roles in areas like AI, cybersecurity, cloud computing, and data analytics. These roles do not always require a traditional four-year college degree. These positions span the gap between technical expertise and human-centered work, making them essential in an AI-driven economy. Unlike traditional blue-collar or white-collar jobs, new-collar opportunities emphasize hands-on experience, some vocational training, and certifications rather than formal academic credentials. Examples include AI-assisted healthcare technicians, cybersecurity specialists, data analysts, cloud computing professionals, and skilled automation technicians. Many companies now value certifications, bootcamps, hackathons, apprenticeships, and hands-on experience just as much, sometimes more. For instance, the IBM AI Engineering Professional Certificate[55] and Google Cloud Certified Generative AI Leader[56] are highly sought after for building and deploying AI models and leading AI initiatives, respectively. In cybersecurity, CompTIA Security+ [57] offers a foundational entry, while the ISC2 (an association for cybersecurity professionals) **Certified Cloud Security Professional** (**CCSP**)[58] and Microsoft Certified: Cybersecurity Architect Expert[59] address the crucial need for cloud security and comprehensive security architecture. For cloud computing, the Google Cloud Certified Associate Cloud Engineer[60] and Microsoft Certified:

54 NccWpAdmin. (2022, August 15). U.S. Cotton Trust Protocol Announces Levi Strauss & Co and Their Legacy Brands as New Members. Trust US Cotton Protocol. https://trustuscotton.org/us-cotton-trust-protocol-announces-levi-strauss-and-legacy-brands-as-members/

55 IBM AI Engineering. (n.d.). Coursera. https://www.coursera.org/professional-certificates/ai-engineer

56 Rifkin, E. (2025, May 14). New Google Cloud certification in generative AI. Google Cloud Blog. https://cloud.google.com/blog/topics/training-certifications/new-google-cloud-certification-in-generative-ai

57 Security+ (Plus) Certification | CompTIA. (n.d.). https://www.comptia.org/en-us/certifications/security/

58 CCSP Certified Cloud Security Professional | ISC2. (n.d.). https://www.isc2.org/certifications/ccsp

59 Bipach. (n.d.). Microsoft Certified: Cybersecurity Architect Expert - Certifications. Microsoft Learn. https://learn.microsoft.com/en-us/credentials/certifications/cybersecurity-architect-expert/

60 Associate Cloud Engineer Certification | Learn | Google Cloud. (n.d.). Google Cloud. https://cloud.google.com/learn/certification/cloud-engineer

Azure Solutions Architect Expert[61] validate essential and advanced skills in cloud platform management. Finally, in data analytics, the Google Data Analytics Professional Certificate[62], IBM Data Analyst Professional Certificate[63], and Microsoft Certified: Power BI Data Analyst Associate[64] equip individuals with hands-on skills in data manipulation, visualization, and business intelligence, demonstrating how targeted certifications are becoming direct pathways to well-paying, high-impact roles. Middle-skills jobs, those requiring more than a high school diploma but less than a university-level bachelor's degree, are expanding across industries. AI-powered diagnostics in healthcare, smart manufacturing, sustainability, and customer experience roles using AI-driven insights are reshaping employment landscapes. These roles are more about working with AI; they are about using smart tools to solve problems, make better decisions, and build the future.[65] These roles all require a blend of technical proficiency and human skills such as critical thinking, communication, and ethical reasoning.

To succeed, students should focus on building a strong foundation in **science, technology, engineering, and mathematics (STEM)** fields, explore hands-on tech learning opportunities, and maintain a growth-mindset, staying open to opportunities. The jobs of tomorrow will be filled by those who are proactive about learning today and passionate about making a difference.

As powerful as AI can be, it also brings with it some serious ethical questions, and tomorrow's leaders need to be ready to face them. AI systems can unintentionally reinforce existing bias, invade privacy, or make decisions that no one fully understands. That is why it is so important for the next generation of students to be not just skilled, but responsible digital citizens.

Students who understand both technology and ethics will be essential in building AI systems that are fair, transparent, and trustworthy. This means asking tough questions: *Who trains the AI? How do we prevent discrimination? Who's accountable if something goes wrong?* Students who aspire to become future leaders must learn how to navigate these challenges, and schools must prioritize ethics, data literacy, and digital responsibility in their curricula.

The future of AI is not just about what we *can* build, it is about what we should build. Students who are passionate about justice, fairness, and the impact of technology on society will be the ones who can shape a better, more inclusive AI-powered world.

---

61 Bipach. (n.d.-a). Microsoft Certified: Azure Solutions Architect Expert - Certifications. Microsoft Learn. https://learn.microsoft.com/en-us/credentials/certifications/azure-solutions-architect/
62 Google Data Analytics. (n.d.). Coursera. https://www.coursera.org/professional-certificates/google-data-analytics?msockid=36d5db1157d26cb720c5cf6956fe6d94
63 IBM Data Analyst. (n.d.). Coursera. https://www.coursera.org/professional-certificates/ibm-data-analyst?msockid=36d5db1157d26cb720c5cf6956fe6d94
64 Bipach. (n.d.). Microsoft Certified: Power BI Data Analyst Associate - Certifications. Microsoft Learn. https://learn.microsoft.com/en-us/credentials/certifications/data-analyst-associate/?practice-assessment-type=certification
65 Ellingrud, K., Sanghvi, S., Dandona, G. S., Madgavkar, A., Chui, M., White, O., & Hasebe, P. (2023, July 26). Generative AI and the future of work in America. McKinsey & Company. https://www.mckinsey.com/capabilities/mckinsey-digital/our-insights/generative-ai-and-the-future-of-work-in-america

Implications for education

As AI reshapes our world across almost every industry, education must evolve to prepare students of today for a future where adaptability, innovation, and ethical awareness are essential survival skills. Schools and universities must align their curricula with workforce trends, equipping students with the new-collar skills needed for careers in AI-driven economies. These skills include:

- **Cultivating adaptability**: With AI blurring the boundaries of industry and creating new types of jobs, students must develop adaptability, the ability to learn continuously and pivot across a variety of disciplines. Future jobs will require workers to integrate knowledge from multiple fields, such as AI in healthcare, finance, or creative industries. Classrooms should make the investment to emphasize interdisciplinary learning, problem-based projects, and hands-on experiences where students apply AI tools across different contexts. By fostering a growth mindset and encouraging curiosity in the classroom, educators can prepare students to succeed in careers that do not yet exist.

- **Encouraging innovation and new-collar skill development**: The rise of *new-collar* roles underscores the importance of technical proficiency combined with creativity. Instead of focusing solely on traditional academic pathways, educators can incorporate hands-on AI literacy, coding, data analysis, and machine learning concepts into a wide variety of subjects. Students can also engage in real-world applications of AI, such as using generative AI for creative projects or exploring AI-driven problem-solving in business simulations. Encouraging students to experiment with the latest AI tools and develop their own projects builds confidence in working with emerging technologies, making them more competitive in the evolving job market.[66]

- **Embedding ethical and governance awareness**: As AI grows increasingly more influential, students must explore and understand the ethical implications. This includes recognizing biases in AI models, working to ensure fairness in decision-making, and navigating data privacy concerns. Ethics should be integrated into computer science curricula, social studies, and business courses, with case studies on real-world AI challenges. Debates, discussions, and role-playing activities can help students analyze different perspectives and think critically about responsible AI development. By fostering this type of ethical reasoning, schools can prepare students to shape AI in ways that benefit society.

To future-proof students of today, educators and administrators must emphasize adaptability, innovation, curiosity, experimentation, and ethical awareness. These skills will not only help students navigate future AI-driven workplaces but also empower them to lead in shaping the

---

66 Correspondent, H. (2020, March 5). IBM bets on 'new collar' skills to help fix employability issues. HT Tech. https://tech.hindustantimes.com/tech/news/ibm-bets-on-new-collar-skills-to-help-fix-employability-issues-story-gnaeBYuGuV94X1f93xOJvK.html

responsible use of AI in society. It is critical to engage the next generation instead of sending a message that they are plagiarizing or cheating.

Leading institutions are actively integrating generative AI and data ethics into their interdisciplinary coursework. For example, Ohio State University is implementing universal AI integration across all student curricula to foster practical application[67], while the University of *Edinburgh's Masters of Science in Data and AI Ethics* offers a comprehensive online program focused on responsible AI development and ethical data management[68]. The **University of Luxembourg's Institute for Digital Ethics** (**ULIDE**)[69] informs curriculum development by providing guidance on digital ethics, including algorithmic bias and data privacy. This trend shows institutions are moving beyond just teaching about AI to integrating AI tools and ethical considerations *into* the learning process across diverse fields.

Skill sets for the AI era

The rapid workforce changes induced by AI have put a spotlight on the role of education in preparation for the next generation. Schools and universities are increasingly viewed as crucial fronts for proactive preparation, ensuring that students graduate with the competencies needed to survive and thrive in an AI-transformed economy. Educators and policymakers must respond by updating curricula, teaching methods, and skill-development priorities from the earliest grades through postsecondary programs.

Recent educational initiatives underscore a global shift towards integrating AI literacy and critical digital citizenship into learning. For instance, **United Nations Educational, Scientific and Cultural Organization's** (**UNESCO**) *Guidance for Generative AI in Education and Research* [70] (updated April 2025) provides a human-centered approach to using generative AI ethically and effectively, emphasizing data privacy, age-appropriate use, and pedagogical design. UNESCO also dedicated the International Day of Education 2025[71] to artificial intelligence, urging member states to invest in training teachers and students for responsible AI use and releasing AI competency frameworks for both students and teachers.

Concurrently, the **Artificial Intelligence for K-12 initiative (AI4K12)** in the United States continues to develop national guidelines for AI education for K-12 students, aiming to

---

67 Millard, K. (2025, June 9). Ohio State announces every student will use AI in class. NBC4i. https://www.nbc4i.com/news/local-news/ohio-state-university/ohio-state-announces-every-student-will-use-ai-in-class/

68 Data and Artificial intelligence Ethics. (n.d.). https://postgraduate.degrees.ed.ac.uk/index.php?r=site/view&edition=2023&id=1092

69 University of Luxembourg. (2025, June 11). University of Luxembourg Institute of Digital Ethics (ULIDE) i Uni.lu. Research EN. https://www.uni.lu/research-en/ulide/

70 Fengchun, M., Holmes, W., & UNESCO. (2025). Guidance for generative AI in education and research. In UNESCO. UNESCO. https://www.unesco.org/en/articles/guidance-generative-ai-education-and-research

71 UNESCO dedicates the International Day of Education 2025 to artificial intelligence. (2025, February 3). UNESCO. https://www.unesco.org/en/articles/unesco-dedicates-international-day-education-2025-artificial-intelligence

foster foundational understanding across all grade levels[72]. Complementing this, the OECD and European Commission unveiled a draft *AI Literacy Framework for Primary and Secondary Education*[73] in May 2025, which outlines essential knowledge, skills, and attitudes across four domains: Engaging with AI, Creating with AI, Managing AI, and Designing AI. This framework[74] emphasizes ethics, inclusion, and social responsibility, preparing students to critically evaluate AI outputs and understand its societal impacts.

Furthermore, the *European Year of Digital Citizenship Education 2025*[75], launched by the Council of Europe, focuses on equipping individuals with the competences needed to thrive in a digitally connected society. This initiative addresses challenges like disinformation, cyberbullying, online hate speech, and the misuse of personal data, promoting critical thinking, digital rights, active participation, and well-being in the digital world across all age groups. These global efforts signify a concerted move towards establishing comprehensive standards for AI literacy and critical digital citizenship, ensuring students are not just consumers but responsible co-creators and ethical participants in the AI era.

Building AI literacy and adaptability at the K-12 level

There is growing consensus that foundational understanding of AI should be taught early, at the K-12 level, if not before. Technology leaders and education experts suggest that students need early exposure to what AI is, how it works, and how it impacts society. The **International Society for Technology in Education (ISTE)**, for example, emphasizes that AI education is important across every subject, not just in computer science classes, stating: *in order to be successful in school and in life, all K-12 students need a foundational understanding of what AI is, how it works, and how it impacts society.*[76]

Initiatives like the AI4K12 project (jointly sponsored by AAAI and CSTA) are developing national guidelines to introduce core AI concepts in age-appropriate ways throughout primary and secondary schooling. These efforts distill AI into *Five Big Ideas*, such as perception, machine

---

72 AICERTs. (2025, June 27). April 2025 AI initiative to advance education for U.S. youth. AICERTs - Empower With AI Certifications. https://www.aicerts.ai/blog/transforming-americas-future-through-artificial-intelligence-a-comprehensive-look-at-the-april-2025-executive-initiative-to-advance-ai-education-for-american-youth/
73 Empowering learners for the age of AI: launch of the draft AI literacy framework and stakeholder consultations. (2025, June 10). European Education Area. https://education.ec.europa.eu/event/empowering-learners-for-the-age-of-ai-launch-of-the-draft-ai-literacy-framework-and-stakeholder-consultations
74 TeachAI | AI Literacy. (n.d.). https://www.teachai.org/ailiteracy
75 Council of Europe. (2025). European Year of Digital Citizenship Education 2025. Retrieved July 6, 2025, from https://www.coe.int/en/web/education/european-year-of-digital-citizenship-education-2025
76 AVID Center. (2023b, December 4). Preparing students to join the AI workforce - AVID Open Access. AVID Open Access. https://avidopenaccess.org/resource/preparing-students-to-join-the-ai-workforce/#:~:text=The%20International%20Society%20for%20Technology,%E2%80%9D

learning, and societal impact, to help curriculum developers and teachers integrate AI topics alongside math, science, and humanities content.[77]

The fundamental premise is that basic AI literacy will soon be as indispensable as computer literacy; today's students will inevitably live and work with AI tools, so they must understand the principles behind them.

In addition to AI-specific knowledge, K-12 educators must increasingly focus on transferable skills and mindsets that will serve students in a fast-changing job landscape. Rather than training kids for any one specific job (which might be automated or altered by the time they enter the workforce), forward-thinking curricula emphasize learning *how to learn* and how to keep up with technology. As one education expert put it, *We shouldn't be educating our students to do a particular job. We now need to be educating our students to be able to be flexible, to be able to retrain themselves, to be able to learn how to learn… because the nature of that job may change over the next few years.* This perspective reflects the reality that adaptability is a key currency in the AI era. Classroom strategies increasingly prioritize problem-solving, critical thinking, creativity, and collaboration, skills less likely to be overtaken by automation and essential for pivoting as needed in one's career.[78]

Project-based learning, cross-domain interdisciplinary projects, and inquiry-based activities are being used to cultivate these competencies. There is also an emphasis on cultivating resilience and a growth mindset in students (sometimes called learning agility), so that they are comfortable continuously updating their skills. The WEF notes that four of the top skills for the next five years are precisely these kinds of self-efficacy skills: resilience, motivation, curiosity, and lifelong learning.[79] By nurturing such traits, schools aim to produce graduates who can navigate the uncertainties of an AI-rich future, whether that means adapting to new tools like ChatGPT in their workflow or entirely shifting career paths multiple times.

Educational content providers are also adapting to include ethical and societal discussions around AI. Lessons on data privacy, algorithmic bias, and the social implications of automation are being introduced at all levels to help students become informed digital citizens. For example, some high school programs now involve students in debates about AI's impact on society or have them examine case studies of AI in fields like healthcare or environmental science. This broad approach to machine learning education helps demystify AI and empower students to see themselves not just as users of technology but as potential shapers of it. UNESCO's guidance for policymakers on AI in education underscores that the nature of employment is likely to change, and thus education systems must prepare students to reskill and upskill

77 AI4K12. (n.d.-b). AI4K12. https://ai4k12.org/#:~:text=The%20Artificial%20Intelligence%20is%20joint-ly%20sponsored%20by%C2%A0AAAI%C2%A0and%C2%A0CSTA

78 AVID Center. (2023c, December 4). Preparing students to join the AI workforce - AVID Open Access. AVID Open Access. https://avidopenaccess.org/resource/preparing-students-to-join-the-ai-workforce/#:~:text=t=also%20talks%20about%20the%20importance,%E2%80%9D

79 Olson, A. (2025, March 3). WEF: Skill gaps are the biggest barrier to transformation. Skillsoft. https://www.skillsoft.com/blog/wef-skill-gaps-are-the-biggest-barrier-to-transformation

throughout their lives.[80] By teaching students about AI early and often, and by honing their ability to adapt, K-12 schools serve as a critical foundation for an agile future workforce.[81]

Future skills in higher education

Colleges and universities worldwide should be reshaping their programs to meet the demands of an AI-driven economy. While there has been a proliferation of new AI-related degrees and courses in higher education, this is a rapidly expanding realm that requires constant attention. Many top universities now offer specialized majors or graduate programs in AI, machine learning, or data science, and even those that do not have standalone AI degrees are rightfully weaving AI components into more traditional disciplines. For instance, business schools have added analytics and AI strategy modules; journalism programs to discuss AI in media; and medical schools teach about machine learning and AI in diagnostics. This interdisciplinary integration reflects an acknowledgement that tomorrow's professionals in every field, from finance to agriculture, will need to understand and leverage AI in their work. As one industry association observed, the rise of AI curricula in academic institutions is shaping the future by preparing the next generation of innovators, engineers, and thought leaders, with an evolution in education aimed at meeting the industry demand while also fostering a deep understanding of AI's societal impact. A key trend in higher education is an emphasis on practical, hands-on experience with AI technology and diving into real-world projects. Universities are partnering with tech companies and employers across all industries to provide students opportunities like internships in AI development, industry-sponsored research projects, or hackathons using AI.[82] Here are some notable examples:

- **Texas A&M University and Wiley/Perplexity partnership**[83]: Texas A&M, alongside Texas State University and several United Kingdom institutions, have partnered with Wiley and Perplexity to integrate AI-powered search and educational tools across campus. This initiative aims to make every degree AI-ready, providing students with hands-on experience using enterprise-grade AI platforms and direct access to trusted scholarly resources. Over 75,000 students benefit from this collaboration, which is designed to equip them with the skills needed to succeed in an AI-driven workforce.

80 AVID Center. (2023d, December 4). Preparing students to join the AI workforce - AVID Open Access. AVID Open Access. https://avidopenaccess.org/resource/preparing-students-to-join-the-ai-work-force/#:~:text=In%20AI%20and%20education%3A%20guidance,%E2%80%9D

81 UNESCO Education Sector & The Global Education 2030 Agenda. (2021). AI and education. In Teacher Taskforce. United Nations Educational, Scientific and Cultural Organization. Retrieved March 29, 2025, from https://teachertaskforce.org/sites/default/files/2023-07/2021_UNESCO_AI-and-education-Guidan-de-for-policy-makers_EN.pdf

82 Association for Advancing Automation. (2024, September 23). AI degrees & universities: shaping the future of artificial intelligence. Automate. https://www.automate.org/ai/blogs/top-ai-degrees-universi-ties#:~:text=An%20emphasis%20on%20practical%2C%20hands,will%20face%20in%20their%20careers

83 Wiley and Perplexity announce new AI search partnership. (2025, May 8). Wiley. https://newsroom.wiley.com/press-releases/press-release-details/2025/Wiley-and-Perplexity-Announce-New-AI-Search-Part-nership/default.aspx

- **University of Toronto and Vector Institute**[84]: The University of Toronto is a founding partner of the Vector Institute for Artificial Intelligence, a leading research hub that bridges academic research with industry needs. Through this partnership, students can participate in research projects, summer internships with AI startups, and co-op programs within Toronto's vibrant tech ecosystem. These experiences emphasize both technical mastery and the ethical, societal impacts of AI, preparing students for practical roles in the field.

- **Jitterbit University partner curriculum**[85]: Jitterbit, a leader in cloud-based integration, has launched a new partner program with dedicated AI training and certification, accessible through Jitterbit University. The program is open to technology partners, including universities, and focuses on practical skills in automation integration, low-code app development, and agentic AI. Participants receive free online training, certifications, and opportunities to collaborate with a global network of industry professionals.

These experiences allow students to apply classroom knowledge to solve concrete problems (for example, using machine learning and data science to optimize a business process or working on an AI ethics committee for a product launch). Such practice not only builds technical proficiency but also cultivates project management, teamwork, and the ability to translate AI innovations into viable solutions, exactly the skills needed in the workforce. In addition, many higher-ed institutions now include courses on ethics and the policy dimensions of AI, ensuring that graduates consider issues of fairness, accountability, privacy, transparency, and societal impacts when deploying AI systems. This holistic training is meant to produce graduates who can navigate both the technical and human aspects of working with AI.

Higher education institutions are also embracing the need for continuous learning. Universities and community colleges are expanding their access to certificate programs, online courses, and executive education in AI and digital skills, recognizing that working adults will cycle in and out of education as career demands and industry needs change. In some regions, consortia of colleges have formed to integrate AI skills into curricula at scale, often with governmental support, so that even two-year programs and vocational training include AI components for relevant fields.[86,87] Furthermore, teachers and faculty themselves are updating pedagogies to

84 Best Schools for Artificial intelligence Programs in 2025 - Nova Scholar. (n.d.). https://www.novascholar. education/blog-posts/best-schools-for-artificial-intelligence-programs-in-2025

85 Lawler, R. (2025, June 26). Jitterbit University launches dedicated partner curriculum and certification designed to meet real-world demands of AI in 2025 — EdTech Innovation Hub. EdTech Innovation Hub. https://www.edtechinnovationhub.com/news/jitterbit-university-launches-dedicated-partner-curriculum-and-certification-designed-to-meet-the-real-world-demands-of-ai-in-2025

86 Palmer, K. (2025, January 23). Community colleges join forces to expand access to AI training. Inside Higher Ed | Higher Education News, Events and Jobs. https://www.insidehighered.com/news/tech-innovation/teaching-learning/2025/01/23/community-colleges-join-forces-expand-access-ai#:~:text=Community%20colleges%20join%20forces%20to,world%20problems%20or%20create%20efficiencies

87 Ascott, E., & Ascott, E. (2024, December 2). How are educational institutions adapting to prepare students for the future of work? Allwork.Space. https://allwork.space/2024/11/how-are-educational-institutions-adapting-to-prepare-students-for-the-future-of-work/#:~:text=Top%20universities%20are%20now%20offering,Google%20for%20direct%20job%20pathways

reflect this new era, for example, using AI tools like tutoring systems or generative AI in the classroom to enhance learning, and at the same time teaching students about those very tools' capabilities and limitations. There is a shared understanding in higher education that lifelong learning is now a fundamental skill; as one educator quipped, a child entering school today will graduate into a world in 2040 where many jobs do not yet exist, but will live, learn, and work in ways that will forever be changed by AI.[88] Colleges are thus striving to instill the mindset that learning does not stop at graduation; successful careers will involve repeatedly acquiring new skills, many of them related to evolving technologies.

Educational institutions at all levels are leaning in to help future-proof their students. From introducing basic AI literacy in elementary schools around the world to offering advanced AI engineering and data science degrees and practical experience in college, these initiatives aim to help prepare the coming workforce with both the hard skills to work with intelligent machines and the human skills to remain relevant when machines take over routine work. The focus is on building a pipeline of talent that is comfortable with technology, creative in problem-solving, ethically grounded, and most importantly, one that is adaptable. This proactive preparation is critical; it not only improves individual career prospects but can also help society at large to manage the transition to an AI-driven economy without leaving large segments of the population behind.

Soft skills versus technical skills

As we prepare students for a future shaped by AI, it is essential to balance technical proficiency with human competencies. While coding, data analysis, and algorithmic thinking are foundational skills for the future, they must be taught alongside human skills including creativity, collaboration, empathy, and critical thinking to foster truly well-rounded learners. These human abilities are what make students not only capable users of technology but responsible innovators who can thoughtfully navigate complex, real-world challenges.

Creativity can fuel innovation and will allow students to imagine new possibilities for AI applications. Collaboration teaches them to work effectively in diverse teams, a critical skill in both academic and workplace environments. Empathy helps ensure that technology is designed with people in mind, respecting different perspectives and avoiding harm. Critical thinking empowers students to question, analyze, and improve the systems they interact with. Embedding these core human values into AI education promotes a more ethical and inclusive approach to technology. This balanced framework can help students understand not only how AI works but also why it matters and how it can be used to serve human needs.

Recent studies from 2025 provide strong empirical evidence that employers increasingly prefer candidates with balanced skill sets that combine technical expertise, adaptability, and human-

88 AVID Center. (2023e, December 4). Preparing students to join the AI workforce - AVID Open Access. AVID Open Access. https://avidopenaccess.org/resource/preparing-students-to-join-the-ai-work-force/#:~:text=Arpan%20Chokshi%2C%20National%20Board%20Certified,He%20points%20out

centric abilities. The *World Economic Forum's Future of Jobs Report 2025*[89] found that while analytical and technology skills remain essential, employers now rank resilience, flexibility, leadership, and social influence among the most sought-after competencies. *Drexel University's 2025 Annual College Hiring Outlook*[90] similarly, highlights that ethical judgment, adaptability, and critical thinking are top priorities for employers across industries. Additionally, the *State of Skills-Based Hiring Report 2025*[91] reveals that 72% of employers believe hiring holistically—considering both technical and soft skills—leads to better organizational outcomes, including improved performance, stronger team cohesion, and higher retention rates. These findings underscore a clear shift: employers value candidates who can navigate complex environments and contribute meaningfully beyond technical tasks.

As AI becomes more deeply embedded in society and our human existence, nurturing this combination of technical skill and human insight will be key to developing the next generation of ethical student leaders and changemakers.

Lifelong learning mindset

In this era of rapid technological change, instilling a lifelong learning mentality in students is essential to their long-term success. AI and automation are constantly reshaping job markets, making agility, adaptability, and continuous skill development more valuable than ever. Schools must move beyond traditional rote learning to foster curiosity, resilience, and self-directed learning habits. Encouraging students to embrace challenges, experiment with new ideas, and view setbacks as opportunities for growth helps them to develop a mindset that empowers them to see learning as an ongoing journey rather than a task that ends with a degree. Project-based learning, inquiry-driven activities, and interdisciplinary coursework help provide students with opportunities to explore complex problems and develop solutions, reinforcing their ability to learn independently. Additionally, the integration of real-world applications of AI, data analytics, and emerging technologies into curricula ensures that students remain engaged with the skills and knowledge most relevant to the evolving workforce. It is critical to embed digital literacy and adaptability training across subjects, helping students navigate new tools, industries, and career shifts throughout their lives. Furthermore, building infrastructure to foster collaboration and mentorship opportunities with professionals, alumni, and industry experts will expose students to the realities of lifelong learning in various careers, reinforcing the importance of continuous upskilling. Teachers and institutions can also encourage a habit of self-reflection, goal-setting, and personal knowledge management, empowering students to take charge of their education beyond the classroom. With access to significant online resources, AI-driven personalized learning platforms, and skill-building programs, students can cultivate their intrinsic motivation to keep learning, staying ahead in an increasingly

89 Zahidi, S. (Director). (n.d.). Future of Jobs Report 2025. In WEForum. https://www.weforum.org/publi-cations/the-future-of-jobs-report-2025/

90 Employers seek ethical, adaptable graduates in 2025 job market. (n.d.). Drexel University's LeBow College of Business. https://www.lebow.drexel.edu/news/employers-seek-ethical-adaptable-gradu-ates-2025-job-market

91 Anonymous. (2025). The State of Skills-Based Hiring Report 2025. https://www.hrmorning.com/wp-con-tent/uploads/2025/06/TestGorilla-The-State-of-Skills-Based-Hiring-2025.pdf

AI-driven world. In the following table, you will find examples of certifications to extend students' AI education beyond the classroom:

Innovation area	Description	Example(s)
Generative AI certifications[92]	AI-focused, hands-on, stackable credentials for all levels	Coursera[93], Google Cloud[94], DataCamp[95], NVIDIA[96], Microsoft[97], IBM[98]
Modular/Micro-credentials[99]	Short, skill-based, stackable courses for personalized learning paths	Coursera, [100]European Skills Agenda[101], Open LMS[102]
AI-driven personalization[103]	Adaptative content, real-time feedback, and tailored learning journeys	Coursera, an AI-powered LMS platform
Flexible learning pathways	Recognition of prior learning, individual learning accounts, and inclusive access	EAEA[104], European Skills Agenda[105]

92 Sanders, K. (2025b, January 28). 15 Best Generative AI Certifications for Upskilling in 2025. The CTO Club. https://thectoclub.com/career/best-generative-ai-certifications/

93 Generative AI for Software Development Skill Certificate. (n.d.). Coursera. https://www.coursera.org/professional-certificates/generative-ai-for-software-development

94 Rifkin, E. (2025b, May 14). New Google Cloud certification in generative AI. Google Cloud Blog. https://cloud.google.com/blog/topics/training-certifications/new-google-cloud-certification-in-generative-ai

95 AI Fundamentals Certification. (n.d.). Datacamp. Retrieved July 6, 2025, from https://www.datacamp.com/certification/ai-fundamentals

96 NVIDIA GenAI and LLMS certification. (n.d.). NVIDIA. https://www.nvidia.com/en-us/learn/certification/generative-ai-llm-associate/

97 Sherzyang. (n.d.). Introduction to AI in Azure - training. Microsoft Learn. https://learn.microsoft.com/en-us/training/paths/introduction-to-ai-on-azure/

98 IBM AI Engineering. (n.d.-b). Coursera. https://www.coursera.org/professional-certificates/ai-engineer

99 Metrospective. (2025, May 9). Designing modular and learner-centered microcredentials for lifelong learning - Metrospective. https://metrospektiivi.metropolia.fi/en/2025-05-08-artikkeli/designing-modular-and-learner-centered-microcredentials-for-lifelong-learning/

100 Moran, J. (2025, June 4). Presenting Coursera's 2025 Global Skills Report: the skills trends shaping the future of education and employment. Coursera Blog. https://blog.coursera.org/presenting-courseras-2025-global-skills-report-the-skills-trends-shaping-the-future-of-education-and-employment/

101 European Skills Agenda. (2025, July 1). Employment, Social Affairs and Inclusion. https://employment-social-affairs.ec.europa.eu/policies-and-activities/skills-and-qualifications/european-skills-agenda_en

102 Prieto, L. M. (2025, May 28). Microcredentials in 2025: The Future of Flexible, Career-Ready Learning. OpenLMS. https://www.openlms.net/blog/education/microcredentials-2025-future-flexible-career-ready-learning/

103 Kondrat, B. S. (n.d.). Top 10 Learning & Development (L&D) trends in 2025. https://www.educate-me.co/blog/learning-and-development-trends

104 EAEA - European Association for the Education of Adults. (2025, June 26). Introducing EAEA's annual theme 2025: Flexible Learning Pathways - European Association for the Education of Adults. European Association for the Education of Adults. https://eaea.org/our-work/campaigns/introducing-eaeas-annual-theme-2025-flexible-learning-pathways/

105 European Skills Agenda. (2025b, July 1). Employment, Social Affairs and Inclusion. https://employment-social-affairs.ec.europa.eu/policies-and-activities/skills-and-qualifications/european-skills-agenda_en

Innovation area	Description	Example(s)
Immersive technologies	Use of VR/AR for interactive, accessible, and engaging learning experiences	Duolingo[106], Kahoot![107], XR-based platforms[108] [109]
Cross-sector collaboration	National/regional platforms integrating education, training, and industry	Lifelong Learning Platform EU[110], CIVIS[111]

Table 7.1: Summary of key innovations in lifelong learning platforms

By fostering curiosity, adaptability, and a proactive learning mindset, education can help to prepare students not just for their first job but for a lifetime of growth, career transitions, and meaningful contributions to society in the face of ever-changing technological advancements.

Classroom strategies and curriculum design

As AI continues to transform the way we live, work, learn, and connect, it is imperative that our education systems evolve accordingly to serve the next generation. Preparing students for the future means much more than teaching them how to use new technologies; it means equipping them with the skills to question, shape, and innovate with these tools in ethical, responsible, and creative ways. Integrating emerging AI concepts across the curriculum not only enriches students' understanding of the world around them but also helps build critical competencies for a workforce increasingly shaped by data, automation, and intelligent systems.

A powerful example of meaningful AI integration comes from an interdisciplinary **project-based learning** (PBL) project involving sixth and third-graders (K-12)[112], who collaborated on interdisciplinary projects using AI tools like SchoolAI and ChatGPT. Projects included creating *choose your own adventure* novels and informational texts for patients of the *Maria Fareri Children's Healthcare Services at MidHudson Regional Hospital*. Students used AI to brainstorm, clarify information, and refine their work, but retained creative control and ownership.

106 Barker, K., MA. (2024, December 2). Adventures is Duolingo's new immersive gamified feature. Duolingo Blog. https://blog.duolingo.com/adventures/
107 Technology Solutions | Kahoot! (2025b, May 21). Kahoot! https://kahoot.com/business/use-cases/technology-solutions/
108 XR4ED | Accelerating innovation in learning and education through EdTech and XR. (n.d.). https://xr4ed.eu/
109 XR2Learn – XR2Learn. (n.d.). https://xr2learn.eu/
110 Info. (2025, February 20). Lifelong Learning Platform's iterative study on cross-sector collaboration in education and training - a new e. LLLPlatform. https://www.lllplatform.eu/post/lifelong-learning-plat-form-s-iterative-study-on-cross-sector-collaboration-in-education-and-training
111 Micro-credentials: from idea generation to delivery. (n.d.). CIVIS - a European University Alliance. https://civis.eu/en/learn/civis-courses/micro-credentials-from-idea-generation-to-delivery
112 From cheating tool to learning Partner: A blueprint for PBL-AI solutions. (n.d.). https://blog.defined-learning.com/from-cheating-tool-to-learning-partner-a-blueprint-for-pbl-ai-solutions

Teachers facilitated discussions on how AI insights shaped student decisions, emphasizing ethical and responsible use. Outcomes included increased student engagement, deeper critical thinking, and pride in producing meaningful, audience-focused work.

Today's classrooms must evolve and go beyond traditional subject silos and foster interdisciplinary collaboration among educators. By embedding AI themes into diverse subject areas, like using data science projects in math, exploring algorithmic bias in social studies, or creating digital art using generative tools. It is imperative for educators to work to demystify AI for students and encourage a more holistic approach to learning. These integrated experiences will help students to see the connections between disciplines and understand how technology is impacting every aspect of society.

Project-based and experiential learning approaches will be vital to this vision. Hands-on simulations, coding clubs, hackathons, AI-driven science fairs, and community challenges give students a sense of agency and ownership over their learning. These environments reflect the real-world workspaces of the future, where problem-solving, collaboration, and iteration are essential. By emphasizing experimentation and creativity, students are encouraged not only to be curious to understand technology but also to reimagine what is possible with it.

Another essential pillar of this transformation is to build systems to create data literacy and analytical thinking from an early age. Introducing spreadsheets, basic programming, and grade-level-appropriate AI tools fosters a deeper understanding of data—how it is collected, interpreted, and applied. These lessons can help students become critical thinkers who can question how algorithms influence their daily lives and who can recognize bias or misuse in automated systems. In a world where daily decisions increasingly rely on data, these skills are fundamental to both personal agency and civic responsibility.

Equally important is instilling a strong foundation in ethical and responsible use of AI technology. Classroom discussions, student-led debates, and case studies focused on real-world AI dilemmas, like deep fakes, facial recognition, social media algorithms, or automated hiring systems, help students grapple with the implications of emerging technologies. These conversations emphasize inclusiveness, fairness, transparency, and accountability, encouraging young people to become conscientious designers, developers, and users of technology.

Beyond the classroom, deep partnerships with industry, community colleges, and technical programs can help students envision their futures in AI-supported careers. Career awareness programs, industry guest speakers, and job-shadowing opportunities introduce students to high-demand roles in cloud computing, cybersecurity, machine learning, and beyond. These experiences are especially critical in connecting students to new-collar and middle-skills opportunities, positions that require specialized training but not necessarily a four-year degree and ensuring that AI education is inclusive and accessible.

To truly prepare students for this evolving workforce, schools must also offer targeted coursework and certification programs that align with evolving industry standards. Whether through classes on AI, digital literacy, automation, or data analytics, or through certification pathways in cloud services and programming, students should have tangible ways to demonstrate their competencies. Internships and apprenticeships deepen this preparation, giving learners real-world experience and mentorship in AI-driven fields.

Ultimately, preparing students for an AI-augmented world requires much more than technical know-how. It calls for developing a mindset of lifelong learning: adaptability, curiosity, and the willingness to keep growing as technology changes. By exposing today's students to emerging trends, continuous learning platforms, and the dynamic nature of modern careers, educators can empower students who are tomorrow's workforce to be resilient, future-ready individuals.

Integrating AI into education is not a luxury; it is a necessity. Through thoughtful, hands-on, and ethically grounded learning approaches, we can ensure that students do not just adapt to the future; they help shape it. Some of the programs and courses that can be considered for the integration of AI include:

- **Career awareness programs**: Develop programs to introduce students to AI-enhanced trades, technical careers, and middle-skills opportunities through career fairs and guest speakers.

- **Industry partnerships**: Build partnerships to collaborate with local businesses, tech companies, and community colleges to offer hands-on workshops and mentorship.

- **AI and digital literacy courses**: Develop coursework to embed AI, automation, and data analytics into curricula across various subjects.

- **Certification programs**: Offer courses that prepare students for industry-recognized credentials in cloud computing, cybersecurity, and machine learning.

- **Internships and apprenticeships**: Provide students with a real-world experience in AI-supported fields through partnerships with tech-driven companies.

- **Project-based learning**: Engage students in interdisciplinary projects that combine their technical skills with problem-solving and ethical considerations.

- **Emphasizing lifelong learning**: Encourage flexibility and adaptability and upskilling by exposing students to continuous learning platforms and emerging job trends.

Educator roles and professional development

As AI transforms learning, educators must shift from traditional instruction to becoming facilitators who guide inquiry-based activities and student-led explorations. Instead of delivering static lectures, teachers can create dynamic learning environments, augmented and supported by AI, where students actively engage with problems, collaborate, and discover solutions independently. Inquiry-based learning encourages students to ask questions, conduct their own research, and develop independent critical thinking skills as they navigate complex subjects. Educators can research and design projects that challenge students to analyze real-world problems, integrate new AI tools for research and problem-solving, and reflect on ethical implications. This hands-on approach ensures that students not only acquire deep technical knowledge but also develop flexibility, adaptability, and creativity, skills essential in an AI-driven workforce.

Several leading **professional development** (PD) programs are specifically designed to equip teachers with actionable strategies for integrating generative AI tools in the classroom, moving well beyond basic tech skills to focus on pedagogy, creativity, and responsible use:

- **Google's Generative AI for Educators**[113] offers a free, self-paced course (with MIT RAISE[114]) on lesson personalization, creative activity design, and workflow automation. Over 80% of teachers report time savings and increased confidence using AI.

- **GenAI Literacy Trainer Essentials**[115] by AI for Education is a six-week online course for instructional leaders, focusing on foundational AI skills, classroom strategies, and ethical use, enabling them to deliver AI PD in their schools.

- **Technical training, pedagogical support, testing revamp, practice networks (TPTP) Support System for Teachers**[116] provides a five-week course and ongoing support, emphasizing responsible use of tools like ChatGPT and context-specific training.

- **EU Academy's Artificial intelligence for teacher professional development**[117] offers webinars and workshops on practical AI uses, creative applications, and ethical considerations.

Many schools also use train-the-trainer models for sustained, peer-led AI integration. These programs go beyond basic tech skills, empowering teachers to use, question, and innovate with AI tools in creative and responsible ways. Additionally, educators play a crucial role in helping to mentor students on the responsible use of AI. As students increasingly interact with generative AI, data analytics, and automation tools, educators must help them navigate these technologies critically and ethically. It is critical for teachers to show students the difference between outsourcing to AI and partnering with AI. Students must see how AI can be a partner, not a shortcut. This conversation includes fostering discussions on plagiarism, bias in AI, data privacy, and the social impact of automation. By modeling ethical reasoning to students, encouraging digital literacy, and guiding students to evaluate AI-generated content with

113 Sanders, S. (n.d.). Generative AI for Educators - Grow with Google. https://grow.google/ai-for-educators/
114 MIT RAISE: Responsible AI for Social Empowerment and Education. (2025, July 3). MIT RAISE. https://raise.mit.edu/
115 Train the Trainer Institute: GenAI Literacy Trainer Essentials — AI for Education. (n.d.). AI For Education. https://www.aiforeducation.io/train-the-trainer-institute-genai-literacy-trainer-essentials
116 Al-Ali, S., & Miles, R. (2025). Upskilling teachers to use generative artificial intelligence: The TPTP approach for sustainable teacher support and development. Australasian Journal of Educational Technology. https://doi.org/10.14742/ajet.9652
117 Artificial intelligence for teacher professional development. (n.d.). Artificial Intelligence for Teacher Professional Development. https://academy.europa.eu/local/euacademy/pages/course/event-overview.php?title=artificial-intelligence-for-teacher-professional-development

discernment, educators can help empower the next generation to use AI as an enhancement rather than a replacement for human insight, ensuring thoughtful and responsible engagement with emerging technologies.

Continuous training and collaboration

As AI technologies evolve to reshape the way in which we provide education, continuous training and collaboration are essential for educators to stay ahead. Teachers' professional development must evolve beyond occasional workshops and become an ongoing process that equips educators with the knowledge and skills to understand AI and to integrate AI tools, data analytics, and **educational technology** (**edtech**) platforms into their teaching. Schools should provide structured learning opportunities such as hands-on training in AI fundamentals, machine learning applications, and the ethical implications of technology in education. Sessions on predictive analysis and data-driven decision-making can help teachers use analytics to personalize instruction and assess student progress more effectively. Additionally, professional development should include training for teachers on emerging edtech platforms, ensuring that educators can confidently implement AI-powered tools like adaptive learning systems, intelligent tutoring programs, and automated assessment tools in their classrooms.

Collaboration is equally important in fostering a culture of continuous learning. Professional development communities such as **teacher learning communities** (**TLCs**)[118] and global **communities of practice** (**CoPs**) have become pivotal in helping educators adapt rapidly to new AI technologies. These collaborative networks enable teachers to share experiences, co-create resources, and develop practical strategies for integrating AI into teaching, from lesson planning and personalized learning to AI-assisted feedback and ethical use. For example, the British Council's global CoP[119] brought together educators from 18 countries to address challenges and opportunities in AI adoption, resulting in actionable insights on AI safety, effective classroom applications, and data privacy. Such forums not only accelerate the responsible uptake of AI but also foster a culture of continuous learning, empowering educators to critically assess and innovate with AI tools while maintaining a strong focus on human interaction and ethical considerations. This collective approach ensures that teachers are not just keeping pace with technological change but are actively shaping how AI enhances education.

Partnering with local industry experts, universities, and tech companies can further help to enrich teacher training by providing insights into real-world AI applications and workforce trends. These partnerships can include a variety of guest lectures, mentorship programs, and hands-on workshops that help bridge the gap between academic knowledge and practical

118 Pan, H. W., & Cheng, S. (2023). Examining the Impact of Teacher learning communities on Self-Efficacy and Professional Learning: an application of the Theory-Driven Evaluation. Sustainability, 15(6), 4771. https://doi.org/10.3390/su15064771

119 Transforming teacher education with AI: Lessons from a global Community of Practice. (n.d.). TeachingEnglish. https://www.teachingenglish.org.uk/publications/case-studies-insights-and-research/transforming-teacher-education-ai-lessons-global

AI applications. By fostering a collaborative approach to professional education and growth, teachers not only enhance their own skill sets but also create a more engaging, future-ready learning experience for their students. Continuous professional development helps to ensure that teachers remain lifelong learners themselves, setting a powerful leadership example for students in an era where adaptability and technological fluency are crucial for success.

Assessing AI integration effectiveness

To ensure that AI-driven education is truly benefiting students, educators must implement strategies for measuring student engagement, skills acquisition, and career readiness. One key approach is tracking engagement through interactive assessments, participation in AI-enhanced activities, and feedback surveys. AI tools can help provide real-time insights into student progress, identifying areas where learners excel or struggle. Educators can also assess skills acquisition by designing project-based assignments where students apply these AI tools, analyze data, or demonstrate critical thinking in technology-enhanced tasks. Certifications in AI literacy, software development and coding, or data analytics can serve as benchmarks for students' preparedness for AI-driven careers.

Leading educational institutions are leveraging advanced analytics and AI tools to drive real-time assessment and measurable improvement in student outcomes. Platforms like Knewton Alta[120] use adaptive learning algorithms to analyze vast amounts of student interaction data, enabling instructors to pinpoint where learners struggle and tailor instruction accordingly, which deepens understanding and boosts retention[121]. AI-powered grading systems such as Gradescope[122] automate assessment, providing instant, detailed feedback and freeing up teachers' time for more targeted support. Universities are also adopting frameworks that prioritize responsible and transparent AI use, ensuring that data-driven insights are used ethically to enhance both teaching and learning[123]. Reports highlight that these AI-driven strategies are not only increasing teaching effectiveness and student engagement but are also bridging learning gaps with unprecedented precision, marking a shift from experimental pilots to institution-wide, outcome-focused implementations.

Educators should measure student progress as well as engage in reflective teaching practices to continuously refine their AI-enhanced lessons. This work involves reviewing student performance data, gathering feedback, and iterating on instructional[124] strategies. For instance, if AI-driven personalized learning tools show gaps in student understanding, teachers can adjust lesson pacing or incorporate more hands-on applications. Peer collaboration and TLCs

120 Alta. (n.d.). https://www.wiley.com/en-us/education/alta
121 ScrumLaunch. (n.d.). ScrumLaunch. https://www.scrumlaunch.com/blog/ai-in-education-transform-ing-learning-and-teaching-in-2025
122 Gradescope | Save time grading. (n.d.-b). https://www.gradescope.com/
123 3 Trends to prioritize in your annual strategy. (n.d.). 2025 AI Shortlist for Higher Education. https://assets.ctfassets.net/1e6ajr2k4140/4pkhlb5YUKH6Xb7T9jTMSf/2506b985233d3f7c05a3d82e5491f4c7/2025_AI_Shortlist_for_Higher_Education_3_Trends-compressed-compressed.pdf.pdf
124 Dent, D., Frazee, J., Shumaker, C., & Wrye, T. (2024, October 23). 2025 EDUCAUSE Top 10. Educause. https://er.educause.edu/articles/2024/10/2025-educause-top-10-1-the--data-empowered--institution

can further support iterative refinement by allowing educators to share insights and best practices. By integrating data-driven decision-making with reflective teaching, schools can ensure that AI tools are used to enhance, not replace, effective instruction, preparing students to navigate and thrive in an increasingly AI-driven workforce.

Bridging the classroom and the real world

Building a broad set of strong industry partnerships and mentorship programs is essential for preparing students for an AI-driven workforce. Collaborations with tech companies, industry giants, local businesses, and academic institutions help to provide students with real-world exposure through internships, hands-on projects, and industry-aligned learning experiences. By engaging with professionals in the world of technology, AI, cybersecurity, data analytics, and automation, students can gain valuable insights into career pathways and the evolving job market. These partnerships help students and educators bridge the gap between classroom learning and workplace application, ensuring that students develop both technical and soft skills necessary for success in AI-integrated industries.

Recent case studies highlight how industry-school partnerships are tangibly improving student career readiness by bridging the gap between classroom learning and real-world workforce demands. For example, in **science, technology, engineering, and mathematics (STEM)** education, collaborations with aviation and geospatial industries have enabled high school students to earn industry-recognized credentials such as remote pilot licenses and aeronautical radio operator certificates, directly preparing them for careers in aviation, surveying, and environmental science[125]. In **Higher National Diploma (HND)** programs, partnerships with businesses provide students with hands-on internships, live industry projects, and curriculum co-design, ensuring academic content remains aligned with current industry needs and equipping students with both technical and soft skills essential for the workplace[126]. Business schools, such as *King's College London*, have run global industry consultancy projects where students work directly with employers on real challenges, significantly boosting their practical experience and employability[127]. These partnerships not only increase the rates at which students graduate with official career readiness designations[128], but also expand professional networks and job opportunities, demonstrating the powerful impact of sustained collaboration between education and industry on preparing students for successful careers.

Schools can enhance these experiences by engaging with and bringing industry experts directly into the classroom through guest lectures, panel discussions, and mentorship

125 Francis, L. (2025, March 20). Bridging the gap: the power of School-Industry partnerships. She Maps. https://shemaps.com/blog/bridging-the-gap-the-power-of-school-industry-partnerships/
126 Mont Rose College of Management and Science. (2025, February 27). The role of industry partnerships in HND Programs I MR College. MR College. https://mrcollege.ac.uk/the-role-of-industry-partnerships-in-hnd-programs/
127 Pracstaging. (2024, December 16). Enhancing Student Employability in 2024-2025: A complete guide for educators. Practera. https://practera.com/complete-guide-for-educators-2024-2025/
128 Perry, A. M. (2025). Unlocking the black box of School–Industry Partnerships: A comparative case study. International Journal of Training and Development. https://doi.org/10.1111/ijtd.70003

programs. Professionals from leading tech firms, startups, and AI research institutions can provide firsthand knowledge about AI trends, ethical challenges, and in-demand skills. Workshops and hackathons can further immerse students in a variety of real-world problem-solving by simulating workplace challenges, encouraging collaboration, and fostering innovation. For example, students could participate in AI-driven experiments, case studies, develop automation solutions for local businesses, or design ethical AI policies for real-world applications.[129]

By integrating industry partnerships into education, schools can create a talent pipeline that aligns with workforce needs while equipping students with relevant experience, networking opportunities, and mentorship. These collaborations not only enhance learning but also provide students with a huge competitive advantage in securing future careers.

Supporting remote and distributed learning models

As remote and distributed work becomes more common across industries, educators must help prepare students to thrive in hybrid and online team settings. Future jobs will require seamless collaboration across time zones and digital platforms, making it essential for schools to help students develop strong communication, self-management, and teamwork skills in virtual environments. Educators can help foster these abilities by integrating remote learning models into the classroom, ensuring students gain hands-on experience with modern collaboration tools.

One key strategy to help schools achieve these ends is to use AI-powered collaboration tools, such as video conferencing, shared digital workspaces, and cloud-based project management platforms. Tools like Microsoft Teams, Google Workspace, and AI-driven scheduling assistants can help students coordinate group projects, manage deadlines, and communicate effectively in virtual settings. Educators should encourage students to engage in asynchronous and synchronous teamwork with fellow students, mirroring real-world remote workflows where employees must collaborate despite working in different locations or time zones.

Global collaborative learning models are increasingly leveraging advanced AI tools to facilitate seamless international student collaboration and multidisciplinary problem-solving. One standout example is the emergence of *Virtual Labs*, where teams of AI agents with specialized expertise, such as AI chemists or biologists, work alongside students and faculty from different countries to tackle open-ended research challenges, with human participants providing high-level guidance and oversight[130]. These AI-driven environments enable real-time, cross-border teamwork, allowing students to co-create solutions to complex global issues while developing critical skills in communication, cultural competence, and ethical AI use.

129 The Future of Jobs Report 2023. (2023). In World Economic Forum. World Economic Forum. https://www.weforum.org/publications/the-future-of-jobs-report-2023/
130 Predictions for AI in 2025: Collaborative agents, AI skepticism, and new risks | Stanford HAI. (n.d.). https://hai.stanford.edu/news/predictions-for-ai-in-2025-collaborative-agents-ai-skepticism-and-new-risks

To further enhance distributed work skills, schools can incorporate global collaboration projects, where students work with peers and teammates from other schools or even international partners. AI-powered platforms now support hyper-personalized learning journeys, real-time feedback, and adaptive content translation, making collaborative projects more inclusive and accessible for diverse international cohorts. Virtual internships and industry-led mentorship programs can also help students simulate the realities of remote work. This shift from isolated learning to AI-enhanced, globally connected classrooms reflects a broader trend toward education ecosystems that are integrated, adaptable, and focused on preparing students for a future defined by both technological innovation and cross-cultural collaboration. By embedding these experiences into the classroom, schools ensure students are prepared for the flexibility and digital proficiency required in AI-driven, distributed workplaces.

Career awareness and guidance

As AI reshapes the nature of work, career awareness and guidance must evolve to showcase the diverse opportunities emerging across industries. Students need to get real-world exposure to a wide range of AI-impacted careers beyond traditional tech roles, including fields like cybersecurity, health tech, creative AI, and smart manufacturing. Educators can provide structured career exploration activities that highlight how AI is transforming different sectors, from AI-assisted medical diagnostics to ethical AI governance and automation-driven operational logistics. By integrating career discussions into various school subjects, educators can help students see how AI can augment and align with their interests and skills, making career pathways more tangible.

Education departments and industry consortia are driving impactful initiatives to integrate career awareness programs in AI-driven fields, ensuring students are prepared for the rapidly evolving workforce. The U.S. government's April 2025 *Advancing Artificial Intelligence Education for American Youth*[131] executive initiative exemplifies this trend by embedding AI literacy and career pathways across K-12 and postsecondary systems, supporting hands-on learning with real-world AI tools, and expanding access to industry-aligned apprenticeships and certifications. Globally, the *European Commission* and OECD have launched the AI literacy framework[132], which not only promotes technical skills but also emphasizes critical, creative, and ethical engagement with AI, preparing students to navigate and shape future job markets. Industry-backed programs further bridge the skills gap by offering free, scalable AI training and career development resources to diverse populations, while large-scale public-private partnerships are increasingly integrating work-integrated learning, internships, and co-op programs into formal education to align with industry needs and boost employability in AI-centric roles. These collaborative efforts reflect a global commitment to making AI career awareness and readiness a foundational component of modern education.

---

131 The White House. (2025, April 23). Advancing artificial intelligence education for American youth. https://www.whitehouse.gov/presidential-actions/2025/04/advancing-artificial-intelligence-education-for-american-youth/
132 Why AI literacy is now a core competency in education. (2025, June 3). World Economic Forum. https://www.weforum.org/stories/2025/05/why-ai-literacy-is-now-a-core-competency-in-education/

To support students in identifying their strengths and aligning them with AI-driven careers, educators can leverage self-assessment tools, mentorship programs, career counseling workshops and related sessions. Interactive activities like career fairs, panels, workplace simulations, and job shadowing can offer students real-world insights. Schools can also introduce students to alternative career pathways, such as new-collar roles that prioritize skills-based hiring over traditional academic degrees. By exposing students to the interdisciplinary nature of AI-related careers, educators can empower students to pursue roles that combine technical knowledge with creativity, ethics, or human-centric problem-solving skills. Ultimately, career guidance should inspire adaptability and curiosity, ensuring students can navigate the impact of AI on the evolving job market with confidence.

Continuous innovation

As AI continues to evolve, schools must actively adapt to ensure both students and educators stay on pace with or ahead of emerging trends. Managing AI advancements requires a culture of continuous learning, where teachers and students engage with industry developments through reading, AI forums, online courses, and conferences. Schools should encourage the participation of both teachers and students in AI-focused communities such as OpenAI, Google AI, and MIT's AI initiatives, where members can discuss breakthroughs, ethics, and practical applications. Online courses from platforms like Coursera, edX, and Udacity offer easy-to-access, up-to-date training on AI concepts, ensuring that educators can integrate the latest AI knowledge into their classroom teaching. Attending AI-related conferences, whether in-person or virtually, exposes both teachers and students to thought leaders, cutting-edge research, and real-world applications of AI, helping them see the evolving role of AI in society. By promoting these opportunities, educators can cultivate a mindset where staying updated on AI trends becomes second nature for the classrooms of the future.

Beyond individual learning, embracing the fast-paced nature of change as part of school culture is essential for preparing students for an AI-driven workforce. Traditional curricula, which have relied on static textbooks and rigid lesson plans in the past, must evolve to accommodate the dynamic nature of AI. Schools should adopt flexible, modular curricula that allow for the integration of emerging AI technologies, real-world case studies, and hands-on tech experimentation. This can involve embedding AI topics into multiple disciplines, teaching ethical considerations in humanities courses, AI-assisted research in science classes, or automation's economic impact in social studies. Schools should also provide space for student-led exploration, encouraging projects where students apply AI tools to solve real-world problems. It is a brave new world.

Creating AI innovation hubs or labs within schools can further support student exploration and adaptability, providing students with direct, hands-on engagement with emerging AI technologies, transforming both learning and career preparation. These spaces house AI-driven software, robotics kits, and interactive learning tools that empower students to experiment with AI concepts. The **European Digital Innovation Hubs** (**EDIHs**)[133], now operational across the EU, offer students and educators access to advanced AI tools, technical expertise, and test-before-invest environments, allowing them to experiment with real-world AI applications and develop practical skills in collaboration with industry partners. Similarly, the *AI Observatory and Action Lab*[134], launched by *EdTech Hub*, serves as a dynamic platform where students and teachers co-design and test AI-powered learning strategies, ensuring that technology is both effective and equitable in real classroom settings. In China, the 2025 *Hainan International Forum on Higher Education Innovation and Development* has spotlighted university-based three-campus models—physical, industrial, and digital—where smart teaching platforms automate class scheduling, personalize learning paths, and provide AI-driven feedback, enabling students to navigate and shape their own educational journeys using cutting-edge AI systems[135]. These hubs not only foster technical proficiency but also cultivate creativity, ethical awareness, and adaptability, equipping students to thrive in an AI-driven future.

By working on AI-based projects, such as training and self-help chatbots, analyzing datasets, or developing machine learning models, students have the opportunity to build on practical experience that prepares them for future careers. Schools can also form AI student clubs, where interested students can collaborate on AI-related challenges, engage in AI hackathons, and share insights with peers.[136] Another key element of supporting students in staying ahead is to foster teacher collaboration and professional development. Schools should provide dedicated time for educators to discuss AI integration in the classroom, share best practices, and refine their teaching strategies. Encouraging educators to work together in learning communities ensures that AI literacy becomes a shared effort rather than an individual task. Schools can also pair up with local universities and tech companies to offer AI-focused workshops and mentorship programs, giving educators direct access to industry knowledge.

Ultimately, adopting AI into education to prepare a future workforce needs to be an ongoing process rather than a one-time initiative. AI advancements will continue to shift the job market, requiring students to develop adaptability and lifelong learning skills. This technology will change the future of work for decades. By embracing AI forums, flexible curricula, and an innovative school culture, educators can ensure students are not just learning about AI but actively engaging with it. Schools that stay ahead of these AI trends will better equip students to navigate the future, where AI literacy and problem-solving skills will be essential in almost every field.

133 European Digital Innovation Hubs. (n.d.). Shaping Europe's Digital Future. https://digital-strategy.ec.europa.eu/en/policies/edihs

134 Hub, E. (2025, June 13). How to unlock learning outcomes in the age of AI? EdTech Hub. https://edtech-hub.org/2025/04/04/how-to-unlock-learning-outcomes-in-the-age-of-ai/

135 Exploring AI-Driven Transformation: 2025 Hainan Higher Education Innovation Forum set for November. (n.d.). RIVER COUNTRY - NEWS CHANNEL NEBRASKA. https://rivercountry.newschannelnebraska.com/story/52892363/exploring-ai-driven-transformation-2025-hainan-higher-education-innovation-forum-set-for-november

136 Peretz, J. (2025, February 12). Reinventing Classrooms with Immersive Innovation Labs® by Inventionland Education. Inventionland Education. https://inventionlandeducation.com/reinventing-classrooms-with-immersive-innovation-labs-by-inventionland-education

Cultivating an adaptable school ecosystem

In an era where AI and technology are reshaping industries at an unprecedented pace, schools must build adaptable ecosystems that evolve along with these AI advancements. This requires culture change, forward-thinking policies, continuous feedback mechanisms, and open minds that stay curious. Rather than rigid curricula and traditional learning models, schools must adopt flexible policies that allow for creativity and iterative updates in response to technological shifts. Advances in AI and workforce automation will continue to transform industries. The skills that students need today may look very different in just a few years. Schools need to develop dynamic curriculum frameworks, incorporating AI literacy, data ethics, and problem-solving skills while allowing room for new emerging technologies to be seamlessly integrated as they become relevant. Regular curriculum reviews, informed by workforce trends, industry collaborations, and technological breakthroughs, can help ensure that students are always receiving an education aligned with future job markets.

Policy developments worldwide are actively supporting flexible curriculum models and dynamic investments in educational infrastructure to better prepare students for a rapidly changing world. India's **National Education Policy** (**NEP**) 2025[137], for example, introduces a flexible, multidisciplinary curriculum that allows students to explore subjects across disciplines, integrates AI-driven platforms for personalized learning, and emphasizes teacher training in modern pedagogical techniques. In Portugal and across the EU, ongoing reforms are modernizing education systems by developing demanding and flexible curricula focused on scientific and cultural knowledge, supporting school autonomy, and aligning vocational and higher education with evolving workforce needs[138]. Globally, there is a marked shift toward hybrid and agile learning models, with investments in digital infrastructure enabling the adoption of project-based learning, micro-credentials, and real-world skill development[139]. These policies are also promoting equity by broadening access to education for adults and underrepresented groups, and by encouraging personalized teaching that respects individual learning paces and styles[140]. Collectively, these initiatives reflect a commitment to building responsive, future-ready education systems through both curricular innovation and robust infrastructure investment.

A critical characteristic of this new world is adaptability and being able to create a continuous feedback loop where students, educators, and administrators actively refine AI integration into the classroom. Schools can benefit from the creation of AI task forces or innovation committees composed of teachers, students, IT specialists, and industry advisors to evaluate emerging AI tools and their effectiveness in classrooms. Regular discussions, surveys, and pilot programs can help to identify what works best and where adjustments are needed. By engaging students

137 Holistic Educare. (2025, March 27). National Education Policy (NEP) 2025 – Key Highlights. https://holisticeducare.in/uncategorized/national-education-policy-nep-2025-key-highlights/
138 Ongoing reforms and policy developments. (n.d.-b). https://eurydice.eacea.ec.europa.eu/eurypedia/portugal/ongoing-reforms-and-policy-developments
139 Motion, E. I., & Motion, E. I. (2025, January 14). 2025 Higher Education trends: 5 key shifts to watch. https://eimpartnerships.com/articles/2025-higher-education-trends-5-key-shifts-to-watch
140 Education GPS, OECD, (2025, July 6), 5:46:58 PM http://gpseducation.oecd.org

in the AI conversation, schools empower them to take ownership of their learning experience while also developing critical thinking about AI's role in education.

Beyond policy and feedback, adaptability can thrive in a culture of experimentation and openness to change. Schools must encourage sandbox environments where teachers can test drive AI-driven tools and methodologies before full-scale implementation. Professional development for educators must be ongoing, with teachers continuously up-skilling in AI literacy, digital tools, and interdisciplinary teaching approaches. Additionally, administrators should provide resources and incentives for AI innovation, recognizing educators who take the lead in integrating AI effectively.

Finally, adaptability must extend beyond the classroom, ensuring that school and community education infrastructures are built to support long-term technological evolution. This includes investing in a robust digital infrastructure, cloud-based learning environments, and significant cybersecurity measures to protect student data while allowing for AI-enhanced personalized learning. By fostering an agile, tech-forward school ecosystem that prioritizes flexibility, ongoing learning, industry collaboration, and iterative improvement, education systems can remain future-ready, preparing students for careers in an AI-driven world while maintaining an ethical and human-centered learning experiences.

Conclusion

The transformative impact of AI on the global labor market has arrived. This change will only accelerate in the years ahead. Nearly every job in every industry in every country will be touched in some way by AI; some will be redefined, some will disappear, and entirely new occupations will be born.[141] Current trends and research indicate that while substantial job displacement will occur, there is a notable potential for net positive job growth if new tech-driven roles can be filled. The World Economic Forum's Future of Jobs Report 2025[142] highlights that 70% of employers now prioritize upskilling their workforce for AI-driven roles, with half planning to reorient their business strategies around AI adoption and two-thirds seeking talent with specific AI skills. TechNet's 2025 white paper[143] calls for robust government investment in upskilling, reskilling, and equitable access to digital skills training, especially for underserved communities, to ensure all workers can adapt and thrive as jobs evolve in a technology-driven economy. Meanwhile, the *European Parliamentary Research Service*[144]

141 Mayer, H., Yee, L., Chui, M., & Roberts, R. (2025, January 28). Superagency in the workplace: Empowering people to unlock AI's full potential. McKinsey & Company. https://www.mckinsey.com/capabilities/mckinsey-digital/our-insights/superagency-in-the-workplace-empowering-people-to-unlock-ais-full-potential-at-work

142 Zahidi, S. (Director). (n.d.). Future of Jobs Report 2025. In WEForum. https://www.weforum.org/reports/the-future-of-jobs-report-2025/

143 Fleming, P., Meghan Dorn, Kate Davis, & TechNet. (2025). AI AND THE WORKFORCE. In TECHNET. https://www.technet.org/wp-content/uploads/2025/02/TechNet-AI-Workforce-White-Paper-2025.pdf

144 Vesnic-Alujevic, L., Saitis, G., & European Parliamentary Research Service. (2025). What role for AI skills in (re-)shaping the future European workforce? In Policy Foresight Analysis (Report PE 765.806). https://www.europarl.europa.eu/RegData/etudes/BRIE/2025/765806/EPRS_BRI(2025)765806_EN.pdf

emphasizes the urgency of closing the AI skills gap through lifelong learning, anticipatory governance, and targeted investment in digital infrastructure, all while maintaining a human-centric and ethical approach to AI development.

The challenge and opportunity lie in navigating this transition. Across these statements, a common priority emerges: preparing the workforce for AI is not only about technical proficiency, but also about fostering adaptability, critical thinking, and ethical responsibility, ensuring that the benefits of AI are broadly shared and that workers are empowered to shape the future of work. Workers who continuously update their skills and embrace AI as a tool are more likely to thrive, whereas those stuck in outdated roles risk falling behind.[145] This emphasizes the role of education and training. By instilling digital skills, adaptability, and a mindset of lifelong learning, we can empower the workforce to leverage AI's benefits rather than be sidelined by its emergence. Proactive measures, from corporate reskilling programs to K–12 AI curricula changes, are now underway to bridge the skill gap and ease workforce transitions. There is no doubt that AI is already reshaping work as we know it; the key is ensuring that people around the world are prepared to shape AI to humane ends and prosper alongside it, rather than be displaced by it. With concerted effort by industry, educators, and policymakers, the AI revolution can become a driver of inclusive growth, unlocking innovation and productivity while creating new opportunities for millions of students and future workers.[146] The future of work in the age of AI will ultimately be what we make of it, and the steps we take today will determine how a future workforce emerges stronger, more skilled, and ready to collaborate with the intelligent machines of tomorrow.[147]

In the next chapter, we look into how educators can enhance their AI skills, learn best practices, and become the instructors of tomorrow.

Questions

1. How might education change in response to the rise of AI across industries?

2. What are the key differences between traditional education and what's needed for the new AI era?

3. What new roles can AI play in supporting teachers, rather than replacing them?

4. How can schools balance technical skill development with ethics and emotional intelligence in an era of AI?

145 Education, I. (2025, March 10). The impact of AI on job roles, workforce, and employment: What you need to know | Innopharma Education. Innopharma Education. https://www.innopharmaeducation.com/blog/the-impact-of-ai-on-job-roles-workforce-and-employment-what-you-need-to-know
146 Leopold, T. (2025). Future of Jobs Report 2025: The jobs of the future-and the skills you need to get them. In World Economic Forum. World Economic Forum. https://www.weforum.org/stories/2025/01/future-of-jobs-report-2025-jobs-of-the-future-and-the-skills-you-need-to-get-them/#:~:text=,likely%2Cneed%20in%20the%20future
147 Yeyati, E. L., & Seyal, I. (2025, March 19). Digital footprints and job matching: The new frontier of AI-driven hiring. Brookings. https://www.brookings.edu/articles/digital-footprints-and-job-matching-the-new-frontier-of-ai-driven-hiring/

5. What is the significance of new-collar jobs, and how can schools and teachers prepare students for them?

6. In what ways can AI further exacerbate or help reduce social and economic inequalities?

7. How can we measure student readiness for an AI-driven workforce?

Exercises

1. **Role analysis—The future of work**: Choose a job or career path that interests you; this could be anything from healthcare to design to software engineering. Research how AI is now impacting that field and identify which aspects are being automated, enhanced, or redefined. Then, make a list of technical and human skills that would make someone more competitive and resilient in that profession. How should those new skills be taught?

2. **Ethics debate—Should AI make critical decisions**: Divide the class into small groups and assign a scenario (e.g., AI in student grading, AI hiring, criminal sentencing, or health diagnostics). One side argues in favor of AI decision-making, while the other presents ethical concerns, such as bias or lack of transparency. This exercise encourages students to think critically about the role of ethics in tech and helps them articulate informed opinions on real-world dilemmas.

3. **Build with AI—Creative collaboration**: Ask students to use a free, age-appropriate AI tool (e.g., ChatGPT for writing, Canva AI for design, or Google's Teachable Machine for basic machine learning) to create a new project such as a story, poster, or presentation. Afterward, they should reflect on and share what the AI helped them do well and what limitations they encountered. This activity builds familiarity with emerging tools while fostering critical thinking about where human creativity still matters most.

4. **Industry interview—Learning from the field**: Have students interview a professional (family member, community member, or guest speaker) who works in a field that is influenced by AI. They should ask how the person's job has changed over time, what AI tools they use (if any), and what advice they would give to students preparing for the future. This helps students connect classroom learning to real-world applications and build career awareness.

5. **Career pathway map—Exploring new-collar jobs**: Students choose a new-collar job, like cybersecurity analyst, data technician, or AI support specialist, and research how to enter the field. They will identify new required skills, key certifications, training programs, and employers who are hiring, then create a visual map or infographic to present their findings. This can help promote exploration of non-traditional education paths and open their eyes to the diversity of opportunities in AI-driven industries. Repeat this exercise regularly.

CHAPTER 8

AI-enhanced Professional Development for Educators

The illiterate of the 21ˢᵗ century will not be those who cannot read and write, but those who cannot learn, unlearn, and relearn.

-Alvin Toffler

Introduction

As AI continues to reshape education, its potential to support and empower educators has become increasingly clear. While much of the public conversation centers on how AI impacts students, this chapter focuses on the transformative opportunities AI offers teachers through personalized professional development, smarter workflows, real-time data, and collaborative support tools.

Teachers are not just users of educational technologies; they are designers of learning experiences, mentors, and leaders in their communities. AI-enhanced PD is not about replacing teacher expertise, but about freeing time, improving precision, and elevating human capacity.

The rise of AI is reshaping how educators plan, teach, and grow in their profession. Importantly, AI is not a replacement for teachers but a powerful assistant that can shoulder routine tasks and provide data-driven insights, freeing teachers to focus on what they do best: connecting with students. Around the world, many teachers are already experimenting with AI tools to save time and reduce burnout. In California, for example, educators have begun using AI to personalize reading materials for students, generate lesson plans, and handle other tasks, all in order to save time and reduce burnout[1]. The **Organisation for Economic Co-operation and Development's (OECD)** 2024 *Education at a Glance* report highlights that teacher attrition rates are rising, with many countries reporting that over 30% of teachers are considering leaving the profession due to stress, workload, and burnout.[2]

Every minute saved on administrative work can be reinvested in student engagement. One estimate suggests that even 30 seconds saved each day adds up to six extra instructional hours over a school year[3], highlighting AI's potential to meaningfully increase time for teaching and professional growth. Educators can leverage AI across a spectrum of tasks to enhance teaching and professional development through various applications of AI and education, from adaptive learning systems and automated grading to intelligent tutoring and smart content creation. Globally, the world needs 44 million additional teachers by 2030 to achieve universal primary and secondary education.[4]

Structure

- Personalized professional development and coaching
- Data-driven instructional design
- Assessment and feedback
- Content creation and enhanced experiences
- Time management and collaboration
- Family and community engagement
- Future-proofing and ongoing evolution
- Best practices

Objectives

This chapter aims to equip readers with a comprehensive understanding of how AI can enhance professional development for educators across all levels of education. By exploring both current applications and emerging innovations, readers will learn how AI can personalize

1 Johnson, K. (2024, July 25). California teachers are using AI to grade papers. Who's grading the AI? CalMatters. https://calmatters.org/economy/technology/2024/06/teachers-ai-grading/#:~:text=Teachers%20use%20AI%20to%20do,laden%20with%20racism%20or%20sexism
2 OECD (2024), Education at a Glance 2024: OECD Indicators, OECD Publishing, Paris, https://doi.org/10.1787/c00cad36-en.
3 Riddell, R. (2017, November 1). IBM's Watson is helping educators choose relevant math lessons. K-12 Dive. https://www.k12dive.com/news/ibms-watson-is-helping-educators-choose-relevant-math-lessons/508599/#:~:text=Thus%20far%2C%20AI%20isn%27t%20turning,hours%20during%20the%20school%20year
4 Global Education Monitoring Report Team. (2023). 2023 GEM Report: Technology in Education: a tool on whose terms? In UNESCO (ED-2023/SANS COTE). UNESCO. https://doi.org/10.54676/JKLA7966

professional learning experiences, support instructional design, and improve the quality and efficiency of assessment and feedback. The chapter also examines how AI-powered tools assist in content creation, time management, and collaboration, allowing teachers to focus more on student engagement and instructional quality. Readers will gain insights into how AI strengthens connections with families and communities, enables better communication with administrators and policymakers, and prepares educators to adapt to ongoing changes in educational technology. Grounded in real-world examples and research-backed strategies, this chapter encourages educators to critically reflect on ethical and practical considerations while embracing the transformative potential of AI to future-proof their skills and enhance their impact in the classroom and beyond.

Personalized professional development and coaching

Continuous PD is vital for educators, and AI offers new ways to personalize teacher learning and coaching. Traditionally, teachers might wait for occasional peer observations or annual workshops for feedback on their practice. Now, AI-powered coaching tools can provide on-demand, individualized feedback and PD recommendations throughout the year. For example, an *AI Coach* platform by *Edthena*[5] allows teachers to guide their own professional growth via a chatbot trained on instructional coaching strategies. Teachers set goals (such as improving class discussions or transitions), and the AI Coach engages them in a reflective cycle, prompting the teacher to analyze their classroom videos or experiences and then suggesting targeted resources. If a teacher notes that discussions are falling flat, the AI might recommend an article on clever ways to get students talking or an icebreaker activity to try. In this way, AI can curate professional development recommendations aligned to each teacher's specific needs, whether it is classroom management tips or strategies for engaging language learners.

Another exciting development is AI-driven instructional coaching for real-time insights. Consider TeachFX[6], an app that uses speech recognition and natural language processing to analyze classroom audio recordings. After a teacher records a lesson, TeachFX produces a private report detailing aspects of their instruction. For instance, the balance of teacher talk vs. student talk, the number of open-ended questions asked, and whether the teacher builds on student responses. Five years ago, such feedback required a human coach painstakingly tallying interactions; now an AI can deliver it instantly. TeachFX does not judge the teacher; it simply surfaces data for reflection, leaving decisions to the educator or mentor. This is personalized coaching in action: a teacher can discover, for example, that students only spoke for 2 minutes in a 30-minute lesson when they assumed it was more. With that insight, they might adjust their strategies to increase student participation. In one case, a teacher using TeachFX realized her students spoke far less than she thought, prompting her to consciously

---

5 Geller, A. (2025, April 3). AI Coach for Teacher PD | Instructional Coaching | Edthena. Edthena. https://www.edthena.com/ai-coach-for-teachers/

6 TeachFX. (n.d.). TeachFX. https://teachfx.com/

allow more student talk: a change that made her classroom more interactive[7]. Nearly all teachers who use such AI coaching tools see improvements like reduced off-task behavior and higher student engagement as they act on the feedback. The following figure shows an educator tapping into their AI coach:

Figure 8.1: Educators need to engage their own AI coach

AI can also facilitate peer observation and mentorship by making it easier for teachers to connect and learn from one another. Scheduling peer observations can be challenging, but AI scheduling assistants (discussed later in this chapter) can help find common planning times for teachers to observe each other's classes or swap videos. Moreover, AI analysis of classroom videos can highlight key moments. For instance, flagging a particularly successful explanation or a missed opportunity for questioning, which a mentor teacher and mentee can later review together. Some platforms are beginning to use machine learning to index teacher videos for specific skills or practices, so a teacher looking to improve, for example, wait time after asking questions, could quickly find examples of colleagues who excel in that area. By intelligently matching teachers for mentorship (e.g., identifying a veteran teacher's strength in project-based learning and suggesting them as a mentor to a newer teacher interested in that domain), AI can strengthen collaborative professional learning networks. While such matchmaking is still emerging, the goal is to build a culture where personalized coaching is available to every teacher, whether through an AI guide or an AI-facilitated human mentor.

Real-world implementations show the promise of AI in teacher coaching. In one school district in *California*[8], an instructional coach leveraged an AI tool to transcribe and analyze teachers' classroom recordings, which provided just-in-time opportunities for reflection outside the usual formal coaching cycle. Teachers who were initially skeptical found the process non-evaluative and helpful; they became more enthusiastic about coaching when they saw concrete

---

7 Noonoo, S. (2023, December 1). Improving your teaching with an AI coach. Edutopia. https://www.edutopia.org/article/improving-your-teaching-ai-coach/
8 Noonoo, S. (2023b, December 1). Improving your teaching with an AI coach. Edutopia. https://www.edutopia.org/article/improving-your-teaching-ai-coach/

improvement in their practice. Importantly, AI coaching tools maintain teacher control over their data, so teachers can practice honest self-reflection and choose what to focus on.

AI expands access to personalized PD and coaching by providing timely, targeted insights and resources to teachers. Whether through an AI mentor that chats with them about their goals, or analytic tools that reveal patterns in their instruction, these technologies support a growth mindset in educators. By integrating AI into professional learning, while still involving human coaches and peers for support, schools can create a coaching ecosystem where every teacher, not just the lucky few, gets the feedback and guidance they need to thrive. It is also important to keep in mind that AI can generate a lot, and an over-reliance on AI as a mentor can lead to a tiredness or fatigue—call it *AI* mentor fatigue—so administrators need to take care not to overwhelm educators, and educators need to be cognizant of over-reliance.

It is important to distinguish between AI that enhances classroom instruction for students and AI designed for educator professional development—this chapter focuses squarely on the latter. While classroom AI tools support student learning through adaptive content, intelligent tutoring, and student behavior and progress tracking, they aim primarily to improve student outcomes. In contrast, AI for PD empowers teachers directly, helping them reflect, grow, and refine their professional skills practice. These systems act as teacher coaches rather than co-teachers. For instance, an AI-powered tutor may help students grasp algebra, but an AI coaching tool helps a teacher better facilitate math discussions or manage transitions more smoothly. Classroom AI emphasizes content delivery to students, whereas teacher-facing AI emphasizes educator skill building, reflection, and professional growth.

This distinction is vital: the former is about delivering learning to students; the latter is about improving teaching and educator skills. AI-enhanced PD tools like Edthena's AI Coach[9] or TeachFX[10] do not instruct students—they listen, analyze, learn, and recommend strategies to educators. It is about supporting the teacher behind the desk in the front of the classroom, not just the students in front of the desk. By doing so, AI helps build stronger educators—who in turn help build stronger classrooms.

Data-driven instructional design

Designing effective instruction requires understanding students' diverse needs and tailoring the curriculum accordingly. AI excels at analyzing data and can empower teachers to make data-driven instructional design decisions: from customizing the curriculum and planning adaptive lessons to differentiating instruction based on student performance data.

One area AI has made inroads is curriculum customization. Rather than a one-size-fits-all curriculum, AI enables dynamic adjustment of content and sequence as explored in *Chapter 6, AI for Diverse Learning Needs*. This kind of AI assistance acts like an intelligent librarian or curriculum specialist at the teacher's fingertips. It saves time hunting for quality resources and ensures better alignment to learning objectives.

9 Geller, A. (2025b, June 9). AI Coach for Teacher PD | Instructional Coaching | Edthena. Edthena. https://www.edthena.com/ai-coach-for-teachers/
10 TeachFX. (n.d.-c). TeachFX. https://teachfx.com/

Teachers are also using generative AI to accelerate lesson planning and adaptation. With AI, creating a lesson plan can sometimes be as simple as describing what you need. For instance, the platform Curipod[11] lets teachers input a topic and instantly generates a ready-to-use interactive lesson, complete with text, images, polls, and discussion questions tailored to that topic. If you have a mixed-ability class learning about photosynthesis, Curipod's AI could produce a lesson with structured explanations and a variety of activities (a poll to assess prior knowledge, an open-ended question to spark discussion, etc.), which you can then tweak as needed. Another tool, Eduaide.AI[12], offers a big variety of resource templates and can generate everything from a differentiated syllabus to **individualized education plan** (**IEP**) suggestions with the ability to easily translate content into 15+ languages for classes with multilingual learners. These tools exemplify how AI assists with adaptive lesson planning: by instantly proposing outlines and materials, AI allows teachers to iterate and adapt lessons more efficiently. Rather than writing a plan from scratch, a teacher can spend time refining an AI-generated plan, incorporating student data or preferences to adapt it further.

A key benefit of AI is the ability to use data to drive differentiation in instruction. Adaptive learning platforms harness algorithms to adjust content difficulty and pace for each student, giving teachers granular insight into student progress. For example, DreamBox Learning[13], an adaptive math platform, analyzes each student's responses in real time and dynamically modifies the next problems or lessons to suit their level. If a student is struggling with two-digit multiplication, DreamBox might backtrack to review simpler concepts or provide visual aids; if another student is excelling, it will present more challenging problems to keep them engaged. This ensures that all students can work at an appropriate pace, and teachers receive analytics on who has mastered which concept. Such AI-driven systems are essentially data-driven differentiation engines: they continuously collect performance data and personalize the learning trajectory for each student. Teachers can then use the dashboard insights to form flexible groups, assign targeted interventions, or adjust whole-class instruction. For instance, an AI dashboard might reveal that five students are at risk of not grasping a concept (perhaps flagged by a series of errors or slow progress); the teacher can then pull those students for a review session, addressing gaps before they widen.

AI's predictive analytics further bolster instructional planning by identifying students who might be at risk academically. Early warning systems powered by machine learning can analyze attendance, grades, engagement metrics, and more to predict which students are likely to struggle or even drop out. For example, a large school district in the Western U.S. implemented a predictive AI system that monitors data from as early as kindergarten to flag at-risk students so counselors and teachers can intervene proactively[14]. The system continuously learns new risk factors and provides a user-friendly dashboard for real-time monitoring of

11 Feel the buzz of 100% participation. (n.d.). Curipod. https://curipod.com/
12 Eduaide.Ai: AI created for teachers. (2025, April 1). https://www.eduaide.ai/
13 DreamBox by Discovery Education. (2025c, February 12). Online math & reading programs for students | DreamBox by Discovery Education. https://www.dreambox.com/
14 Concurrency. (2024, June 11). AI early warning system predicts At-Risk K-12 students – concurrency. https://concurrency.com/case-study/ai-early-warning-system-predicts-at-risk-k-12-students/#:~:text=Predictive%20AI

these predictions. In a classroom context, this means a teacher could receive an alert that a certain student's pattern of low quiz scores and absenteeism indicates they are at high risk in math, even if the student has not outright failed yet. With that knowledge, the teacher might adapt the upcoming lessons to include more reinforcement for that student, involve a specialist, or communicate with the family, thus effectively adapting the instructional design based on predictive data.

Case on Mr. Jules's 5th-grade reading class

Mr. Jules teaches a diverse class of 5th-graders with varying reading levels and interests. To meet all their needs, he uses two different AI tools:

- **Adaptive AI for real-time personalization with choice Texts**: During independent reading time, Mr. Jules uses *Choice Texts by eSpark*.[15] As students log in, the AI instantly adapts reading passages for each child's interest—sports, science, animals, or outer space—while still targeting the same comprehension skill (e.g., identifying main ideas). If a student struggles mid-lesson, the AI detects competency and confusion based on interaction patterns and adjusts the difficulty level or offers a hint on the spot.

  Result: Every student experiences a personalized reading session tailored to their current mood, level, and interests—in real time.

- **Predictive AI for long-term planning with panorama student success[16]**: For a broader long-term strategy, Mr. Jules turns to *Panorama*, a predictive analytics platform. It aggregates months of assessment data, behavior trends, and attendance patterns to flag students at risk of falling behind. The platform suggests interventions, like small group support or home communication, which Mr. Jules can schedule over the coming weeks.

  Result: Mr. Jules plans lessons and student support proactively, months before potential learning gaps widen.

To illustrate how these AI capabilities come together, consider planning a unit on reading comprehension in Mr. Jules's diverse 5th-grade class. Using an AI-driven system, a teacher might do the following:

- **Customize the curriculum content**: Use an AI tool to find reading passages on topics interesting to each student (sports, music, animals, etc.), aligned to the same comprehension skill. In fact, the edtech program Choice Texts by eSpark[17] does

---

15 eSpark Learning. (2024, October 1). Differentiate your math, reading, and writing instruction | eSpark. eSpark. https://www.esparklearning.com/
16 Panorama. (2020, November 3). Predictive Analytics in Telecom - Panorama Software. https://panorama.com/predictive-analytics/
17 eSpark Learning. (2024, October 1). Differentiate your math, reading, and writing instruction | eSpark. eSpark. https://www.esparklearning.com/

exactly this; it leverages AI to generate custom reading passages and questions for each student based on their personal interests. A student who loves animals might get a passage about wildlife conservation, whereas another who loves space might read about Mars, both targeting the day's skill. The teacher no longer has to manually search for multiple texts; AI creates them on the fly.

- **Maintain alignment to standards**: AI-powered tools like eSpark's Choice Texts[18] ensure alignment with educational standards by integrating a variety of standards directly into the learning content generation process. Each AI-generated reading passage is crafted to target specific reading skills and specific standards, such as those outlined in the *U.S. Common Core State Standards*. This is achieved through a combination of designed prompts and the development of rigorous learning design frameworks that guide the AI in producing content and lessons tailored to the intended instructional objectives. These AI tools employ rigorous rubrics to maintain student age-appropriateness and instructional quality. This comprehensive approach allows educators to help provide personalized reading materials that are both engaging and pedagogically sound, without the need for manual curation.

- **Plan adaptive lessons**: With data from previous assignments, the teacher asks an AI assistant like Khan Academy's Khanmigo[19] for help grouping students and planning differentiated activities. Khanmigo can analyze student performance and suggest, for example, *Group A could work on an independent project since they have mastered these skills, while Group B would benefit from a guided practice on inference*, essentially an AI co-planner. It also tracks student progress in real-time during the lesson, giving the teacher live insights into who is answering correctly or who seems stuck[20].

- **Differentiate on the fly**: As students work, an AI system integrated with their practice (maybe through an intelligent tutoring system on their tablets) adjusts reading difficulty. If a student breezes through questions, the AI serves a more complex text; if another struggles, it might provide hints or switch to a more accessible passage. The teacher's dashboard updates to show these adjustments, highlighting which students might need one-on-one support. Platforms like Knewton Alta[21], already mentioned in *Chapter 6, AI for Diverse Learning Needs*, have demonstrated this kind of functionality; they track various performance metrics to identify learning gaps and suggest adjustments in strategy.

At the end of the unit, not only has each student received a personalized learning experience, but the teacher has a wealth of data to reflect on. Perhaps the AI-generated content revealed

18 eSpark Learning. (2024, October 1). Differentiate your math, reading, and writing instruction I eSpark. eSpark. https://www.esparklearning.com/
19 Meet Khanmigo: Khan Academy's AI-powered teaching assistant & tutor. (n.d.). https://www.khanmigo.ai/
20 NoAILabs. (2024, December 10). Learning with AI// more productive with models and tools. Medium. https://noailabs.medium.com/learning-with-ai-more-productive-with-models-and-tools-77ca2b2b7ea-d#:~:text=teachers%3A
21 Alta. (n.d.). https://www.wiley.com/en-us/education/alta

new student interests, or the adaptive system identified an unnoticed misconception common to many students, informing the teacher's next unit planning. The data-driven approach to instructional design that AI enables leads to a more responsive curriculum, one that evolves based on evidence of what students need, rather than sticking rigidly to a preset plan.

In sum, AI empowers educators to design instruction that is both personalized and flexible. By leveraging AI tools for curriculum customization, adaptive lesson planning, and differentiation, teachers can ensure that each student's learning experience is tailored, addressing their strengths, weaknesses, and interests. As the *World Economic Forum Annual Meeting 2025* report[22] put it, AI can handle the heavy lifting of processing data and adjusting difficulty, while teachers provide the emotional intelligence and mentoring, together delivering truly learner-centric education. The result is a classroom where the curriculum is not static, but a living design continually refined by real-time insights and smart recommendations.

Assessment and feedback

Assessment and feedback are core parts of teaching where AI has shown tremendous potential to increase efficiency and effectiveness. Grading stacks of papers or monitoring every student's engagement can be incredibly time-consuming for educators. AI tools can automate many of these processes, providing faster feedback to students and richer analytics to teachers. However, the rise of automated grading also raises evolving policy concerns around academic integrity, potential bias in assessment algorithms, and equity of access, sparking active debates about inclusiveness, transparency, accountability, and fairness in AI-driven education systems. Let us explore how AI handles automated grading and feedback, powers intelligent tutoring systems that give students instant guidance, tracks student behavior and engagement for intervention, generates insightful progress reports and visualizations, and even predicts which students might need extra help. These advances not only save teachers time but also improve the timeliness and quality of feedback that students and parents receive.

Automated grading and instant feedback

One of the most teacher-friendly applications of AI is automated grading. Anyone who has graded dozens of essays or homework assignments knows how it can consume evenings and weekends. AI-driven grading tools can take over repetitive grading tasks, from marking multiple-choice quizzes to providing initial feedback on essays.

Consider Writable[23], an AI-powered writing evaluation tool. In this article[24] that showcases the use of AI by California teachers, one veteran teacher shares her testimonial on how she piloted

22 Haoyang, D. L., & Towne, J. (2025, January 9). How AI and human teachers can collaborate to transform education. World Economic Forum. https://www.weforum.org/stories/2025/01/how-ai-and-human-teachers-can-collaborate-to-transform-education/#:~:text=AI%20systems%20excel%20at%20tasks,time
23 Writable. (2024, March 29). Home - Writable. https://www.writable.com/
24 Johnson, K. (2024b, July 25). California teachers are using AI to grade papers. Who's grading the AI? CalMatters. https://calmatters.org/economy/technology/2024/06/teachers-ai-grading/#:~:text=automates%20grading%20writing%20assignments%20and,hand%20out%20more%20writing%20assignments

Writable in her high school English classes and reported it was the best year yet in her nearly three decades of teaching. Why? Because the AI could automatically grade student essays and provide detailed feedback on writing quality within moments, which meant students got immediate pointers on how to improve. Roberts found that because feedback was so quick, she could assign more frequent writing exercises; students wrote more, revised more, and improved faster. By mid-year, students who previously struggled to write a coherent paragraph were completing multi-paragraph essays with evidence and reasoning; she attributed this growth in part to the rapid, iterative feedback cycle enabled by AI. Automated feedback told her students how to improve faster than she could on her own, allowing her to increase the volume of writing practice without overwhelming herself with grading. Of course, she still reviewed the AI's assessments for accuracy (especially for edge cases), but the heavy lifting was done by the machine. Teachers can incorporate AI-generated feedback into rubric-based grading by leveraging AI suggestions to help inform comments on specific dimensions such as essay organization, argument strength, or use of evidence. For instance, they might cross-check AI feedback on grammar and coherence to support scores in the writing mechanics and clarity of expression sections of a given rubric, ensuring alignment with grading criteria while saving time.

AI grading is not limited to writing. Tools like Gradescope[25] (widely used in higher education and now trickling into K-12) use AI to group similar student answers together for faster scoring of open-response questions. For instance, on a short-answer science quiz, Gradescope might detect that 15 students wrote essentially the same incorrect answer. The teacher can then grade that answer once and apply the comment to all, rather than writing *Check your units* 15 times. AI also helps maintain consistency and objectivity in grading, reducing the inadvertent bias or fatigue that can affect human graders.

Beyond grading, AI can provide immediate feedback to students through intelligent tutoring systems. An **intelligent tutoring system** (**ITS**) is like a software tutor that gives students hints, explanations, and corrections in real time as they work through problems. A classic example is Carnegie Learning's MATHia[26], which uses AI to guide students step-by-step through algebra problems, offering tailored hints when a student is stuck and feedback when they make an error. Systems like this leverage AI to adapt their feedback to the student's responses, providing easier hints if the student is really struggling, or more challenging prompts if the student is ready to be stretched. The result is that students get instant feedback on their work, rather than waiting for the next day when the teacher returns their paper. Research has shown that immediate feedback is crucial for learning; students can correct misconceptions in the moment and build on their understanding right away.

From the teacher's perspective, the data from these AI tutoring interactions is incredibly valuable. The software can pinpoint common errors (e.g., a majority of the class might be misapplying a formula), alerting the teacher to address that in a review. It essentially conducts

25 Gradescope | Save time grading. (n.d.-b). https://www.gradescope.com/
26 MATHIA | Carnegie Learning. (n.d.). Carnegie Learning. https://www.carnegielearning.com/solutions/math/mathia/

formative assessment continually in the background. As an example, the AI in Quizizz[27], a popular quiz platform, now goes beyond just grading student answers. It can adjust question difficulty on the fly and even auto-correct grammar in student responses, then redesign upcoming questions to better reflect real-world scenarios if it detects misconceptions. A teacher using Quizizz might see in the live report that the AI switched a few questions to easier ones for certain students who were performing poorly, to rebuild their confidence or re-teach a concept. Meanwhile, advanced students got more complex scenarios. Such responsiveness was not possible with static paper quizzes. By automating the routine aspects of assessment and adding a layer of adaptivity, AI helps ensure every student receives appropriate challenge and support, and every teacher gets meaningful feedback data without extra work.

Engagement tracking and behavioral insights

Assessment is not only about academic work; it is also about knowing how students are engaging in class. AI systems can monitor and analyze student behaviors and interactions, alerting educators to issues that might require attention. For instance, AI can track online learning behaviors, which videos a student watched, how long they stayed on a question, their click patterns, and flag disengagement. A simple example is an online learning platform noticing a student rapidly clicking next without reading content, suggesting they are disengaged or frustrated. The platform could notify the teacher or even pop up a gentle reminder to the student, like, **It looks like you are skipping a lot; is everything okay?**

In physical classrooms, experimental AI systems use computer vision to gauge student engagement (though these raise privacy concerns and are used cautiously). Some schools have tested cameras with AI that observe student facial expressions or posture to estimate who is confused or bored. A less invasive approach, and one more commonly adopted, is wearable or device-based tracking of participation. For example, Classcraft[28], a gamified behavior management platform, uses AI to help track and reward student behaviors in class. Teachers define positive behaviors (like helping a peer or participating in a discussion), and students earn points in a game when those behaviors are observed. Classcraft's AI can analyze patterns, perhaps noticing that a usually active student has been quiet for several days, which might prompt the teacher to check in with them. By turning behavior tracking into a game, students are motivated to stay engaged, and the AI ensures no one slips under the radar. It essentially automates the process of noting class participation and engagement, which is hard for a teacher to do in real time for every student.

Another aspect is behavioral early warnings. AI can combine data on discipline referrals, attendance, and class engagement to predict if a student is at risk of behavioral issues or disengagement. For example, a system might learn that when a student's homework submission rate drops below 50% and they have been absent three times in a month, the probability of them failing the class or having a behavioral incident rises sharply. The AI could then alert the teacher and school counselor to intervene. This proactive stance is part of many *Early*

27 Quizizz. (n.d.). Quizizz. Retrieved April 5, 2025, from https://quizizz.com/?lng=en
28 HMH Classcraft | HMH. (2024, April 18). https://www.hmhco.com/programs/classcraft

Warning Systems being adopted in districts to reduce dropouts. Wisconsin, for instance, has a **Dropout Early Warning System**[29] (**DEWS**) that uses an algorithm to predict which middle schoolers are unlikely to graduate on time, allowing schools to provide support years before the graduation date. Similarly, at the classroom level, a teacher armed with AI-driven behavior insights can reach out to a struggling student before the report card or detention slip, perhaps connecting them with resources, communicating with parents, or adjusting their seating or group to improve engagement.

Richer assessment data and feedback loops

AI does not just expedite grading; it also transforms raw scores into meaningful visualizations and reports. Data-driven progress reports and visualizations help teachers, students, and parents see the story behind the numbers. Modern learning platforms often include analytics dashboards that use AI to highlight trends: for instance, a chart showing a student's mastery levels across different standards, or a heatmap of which homework questions had the highest error rates. Such insights are incredibly valuable for a teacher planning a review session or deciding what to re-teach. Instead of relying on gut feeling or a cursory glance at the gradebook, the teacher has a clear, data-backed picture of class performance. The AI essentially acts as a data analyst, freeing teachers from manual number-crunching.

For students and parents, AI can tailor progress feedback to be more understandable. Some AI-driven systems[30] create student-facing reports that explain learning progress in plain language, sometimes even with a bit of friendly AI narration. At the same time, it might alert the teacher that the student is struggling with inference questions, prompting the teacher to give targeted practice. By visualizing data (graphs of reading speed over time, pie charts of mastered vs. unmastered skills, etc.), AI helps make progress tangible. Parents appreciate these clear visuals and notifications: many learning platforms will automatically notify parents if certain conditions are met, say, if a student's grade drops below a threshold or if they have not logged into the learning system for a week. Such notifications can be generic, but with AI, they can be more nuanced. Some systems even auto-send motivational messages or study tips to students based on their performance patterns.

One important contribution of AI to assessment is identifying at-risk students early (overlapping with predictive analytics mentioned earlier in this chapter). By analyzing assessment data alongside other metrics, AI can predict which students might fail a course or a standardized exam in advance, so teachers can intervene. A case study[31] from a large district showed an

29 Takeaways from Our Investigation into Wisconsin's Racially Inequitable Dropout Algorithm – The Markup. (2023, April 27). https://themarkup.org/the-breakdown/2023/04/27/takeaways-from-our-inves-tigation-into-wisconsins-racially-inequitable-dropout-algorithm#:~:text=Takeaways%20from%20Our%20 Investigation%20into,how%20likely%20middle%20school
30 AllHere | Family engagement. (n.d.). Allhere. https://www.allhere.com/#:~:text=We%20foster%20fami-ly%20engagement%20in,support%20in%20their%20preferred%20language
31 Concurrency. (2024b, June 11). AI early warning system predicts At-Risk K-12 students – concurrency. https://concurrency.com/case-study/ai-early-warning-system-predicts-at-risk-k-12-students/#:~:tex-t=An%20early%20warning%20system%20was,friendly

AI early warning system successfully flagged students as early as kindergarten who were at risk of academic challenges later, enabling guidance counselors to provide support before problems escalated. On a smaller scale, a middle school teacher might get an AI-generated list of five students who, based on their assessment trends and engagement, are projected to score below proficiency on the upcoming state test, while there is still time to provide remediation or one-on-one tutoring. These are insights a busy teacher might not infer unaided, especially when teaching 100+ students. In one survey done by Impact Research[32], teachers noted that AI was helping them spot and assist students in need as often, if not more than, it was helping students directly, highlighting a shift in how we think about AI in classrooms. It is not just about students cheating with AI (a common fear in headlines); it is also about teachers using AI to help students succeed.

Finally, AI can also assist in more specialized assessment scenarios. For instance, in special education, AI tools can help track the progress of students on their IEP goals by analyzing observational data and work samples, giving special educators visual progress reports to share in meetings. AI-powered speech and language assessment apps can evaluate a student's reading fluency or pronunciation instantly, which is useful for language teachers or therapists. These targeted feedback tools enrich the overall picture of a student's abilities beyond what a traditional test might capture.

Content creation and enhanced experiences

Creating engaging educational content and experiences is a time-intensive part of teaching: whether it is designing lesson materials, finding the right resources, or creating enriching activities that capture students' imaginations. AI is proving to be a creative partner for teachers, helping with content creation and curation and enabling enhanced learning experiences like simulations and virtual labs. AI can also improve language accessibility and inclusiveness in content, ensuring all students can benefit. Let us discuss how educators are using generative AI to produce high-quality instructional materials in a fraction of the time, how AI-curated libraries suggest just the right video or reading at the right moment, and how AI-driven simulations provide interactive experiences that would be hard to manage otherwise. In this section, we will also look at how AI is making content more accessible through translation and adaptive presentation. In the following table, you will find examples of different types of instructional materials and how AI can assist:

Content type	AI use case
Lesson planning	AI suggests standards-aligned lesson plans, adapts pacing guides, and recommends materials based on learning objectives.
Quizzes	AI auto-generates multiple-choice and open-ended quizzes tailored to student proficiency levels.

32 ChatGPT Used by Teachers More Than Students, New Survey from Walton Family Foundation Finds. (n.d.). Walton Family Foundation. https://www.waltonfamilyfoundation.org/chatgpt-used-by-teachers-more-than-students-new-survey-from-walton-family-foundation-finds

Content type	AI use case
Simulations	AI powers interactive labs and role-play scenarios, offering real-time feedback in science, history, and more.
Translations	AI tools instantly translate lesson content and instructions to support multilingual learners.
Parent newsletters	AI drafts personalized updates based on classroom activity logs and student progress data.
Video/reading curation	AI curates age and topic-appropriate multimedia resources aligned to current lessons.
Accessibility tools	AI adapts content format (e.g., text-to-speech, dyslexia-friendly fonts, simplified summaries).
Worksheet generation	AI creates practice worksheets or extension activities based on class performance trends.
Parent teacher conference scheduling	AI auto-schedules meetings based on availability and preferences and sends reminders to families.
Administrative emails	AI drafts professional emails to parents or staff for events, reminders, or behavioral updates.

Table 8.1: AI use cases for educator content creation

Generating lesson content has become one of the most popular applications of AI among teachers, especially with the advent of user-friendly generative AI like OpenAI's ChatGPT. Teachers are using AI tools to generate everything from quiz questions and worksheets to example essays and educational games. According to a Walton Family Foundation survey[33], 71% of teachers said AI tools are essential for student success, and many have begun using AI to craft materials and activities.

Generative AI specialized for education is also on the rise. Tools like Canva's Magic Write[34] and Slidesgo's AI Presentation Maker[35] assist in creating visual content. Magic Write can generate writing ideas or even entire slide decks based on a prompt, while Slidesgo's AI will make a draft presentation in minutes given a topic and desired tone, expediting what could take a couple of hours to assemble manually and giving teachers more time to plan interactive activities around the content.

---

33 ChatGPT Used by Teachers More Than Students, New Survey from Walton Family Foundation Finds. (n.d.). Walton Family Foundation. https://www.waltonfamilyfoundation.org/chatgpt-used-by-teachers-more-than-students-new-survey-from-walton-family-foundation-finds
34 Magic Write: Online AI Text Generator. (n.d.). Canva. Retrieved April 5, 2025, from https://www.canva.com/magic-write/
35 Slidesgo. (n.d.). Free Google Slides themes and Powerpoint templates | Slidesgo. https://slidesgo.com/

Another content chore where AI shines is question generation and variant creation. Teachers often need multiple versions of questions (for differentiation or simply to discourage copying). AI can take an existing question and generate similar ones with different numbers or contexts. This means a teacher can input one base question and get a whole bank of leveled questions back. Likewise, AI can suggest realistic scenarios for applying a concept, adding relevance to content. For instance, an economics teacher might ask AI for examples to illustrate supply and demand beyond the classic price of milk scenario, and get fresh, creative contexts (maybe the surge in demand for a new video game console) to use in class discussions. It is important to note that while generative AI can accelerate content creation, it may struggle or hallucinate in subject areas like history or ethics where factual precision and nuanced interpretation are critical. AI tools can inadvertently generate false or inaccurate information, oversimplified narratives, or biased examples—especially when addressing complex or sensitive topics. Educators should carefully review and fact-check AI-generated content in these areas to ensure alignment with curriculum standards and ethical teaching practices. In the following table, you will find examples of sensitive topics where AI-created content can cause risk:

Subject	Risk of reliance on unchecked AI
History	Risk of inaccuracies, oversimplified accounts, or biased portrayals of events and figures.
Civics and government	Potential for political bias or misrepresentation of current events and policy debates.
Ethics and philosophy	AI may lack the nuance required to address moral complexity or diverse cultural perspectives.
Health and human sexuality	Risk of providing outdated, inappropriate, or culturally insensitive information.
Race, identity, and social justice	AI may reflect embedded biases or omit critical context, leading to problematic representations.

Table 8.2: Sensitive subjects prone to AI risk

Content curation is another area where AI lightens the load. Educators are inundated with resources on the internet, and finding the right one (be it a video, article, or simulation) can be like finding a needle in a haystack. AI recommendation engines can sift through repositories of **Open Educational Resources (OER)** and present a tailored selection to a teacher. Systems like Google Classroom's assistive features[36] or Microsoft's Education Insights[37] use AI to recommend enrichment or remedial resources based on student performance. For example, if a group of students struggled with a math homework on fractions, the system might suggest

36 Classroom management Tools & Resources - Google for Education. (n.d.). Google for Education. https:// edu google.com/workspace-for-education/products/classroom/?modal_active=none
37 Team, M. E. (2024, July 18). Use data to support your students with Education Insights | Microsoft Education Blog. Microsoft Education Blog. https://www.microsoft.com/en-us/education/blog/2023/08/use-data-to-support-your-students-with-education-insights/?msockid=36d5db1157d26cb720c5cf6956fe6d94

a specific video or an interactive fraction game for those students, directly within the teacher's workflow. This targeted curation ensures students get supplemental content matched to their needs without the teacher spending hours searching.

AI is also enabling interactive and immersive content that was previously hard to create. Interactive simulations and virtual labs are prime examples. Companies like Labster[38] have developed virtual science labs where students can perform experiments in a game-like 3D environment. What makes Labster particularly powerful is its AI-driven virtual lab assistant, a friendly drone character named *Dr. One*, that guides students through experiments. Dr. One provides real-time feedback and hints. If a student forgets a step or makes an error in the simulation, Dr. One chimes in with a tip, much like a teacher would in a real lab. The AI assistant makes the virtual lab experience more engaging and educational by ensuring students learn from mistakes rather than getting stuck. Teachers benefit because students can conduct complex experiments (like gene editing or chemical titrations) virtually, with the AI ensuring safety and guiding learning. This might be impossible to do hands-on in a typical classroom due to equipment, safety, or time constraints. By offloading some guidance to AI in the simulation, teachers can focus on debriefing the conceptual understanding. As Labster notes, instructors appreciate that the AI assistant in the simulation allows them to focus on more in-depth discussions and personalized support during class time, while the basics are handled in the virtual lab.

Beyond labs, AI is enhancing experiences through adaptive learning games and scenarios. Imagine a history teacher using an AI-powered role-playing game where students chat with historical figures. The AI controls the characters, adjusting their responses to student questions. This is not far-fetched; Hello History app[39] by *Humy* is already using cutting-edge artificial intelligence technology to create interactive experiences that allow people to engage and learn from historical figures. This AI-powered experience offers users the chance to have conversations with those who have shaped our world, and to gain insight into their lives, thoughts, and beliefs. These kinds of AI-driven simulations create immersive learning experiences that can deepen understanding and empathy.

When using AI-generated materials, educators should create or adopt a verification routine to ensure accuracy, appropriateness, freedom from bias, and instructional alignment. One effective strategy is to run AI outputs through a second tool—such as plagiarism checkers, fact-checking websites, or educational content validators—to cross-check and verify key facts and identify potential errors or bias. Teachers can also develop a simple checklist that includes questions like:

- *Is this factually accurate?*

- *Do I know the source of the material?*

- *Does this align with my curriculum standards?*

---

38 Meet Dr. One: Labster's lab assistant. (n.d.). https://www.labster.com/blog/meet-dr-one#:~:text=-match%20at%20L157%20Dr,This%20guidance%20fosters%20an
39 Hello History - Chat with AI Generated Historical Figures. (n.d.). https://www.hellohistory.ai/

- *Could this content be perceived as culturally insensitive or biased?*

- *Would I be comfortable presenting this in a diverse (or any) classroom setting?*

For high-stakes subjects like history, ethics, or health, educators should supplement AI-generated content with peer-reviewed papers or textbook-based sources and, when possible, consult with colleagues for an extra layer of review. By applying these quality assurance steps, teachers can be more confident that they can safely and effectively integrate AI-generated materials into their classrooms.

Another facet is language translation and accessibility in content. AI has made real-time translation commonplace, which is a boon for classrooms with multilingual students or for sharing content with parents who speak different languages. For example, Microsoft's Immersive Reader[40] uses AI to provide reading support: it can instantly translate a passage into dozens of languages, read it aloud, break it into syllables, or apply picture dictionaries for vocabulary. A teacher preparing a handout can, with Immersive Reader's help, ensure that a Spanish-speaking newcomer student can see the Spanish translation alongside the English text, and hear both read out. Similarly, AI speech recognition can generate captions for any video or even live teacher lectures, improving accessibility for students who are deaf or hard of hearing. Tools like Notta[41] transcribe spoken words into text in real-time, which means a teacher could speak in class and an AI app could display live captions on a screen or on students' devices, effectively an instant accommodation that used to require specialized services.

For translation in family engagement (which we will discuss more in the next section), AI is transformative as well. But within the classroom, think of an English literature teacher who wants to include a short story that is only available in English, but he or she has a student who has just arrived from China. Using AI translation (like Google Translate[42] or DeepL[43]), he or she can get a reasonably accurate Chinese version of the story to provide to that student. While machine translations are not perfect, they have improved dramatically, and many education platforms integrate them with a single click. The earlier-mentioned Eduaide.AI platform[44], for instance, can translate generated content into 15+ languages instantly; so a teacher generating a worksheet can immediately produce versions in Spanish, Arabic, or Vietnamese for those who need it. This level of accessibility used to require hiring translators or spending hours with a dictionary; now it is nearly instantaneous.

AI also helps in creating alternative content formats for diverse learners, as we explored in *Chapter 6, AI for Diverse Learning Needs*. The beauty is that AI can take one piece of core content

---

40 Immersive Reader. (n.d.). https://www.microsoft.com/en-us/edge/features/immersive-reader?msockid=36d5db1157d26cb720c5cf6956fe6d94&form=MA13FJ
41 About us | Notta. (n.d.). https://www.notta.ai/en/about
42 Understand your world and communicate across languages. (n.d.). Google Translate About. https://translate.google.com/about/?hl=en
43 Secure and scalable AI translation for enterprises | DeepL (n.d.). https://www.deepl.com/en/products/translator
44 Eduaide.Ai: AI created for teachers. (2025b, April 1). https://www.eduaide.ai/

and transform it into multiple ways to fit different needs. Teachers in inclusive classrooms find this especially useful; they can differentiate materials more readily.

Let us not forget content creation for pure efficiency: things like drafting emails, writing rubrics, or creating visuals. Many teachers use AI to draft parent newsletters or stylize text. AI image generation (while used carefully in education) can also create diagrams or illustrations for worksheets when open-license images are hard to find. For example, a biology teacher could use an AI image generator to create a custom diagram of a cell labeled in Spanish, if such a resource does not exist. These uses are auxiliary but contribute to saving teacher time and enhancing the materials students see.

In the end, AI-assisted content creation means teachers can spend more time on the art of teaching rather than the drudgery of material prep. In practice, teachers combining their expertise with AI creativity are producing materials that are engaging, diverse, and adaptable. Students, in turn, experience a richer array of learning activities: from AI-curated videos that speak to their interests, to choose-your-own-adventure stories generated on the fly, to virtual experiments with an AI guide by their side. Content creation and curation are often where teachers pour their passion; with AI's help, they can amplify that creativity and reach every learner more effectively.

Time management and collaboration

Time is one of an educator's most precious resources, and it is always in short supply. From planning lessons and grading to managing classroom needs, teachers juggle a constant and never-ending stream of tasks. AI can serve as a virtual assistant for educators by automating routine duties like scheduling, generating reports, and drafting communications to parents and administrators—freeing up valuable time for instruction, mentoring, and creativity. For administrators, AI helps enhance schoolwide coordination by streamlining resource allocation, budgeting, policy compliance, and meeting logistics. These tools ensure that principals, support staff, and teachers have timely access to shared information, supporting more efficient collaboration and informed decision-making across the school.

Smarter scheduling and organization

Managing schedules and routines, from daily class schedules to parent-teacher conferences, can be a complex puzzle. AI-powered scheduling tools are now tackling these challenges. For instance, some schools use AI scheduling software to automatically generate master schedules that accommodate teacher preferences, student course requests, and room availabilities, something that traditionally took administrators weeks of work. These algorithms can consider hundreds of variables (teacher free periods, course conflicts, class size limits, etc.) and produce an optimized schedule in minutes. A famous example[45] comes from outside the classroom:

---

45 Coleman, E. (2023, July 10). How One City Saved $5 Million by Routing School Buses with an Algorithm. Route Fifty. https://www.route-fifty.com/digital-government/2019/08/boston-school-bus-routes/159113/#:~:text=But%20even%20with%20tradeoffs%2C%20using,saved%20back%20into%20classroom%20initiatives

Boston Public Schools used an algorithm to optimize its bus routing and school start times. In 30 minutes, the AI produced routes that were 20% more efficient, cutting 50 buses from their fleet and saving the district $5 million in a year, savings they redirected into classroom initiatives. Impressively, this was achieved without making bus rides or walk times longer, meaning the algorithm found a win-win solution that human planners had missed. While that example is district-level, it underscores how AI can solve scheduling problems far more efficiently than manual methods.

Task prioritization is another area AI can help with. Teachers often maintain long to-do lists. AI task management apps can prioritize these based on deadlines or even estimated effort. While not every teacher is using such assistants yet, the technology exists and is improving rapidly in consumer productivity tools. The following are some examples of different task prioritizations:

- **Daily workflow transformation**:
  - **Lesson planning**: AI-powered tools streamline lesson planning, allowing educators to generate and adapt lesson content quickly.
  - **Administrative tasks**: AI tools can be used to adapt curriculum materials and provide real-time translation, significantly reducing the time teachers spend on administrative work and material adaptation for diverse classrooms.
  - **Student feedback**: Teachers use AI to create rubrics, generate feedback, and provide students with multiple opportunities for revision and improvement.

- **Weekly workflow experience**:
  - **Time savings**: AI can help manage paperwork and documentation, reducing the pressure to complete administrative cycles by the end of the week. This gives them more time to interact meaningfully with students and lessens the need to take work home.
  - **Professional growth**: AI mentors and leadership tools can provide on-demand support for handling challenging situations, developing professional growth plans, and preparing for evaluations. This support is especially valuable for new leaders or those without a formal handover, helping them navigate their roles more confidently.
  - **Collaboration and ownership**: Participating in the development and refinement of AI tools fosters a sense of ownership and trust among educators.

In the following table, you will find an example of how AI can assist an educator in their weekly tasks:

Day	AI enabled activities	Impact on educator workflow
Monday	Use AI to generate lesson plans and adapt materials for English language learners	Saves hours on planning, supports diversity
Tuesday	AI-assisted grading and feedback for assignments	Immediate feedback, more time for students
Wednesday	Professional learning with AI mentor (leadership support)	On-demand guidance, less stress
Thursday	Data analysis of student performance with AI insights	Targeted interventions, informed teaching
Friday	Prepare documentation and reports using AI tools	Faster admin, more time for reflection

Table 8.3: Week in the life of an AI-enabled educator

An interesting AI application in classrooms is automated attendance and notifications, which ties into time management by reducing the time teachers spend calling roll or tracking down absent students. Systems using computer vision or simple sensors can log when students arrive (some schools use **Radio Frequency Identification** (**RFID**) cards or even facial recognition for attendance, though the latter raises privacy issues). Assuming consent and ethical use, an AI could mark attendance in seconds as students walk in, then immediately send an automated notification to parents for any student who is absent. This not only saves teachers' time but also triggers early parent intervention for unexcused absences. Platforms like AllHere[46] (mentioned earlier in this chapter) take it further by engaging families in two-way texting, with a proactive outreach approach that can reduce chronic absenteeism and the burden on school staff to manually make phone calls or send messages and emails.

Streamlined collaboration with administrators

Teachers and administrators share the goal of improving student outcomes, but communication between them can sometimes be fragmented. AI tools can enhance this collaboration by ensuring both parties have up-to-date data and by reducing the bureaucratic overhead that often strains these relationships. For example, many administrators require teachers to submit reports: weekly lesson plans, assessment results, or compliance checklists. AI can simplify this by auto-generating reports from existing data. If a teacher maintains grades in an electronic gradebook, an AI system can compile a summary report for the principal, highlighting class averages, number of failing students, etc., without the teacher manually compiling it. In fact, AI is automating report generation in many fields, and education is no exception. The teacher can then review and edit the draft for accuracy and nuance, and the administrator receives a

46 AllHere | Family engagement. (n.d.-b). Allhere. https://www.allhere.com/#:~:text=What%20does%20 it%20do%3F

thorough update. This kind of automation ensures that policy compliance and reports, such as documenting progress for special education, is done accurately and on time, without eating into hours of a teacher's day.

Collaboration also improves when decisions are data-informed. AI systems that provide dashboards accessible to both teachers and administrators create a shared understanding of how students and classes are doing. Instead of an administrator walking into a meeting with one set of data and a teacher with another, they might both look at a common AI-driven dashboard. For example, a principal could see from the system that Ms. Lee's 3rd-period algebra class has a higher homework completion rate and better quiz scores than her 4th-period class. The AI might highlight that difference and even analyze potential reasons (perhaps the 4th period is right after lunch and many students are tardy, missing instruction). Armed with this information, the principal and teacher can collaboratively discuss strategies: maybe adjusting the schedule or providing additional support to the 4th period. In the past, such conversations might rely on anecdote or partial data; AI makes the relevant data points readily available, focusing collaborative meetings on solutions rather than on figuring out the facts.

Administrators also benefit from AI in resource allocation and budgeting, which in turn helps teachers by ensuring needs are met. AI can analyze spending patterns, enrollment trends, and usage of resources to recommend where to allocate the budget for maximum impact. For instance, an AI analysis might reveal that a set of math software licenses is not being used fully in one school, but another school has a higher demand, prompting the district to redistribute licenses more efficiently. Or it might forecast an increase in English language learner enrollment at a particular school and suggest allocating more funds for bilingual aides there. By optimizing resource use, AI helps ensure teachers have what they need (materials, support staff, training funds) without waste.

One concrete example of AI aiding resource decisions is in staffing. Some districts use predictive models to anticipate student enrollment changes and thus adjust hiring. An AI might combine local birth rates, housing development data, and migration trends to predict next year's students per grade. The administration can then transfer or hire teachers accordingly, avoiding last-minute scrambles that often place a burden on teachers (like suddenly large class sizes or mixed-grade classes). Similarly, AI can help with substitute teacher scheduling by predicting high absence days (e.g., around flu season) and ensuring a larger substitute pool on those days.

For collaboration with administrators, AI also ensures policy compliance is less of a headache. Schools operate under many regulations (state or government standards, IEP legal requirements, etc.). AI can monitor these in the background, for example, checking that every student's accommodations were provided in digital learning platforms, or that required safety drills were logged each month, and then gently prompt the responsible staff if something is missing. This reduces the chance of human oversight errors and the dreaded scenario of scrambling during an audit or review. It also means teachers and principals spend less meeting time on compliance talk, because they trust the system to keep track and alert them only when something is off.

AI as a collaborative partner in decision-making

Beyond automating routine tasks, AI is increasingly acting as a decision-support tool for school leadership, which indirectly benefits teachers. For instance, when school leaders consider a new initiative (like a different curriculum or a policy change), AI can assist by running simulations or analyzing data from other contexts. We will cover policy and future planning in the next section of this chapter, but it is worth noting here how collaboration is enhanced when AI provides evidence for decisions. Administrators are often flooded with proposals and data; AI can synthesize research findings or outcomes from similar regions or districts to inform local decisions. Another collaborative aspect is feedback on policy implementation. Once a new policy or program is rolled out, AI can quickly analyze its impact and report back. This kind of rapid-cycle evaluation strengthens collaboration because it grounds discussions in data rather than opinions.

Lastly, AI can handle many communication tasks that facilitate collaboration. Writing emails, newsletters, or announcements can be partially automated. These small time-savers add up; AI tools can summarize long email threads or meeting transcripts, so if a teacher missed a meeting, the AI provides a bulleted recap rather than the teacher reading through pages of notes.

Automating administrative drudgery and providing intelligent insights allows educators and administrators to collaborate with less friction and more focus on students. The ultimate payoff is that teachers can invest their time in planning creative lessons, mentoring students, or engaging in PD (the human-centric work that AI cannot replace), while AI quietly keeps the gears of school operations turning efficiently in the background.

Family and community engagement

Educating a child is a partnership between the school and the family (and by extension, the wider community). Effective communication and engagement with parents and the community can greatly enhance student success. AI is proving to be a valuable tool in bridging gaps and strengthening these partnerships. It can facilitate smoother parent-teacher communication by breaking language barriers and providing timely updates, enable automated notifications to keep parents informed, support broader community outreach and engagement initiatives, and even assist in analyzing community feedback to guide school decisions.

Breaking language barriers and enabling 24/7 communication

One of the most practical ways AI is boosting family engagement is through language translation and accessibility. In many schools, teachers may not speak all the languages of the families they serve. This used to mean relying on human translators or sending home limited communications. Now, AI-powered communication apps like TalkingPoints[47] have changed the game with a two-way multilingual messaging platform that uses AI to translate messages between teachers and parents in over 150 languages. TalkingPoints has been hugely successful: it is reportedly used in two out of three U.S. schools[48], reaching over 5 million families, and has led to improved attendance and even test scores, especially for underserved students, by bringing families into the loop more effectively. Teachers find that parents who previously hesitated to communicate (due to language or timing) are now more responsive. What is impressive is the translation quality: modern AI translation is sophisticated enough to capture tone and context fairly well. Teachers also appreciate features like translated video captions; they can record a short video message, and the platform will overlay captions in the family's language. Imagine sending a quick video of students doing a science experiment with captions in Chinese or Arabic for those families; it creates inclusion that was logistically very hard to achieve in the past.

While systems like TalkingPoints have been widely praised for their impact, implementation can face pitfalls if teachers are not properly trained in using the platforms or if families do not fully understand how to access and respond to messages in the system. Some districts have reported challenges with inconsistent usage, overly automated or incorrect communication, or misunderstandings due to nuanced language that even advanced AI can misinterpret. To mitigate these issues, districts should develop clear onboarding plans and provide training for both staff and families, encourage opt-in use with personalized introductions, and establish norms for when to rely on AI versus human follow-up to ensure clarity and trust.

Beyond translation, AI enables round-the-clock communication in a manageable way. Chatbot technology is being used to ensure parents can get answers to common questions anytime without waiting for office hours. For example, some school districts have experimented with AI chatbots[49] (like the Ed chatbot in Los Angeles Unified, built by *AllHere*) that parents and students could ask questions about school policies, schedules, or resources. The idea is that instead of calling the front office and being put on hold, a parent could text or speak to an AI assistant and get an instant answer. While LA's initial rollout faced some issues[50] and was paused, the concept remains powerful, especially for districts with limited administrative staff.

To foster effective AI-powered community engagement, schools and districts should follow a few simple design principles when crafting messages and deploying these types of tools.

47 Edwards, L. (2024, October 28). TalkingPoints: How to use it to connect with families. Tech & Learning. https://www.techlearning.com/how-to/talkingpoints-how-to-use-it-to-connect-with-families#:~:text-t=What%20are%20the%20best%20TalkingPoints,features
48 Edwards, L. (2024, October 28). TalkingPoints: How to use it to connect with families. Tech & Learning. https://www.techlearning.com/how-to/talkingpoints-how-to-use-it-to-connect-with-families#:~:text-t=What%20are%20the%20best%20TalkingPoints,features
49 Young, J. R. (2024, May 2). Los Angeles School District launched a splashy AI chatbot. What exactly does it do? EdSurge. https://www.edsurge.com/news/2024-05-02-los-angeles-school-district-launched-a-splashy-ai-chatbot-what-exactly-does-it-do#:~:text=,systems%20used%20in%20the
50 $3 million chatbot lasts three months in LA schools. (n.d.). Privacy International. https://privacyinternational.org/examples/5432/3-million-chatbot-lasts-three-months-la-schools#:~:text=Los%20Angeles%20public%20schools%20have,school%20system%20after%20only

Messages should be concise, making them easy to read and understand quickly, especially on mobile devices and for non-native speakers. The messages should maintain a human tone—warm, respectful, and conversational—to help build trust and avoid sounding overly robotic or automated. All communications must be provided in multi-lingual formats, using high-quality AI translation to reflect the linguistic diversity of parents and families while allowing for parent input in their preferred language. Finally, these systems should be opt-out friendly, giving families more control over their communication preferences and avoiding the feeling of being overwhelmed or monitored. These principles ensure transparency, inclusivity, clarity, and a stronger sense of partnership between schools and communities.

Automated notifications are also keeping parents and guardians more informed than ever. Most schools already use robocalls or SMS blasts for things like weather closures or important events. AI takes this up a notch by personalizing and targeting notifications based on data. For example, instead of sending a generic message about missing assignments, an AI system could detect that a particular student has missed three homework assignments in math and automatically send a gentle, personalized alert to the parent or guardian. This kind of notification, generated by AI scanning the gradebook, is far more actionable than a generic progress report. Also, it can be translated or delivered via the parent's preferred channel (text, email, app notification).

Amplifying community voice and outreach

Engaging the broader community: local organizations, voters, and community members without children in school, is also important for schools (for support, funding, etc.). AI can assist in community engagement and outreach by analyzing community feedback and helping tailor communications to community interests.

One way is through sentiment analysis and trend detection on community input. Schools often collect feedback via surveys, public forums, or social media. It is challenging for administrators to read every comment or discern patterns in hundreds of free-response survey answers. Tools like Social Pinpoint's Analysis Assistant[51] use machine learning to uncover sentiment, themes, and insights from engagement data in real-time. This means a school board can quickly understand the community's mood and get an AI-generated summary from social media posts or survey responses. Armed with this, school leaders can address the biggest worries proactively. It ensures community voices are quantified and heard, even if not everyone can attend meetings. AI can also help support cultural responsiveness by tailoring communications not just linguistically, but contextually assisting in adjusting messages to reflect local holidays, community events, and cultural norms, ensuring families receive accurate information that feels relevant and respectful to their specific backgrounds and schedules.

Another aspect is personalizing content for community outreach. A city or school might want to keep the wider community informed about school successes or needs. AI can analyze what

---

51 Dev, X. (2024, March 22). Reporting & insights. Social Pinpoint. https://www.socialpinpoint.com/platform/reporting-insights/

type of content engages the community by looking at past interactions, and then help generate relevant communications. For instance, an AI might find that social media posts about student achievements get a lot of positive engagement from the community. On the flip side, if there is misinformation swirling in the community, AI social listening tools (like Brandwatch[52]) can flag trending topics so the school can respond.

Social media listening powered by AI helps schools maintain a good relationship with the community by responding promptly to concerns and highlighting positive stories.

For broader outreach, AI can assist in segmentation and targeted communication. Community members have different interests, some care about sports, others about academic accolades, others about financial efficiency. AI can analyze who clicks on or opens what type of content in newsletters or on websites. Then, it might recommend segmenting the newsletter: sports enthusiasts get a headline about the football team's championship, while others get a highlight on a new STEM lab, etc., all within the same newsletter but ordered based on interest profiles (derived from AI analysis). This kind of personalization, common in marketing, can increase engagement from community stakeholders by showing them the aspects of school news they value most.

Furthermore, AI can ensure inclusive outreach. Sometimes, certain communities (perhaps non-native English speakers or specific neighborhoods) might be less engaged due to lack of tailored communication. AI translation and content adaptation can help reach these groups effectively. We discussed translation for parents, but that can extend to community newsletters, flyers, etc., ensuring everyone in the community, regardless of language or disability, can access information (through translated text or text-to-speech for visually impaired community members).

Lastly, AI can help plan and evaluate community initiatives through scenario analysis. If a district is considering hosting a community tech night or a new adult education program, AI could analyze census and local data to predict interest or attendance, helping tailor the program to community needs. While not a direct engagement tool, this use of AI ensures that efforts to engage the community are data-informed and more likely to succeed.

In practical terms, teachers and principals feel the impact of these AI-supported engagement strategies. Teachers, for one, note that when communication with families improves, students come to class better prepared and supported. From the community side, when the community feels heard and informed, they tend to support schools more, volunteering, or simply promoting the school's reputation. In an era where partnership is key, AI becomes the connective tissue that keeps everyone on the same page in the educational journey of each child.

Future-proofing and ongoing evolution

The educational landscape is continually evolving, from pedagogical approaches to the skills students' need for the future, and AI is accelerating that evolution. To truly leverage

---

52 Brandwatch. (n.d.). Brandwatch | The social suite of the future. https://www.brandwatch.com/

AI, educators and policymakers must future-proof education by anticipating changes and continually updating practices. This means preparing students (and teachers) for a world where AI is ubiquitous and using AI for scenario planning and risk analysis to make resilient long-term decisions. It also involves using AI insights for informed policy recommendations and gathering feedback on policy implementation to adapt quickly. Let us discuss how AI can help education systems stay ahead of the curve: by simulating possible futures, informing strategic planning, and ensuring that professional development and curricula evolve alongside technological advances. We will also highlight the importance of ongoing teacher training and ethical considerations, so that the human element, teachers' mentorship and guidance, remains central even as AI's role grows.

AI in strategic foresight and policy

One of AI's powerful capabilities is running complex models and simulations, essentially asking *what if?* with data. In education, this can translate to scenario planning at the school, city, or even national policy level. For example, a district or area might use AI to simulate the impact of various policy changes, such as adjusting school start times, changing class sizes, or introducing a 4-day school week. We saw a glimpse of this in the Boston example[53]: after optimizing bus routes, the Boston team developed an algorithm that allowed for unprecedented insight into the implications of changing school start times. They could tweak parameters (like swapping high school and elementary start times) and see projected outcomes on transportation, cost, and equity. In fact, the algorithm found a solution that would have dramatically reduced early start times for students (especially benefiting those historically disadvantaged by the old schedule). Although the proposed change faced public resistance, the point is that AI provided clear evidence and a balanced solution that human planning had not achieved in decades. This kind of scenario planning can be applied to academic policies too. A state education department could ask: *What if we require an extra year of math for graduation?* and have an AI project the outcomes: how many more math teachers would be needed, the potential increase in college-readiness, the risk of higher dropout if support is not sufficient, etc. Armed with these simulations, policymakers can make more informed policy recommendations and decisions, ideally avoiding unintended consequences. In the following table, you will find three *what if* policy scenarios:

Policy scenario	How AI simulations could model effects
What if schools moved to a 4-day instructional week?	AI could model impacts on learning outcomes, attendance patterns, and family logistics by analyzing historical data from similar districts and projecting effects on academic performance, childcare demand, and teacher retention.

---

53 Coleman, E. (2023b, July 10). How One City Saved $5 Million by Routing School Buses with an Algorithm. Route Fifty. https://www.route-fifty.com/digital-government/2019/08/bos-ton-school-bus-routes/159113/#:~:text=Now%20in%20its%20third%20year,such%20as%20school%20start%20times

Policy scenario	How AI simulations could model effects
What if all students received AI tutoring support starting in Grade 3?	AI could simulate academic growth trajectories, identify equity gaps (e.g., device access), and project long-term gains in literacy and math. It could also highlight areas requiring continued human support and forecast teacher training needs.
What if graduation requirements included AI literacy and digital ethics?	AI could assess impacts on course scheduling, staffing needs, and alignment with workforce trends. Simulations could also forecast student preparedness for AI-driven careers and model community sentiment toward the policy.

Table 8.4: What if policy scenarios

AI's predictive ability is also being harnessed to future-proof the curriculum and workforce development. For instance, labor market AI models can analyze trends and suggest which skills students should be learning to be prepared for jobs 10–20 years from now. If AI forecasts a boom in renewable energy technology careers, a district or area might proactively invest in STEM and environmental science programs. Likewise, if models predict that routine coding might be largely automated (needing more emphasis on creative and complex problem-solving instead), schools can adjust their computer science curricula accordingly. This is part of future-proofing education: ensuring that what we teach and how we teach evolves in step with societal needs. A *World Economic Forum* article[54] noted that *educational institutions must invest in both AI infrastructure and teacher training, while also ensuring this tech is available to all students*, emphasizing that preparing for the future is not just about tech but also equity and teacher readiness. That means as AI becomes more integrated, schools must continuously train teachers in AI literacy and ethical use, so they can in turn guide students. It is an ongoing evolution, not a one-off change.

While AI excels at modeling complex scenarios—such as student enrollment shifts, transportation efficiency, or school staffing needs—it has clear limitations when it comes to capturing the full human and ethical dimensions of education policy. AI can also simulate the logistical outcomes of a decision, like adjusting school start times or adding graduation requirements, but AI cannot understand or account for the moral implications, community values, or emotional impact on students and families in the same way that a human can. Predictive models may suggest what is possible or efficient, but they cannot determine what is right, trustworthy, or problematic—these judgments require human deliberation, cultural understanding, and ethical reflection. Policymakers must use AI as a decision-support tool, not a substitute for inclusive, values-based leadership.

---

54 Haoyang, D. L., & Towne, J. (2025, January 9). *How AI and human teachers can collaborate to transform education*. World Economic Forum. https://www.weforum.org/stories/2025/01/how-ai-and-human-teachers-can-collaborate-to-transform-education/#:~:text=AI%20systems%20excel%20at%20tasks,time

Continuous improvement and adaptation

In a future-proof mindset, nothing is *set and forget*, policies and practices should continuously improve based on data (which AI can supply). This is where feedback on policy implementation comes in. After rolling out an AI initiative or any new policy, AI tools can analyze the outcomes and report what is working and what is not, faster than traditional evaluation methods. For example, suppose a district or area implements a new AI-driven math tutoring software for all middle schoolers. Rather than waiting for end-of-year test scores to judge its effect, AI analytics within the software could give real-time feedback: usage patterns, improvement rates, which types of students benefit most, etc. If the data shows that only 30% of students are using it regularly, the district or area can intervene mid-year (perhaps more training or integration into class), rather than declaring the initiative a failure later. This agile approach to implementation is common in business (fail fast, iterate), and education can adopt it with AI help. Essentially, AI enables evidence-based iteration of educational programs and policies.

Another aspect of future-proofing is addressing the ethical and societal implications of AI in education proactively. As AI is integrated, educators and policymakers have to consider issues like data privacy, algorithmic bias, and the role of human judgment. Best practices (which we will cover in the next section) include developing guidelines for AI use. This kind of policy guidance, in response to AI's rise, helps future-proof by building a culture of responsible AI use from the start.

In the following table, a few examples of AI in professional development planning dashboards are shown:

Platform or tool	AI features for educator professional development	Example use cases
Coursera	Skills proficiency tracking, personalized course recommendations	Targeted PD, skills benchmarking
SOLVED DATA+	Natural language queries, actionable feedback, coaching analytics	Classroom engagement, multi-tiered system of supports prep
Cengage insights	Real-time student learning analytics, AI-driven improvement plans	Early intervention, PD focus
General EdTech tools	Automated continuing education unit tracking, resume or curriculum vitae generation, micro-course curation	Compliance, self-directed PD

Table 8.5: AI features for educator development

It is also about ensuring teachers remain central. As *Sal Khan* (founder of Khan Academy) noted[55], AI will not replace teachers but will enhance their abilities and allow for more personalized interactions with students. Future-proofing education means shaping AI's role to amplify human teaching, not diminish it. That involves policies on AI, for example, a policy might state that AI-generated feedback to students should always be reviewed by a teacher or that AI should be used to free teacher time for mentorship (and measure if that is happening). Keeping such principles at the forefront ensures that as AI technology evolves (which it is, rapidly), the implementation evolves with a clear vision that education is ultimately a human endeavor.

Predictive analytics for at-risk students, discussed earlier, is also a future-proofing measure on an individual level; catching issues early is essentially future-proofing a student's academic career. By scaling that up, an education system future-proofs its outcomes by addressing problems like dropout or achievement gaps before they fully materialize.

From the teacher's perspective, future-proofing and ongoing evolution backed by AI mean they are never stagnating. Professional development becomes a continuous, AI-curated journey (tying back to personalized PD). One can envision a future where an AI system reminds a teacher, **It has been 2 years since your last training on digital assessment tools; since then, new AI assessment methods have emerged. Here are two micro-courses you might take to stay up to date.** Teachers would essentially have an AI mentor ensuring their skills evolve over time.

Building resilience with AI insights

Another forward-looking use of AI is **risk analysis and crisis planning**. Schools face potential disruptions: natural disasters, pandemics (as we learned), and economic downturns. AI can assist in creating robust contingency plans by simulating different scenarios. For example, an AI could help devise the optimal way to shift to remote learning if needed again, learning from the data of 2020–2021 to suggest, say, which students need devices or how to schedule to maximize engagement. For school safety drills, AI can model emergency evacuation times or the impact of certain safety measures. While we hope to not need these, having AI-aided plans is like an insurance policy, it is part of future-proofing to be ready for various futures.

Finally, a big part of future-proofing is continuously asking, *What's next?* and embracing a mindset of ongoing evolution. Future-proofing education in the age of AI involves a partnership between human foresight and AI insight. Educators and policymakers define the values and goals (e.g., equity, preparing well-rounded citizens), and AI provides the analytical muscle to explore how best to achieve them in a changing world. It means committing to ongoing learning, adaptation, and strategic innovation. Perhaps the most important element is recognizing that AI itself is an evolving tool; what it can do today is not its limit. Therefore, an education system attuned to AI's evolution, ready to adopt new capabilities when beneficial

55 NoAILabs. (2024b, December 10). Learning with AI// more productive with models and tools. Medium. https://noailabs.medium.com/learning-with-ai-more-productive-with-models-and-tools-77ca2b2b7ead#:~:-text=Sal%20Khan%20believes%20that%20AI,more%20personalized%20interactions%20with%20students

and ready to impose new rules when needed, will be best positioned to harness AI for good. The work is never done, but with AI aiding reflection and planning, the system can continually renew itself. In essence, future-proofing education means creating a responsive, data-rich, and innovative ecosystem, one where AI is leveraged to make informed decisions swiftly, and where educators are empowered to focus on the human aspects of teaching that only they can do. With that synergy, the education system can confidently navigate the future, no matter what it holds. ·

Best practices

As AI becomes a more integral part of the educational toolkit, it is crucial to follow best practices to ensure that these technologies are used effectively, ethically, and in a way that truly supports teaching and learning. Here, we outline some best practice guidelines for educators and administrators embracing AI. These recommendations synthesize lessons learned from early implementations and expert advice, and they aim to help you maximize AI's benefits while mitigating potential pitfalls. By adhering to these principles, schools can create an environment where AI augments human capabilities and maintains trust among all stakeholders:

- **Keep humans in the loop**: Always remember that AI is a tool to assist, not replace, the educator. Maintain human oversight of AI-driven processes, especially those affecting student evaluation or well-being. For example, if an AI grades essays or provides feedback, a teacher should review a sample of the feedback to ensure it aligns with curriculum goals and student needs[56]. Human judgment is essential to catch errors (AI might mis-grade a creative but correct approach) and to provide the empathetic context that AI lacks. AI might flag a student as at-risk, but a counselor or teacher should interpret that with knowledge of personal circumstances. Always use AI recommendations as a starting point, not the final word.

- **Transparency and consent**: Be transparent with students, parents, and staff about how AI is being used. If you are using an AI tutoring system or a chatbot, explain its purpose and limits. For instance, let students know that an AI will be giving them practice questions or feedback, but that you will monitor and help as needed. Obtain necessary consents for data use, especially if student data is involved. Parents are more likely to support AI interventions if they understand the benefits and know that safeguards are in place. Also, consider giving opt-out options: not every family may be comfortable with certain AI uses, and providing alternatives (like opting out of AI-generated feedback in favor of traditional feedback) can build trust.

- **Data privacy and security**: Ensure that any AI tools comply with privacy laws and that student data is protected. Stick to reputable platforms that have robust data security measures. Avoid inputting sensitive personal information into AI systems

---

56 Noonoo, S. (2023c, December 1). Improving your teaching with an AI coach. Edutopia. https://www. edutopia.org/article/improving-your-teaching-ai-coach/

unless you are sure of how that data is stored and used. For instance, if using a service to transcribe student speech or analyze their writing, confirm that the data won't be improperly stored or sold. When in doubt, consult IT or leadership before using a new AI service with student data.

- **Address bias and fairness**: AI systems can inadvertently perpetuate biases present in their training data. It is important to be mindful of this and to check AI outputs for bias. For example, if an AI is used to identify students for gifted programs or disciplinary action, scrutinize those recommendations for any patterns that suggest bias (e.g., disproportionately flagging or favoring a certain demographic). Use AI as one input among many, rather than the sole basis for such decisions. Additionally, expose students to discussions about AI bias. This turns a best practice into a learning opportunity: students can learn to critically evaluate AI, aligning with digital literacy goals.

- **Quality over hype**: Not every shiny AI tool will be right for your classroom. Choose tools that have demonstrated efficacy or have credible backing. Look for evidence (case studies, pilot results) that an AI application actually improves outcomes or saves time in practice. It is easy to be dazzled by bold claims, but best practice is to pilot on a small scale, gather feedback from teachers and students, and scale up what works.

- **Continuous training and support**: Provide ongoing professional development for educators on how to use AI tools effectively. A one-time workshop is not enough because the tools evolve, and teachers often discover new needs after initial use. Establish a community of practice or regular check-ins for teachers to share tips and troubleshoot issues with AI tools. Encourage teachers to become learners alongside their students when it comes to AI. A growth mindset can alleviate the pressure to be perfect from day one.

- **Student-centered implementation**: Always align AI use with pedagogical goals and student benefit. Use AI to enhance differentiation, not to oversimplify. For instance, if AI offers personalized practice, ensure it aligns with each student's learning plan and does not become a meaningless drill. Solicit student feedback on AI tools and use that feedback to adjust usage. Maintain a balance of AI and non-AI activities to cater to different learning preferences and to develop students' interpersonal skills and creativity, which AI cannot substitute. In short, keep the focus on learning outcomes, using AI as a means to that end.

- **Ethical use and academic integrity**: With generative AI (as text generators), establish clear guidelines for what is acceptable use in academic work. Teach students about plagiarism and the proper way to use AI, for example, using it to brainstorm or outline is different from having it write an entire essay. Many schools now have AI usage policies in their honor codes[57], e.g., students must cite any AI assistance used in

---

57 Johnson, K. (2024c, July 25). California teachers are using AI to grade papers. Who's grading the AI? *CalMatters*. https://calmatters.org/economy/technology/2024/06/teachers-ai-grading/#:~:text=burn-out%20www,laden%20with%20racism%20or%20sexism

assignments. This not only preserves academic integrity but also prepares students for a future where knowing how to ethically use AI is a key skill. Similarly, as a teacher, if you use AI to help draft a lesson or write a report, it is good practice to double-check all facts as AI can hallucinate inaccuracies, and to be transparent if needed about AI contributions. This builds a culture of honesty and critical evaluation.

- **Monitor and evaluate impact**: Treat AI implementations as you would any initiative: collect data and evaluate their effectiveness. Determine key metrics (student engagement, achievement gains, time saved, etc.) and see if the AI tool is meeting expectations. Use surveys or analytics to gather evidence. Be ready to pivot or discontinue use if it is not delivering benefits or if it is causing unintended negatives (like students becoming too dependent or anxious about an AI). On the other hand, amplify what works by sharing success stories. Perhaps an automated reading coach AI significantly improved reading fluency in one class; consider expanding that and documenting the process so others can learn from it.

- **Ensure inclusivity and equity**: Make sure AI tools do not widen the digital divide. All students should have access to the AI's benefits. If an AI requires devices or internet at home, provide alternatives or school access for students who lack those resources. Also, design AI usage that is sensitive to diverse learners. For instance, an AI tutor that only speaks is not ideal for a deaf student without captioning. Push vendors or use features that include multiple modes (text, audio, visuals). When using AI analytics to make decisions, ensure that historically marginalized groups are not disadvantaged by the algorithms. Keep equity at the center of AI initiatives: the promise of AI is that it can help personalize learning for all, but that only holds if all students are accounted for in design and deployment.

By following these best practices, educators can create an environment where AI is a trusted assistant, one that provides educators with valuable insights into student learning and assists with time-consuming tasks without undermining the human connections at the heart of education. Importantly, these practices cultivate an ethical, reflective culture around AI. Education is often about modeling for students how to approach new challenges. By thoughtfully integrating AI, celebrating its advantages and candidly addressing its flaws, teachers model adaptability and lifelong learning. The previously mentioned best practices are not one-and-done steps but ongoing habits: checking for bias, keeping communication open, updating skills, and reviewing outcomes. In essence, they boil down to *Trust the AI, but verify* and maintain the teacher's role as the professional decision-maker. When educators follow that approach, AI truly becomes a partner in education, not a threat.

Conclusion

AI in education is here, in our classrooms and offices, quietly transforming how we teach, learn, and collaborate. Now that we have explored how AI can support cognition and efficiency, we turn to its role in the more delicate and sensitive territory of emotion, empathy, and social growth—where the stakes are not just academic, but deeply human.

This chapter has traveled through the many facets of an educator's work and shown that at each stage, from planning lessons to engaging families to shaping future policy, AI can be a powerful enabler. It empowers teachers with insights from data that would be impossible to parse manually, it shoulders mundane tasks to let teachers focus on human connections, and it opens up new possibilities for personalized and engaging learning experiences.

AI can enhance professional development for educators by serving as a coach, analyst, creator, and connector. It brings a wealth of support that, used wisely, can make teaching more effective and sustainable. Imagine a school day where routine tasks are minimized, where every lesson is informed by real evidence of what each student needs, where feedback loops with students and parents are immediate and meaningful, and where teachers have more bandwidth to innovate and inspire. This vision is increasingly within reach. Together with our AI assistants, we can continue to transform education to be more inclusive, effective, and responsive than ever before, ensuring that every educator and every student is prepared to thrive in the world ahead.

In the next chapter, we will discuss how AI can support students' **social-emotional learning (SEL)**. While SEL is considered to be primarily about human-centered relationships, AI has the potential to augment and support SEL in educational settings in new and interesting ways. We will share implementation techniques and classroom strategies to help you start incorporating AI for SEL.

Questions

1. How might AI shift the role of teacher from delivering information to designing a human + machine learning experience, and are current professional development models preparing educators for this transformation?

2. If AI can analyze every classroom moment and student interaction, what does it mean for a teacher's professional growth to be data-rich, and how to keep it deeply personal?

3. How can we ensure that AI-enhanced feedback loops for teachers lead to meaningful change rather than overwhelming micro-management and over-evaluation?

4. What would a truly AI-augmented peer mentoring culture look like? How could a culture change transform how educators connect, reflect, and improve together?

5. In what ways can AI in PD unintentionally build on and reinforce inequity, especially among schools or educators with differing levels of access, tech fluency, or support?

6. Imagine a future where every teacher has a personalized AI mentor, growing with them year by year. What might that change about how we define career progression in education?

7. How might AI in PD help teachers become not just consumers of professional knowledge, but co-creators, experimenters, and innovators within their own

ecosystems? How can teachers provide reinforcement learning to the AI models using experience and classroom data?

8. How can AI-powered PD elevate the voices and experiences of underrepresented educators and school districts, and what guardrails do we need to create to prevent bias in how recommendations or insights are surfaced?

9. What does responsible and ethical implementation of AI in professional development look like when teacher data, student voices, and learning artifacts are all being analyzed at scale? Is there any data that should be off limits?

Exercises

In small groups, discuss and explore the following topics:

1. How PD needs to evolve to prepare for the shifting role of teachers in an AI-rich classroom.

2. Balancing quantitative AI insights with qualitative, human dimensions of teaching practice.

3. The emotional and psychological impact of constant AI-driven feedback, and how it supports or hinders teacher freedom and agency.

4. Rethinking mentorship beyond in-person observations using intelligent video indexing, smart scheduling, and cross-school or even international educator collaboration.

5. The risks of a world of AI haves and have-nots in professional learning, and how to build more inclusive AI ecosystems.

6. Rethinking tenure, evaluation, and growth based on a living portfolio of AI-assisted learning and teaching evolution based on classroom data, PD, and career goals.

7. The shift from PD as something done to teachers, to something co-constructed *with* teachers, using AI as a collaborator and partner.

8. Equity in algorithmic mentorship, spotlighting diverse teaching strengths, and avoiding one-size-fits-all AI solutions. Leveraging reinforcement learning to improve models based on human feedback.

9. Transparency, security, privacy, inclusiveness, consent, data sovereignty, and how to build trust in AI systems that see deeply into classroom practice.

CHAPTER 9

AI in Supporting Social-emotional Learning

Emotional intelligence is the ability to recognize, understand, and manage our emotions, as well as to recognize, understand, and influence the emotions of others.

-Daniel Goleman

Introduction

The integration of AI in supporting **social-emotional learning** (SEL) within educational settings allows instructors to customize learning and think about the broader landscape of education, exploring beyond academic pursuits. SEL takes shape with the intentional teaching of many interpersonal skills that help students thrive in diverse situations throughout their lives. Over time, the value of SEL has been understood to have a profound impact on students' overall development and well-being. It helps students develop critical life skills such as emotional regulation, strong collaboration strategies, empathy, and effective communication. Through a supportive and inclusive environment, instructors can leverage SEL strategies to promote positive relationships between students, enhance academic performance, and reduce behavioral issues. SEL can also support student growth and development by leveraging AI tools and applications, navigating complex social situations, building greater emotional resilience, and exploring moral and ethical scenarios in a safe environment. In essence, AI can be a strong supporter to help teach SEL in addition to demonstrating and reinforcing SEL through its own behavior. AI integration with SEL has the potential to accelerate the instruction of our youth, creating well-rounded, emotionally intelligent, and socially responsible contributors to society, preparing students for success both in school and in life.

Structure

- Historical foundations of social-emotional learning
- Community, engagement, and safety
- Reflection, identity, and self-esteem
- Social interaction, empathy, and collaboration
- Scaffolding emotional growth
- Moral and ethical reasoning
- Classroom strategies for implementing AI for SEL
- Ethical and practical concerns
- Future direction

Objectives

This chapter aims to explore the integration of AI into SEL strategies, from the historical foundations of SEL to examining core strategic components such as community engagement, self-esteem, and empathy. We will highlight the potential SEL classroom strategies that are prime for the integration of AI and briefly address both ethical and practical concerns. The advantages of integrating AI into students' social-emotional education are numerous, facilitating the development of a holistic approach to student development.

Historical foundations of social-emotional learning

SEL has roots going back to ancient Greece and the age of *Plato*. Once again, we call on the philosophy of Plato to help explain the origins of educational concepts that are still prevalent today. In Plato's famous text *The Republic,* he not only discussed the benefits of a strong basic education but also the need for building a strong moral character and a sense of good judgment. While not a new concept, how we think about and teach SEL to our children continues to evolve in today's educational systems.

During the early 20th century, educators and psychologists began to recognize the important role of social and emotional development in the early stages of childhood. *John Dewey's* philosophy on how young children and school-age students should learn was one of pragmatism; teachings around the entire developmental experience, including SEL, along with academic learning.[1] Dewey believed that emotion drives the desire to learn and valued real-life experiences as part of the learning journey. Developing strong social and emotional skills at a young age is important for the overall well-being of society by establishing acceptable behavioral norms.

Today, SEL is seen as a vital component of every child's educational journey. The integration of AI to support SEL strategies can be a useful classroom strategy. For example, by using AI tools such as Classcraft[2], teachers can gamify SEL learning as students are awarded badges for demonstrating positive behaviors such as self-management, responsible decision making, social awareness and emotional regulation.

Key theories and models

While many different theories exist explaining how people learn, there are several that stand out as having shaped the development of SEL. Introduced in the 1980s, *Howard Gardner's* theory of *Multiple Intelligences* expanded the categories in which humans learn beyond the basic senses of vision, hearing, and touch. His theory included eight different yet interconnected intelligences that shape human experience, with interpersonal and intrapersonal intelligences holding true to the learnings of social and emotional engagement between people.[3] Interpersonal intelligence touches on the responses and understanding of others' feelings, emotions, desires and motivations. Intrapersonal intelligence is the inward focus of understanding about one's feelings, emotions, beliefs, and values. Gardner believed that the importance of understanding the motives of oneself and others assists in overall cognitive development and paved the way for further concepts related to SEL.

Daniel Goleman's theory on **emotional intelligence** (**EI**) provided an additional stepping stone to the popularization of SEL. Goleman's EI theory helped educators more fully understand that intellectual knowledge was not the only important component in learning. EI refers to the ability to understand and pick up on the subtle nuances of human interaction and the way someone responds verbally or non-verbally in different situations.[4] Based on his theory of EI, Goleman developed a framework to assist in the development and teaching of EI. His framework touched on five components, including social skills, empathy, self-regulation, motivation, and self-awareness.[5] These components work together to inform the broader understanding of one's own emotional intelligence.

1 Simply Psychology. (2024a, February 1). John Dewey on Education: Impact & Theory. https://www.simplypsychology.org/john-dewey.html

2 HMH Classcraft. (2024, April 18). https://www.hmhco.com/programs/classcraft

3 Simply Psychology. (2025, March 26). Gardner's Theory Of Multiple Intelligences. https://www.simplypsychology.org/multiple-intelligences.html

4 NeuroLaunch.com. (2024, October 18). Goleman's Theory of Emotional Intelligence: A Comprehensive Exploration. https://neurolaunch.com/goleman-theory-of-emotional-intelligence/

5 Hcsuper. (2022, November 29). Daniel Goleman's Emotional Intelligence Theory: Explanation and Examples | Resilient Educator. Resilient Educator. https://resilienteducator.com/classroom-resources/daniel-golemans-emotional-intelligence-theory-explained/

The **Collaborative for Academic, Social, and Emotional Learning** (CASEL) was founded in 1994, bringing together a large network of people, including researchers and educators, to advance the field of SEL.[6] CASEL's work included the development of a comprehensive framework for SEL, the *CASEL wheel*.[7] This framework includes five core components: self-awareness, self-management, responsible decision-making, social awareness, and relationship skills, all surrounded by a network where students engage in learning, including home, schools, and communities. This framework became the foundation for current SEL programs and practices being adopted by educational systems around the world. For example, a 2024 study[8] published in the *International Journal of Emotional Education* discussed how European initiatives in education are connecting to the CASEL framework, showing the importance of SEL in a school context.

Integration of SEL in education

The integration of SEL into schools has grown significantly since the early 2000s as a result of research. Much of the research conducted is based on the SEL theories and models described earlier in this chapter. Overall, research has provided strong evidence that SEL impacts children's success with academics, mental health, and social behavior. A research brief titled *Evidence for social and emotional learning in schools* by the *Learning Policy Institute* discussed the results from 12 separate studies focused on PreK-12 grade levels on the effects of SEL integration in the classroom.[9] In all cases, positive impact was reported on students' social and emotional competencies, relationships with others, appropriate situational behaviors and academic performance. In addition, a reduction in emotional distress and poor behavioral responses was also noted.

In response to research on SEL, more and more global educational systems are integrating SEL practices into their curriculum at every grade level and within policy itself. For example, in 2003, the *Illinois State Board of Education*, in partnership with CASEL and the *Illinois Children's Mental Health Partnership*, created and adopted SEL standards across their school system for all K-12 students.[10] This broad adoption set a precedent for other U.S. states to follow and is now considered a best practice within most educational settings.

Internationally, the integration of SEL in the classroom has also gained traction. Organizations such as the **United Nations Educational, Scientific and Cultural Organization (UNESCO)**[11]

---

6 About CASEL - CASEL. (2024, February 29). CASEL. https://casel.org/about-us/

7 Fundamentals of SEL - CASEL. (2024, November 27). CASEL. https://casel.org/fundamentals-of-sel/

8 Cavioni, V., Broli, L., & Grazzani, I. (2024). Bridging the SEL CASEL Framework with European educational policies and assessment approaches. International Journal of Emotional Education, 16(1), 6–25. https://doi.org/10.56300/ultx1565

9 Greenberg, M. T. (2023). Evidence for social and emotional learning in schools [Research brief]. https://files.eric.ed.gov/fulltext/ED630375.pdf

10 Social and emotional learning. (n.d.). Illinois State Board of Education. Retrieved April 12, 2025, from https://www.isbe.net/sel

11 Social Emotional learning. (n.d.). UNESCO MGIEP. https://mgiep.unesco.org/sel-for-everyone

and the **Organisation for Economic Co-operation and Development (OECD)**[12] have helped shape global policy and advocated for the adoption of SEL practices in the classroom curriculum. They promote SEL's role in determining positive life outcomes and supporting global peace.

More recently, research around the integration of AI in support of SEL has emerged. In a 2024 study, published in the *Journal of Research in Innovative Teaching & Learning,* the findings indicated that the integration of AI in educational settings showed an increase in engagement, promotion of mental well-being, empathy development, and greater opportunities for personalized learning among test subjects.[13] While there are many positives to the integration of AI in SEL, concerns are also arising as students view AI technologies as a safe zone to express their innermost secrets. Sharing feelings and other thoughts without fully understanding the privacy implications that exist and what data is retained can lead to harmful consequences. To help students better understand the implications and concerns, Common Sense Media partnered with CASEL to further apply the *CASEL wheel* to the digital space with a goal to help students navigate difficult online situations, leveraging social and emotional skills.[14]

In our post-global COVID-19 pandemic world, the increase in online social activities, brought on by the necessary seclusion during the pandemic, has changed how students engage with each other, form their values, and understand nuances in online situations. Studies show that the pandemic affected the academic and social-emotional growth of millions of students around the world, putting many behind in reaching targeted grade-level milestones.[15] The long-term effects, both positive and negative, of the global COVID-19 pandemic are yet to be fully understood; however, the importance of SEL is further reinforced as a critical component of ongoing development throughout life, especially in response to disruptive events that plague mental health.

SEL has come a long way since Plato espoused the need for developing a strong moral character in addition to strong academic knowledge. SEL is now being adopted as a key component of education in classrooms around the world. With the increase of SEL and AI integration, students will need to learn how to best succeed in an increasingly complex and connected world.

Community, engagement, and safety

As students develop, the intersection of SEL and academic instruction becomes increasingly important. From the time children are born, they begin to process the understanding of emotion

12 OECD (2024), Social and Emotional Skills for Better Lives: Findings from the OECD Survey on Social and Emotional Skills 2023, OECD Publishing, Paris, https://doi.org/10.1787/35ca7b7c-en.
13 Sethi, S. S., & Jain, K. (2024). AI technologies for social emotional learning: recent research and future directions. Journal of Research in Innovative Teaching & Learning, 17(2), 213–225. https://doi.org/10.1108/jrit-03-2024-0073
14 Abrams, Z. (2025, January 1). Classrooms are adapting to the use of artificial intelligence. American Psychological Association. https://www.apa.org/monitor/2025/01/trends-classrooms-artificial-intelligence
15 Research Brief: Social-Emotional Learning (SEL) in response to COVID-19 | Rutgers CESP. (n.d.). Rutgers CESP. https://cesp.rutgers.edu/resource/social-emotional-learning-covid-response

from different cues they receive, such as the smile from mom or dad or the tone of voice used in response to behavior. As they get older, acceptable behaviors are learned from families and the community through cooperative play on the playground or in other social settings. By the time children are school age, basic social and emotional behaviors are forming as they add in more structured academic learning. These early interactions with adults and other children begin to shape the trajectory of life. By fostering a safe and inclusive classroom environment that leverages SEL frameworks in addition to academic instruction, societies can create a sense of support and belonging among students.

Building community

The integration of AI and SEL can also play a significant role in building a supportive community. The facilitation of strong communication, monitoring of student interactions, and providing personalized support are examples of how AI and SEL can work together for the betterment of students.

SEL's focus on the development of emotional and social skills, combined with AI's ability to enhance these efforts in the classroom, has the potential to create a positive classroom environment for all. Leveraging AI platforms, such as Constructive Feedback Generator[16], which assists students to give and receive feedback in a positive and constructive manner, is one example of the integration that is taking root. These tools are designed to help students grow and make positive, actionable changes in their behavior. They also have the potential to alert instructors to harmful comments, giving teachers the early cues to intervene when necessary to maintain a positive classroom atmosphere. The following figure shows an educator facing a student who is surrounded by AI assistants:

Figure 9.1: *Students will be supported by AI in all they do*

---

16 Free AI Constructive Feedback Generator (No login required). (n.d.). https://galaxy.ai/ai-constructive-feedback-generator

Enhancing engagement

One of the largest benefits of AI in the classroom is its ability to create and enhance personalized learning through adaptive learning systems. Adaptive learning platforms, as discussed in *Chapter 6, AI for Diverse Learning Needs*, use AI to create personalized learning plans that align with each student's diverse learning needs. A critical factor for effective learning is engagement, in which adaptive learning platforms excel. By adjusting to a student's performance in real-time, providing immediate and actionable feedback, and keeping students engaged, these platforms have the potential to assist teachers in creating positive learning environments for all.

One technique to enhance engagement, motivate and educate students in the classroom is through AI-powered gamification. Gamifying learning allows students to earn points, badges, or compete for leaderboard status, encouraging positive engagement and competition. By gamifying SEL, students have the benefit of learning positive responses and behaviors that will gain them status and levels. One example is Classcraft, which is designed as a multiplayer gamified learning experience for SEL in the classroom.[17] Teacher monitoring is encouraged in Classcraft to assist students on their path to success. Many of the game components are team-based, encouraging greater community engagement with peers to solve problems collaboratively. Gamified learning not only motivates students to participate actively but is also an enjoyable way to learn, leading to greater peer and classroom engagement.

Safety measures

Ensuring student safety is a top priority for educators both in online forums and offline interactions. AI has the ability to monitor student interactions and can enhance safety measures by detecting potential risks. Integration with SEL frameworks provides an added advantage for teaching students how to best navigate different situations they encounter daily in a safe and respectful way. For instance, AI can analyze online communications for signs of cyberbullying, harassment, or other harmful behaviors. When such issues are found, the system can alert parents or guardians and teachers, helping them to take action to protect students. This intervention reinforces the importance of social awareness, empathy and relationship skills, all critical components of SEL.

While AI algorithms can be used for the good of SEL, we would be remiss not to mention protecting our students from the potential harm AI systems can have, such as bias and privacy concerns.[18] At the core of SEL is the belief that the overall well-being of society is created by establishing acceptable behavioral norms. If bias is introduced through the use of AI, the ramifications can be great, as inappropriate behaviors would be encouraged and potentially

---

17 Edwards, L. (2022, October 7). What is Classcraft and How Can It Be Used to Teach? Tips & Tricks. TechLearningMagazine. https://www.techlearning.com/how-to/what-is-classcraft-and-how-can-it-be-used-to-teach-tips-and-tricks
18 AI in education: What are the risks and challenges? (n.d.). https://www.9ine.com/newsblog/ai-in-education-what-are-the-risks-and-challenges

proliferate throughout the classroom. The oversight instructors have in classroom settings is critical when integrating AI with SEL to ensure proper use and the positive outcomes expected. In the following table, you will find examples of helpful AI support versus harmful surveillance in the context of privacy concerns:

Helpful	Harmful
Real-time feedback in a controlled environment	Monitoring of private chats without consent
Teacher-initiated AI monitoring with human oversight	Automated disciplinary action
Opt-in SEL tool use	Data collection without transparency

Table 9.1: Privacy boundary examples with AI use in SEL situations

By leveraging AI platforms with SEL strategies, a more inclusive, engaging, and secure learning environment can be created. One that fosters the social-emotional development of students, leading to a safe learning environment. As AI integration with SEL continues to evolve, its potential to transform education will make it an invaluable asset in classrooms.

Reflection, identity, and self-esteem

By promoting self-reflection, supporting identity formation, and boosting self-esteem, AI has the potential to transform education, ensuring students develop the skills to self-assess not only their academic learning but also their social-emotional engagement with others. Educators also have a role to play by leveraging AI tools to create personalized and engaging learning experiences that support students' growth and well-being, along with that of the whole class.

Self-reflection

AI applications have great benefits in promoting self-reflection among students. Self-reflection is the process of thinking deeply about one's own experiences and emotions to gain additional insight and understanding of who one is. AI has the ability to intensely question students, encouraging them to reflect more deeply on their learning experiences and emotional responses.[19] For example, AI can analyze students' learning data and provide targeted reflection questions that guide the student to fully self-evaluate their learning strategies and outcomes.[20] This process helps students develop skills to monitor and control their own learning more effectively. In addition, AI tools can produce real-time feedback to students, enabling them to adjust their academic and social-emotional learning strategies in real time, thereby enhancing their overall effectiveness.

19 Stanford Graduate School of Education. (2023, December 1). Enhancing Reflective Practices with AI - IT Teaching Resources. IT Teaching Resources. https://teachingresources.stanford.edu/resources/enhancing-reflective-practices-with-ai/
20 Learnomics - AI in Education. (2024, September 19). How can AI facilitate metacognitive strategies in teaching and learning? https://mylearnomics.com/ais-role-in-metacognitive-teaching-strategies/

Supporting identity formation

With the increased blending of online and real-world engagement, we are seeing how AI can play a pivotal role in a student's formation of their own identity. Identity formation is an ongoing process whereby an individual explores their values, affiliations and beliefs to develop a sense of self. This is especially important as we explore the integration with SEL strategies and the need to ensure a balanced approach is taken by students and instructors.

The benefits of AI integration with SEL strategies in supporting students as they explore their identity include the ability of AI tools to:

- Assist educators in creating safe spaces for students to express themselves in different ways.
- Allow students to explore different aspects of their identities through engaging and interactive activities both independently and with others.
- Create a safe space for students to ask questions without any judgment.

Some of the risks[21] of AI influence on SEL strategies as students explore and have more online connections, including:

- Constant exposure to idealized images and lifestyles leads to low self-esteem.
- The anonymity of online engagement can lead to cyberbullying, among other negative behaviors.
- Reduced in-person engagement and face-to-face social skills practice.

By discussing some of the concerns raised in recent discussions and research surrounding the increased use of social and digital platforms, the possible interventions become apparent. Strong guidelines for online use, a focus on student safety, encouraging in-person engagement, especially in classroom settings, and implementing SEL strategies throughout K-12 can assist in supporting students in this critical phase of development.

Boosting self-esteem

Boosting self-esteem, one's overall sense of worth, leads to benefits such as improved mental health, better social relationships, the ability to adapt to challenges and changes, and a greater commitment to achieving goals. AI tools have the ability to significantly contribute to boosting a student's self-esteem by providing positive reinforcement and other support throughout their education. For example, the Feeling Great application uses a chatbot powered by AI, along with interactive courses to engage with students. Their goal is to increase self-esteem and emotional well-being by reducing negative thoughts and feelings.[22] An example of a

---

21 Weir, K. (2023, September 1). Social media brings benefits and risks to teens. Psychology can help identify a path forward. American Psychological Association. https://www.apa.org/monitor/2023/09/protecting-teens-on-social-media
22 Feeling Great app FAQs. (n.d.). https://www.feelinggreat.com/faqs

prompt to use in the Feeling Great application is **If your feelings today were a color, what color would they be and why did you choose that color?** This type of prompt helps the student reflect on their emotional state, at the moment, in a creative and non-threatening way. Kahoot! is another example of an AI-driven interactive learning platform that encourages student engagement through fun learning experiences, reinforcing self-worth through celebrating progress.[23] Leveraging AI platforms can help students boost their self-esteem and help them feel confident in their ability to conquer any challenge.

Social interaction, empathy, and collaboration

Social interactions in today's world are more complicated than ever before. The way students access technology, whether via a computer or cell phone, the number of applications and AI algorithms working behind the scenes to share what it thinks you need to see and learn, is overwhelming. Students, teachers and parents or guardians not only need to pay attention to social-emotional learning in an interconnected world, they also need to pay close attention to what and how students are being exposed to different influences in their SEL journey. AI platforms are emerging as strong supporters of SEL and can be extremely helpful in classroom settings, facilitating social interactions and ensuring students exhibit empathetic and collaborative behaviors.

Facilitating social interaction

AI social networking tools can positively enhance student interactions, especially when introduced in a classroom for learning purposes. In-class social networking tools such as Nearpod, an interactive learning platform leveraging AI to help instructors engage their students and deepen peer-to-peer learning through collaborative learning lessons and social networking tools.[24] These social teaching platforms use AI algorithms to connect students with similar interests or skills, encouraging them to collaborate on projects and assignments. In relation to other, more traditional collaborative tools such as Google Docs, Nearpod is designed to provide synchronous, teacher-led, real-time interactivity with instant feedback. In a study titled *The Impact of Artificial Intelligence (AI) Technology on Students' Social Relations,* the results indicated that while AI use for social purposes in the classroom was shown to improve learning outcomes and efficiency, it can create social inequality and a strong dependence on technology itself.[25] Social discussion forums are another use of AI in the classroom. A student's contributions can be monitored and then relevant topics or connections with other students can be recommended, encouraging more meaningful conversations with others. Not only can AI monitor individual contributions, but it can also provide real-time feedback to a group, ensuring that conversations and other social interactions are positive and productive.

23 "It's taken over the school by storm!": teachers at Bishop O'Dowd Hig. . . (2022, September 16). Kahoot! https://kahoot.com/what-is-kahoot/
24 Nearpod: Foster a love of learning in every student. (n.d.). https://nearpod.com/
25 Amanda Puteri, S., Saputri, Y., & Kurniati, Y. (2024). The Impact of Artificial Intelligence (AI) Technology on Students' Social Relations. BICC Proceedings, 2, 153–158. https://doi.org/10.30983/bicc.v1i1.121

By assisting with these interactions, AI helps students develop strong social skills such as teamwork, communication, and conflict resolution.

Developing empathy

Empathy is one of the soft skills that is difficult to teach, yet is critical as a foundation for social interactions and strong communication. SEL strategies aim to teach empathy through role-playing and other activities that require students to reflect on the situation. AI can play a significant role in nurturing this skill and transforming how empathy is taught. **Virtual reality (VR)** experiences and simulations can be an effective tool where students are immersed in complex social situations that then require them to navigate and practice empathy.[26] AI has the ability to create these situations in a safe environment, effectively allowing students to practice and develop their skills. Additionally, AI can review responses and provide personalized, real-time feedback to help students improve empathy skills by reflecting on the experience.

Collaborative learning

AI is having a profound influence on collaborative learning in our global society. As students jointly author, work together on assignments, and capture ideas using technology, they respond with feelings of greater accountability and engagement. The ability of AI to assist in assessing the skills and contributions of an individual in a group activity drives inclusive learning experiences. With each group member having an understanding of how other members are engaging with the content and discussions, teamwork is promoted. AI platforms such as Slack, Microsoft Teams, and Google Workspace are designed to effectively connect groups of people together and drive greater efficiency through AI-powered capabilities like automatic note summarization, real-time translation and task generation.[27] The integration of AI with SEL is continuing to evolve and transform education in new and exciting ways, building skilled students who will be ready with strong leadership and collaboration skills to take on the world.

Scaffolding emotional growth

Emotional scaffolding refers to support provided to students to help them develop their overall emotional well-being, including emotional resilience and regulation. AI applications can play a significant role in building emotional capabilities with tools that assist students in managing their emotions, promoting strong mental stability through mindfulness, and providing a personalized emotional support plan.

---

26 Jamaluddin, N. S., & Mokhtar, M. (2025). Teaching Empathy: How AI Can Support the Development of Soft Skills in Education. International Journal of Academic Research in Business and Social Sciences, 15(3). https://doi.org/10.6007/ijarbss/v15-i3/24469

27 Mahendra, S. (2024, December 5). Collaborative learning with AI tools. Artificial Intelligence +. https://www.aiplusinfo.com/blog/collaborative-learning-with-ai-tools/

Many of the AI applications that support students in their emotional growth assist by providing real-time feedback and intervention techniques that students can leverage as they work to regulate their emotions daily. In a recent study titled *Emotion recognition for enhanced learning: using AI to detect students' emotions and adjust teaching methods,* it was found that, through the use of AI facial recognition technology, students who appeared happy or joyful were more likely to be engaged with learning and process teachings more deeply. Those who appeared sad or frustrated, often associated with negative emotions, were more distracted and experienced cognitive overload, hindering engagement and learning.[28] Building the emotional stability of our youth is one of the key strategies of SEL and mindfulness applications, such as Headspace[29], and emotion tracking tools, like *The Momentary Emotion Assessment Tool*[30], can help students manage and regulate their emotions through targeted intervention techniques. An example of how a teacher may use The Momentary Emotion Assessment Tool in their daily instruction to support a student's emotional awareness and classroom engagement is through the following steps:

1. **Set the routine** through a 5-minute check-in with students to create a calm environment at the start of the time together.

2. **Present the tool,** asking students to select how they are feeling right now from either a list of emotions or emojis.

3. Offer an **optional reflection prompt** asking students to reflect further on their current emotional state, such as, `What is one word to describe why you feel this way?`

4. **Review responses** by quickly scanning the feedback to identify which students may need support throughout the day.

5. **Check in** one-on-one with students who indicate they may need help and offer different mindfulness strategies like deep breathing or quiet spaces.

6. **Track trends** over time to identify patterns.

With the integration of AI into mindfulness applications, these tools use AI algorithms to monitor students' emotional states during activities and show positive potential in supporting educational strategies and adaptive learning plans that support each student's individual emotional needs.[31]

Continuously challenging students in the classroom and providing constructive feedback, with the assistance of AI tools designed to detect areas needing greater emotional support, has

28 Salloum, S.A., Alomari, K.M., Alfaisal, A.M. et al. Emotion recognition for enhanced learning: using AI to detect students' emotions and adjust teaching methods. Smart Learn. Environ. 12, 21 (2025). https://doi.org/10.1186/s40561-025-00374-5

29 Meditation and sleep made simple - Headspace. (n.d.). Headspace. https://www.headspace.com/

30 The Momentary Emotion Assessment Tool | EdInstruments. (n.d.). https://edinstruments.org/instruments/momentary-emotion-assessment-tool

31 Vistorte, A. O. R., Deroncele-Acosta, A., Ayala, J. L. M., Barrasa, A., López-Granero, C., & Martí-González, M. (2024). Integrating artificial intelligence to assess emotions in learning environments: a systematic literature review. Frontiers in Psychology, 15. https://doi.org/10.3389/fpsyg.2024.1387089

the potential to lead to stronger emotional resilience. This resilience enables students to adapt more readily to difficult situations and move forward with a positive mindset.

As students engage in conversations with AI tools such as chatbots that can recognize their emotional state, they will receive appropriate feedback and interventions. Students can receive feedback that helps them understand their emotions and how to access the help they need, whether that is through other AI tools or human intervention. In developing a strong emotional scaffolding, research indicates that AI can effectively assess, teach, and reinforce SEL skills.[32] By leveraging AI technologies in the classroom, educators can benefit from the creation of a more adaptive learning environment supporting the social-emotional development of all students.

Moral and ethical reasoning

In *Chapter 10, Data Security and Ethical Considerations in AI*, we discuss ethical AI in detail in reference to the development and use of AI that adheres to principles of fairness, transparency, accountability, inclusiveness, safety, and privacy. It is also covered later in this chapter, and here we focus on the teachings of ethics and moral reasoning and the power AI lends to these scenarios. Specifically, AI can assist educators in challenging students to think critically and question ethical dilemmas. Instructors can create immersive experiences and utilize AI platforms, such as Mentimeter[33], which allows teachers to develop presentations with polling and feedback options, engaging students and enabling them to discuss and analyze different ethical topics and viewpoints. Mindsmith[34], another AI tool, allows educators to custom-design e-learning courses that incorporate various ethical situations, further ensuring students understand concepts and implications of ethical decisions.

By incorporating AI in the classroom, teachers are better able to adopt a more analytical and outcome-oriented approach to ethical dilemmas, while also highlighting other SEL strategies such as empathy. By utilizing AI tools, instructors can further encourage critical thinking, diving deep into moral and ethical issues through structured AI debate platforms and ethical dilemma games. Kialo Edu[35] is an example of a debate platform that encourages logical reasoning and can improve oral skills on ethical topics. AI-generated quizzes are another option for instructors to leverage for encouraging comprehensive learning and reasoning. An example of an AI quiz platform is Socrative[36], which allows instructors to create questions, administer the quiz, and then adjust their teaching based on instant feedback.

32 Vistorte, A. O. R., Deroncele-Acosta, A., Ayala, J. L. M., Barrasa, A., López-Granero, C., & Martí-González, M. (2024). Integrating artificial intelligence to assess emotions in learning environments: a systematic literature review. Frontiers in Psychology, 15. https://doi.org/10.3389/fpsyg.2024.1387089
33 Mentimeter home page. (n.d.). https://www.mentimeter.com/. Retrieved April 17, 2025, from https://www.mentimeter.com/
34 Mindsmith - eLearning development with Generative AI. (n.d.). https://www.mindsmith.ai/
35 Kialo Edu: The free tool for thoughtful, inclusive class discussion. (n.d.). Kialo. https://www.kialo-edu.com/
36 Socrative. (2025, March 18). Home - socrative. https://www.socrative.com/

To practice ethical decision-making skills, AI simulations can be used to help with real-world situations. VR experiences provide a controlled environment in which students have an opportunity to practice navigating complex moral and ethical situations. VR platforms like ENGAGE[37] offer a compelling environment for students to engage and apply their learned ethical reasoning.

AI tools used by students to explore diverse viewpoints, develop critical thinking, and sharpen reasoning skills will continue to play a role in inspiring students to learn and practice real-world ethical and moral dilemmas in a safe environment. This AI tool engagement has the added benefit of aligning to CASEL's responsible decision-making competency, empowering the direct application of empathy, critical thinking, and ethical reasoning in a socially responsible way. However, challenges remain in ensuring AI platforms are developed in a way that allows them to guide students appropriately through increasingly complex ethical dilemmas.[38] As AI continues to evolve, its potential to become an invaluable asset in all classrooms will continue to grow.

Classroom strategies for implementing AI for SEL

Incorporating AI into SEL coursework is manageable for most educational institutions or independent educators, given the many applications now available. In this chapter, we have discussed many of the AI-focused applications used for different purposes of the SEL curriculum. These SEL strategies supported by AI include:

- **AI-driven emotion recognition**: Provides the ability for instructors to monitor students' emotions in real-time. AI applications will give immediate feedback and suggested interventions to assist students in managing their emotions and reactions to specific situations.

- **Interactive role-playing games**: Simulate different social scenarios in a safe environment, requiring SEL learnings such as ethical decision-making and empathy.

- **VR experiences**: Immersive experiences for students to safely explore complex social-emotional situations from different diverse viewpoints.

- **Adaptive learning platforms**: Personalized learning content, based on feedback, to engage each student based on their specific needs.

- **AI-powered chatbots**: Offer custom emotional support, guidance and recommendations as students interact with them through natural conversation.

37 ENGAGE. (2025, March 31). Spatial Computing Artificial Intelligence - ENGAGE XR. ENGAGE XR. https://engagevr.io/

38 Miller, J. (2025, February 13). Are artificial moral agents the future of ethical AI? | Tepperspectives. Tepperspectives. https://tepperspectives.cmu.edu/all-articles/are-artificial-moral-agents-the-future-of-ethical-ai/

- **Collaborative learning platforms**: Enhance peer-to-peer interactions and teamwork through monitoring student interactions.

- **Ethical dilemma games**: Encourage students to think critically about ethical and moral issues introduced through structured scenarios.

Careful considerations in the implementation of AI in the classroom are necessary to ensure the intended outcomes are achieved. Especially with topics aligned to SEL, which impact student mental health, engagement with others and achievement. Practical steps to implement AI for SEL include:

1. **Select an AI-driven platform or tool** that is designed specifically to meet the goals and outcomes desired.

2. **Align to accessibility standards** and ensure that your tools are trained on diverse data sets and offer customizable, accessible interfaces that work with different assistive technologies.

3. **Set up** by installing the software on classroom devices or working with the appropriate departments at the educational institution to ensure correct configuration for proper use, security, and outcome accuracy.

4. **Continually monitor** the tool for accuracy of output, ethical adherence and alignment to outcomes and goals.

5. **Intervene as needed** if the tool veers away from its intended purpose or outcomes. Realignment of the configuration requirements, choice of a new tool, or additional human intervention, along with the AI solution, may be necessary.

6. **Regularly review** the data collected by the tool to understand trends and adjust teaching strategies accordingly.

These steps provide a structured approach for educators to implement AI strategies for SEL in the classroom. The intent is to encourage more student interaction in a collaborative learning environment through fun and engaging techniques.

Ethical and practical concerns

When integrating AI into the classroom for SEL, ensuring student privacy and data security needs to be top of mind. As discussed robustly in *Chapter 10, Data Security and Ethical Considerations in AI,* AI tools often collect personal information that students and instructors enter into the application or tool to use for analysis and the training of AI models. This data is usually sensitive information about students that includes, for example, academic performance, behavior patterns, and emotional state To protect this information, schools and educators must implement strong security measures for AI tool access, such as encryption and multi-factor authentication. Compliance with regulations like the **General Data Protection Regulation** (**GDPR**) and the **Family Educational Rights and Protection Act** (**FERPA**) will also guide educators to safeguard student information and privacy.

Putting safeguards in place to protect student privacy and data is a great first step to ensure the security of information. However, it often is not enough. Studies suggest that additional focus on appropriate use of sensitive data, AI ethical instruction and ongoing training will further protect students and support educators in a quickly evolving AI landscape.[39]

Cooperation between AI developers, policymakers and educators is essential for AI applications, developed for educational purposes, to be created in a fair and unbiased way. Unfortunately, AI algorithms have the potential to inadvertently perpetuate biases as a result of model training or retraining. To help mitigate bias, the use of diverse datasets when training AI models is essential. By being aware of the potential for bias in AI tools, educators can be on the lookout for unfair AI output and work to create inclusive learning environments for all students. Further techniques can be employed, such as data audits and algorithmic fairness interventions, to help identify and address biases in AI-driven SEL programs.[40] An example of an algorithmic fairness intervention when considering emotional recognition tools, whereby the data set used to train the model uses facial expressions from neurotypical individuals, has the potential to fail to recognize emotions in others outside of that data set. A fairness intervention would involve intentionally diversifying the training data set to include different facial expressions from people of all abilities, neurotypes, ages, races, etc. This will ensure the algorithm performs equitably for the broadest group of users possible.

To appropriately implement AI for SEL in the classroom, resource limitations, technical issues and training curriculum need to be considered. Schools may have difficulty in sourcing, implementing and safeguarding the necessary technology, along with training staff to effectively use and monitor AI tools. Software compatibility within the existing technical architecture and maintenance of AI systems can also pose challenges to the seamless integration of AI into educational practices. To overcome many of these challenges, educational institutions can partner with technical non-profit organizations, technical companies and apply for grants, helping to ensure all mitigation techniques are considered.[41] Another strategy would be to include an opt-in student consent process, for example, by providing a clear explanation of the tool and asking the student to sign a digital consent form in order to participate. It would be important to include the option to decline without any penalty to their grade or impact on their classroom participation. By understanding and addressing these practical concerns, educators can take advantage of the full potential of AI to support SEL goals for every student.

Future direction

Emerging trends in AI are taking place at lightning speed. The development of more sophisticated AI tools used for the development of SEL, such as VR, sentiment analysis,

39 Nguyen, K.V. The Use of Generative AI Tools in Higher Education: Ethical and Pedagogical Principles. J Acad Ethics (2025). https://doi.org/10.1007/s10805-025-09607-1

40 Federation of American Scientists. (2024, December 13). Modernizing AI fairness analysis in education contexts. https://fas.org/publication/modernizing-ai-fairness-analysis-in-education-contexts/

41 Yu, J.H., Chauhan, D., Iqbal, R.A. et al. Mapping academic perspectives on AI in education: trends, challenges, and sentiments in educational research (2018–2024). Education Tech Research Dev 73, 199–227 (2025). https://doi.org/10.1007/s11423-024-10425-2

gamification, coaching chatbots and wearable devices is being explored.[42] These technologies will continue to refine and offer personalized support to students, resulting in increased social engagement and learning, empathy development, and promotion of well-being and mental health.

The long-term effects of AI on SEL and education will be impactful. With AI's ability to personalize learning experiences, students will be able to engage deeply with technology designed specifically to help them develop essential social-emotional skills. These skills, such as emotional regulation, self-awareness, social collaboration, and ethical reasoning, are critical to developing students and their overall success.

As discussed throughout this chapter, the key takeaways with the integration of AI in the classroom and SEL can be summed up as:

- AI has the ability to greatly enhance SEL strategies by helping to create emotionally supportive and inclusive environments.

- Ethical use and implementation are essential by paying particular attention to privacy, security and transparency.

- Collaboration between educators, students, developers, parents and policymakers is key to success.

- The future of AI and SEL integration is strong, and the use of AI in the classroom for both emotional and academic use will become central to instruction in the very near future.

Ongoing research will continue to be needed, as AI technologies advance, to ensure privacy and safety standards are upheld. Addressing ethical concerns, fostering collaboration across organizations, and ensuring the effective integration of AI in education and SEL will be critical as more AI applications and technologies become available for student use. AI's potential to transform SEL and support students' emotional and academic growth will only increase in the future, becoming an invaluable tool supporting the success of both educators and students.

Conclusion

Within educational settings, AI holds significant promise for boosting students' emotional and social skills. By leveraging AI responsibly, schools can create inclusive and supportive environments that promote students' social-emotional development and overall success in a complex world. Ethical considerations, data privacy, and the need for ongoing collaboration among all stakeholders are essential for ensuring the effective and fair use of AI in educational settings. As AI technologies advance, continuous research and cooperation among AI developers, policymakers, educators and parents or guardians will be essential to address

---

42 Sethi, S. S., & Jain, K. (2024b). AI technologies for social emotional learning: recent research and future directions. Journal of Research in Innovative Teaching & Learning, 17(2), 213–225. https://doi.org/10.1108/jrit-03-2024-0073

ethical concerns and ensure privacy and security standards and regulations are adhered to. The incredible potential of AI in supporting students' emotional and academic growth will likely increase in the future, making AI an integral tool for educators and students alike.

In the next chapter, we will cover data security and ethical considerations in AI across a multitude of dimensions. As educators worry about plagiarism in their classroom, students are curious and excited to explore how AI can augment their educational journey. Considerations of data, security, privacy, and ethical AI use are explored within different types of educational instruction and at every level.

Questions

1. What are the ethical considerations of using AI to monitor students' emotions?

2. How can role-playing games help students develop empathy and moral and ethical decision-making skills?

3. What diverse social-emotional scenarios are best leveraged for a virtual reality experience?

4. How can personalized learning content improve student engagement and emotional growth?

5. What student information could be used to tailor learning experiences for their individual needs?

6. How can monitoring student interactions enhance teamwork and social skills?

Exercises

1. Organize a role-playing game, leveraging an AI application, where students simulate a conflict resolution scenario. After the activity, have a group discussion on the decisions made and both positive and negative intrapersonal interactions exhibited.

2. Utilize an adaptive learning platform to create personalized SEL activities for each student. Monitor their progress and adjust the content based on their feedback and responses.

3. Introduce students to an AI chatbot, like ChatGPT. Encourage them to interact with the chatbot and reflect on the guidance and recommendations provided.

4. Set up a collaborative project where students work in small teams using a chosen AI platform designed for collaboration. Monitor their interactions and provide feedback on their teamwork and cooperation skills.

5. Offer students 3-5 examples of ethical dilemmas and encourage them to leverage AI tools to solve. Facilitate a discussion on the solutions presented and the moral and ethical reasoning behind them.

CHAPTER 10

Data Security and Ethical Considerations in AI

Education is not preparation for life; education is life itself.

-John Dewey

Introduction

This chapter will explore the core themes of: security, fairness, transparency, accountability, inclusiveness, and privacy. In an era when algorithms increasingly influence disciplinary decisions, grades, and learning opportunities, we must ask: *Are these systems treating everyone fairly? Do we understand how they work? Who is responsible when they make a mistake?* The stakes are high.

AI algorithms now sit in the front row of the classroom, in the teacher's lounge, the student's pocket, and in the principal's office. They are analyzing homework for plagiarism review, predicting student achievement paths, flagging risky behavior to administrators, and even creating lesson plans. Each promise of efficiency brings an equal-and-opposite question of ethics. Are these systems amplifying or removing bias? Does the constant gaze of the algorithms protect learners or entrench surveillance in our schools? Will automation narrow achievement gaps—or quietly widen them for the very students it claims to help? The answers depend on how rigorously we address security, fairness, transparency, accountability, inclusiveness, and privacy at every step of the design and use of AI.

Ethical AI is not an ancillary or peripheral ideal, but the foundational scaffolding that holds educational innovation upright. Without robust security, biased audits, and shared accountability, automated systems will default to existing power imbalances—magnifying surveillance, eroding privacy, and funneling opportunity along familiar fault lines. By threading each section of this chapter through the central stakes of bias, surveillance, and inequity, we hope to equip readers to question and test every new AI tool against a single mandate: Does it make learning more just, or merely more automated?

Structure

This chapter covers the following topics:

- Fundamentals of data security
- Key ethical challenges in AI in education
- Global AI policies in education
- Legal and ethical considerations in AI for education
- Responsible use of AI by students
- Guidance for educators in security and ethical AI use
- Role of parents or guardians in ethical AI use

Objectives

In this chapter, we explore both the foundational elements of online security and the ethical implications of using AI in education, focusing on how we can ensure that AI technologies are designed, deployed, and used responsibly. Data security and ethical AI are not just about protecting individuals and their content from harm and misuse, but also about promoting inclusiveness, equity, and empowerment in educational settings. We will examine the responsibilities of different stakeholders: students, educators, parents or guardians, and policymakers in data security and making ethical choices related to the use of AI. We will also discuss the principles for evaluating AI models in education, ensuring that the technologies employed are not only effective but also aligned with safety and privacy standards and the values that educators, students, and society hold dear.

Fundamentals of data security

Data security is a critical component of online safety and privacy, especially with the increased presence of cyber activities from social media and news to banking and consumer or business purchasing. With AI in the classroom, understanding the fundamentals of data security and protecting sensitive student, family, teacher and institutional information against threats is essential.

Basic security concepts

Educators and administrators in schools need to be familiar with fundamental cybersecurity principles to protect student and staff data. In practice, a few core security concepts can help lay the groundwork for safer use of technology in education. These security concepts include:

- **Encryption (including data at rest and data in transit)**: Encryption means scrambling data so that only authorized parties can read it. **Data at rest** refers to data that is stored on a device or server, and **data in transit** refers to data that is moving over a network. Both of these data types should be encrypted. In practice, an urban middle school should encrypt report card files stored on its server and use the HTTPS secure protocol to securely transmit student test scores to state databases, ensuring no personal data is exposed during transfer or storage.

- **Secure networks including firewalls, VPNs, and access controls**: A secure school network should act like a protected classroom—only those with permission should get in. Firewalls are digital gatekeepers that block unwanted traffic from entering or leaving the school's network, much like a security guard at the door. **Virtual Private Networks (VPNs)** create an encrypted tunnel for data; a district staff member working from home could use a VPN to safely connect to the school's secure network without exposing data to the wider internet. Access controls enforce who can access what resources. By using strong passwords and role-based permissions, schools can help ensure each user (students, teachers, or administrators) only sees the information they need. For example, a high school should use a firewall to block suspicious external traffic and require teachers working remotely to connect via VPN. **Role-based access control (RBAC)** limits students' access to their own grades, while teachers can view only their class rosters.

- **Multi-factor authentication (MFA)**: MFA adds an extra step to verify a user's identity beyond just a password login. Common forms of MFA include a one-time code sent to a teacher's phone or email, or a fingerprint scan, used in addition to the usual login password. In practice, a teacher logging into the school's gradebook system might enter her password and then be prompted to enter a code from her smartphone. This second factor of authentication ensures that even if someone guesses or steals the password, they cannot access the account without the authorized device or biometric. In practice, a rural district should use MFA to reduce unauthorized logins. When a student accidentally discloses their login credentials, an attacker will not be able to access the grade system without the teacher's mobile authentication code and permission.

- **Data minimization**: Data minimization represents the collection and storage of only the data that is truly needed for educational purposes. The less sensitive information a school stores, the less attractive it is to hackers and the less damage caused if a breach occurs. In practice, a school district might decide not to collect student social security numbers or detailed family financial data unless absolutely necessary. Not only does data minimization protect privacy, but it also helps schools comply with student data privacy laws by limiting unnecessary exposure of personal information. For example, an elementary school should redesign its enrollment forms to exclude unnecessary fields like parent income level and use instead anonymous codes for free lunch eligibility, reducing the storage of sensitive personal and financial data.

These important and practical steps help schools shift from reactive to proactive cybersecurity, reducing risk while promoting safe, ethical use of technology in the classroom.

Threats and vulnerabilities

Educational institutions continue to face a range of cybersecurity threats, and understanding these dangers is the first step to mitigating them. The *U.S. Department of Education* warns that phishing and out-of-date software are two critical weaknesses often exploited in school cyberattacks.[1] In other words, human error (falling for email scams) and technical gaps (unpatched systems) open the door to many security incidents. The following are some of the most common threats and vulnerabilities in school environments, along with their impact:

- **Phishing and email scams**: Phishing is a social engineering attack where criminals send fake emails or messages that trick users into revealing credentials or clicking malicious links. In a school setting, a teacher or administrator might receive an email that looks like it is from their principal or a trusted vendor, asking them to reset their password or open an attachment. If they fall for it, the attacker can steal login details or install malware on their machine. Phishing is quite common. Training and vigilance are key because a single click on a deceptive email can bypass even the best technical defenses. In fact, phishing was the entry point in roughly one-third of cyber-attacks on K-12 schools in recent years[2], underscoring how frequently these scams target educators and staff.

- **Hacking and unauthorized access**: Hacking in this context refers to attackers exploiting vulnerabilities or weak credentials to gain unauthorized access to school systems. This could range from an external hacker bypassing network defenses to a student guessing a weak administrative password. Once inside, the unauthorized user can view or steal sensitive information. A notable real-world example occurred in Chicago Public Schools, where hackers exploited a software vulnerability in a third-party vendor and stole private information for over 700,000 students, publishing it on the dark web[3]. Such breaches expose students' personal data (names, birthdates,

---

1 K-12 Cybersecurity. (n.d.). U.S. Department of Education. https://www.ed.gov/teaching-and-administration/safe-learning-environments/school-safety-and-security/k-12-cybersecurity#:~:text=Cyber%20incidents%20in%20K,phishing%20email%20and%20outdated%20software

2 K-12 Cybersecurity. (n.d.). U.S. Department of Education. https://www.ed.gov/teaching-and-administration/safe-learning-environments/school-safety-and-security/k-12-cybersecurity#:~:text=Cyber%20incidents%20in%20K,phishing%20email%20and%20outdated%20software

3 Koumpilova, M. (2025, March 7). Hackers expose information for 700,000 current and former Chicago students, district says. Chalkbeat. https://www.chalkbeat.org/chicago/2025/03/07/cps-student-data-exposed-in-hacker-attack/#:~:text=In%20a%20ransomware%20attack%20last,web%2C%20district%20officials%20said%20Friday

student IDs, and even medical or disability records) and erode trust between families and schools. The impact, however, is serious–confidential data can be leaked or altered, and the school may face legal consequences under privacy laws. Keeping software updated and enforcing strict access controls (as described in the *Basic security concepts* subsection) are vital to closing the holes that hackers target.

- **Ransomware attacks**: Ransomware is one of the most significant and disruptive cyber threats facing schools today. In a ransomware attack, hidden applications lock or encrypt the school's files and systems, and the attackers then demand a ransom or payment to unlock them. This can paralyze the school's IT systems–databases, email, and learning management systems–bringing teaching and administrative operations to a halt. Unfortunately, K-12 schools have become frequent targets of ransomware in recent years. Hundreds of U.S. school districts have suffered ransomware attacks; between 2016 and 2022 alone, at least 325 ransomware incidents on school districts were publicly reported, with dozens more in 2023[4]. These attacks can have debilitating consequences. For instance, a 2022 ransomware attack on the *Los Angeles Unified School District* (the second-largest school district in the U.S.) led to a massive data leak when the attackers published the stolen files with highly sensitive student health records, including the psychological evaluations of about 2,000 students[5]. In addition to these breaches, ransomware often forces schools to temporarily close or revert to pen-and-paper operations because critical systems are no longer functioning. This means lost classroom time and chaos in everything from attendance to accessing digital textbooks. Even if a school has backups and refuses to pay the ransom, restoring systems can take days, weeks, or months. Ransomware can directly impact student safety (by exposing private information), disrupt learning continuity (when classes or records are inaccessible), and erode institutional trust (parents may question the school's ability to safeguard their children's information).

Overall, these online threats illustrate why cybersecurity is a serious component of student safety. Whether it is a deceptive email or a network break-in, the vulnerabilities in school technology can translate into real harm—interrupted learning, privacy violations, financial losses, and damage to a school's reputation. Proactive defenses and awareness are essential to counter these growing risks. Introducing AI systems without careful consideration to data security and privacy has the potential to augment these risks by increasing data exposure, adding complexity, and introducing new vulnerabilities. Without a strong focus on understanding data security vulnerabilities and systematic implementation, the introduction of AI could unintentionally weaken the protections educational institutions are trying to strengthen.

4 Quraishi, A., Sen, A., Pham, S., Corral, A., & Johnston, T. (2024, August 27). Ransomware attacks on schools threaten student data nationwide. CBS News. https://www.cbsnews.com/news/school-ransomware-attacks-threaten-student-data/
5 Kapko, M. (2023, February 27). Los Angeles school district confirms sensitive student data leaked. Cybersecurity Dive. https://www.cybersecuritydive.com/news/los-angeles-schools-ransomware-health-records/643611/#:~:text=,as%20part%20of%20the%20attack

Risks to students and families

When student data is not properly handled or is compromised, several risks emerge that can negatively impact students and families. Protecting privacy is not just a formality or a legal requirement; it is crucial for safety and fairness. Some major risks associated with improper data handling in education include:

- **Identity theft and fraud**: If hackers or unauthorized individuals obtain private personal student information, they can use these details, like names, birthdates, or social security numbers, to commit identity theft. For example, a recent breach of a major student information system, PowerSchool, exposed students' names, contact details, dates of birth, medical information, and even social security numbers.[6] In such cases, these criminals might attempt to open fraudulent credit card accounts or loans using a student's identity. Young people are often easy targets for identity theft because it might go unnoticed for years until the student is older. A data breach can thus lead to long-term financial and legal problems for students and their families.

- **Student profiling and unfair labeling**: Schools are increasingly using data analytics and even AI tools to track student performance, health, and behavior. The intention is often to identify students who need extra support, but there is a risk that algorithms could potentially mislabel or unfairly profile students or group them into unfair clusters. If data is interpreted without human context, a student might be flagged as high risk, for example, or placed on a watchlist due to an algorithm's judgment without context. For instance, predictive models have been shown to exhibit biases based on data they have been trained on—one study in higher education found that certain algorithms were more likely to incorrectly predict poorer outcomes for Black and Hispanic students compared to their peers[7]. This kind of profiling can be problematic as it can lead to lowered expectations for, or different treatment of, students based on biased data or flawed data analysis. Moreover, once a student is labeled by a system (e.g., as a likely disciplinary case or a low performer), that label can follow them and influence how teachers and administrators treat them throughout their academic career, creating a self-fulfilling prophecy or reinforcing bias.

- **Unintended data sharing**: A big concern to be wary of is that student information may be shared outside the school or the district in ways that students and parents never intended. Many educational online services, applications, and platforms are run by vendors and third-party companies. If those companies are not careful, data can be passed on or sold to advertisers, data brokers, or other external partners. In

---

6 Arghire, I. (2025, January 21). Students, educators Impacted by PowerSchool Data Breach. SecurityWeek. https://www.securityweek.com/students-educators-impacted-by-powerschool-data-breach/#:~:text-t=The%20data%20breach%20led%20to,or%20banking%20information%20was%20affected

7 Mowreader, A. (2024b, July 19). Predictive models in higher ed disadvantage some students. Inside Higher Ed | Higher Education News, Events and Jobs. https://www.insidehighered.com/news/student-success/academic-life/2024/07/19/predictive-models-higher-ed-disadvantage-some#:~:text=Researchers%20found%20some%20models%20predict,either%20prediction%20outcomes%20or%20accuracy

fact, research has revealed that an overwhelming majority of education technology applications share student data with outside entities. One analysis found that 96% of common K-12 school apps were transmitting students' personal information to third-party companies,[8] and about three-fourths of the time, this included sharing data with advertisers or other businesses that could profit from it[9]. This means that a student's study habits or personal details could end up in the hands of marketing firms or other unknown parties. Such unintended sharing will violate trust and expose students to targeted advertising or other uses of their data that have nothing to do with education. It is a risk that often goes unnoticed and unenforced by schools unless they thoroughly vet the privacy practices of each tool they use. A significant and recent illustration of proactive data privacy measures in education comes from New York State's actions[10] in early 2025. To enhance student data privacy and comply with Education Law 2D, New York schools restricted K-12 student access to non-core Google services like YouTube, Google Maps, and Google Translate, effective March 2025. This decision ensures student data is not entered into or stored in services that do not meet state privacy standards, with only essential tools such as Docs, Slides, and Sheets remaining accessible to students. This initiative, driven by a commitment to safeguarding student information and preventing unintended data sharing with third parties, allows teachers to retain access for instructional purposes while enforcing strict boundaries for student data security. This example serves as an inspiring model for other educational institutions aiming to prioritize data privacy in an increasingly digital learning landscape by demonstrating how to audit proactively, restrict vendors, and take concrete steps to mitigate the risks of unintended data sharing.

Importance of infrastructure and IT support

Given the high stakes, schools must prioritize a safe, secure, and strong technology infrastructure and draw on **information technology** (**IT**) support to maintain student safety. Most K-12 institutions do not have extensive in-house cybersecurity teams, so collaboration with vendors and district-level IT professionals and administrators is essential. K-12 school systems are often described as target-rich, cyber-poor because they present highly attractive targets for cybercriminals while simultaneously lacking the resources, robust protections and expertise to defend themselves effectively[11]. In 2024 alone, K-12 institutions experienced a 92% increase in ransomware attacks, with 36% of all ransomware attacks in the education

8 Arundel, K. (2023, January 9). Nearly all ed tech apps share students' personal information. K-12 Dive. https://www.k12dive.com/news/school-apps-share-student-personal-information/639913/#:~:-text=,25%20Children%27s%20Online%20Privacy

9 Arundel, K. (2023, January 9). Nearly all ed tech apps share students' personal information. K-12 Dive. https://www.k12dive.com/news/school-apps-share-student-personal-information/639913/#:~:-text=,25%20Children%27s%20Online%20Privacy

10 Client challenge. (n.d.). https://www.uvstorm.org/article/2047261

11 Cybersecurity for K-12 Education | CISA. (n.d.). Cybersecurity and Infrastructure Security Agency CISA. https://www.cisa.gov/K12Cybersecurity#:~:text=adversaries%20have%20targeted%20our%20Kindergar-ten,often%20without%20the%20proper%20protection

sector targeting these schools[12]. A recent report[13] found that 82% of K-12 schools suffered cyber incidents, including ransomware, phishing, and data breaches. Schools hold vast amounts of sensitive data—student records, financial information, and health details—and provide critical community services such as meals and counseling, making successful attacks especially damaging. However, many schools operate with limited IT budgets, outdated security protocols, and insufficient cybersecurity staff, making them vulnerable to sophisticated attacks that increasingly exploit human factors like phishing[14] (a cyberattack where attackers impersonate trusted sources to trick people into revealing sensitive information or clicking on malicious links) and social engineering[15] (the manipulation of people into performing actions or divulging confidential information, often by exploiting trust or emotions). This combination of high-value data and systemic underinvestment in cybersecurity infrastructure creates a perfect storm, leaving K-12 systems exposed and in urgent need of stronger defenses and strategic investments to protect students, staff, and communities[16]. By working hand-in-hand with school or district IT staff, educators and policymakers can ensure that security measures (like those described in the *Basic security concepts* subsection in this chapter) are properly implemented and maintained. For example, IT specialists can configure firewalls, set up network monitoring, and manage identity access controls, creating a safer digital ecosystem for the entire school.

One critical area where IT support is necessary is in system maintenance and updates. Outdated software and unpatched systems can be a major vulnerability, as noted, cybercriminals frequently exploit known weaknesses when schools have not applied the latest security updates. A dedicated IT team can perform regular vulnerability assessments and promptly install important updates or patches to fix software bugs or issues. This proactive maintenance shuts the doors that attackers might use. It also involves routine tasks like updating antivirus software, renewing security certificates, and replacing old hardware that cannot be secured. Schools that can stay current with updates drastically reduce the risk of a breach; conversely, neglecting updates is like leaving a school's back door unlocked. IT professionals often maintain detailed schedules to review these updates and can test the updates prior to implementation to make sure they do not disrupt classroom technology and other activities. Moreover, IT staff develop and enforce data protection policies—for instance, guidelines on how teachers should store sensitive information (preferably on secure, school-managed cloud drives rather than personal devices) and rules for how to use student data. Having clear policies, supported by technology (like automatic backups and encryption), ensures that even if an incident happens, the damage is limited and data can be restored. Regular backups maintained by the IT department mean that in a scenario like a ransomware attack, the school can recover

12 Sanchez, M. (2025, May 14). How schools can strengthen cybersecurity in 2025. UDT. https://udtonline.com/how-schools-can-strengthen-cybersecurity-in-2025/

13 2025 CIS MS-ISAC K-12 Cybersecurity Report: Where Education Meets Community Resilience. (2025, March 6). CIS. https://www.cisecurity.org/insights/white-papers/2025-k12-cybersecurity-report

14 Kosinski, M. (2025, July 9). Phishing. IBM. https://www.ibm.com/think/topics/phishing

15 IBM. (2025, July 9). Social Engineering. IBM. https://www.ibm.com/think/topics/social-engineering

16 ArmorPoint, V. A. (2025, May 21). What to know about the newest cyberattack strategy putting K-12 schools at risk. eSchool News. https://www.eschoolnews.com/it-leadership/2025/05/21/newest-cyberattack-strategy-k-12-schools/

important data without having to pay the hackers' ransom money. Periodic security audits led by the IT department can reveal weak points in the system (such as unnecessary accounts or misconfigured permissions) before an attacker finds them.

Perhaps the most important element is developing a culture of security awareness among all stakeholders: teachers, students, administrators, and technology staff all must play a role. Technology alone cannot secure a digital environment; people's behaviors play a huge role. This is part of the reason why ongoing cybersecurity training and education are crucial in schools. IT support teams and leaders should offer regular training sessions or resources that teach staff and students how to recognize dangerous phishing emails, use strong passwords, and follow safe practices online. For example, teachers might receive regular training on spotting suspicious email attachments, and students should receive lessons on creating secure passwords or protecting their personal information on school devices. Such training can help to demystify cybersecurity and empower everyone to act as a front-line defender. Administrators can underscore the importance of reporting any odd computer behavior or potential phishing attempts without fear of blame. When all members of a school community treat cybersecurity as an important part of their daily responsibility, the overall risk drops significantly. Leadership (including school principals and district officials) can further support this culture by prioritizing cybersecurity in budgets and policies, ensuring that it is not an afterthought but an integrated part of educational planning. In fact, federal agencies like the **Cybersecurity and Infrastructure Security Agency (CISA)** emphasize the need to raise awareness and change risky behaviors in K-12 settings, providing tools and guidance to help schools improve their security posture[17]. By making cybersecurity a shared mission, rather than just the IT department's job, schools can create an environment where technology can be used for learning with far greater confidence in its safety.

Cybersecurity in education technology settings is a collective responsibility. Understanding basic security concepts gives administrators, educators, and students the tools to protect themselves. By being aware of threats and vulnerabilities, schools can remain vigilant and prepared for potential incidents. And most importantly, leveraging strong infrastructure and IT support builds a resilient foundation, enabling a more proactive and unified response to cyber risks. By investing in these technology areas, educational institutions can safeguard the privacy and continuity of learning for all, even in the face of evolving digital threats, with the implementation of AI in the classroom.

Key ethical challenges in AI in education

In AI-powered classrooms, every glance, every click, query, answer, and pause a student makes can turn into useful data. Modern educational AI tools can continuously collect and process data from student interactions. As AI becomes more deeply integrated into education, it brings with it several ethical challenges that must be addressed to ensure its responsible use. Let us discuss the primary ethical concerns surrounding AI in education, including data privacy,

17 About CISA | CISA. (n.d.). Cybersecurity and Infrastructure Security Agency CISA. https://www.cisa.gov/about

equity and accessibility, bias in AI models, and the autonomy of teachers and students. These issues impact the effectiveness and fairness of AI systems and must be carefully considered to ensure that AI benefits all students, educators, and stakeholders equitably.

AI detection systems, increasingly used to uphold academic integrity, often produce false positives, wrongly flagging genuine student work as AI-generated. Even with false positive rates as low as 1–4%, thousands of students each year may face unwarranted accusations, risking academic penalties, emotional distress, and even expulsion[18]. These errors disproportionately impact non-native English speakers and neurodivergent students, whose writing styles are more likely to be misclassified[19]. The consequences are profound: a single mistaken flag can jeopardize a student's academic record and future, underscoring the urgent need for more reliable detection methods and fairer institutional responses.[20]

As an example, let us meet *Chloe*. Chloe was days away from her high school graduation when an unexpected email shattered her excitement. The principal informed her that an AI-powered plagiarism detector had flagged her final history essay as likely written by AI, accusing her of academic dishonesty. In an instant, Chloe's years of hard work and integrity were called into question by an opaque algorithm. Panicked, she scrambled to gather proof that she alone wrote every word, digging up early drafts and Word version timestamps to demonstrate her writing process. Sitting in the administrator's office, she felt betrayed that a machine's judgment could override her teacher's trust and frustrated that her hard work was not being acknowledged. Chloe was not alone—at a university in Texas, an entire class of seniors faced a similar nightmare when an instructor used ChatGPT itself to test their essays and nearly derailed their graduation[21]. In another case, a college student suffered full-blown panic attacks after being falsely accused by an AI writing detector[22]. These real incidents set an alarming precedent: when schools lean on unproven AI detection tools, innocent students can be branded as cheaters, jeopardizing their education and mental well-being.

These stories highlight urgent questions of fairness and transparency in educational AI. It feels unfair that a secretive algorithm could ruin a student's reputation without clear evidence. Even worse, if nobody could fully explain how the AI decides their work was suspicious, imagine the system was a black box, offering no feedback or chance for defense. In Chloe's story, was

18 Perry, C. (2025, July 2). Student Falsely Accused By AI Detectors: False Positive. AI Detector | ChatGPT Detector | AI Humanizer - Undetectable AI. https://undetectable.ai/blog/student-falsely-accused-by-ai-detectors/

19 Tilawat, M. (2025, July 11). AI Cheating in Schools: 2025 Global Report on Student Use, Detection Failures & Policy Gaps. All About AI. https://www.allaboutai.com/resources/ai-statistics/ai-cheating-in-schools/

20 Hirsch, A., Hirsch, A., & Hirsch, A. (2024b, December 12). AI detectors: An ethical minefield. Center for Innovative Teaching and Learning -. https://citl.news.niu.edu/2024/12/12/ai-detectors-an-ethical-minefield/

21 Verma, P. (2023, May 19). A professor accused his class of using ChatGPT, putting diplomas in jeopardy. The Washington Post. https://www.washingtonpost.com/technology/2023/05/18/texas-professor-threatened-fail-class-chatgpt-cheating/

22 Jimenez, K. (2023b, April 13). Professors are using ChatGPT detector tools to accuse students of cheating. But what if the software is wrong? USA TODAY. https://www.usatoday.com/story/news/education/2023/04/12/how-ai-detection-tool-spawned-false-cheating-case-uc-davis/11600777002

the AI biased by her writing style or limited English fluency? Research shows these detectors often misread simple or non-native English as AI-generated—one study found over half of essays by non-native speakers were falsely flagged, whereas native writers were almost never mislabeled[23]. In other words, the very students working hardest to overcome language barriers could be unjustly punished due to algorithmic bias. Chloe's case and others like it illustrate how a lack of transparency and unchecked bias in AI systems can lead to false accusations that devastate student morale. Her story ends on a relieved note—her evidence eventually cleared her name, and the school dropped the charge. But the damage was done, and Chloe left for college acutely aware that AI in education, if used without care, can erode trust.

Data collection and use

For AI models to be most effective, they require access to a large range of data. Data is used to create more personalized learning experiences and optimize teaching methods. For example, an adaptive math program might use telemetry to record how long a student spends on each question, which problems they got right or wrong, and even the specific errors made. In fact, some platforms gather incredible volumes of information—DreamBox, for instance, might log 50,000 data points per hour as students work through lessons[24]. All of this data is processed in the background by algorithms that look for patterns and insights.

AI education tools typically gather several key categories of student data, such as:

- **Performance metrics**: These include grades on assignments, quizzes, test scores, and skill mastery levels. Essentially, it is important to include any measure of how well a student is doing on academic tasks.

- **Engagement logs**: Data that tracks how the student is learning. This type of data can include the time spent on each task or resource, login frequency, the number of attempts a student makes to answer a question, clickstream data through a lesson, or whether they watch instructional videos to the end. Engagement data can help show how attentive and persistent a learner is with the material.

- **Demographic or personal data**: Basic student information (age, grade level, or demographic background, learning preference profiles). A platform might capture a student's reading level or whether they have special education needs. This context can help AI tailor the experience. Of course, any personal data collected is usually what the school or student has entered into the system, and it is subject to privacy rules.

---

23 AI in Schools: Pros and Cons. (2024, October 24). College of Education. https://education.illinois.edu/about/news-events/news/article/2024/10/24/ai-in-schools--pros-and-cons
24 Dreambox Learning – A teaching assistant for every student in your math class. - Digital Innovation and Transformation. (2019, November 13). Digital Innovation and Transformation. https://d3.harvard.edu/platform-digit/submission/dreambox-learning-a-teaching-assistant-for-every-student-in-your-math-class/#:~:-text=Dreambox%E2%80%99s%20program%20collects%20an%20average,and%20between%20les-sons%E2%80%94dynamically%2C%20instantaneously%2C%20and

Data ownership

As K-12 education becomes more data-driven, the question of who owns student learning data is increasingly important. Traditionally, schools have acted as stewards of this information, managing and securing vast amounts of data to inform instruction and comply with regulations[25]. However, there is a growing movement advocating for greater student ownership, recognizing that when students have access to and control over their own data, it can foster autonomy, engagement, and personalized learning pathways[26]. The following table compares the advantages and drawbacks of school-ownership versus student-ownership of learning data:

Aspect	School-ownership of learning data	Student-ownership of learning data
Pros	• Centralized management and security • Easier compliance with legal and policy requirements • Streamlined data analysis for school improvement	• Empowers students with control and transparency • Increases engagement and responsibility • Supports personalized learning and student agency
Cons	• Limits student agency and transparency • Risk of data misuse or lack of student consent • May reduce student motivation and trust	• Potential challenges in ensuring data security • Difficulties in standardizing data management • May require significant support and education for students

Table 10.1: *Comparison of school vs. student ownership of learning data*

As schools continue to adopt new technologies and personalized learning models, finding the right balance between institutional stewardship and student agency will be crucial for maximizing both the ethical use and educational value of learning data.[27]

Data privacy and security

While AI in education relies heavily on data collection to function effectively, making the protection of student data a critical aspect of ethical AI is necessary. AI models require access

---

25 The Importance of Data Ownership in K-12 - Blog | Pear Deck Learning. (n.d.). https://www.peardeck.com/blog/the-importance-of-data-ownership-in-k-12

26 Student Privacy Compass. (2021, January 15). Student data? Who owns it? https://studentprivacycompass.org/student-data-who-owns-it/

27 The Center - Student Data Literacy. (n.d.). https://sites.google.com/view/thecenter-iowa/learner-centered-mtss/student-data-literacy

to a range of student data, which may include demographic details, academic records, online interactions, and even emotional responses to learning materials. Although beneficial, this extensive data collection also creates significant privacy risks, particularly for vulnerable groups such as minors.

Protecting this data from unauthorized access, ensuring it is used only for its intended purposes, and making sure students' privacy rights are respected are central ethical considerations. The GDPR[28] in the European Union and the **Family Educational Rights and Privacy Act (FERPA)**[29] in the United States are two examples of legal frameworks designed to safeguard student privacy. These laws give students and parents or guardians rights over how their personal data is used and shared. However, AI systems may still operate in ways that circumvent or misunderstand these protections, creating opportunities for misuse or breaches of privacy.

A critical issue is determining who owns the data collected by AI systems. Should students and their families have more control over the data generated? And to what extent should informed consent be required before collecting and using this data? Ensuring that students and their families are fully aware of how their data is being used and are able to consent to its collection is key to maintaining trust and upholding privacy rights. Some practical considerations to ponder include:

- Schools and educational institutions must be transparent about the types of data they collect and how it will be used.

- AI developers should ensure compliance with privacy laws and best practices for data protection.

- Teachers and administrators should be educated about data security risks and how to mitigate them.

Equity and accessibility

One of the most significant advantages of AI in education is its potential to personalize learning for students with diverse needs. However, without careful implementation, AI can exacerbate existing inequalities in education, especially concerning access and affordability.

Think about the digital divide; while AI offers incredible opportunities for personalized learning, it also requires access to digital devices and the internet. Students from lower-income families, those in rural areas, and those attending underfunded schools may not have the necessary access to these technologies, creating a digital divide. This divide could mean that AI-driven educational tools benefit only certain groups of students, while others are left behind.

---

28 General Data Protection Regulation (GDPR) – legal text. (2024b, April 22). General Data Protection Regulation (GDPR). https://gdpr-info.eu/

29 U.S. Department of Education. (2011). The Family Educational Rights and Privacy Act. https://www.ed.gov/media/document/eligible-studentspdf-102019.pdf

On the other hand, AI can be a powerful tool in supporting students with learning disabilities or special educational needs. For instance, AI can provide individualized learning plans, speech-to-text tools, or reading comprehension aids for students with dyslexia or other challenges. Yet, ensuring that these AI tools are affordable and available to all students is crucial. Otherwise, AI could inadvertently widen the gap in educational opportunities.

AI systems must also be inclusive of cultural and linguistic diversity. Many AI tools are developed in English-speaking countries or Western contexts, which can result in biases or limitations when applied in non-Western cultures or for students who speak languages other than English. Ensuring that AI tools are culturally sensitive and linguistically adaptable is essential to promoting equity in education. Practical considerations in the realm of equity and accessibility include:

- AI tools must be designed to be accessible to all students, with particular attention paid to underprivileged communities and those with special educational needs.

- Schools should provide equal access to devices and internet connectivity, working to bridge the digital divide.

- AI models should be built with global education standards in mind, ensuring that they are culturally and linguistically adaptable.

India's AI for All initiative stands out as a successful equity-focused policy model, demonstrating how large-scale, inclusive AI education can be achieved and replicated globally. Launched through a collaboration between the Ministry of Education, **Central Board of Secondary Education (CBSE)**, and Intel, *AI for All* offers a self-paced, internet-based program designed to make AI literacy accessible to millions—including students, professionals, and older adults—regardless of background or prior experience[30]. By 2024, the initiative had reached 15,000 training institutes and aimed to empower up to 2.5 million learners nationwide, emphasizing digital literacy, critical thinking, and ethical AI use[31]. The program's modular, scalable design and focus on bridging industry-academic gaps have led to marked improvements in learning outcomes and employability, with 400,000 students lifted out of learning poverty and an 18% reduction in those lagging behind grade level[32]. India's approach, combining public-private partnerships, accessible content, and real-time data for targeted interventions, offers a replicable blueprint for other countries seeking to promote equity and future-readiness through AI in education.

30 Team, C. (2021, July 30). Intel launches 'AI For All' initiative in collaboration with CBSE, Ministry of Education - CRN - India. CRN - India. https://www.crn.in/news/intel-launches-ai-for-all-initiative-in-collaboration-with-cbse-ministry-of-education/

31 Desk, I. T. E. (2024, March 21). India's youth set to embrace AI: 15,000 ITIs introduce groundbreaking curriculum. India Today. https://www.indiatoday.in/education-today/news/story/15000-itis-introduce-groundbreaking-curriculum-indias-youth-curriculum-edtech-2517601-2024-03-21

32 How AI is transforming teacher effectiveness and learning outcomes in India. (n.d.). BCG Global. https://www.bcg.com/industries/social-impact/client-success/ai-leading-to-greater-educational-outcomes-in-india

Bias and fairness in AI systems

One of the most pressing ethical issues with AI in education is bias. AI models are trained on vast amounts of historical data, which means that if the data used to train these systems is biased and reflects existing inequalities, whether intentionally or unintentionally, the algorithmic decisions or outcomes they produce can perpetuate or even exacerbate those disparities. Model bias refers to systematic errors built into an AI system due to flawed assumptions, limited training data, or an overly simplistic design, causing the model to consistently misinterpret or misrepresent reality. Output bias, in contrast, is reflected in the actual results or predictions produced by the AI, which may be skewed or unfair due to model bias, biased data, or external influences. In essence, model bias shapes how the AI thinks, while output bias is seen in how it acts, and both can negatively impact fairness and accuracy in AI-driven decisions.

In education, biased AI tools could lead to unfair grading[33], biased admissions processes[34], or the marginalization of certain student groups[35]. Understanding and mitigating bias in AI models is, therefore, crucial to ensuring fairness in the educational experiences of all students. In 2020, for example, the UK's A-level standardization algorithm used past school performance data to moderate exam grades, which resulted in many students from lower-performing schools receiving downgraded marks and sparked a national outcry before the policy was reversed[36]. In September 2024, *Education Week* reported that 20 percent of Black high school students were falsely accused of using AI to cheat—compared to 7 percent of white and 10 percent of Latino students—largely due to flawed AI detection algorithms that disproportionately flag writing by students of color.[37]

In everyday classroom tools, bias can be subtler but equally harmful. Consider an adaptive learning platform that recommends math exercises based on a student's past performance: if its training dataset overrepresents learners from well-resourced districts, the system may interpret slower problem-solving by students from under-resourced schools as a lack of ability rather than unmet support needs. Consequently, it steers those students toward easier

33 Hunt, M. (2020, September 24). UK government drops exam grading algorithm in the face of public anger - Global Government Forum. Global Government Forum. https://www.globalgovernmentforum.com/uk-government-drops-exam-grading-algorithm-in-the-face-of-public-anger/

34 Journal of Blacks in Higher Education. (2024, July 22). Study uncovers racial bias in university admissions and Decision-Making AI algorithms. The Journal of Blacks in Higher Education. https://jbhe.com/2024/07/study-uncovers-racial-bias-in-university-admissions-and-decision-making-ai-algorithms/

35 Ashwini, K. P. & United Nations. (2024). Report of the Special Rapporteur on contemporary forms of racism, racial discrimination, xenophobia and related intolerance. In Human Rights Council (Report A/HRC/56/68; pp. 1–3). https://documents.un.org/doc/undoc/gen/g24/084/20/pdf/g2408420.pdf

36 Walsh, B. (2020, August 19). How an AI grading system ignited a national controversy in the U.K. https://www.axios.com/2020/08/19/england-exams-algorithm-grading

37 Klein, A. (2024e, October 24). Black students are more likely to be falsely accused of using AI to cheat. Education Week. https://www.edweek.org/technology/black-students-are-more-likely-to-be-falsely-accused-of-using-ai-to-cheat/2024/09

problems, limiting their challenge and growth. As the 2023 *EDUCAUSE Horizon Report*[38] cautions, *use of particular algorithms may lay bare intrinsic biases that may not be apparent at first but may be more apparent as time goes on and certain trend lines develop.*

Bias can enter AI systems in multiple ways:

- **Skewed or incomplete training data**: If the historical records used to train an AI overrepresent certain groups (i.e., students from affluent schools), the model learns those patterns as normal.

- **Feature proxies**: Data fields that correlate with protected attributes—like zip code or past test scores—can become unintended stand-ins for race or socioeconomic status.

- **Design assumptions**: Algorithmic choices (such as how much weight to give past performance versus peer benchmarks) often reflect developers' own perspectives, which may not generalize fairly across all student populations.

Developers must ensure that diverse data sets are used to train AI models and that algorithms are regularly audited for signs of bias; in essence, they must go further than compliance checklists: they must embed ethical practices throughout the AI development lifecycle, and recognize that the pathways differ by context. Commercial software engineers, often driven by scalability and market timelines, may focus on robust, performant systems that meet broad customer demands. In contrast, educational technologists—whether within university research labs or mission-driven edtech startups—operate under different incentives and constraints. They typically engage in stakeholder-centered processes such as **Institutional Review Board (IRB)** approvals, educator co-design sessions, and iterative user testing to surface and address potential harms before scaling up.

For example, the *U.S. Department of Education's* January 2024 guide *Designing for Education with Artificial Intelligence*[39] was built on more than 20 public listening sessions with students, teachers, parents, and administrators, demonstrating how institutional developers can systematically gather feedback on fairness, privacy, and usability before finalizing AI designs. A prominent U.S.-based example of AI bias in education is the incorrect flagging of **English as a Second Language (ESL)** students by automated plagiarism and AI-detection systems like

38 Pelletier, K., Robert, J., Arbino, N., Muscanell, N., McCormack, M., Reeves, J., McDonald, B., Grajek, S., & EDUCAUSE. (2023). 2023 EDUCAUSE Horizon Report: Holistic Student Experience Edition. EDUCAUSE. https://library.educause.edu/-/media/files/library/2023/9/2023hrholisticstudentexperience.pdf?hash=1F93517550D48DFD13698ED5203F1CC7B43C6E5D&la=en

39 Cardona, M. A., Ed. D., U.S. Department of Education, Rodriguez, R. J., Khan Academy, GoGuardian, Worcester Polytechnic Institute, EDSAFE AI Alliance, Carnegie Learning, Merlyn Mind, TeachFx, Alchemie Solutions, Inc., Digital Promise, Khan Academy, GoGuardian, Worcester Polytechnic Institute, EDSAFE AI Alliance, Carnegie Learning, Merlyn Mind, TeachFx, . . . Digital Promise. (2024). Designing for Education with Artificial Intelligence: An Essential Guide for Developers (By Office of Planning, Evaluation and Policy Development). https://files.eric.ed.gov/fulltext/ED661949.pdf

Turnitin[40]. These tools, widely adopted across American schools and universities, sometimes incorrectly identify authentic student writing as either plagiarized or AI-generated, particularly when the writing style or language usage differs from native norms. Such false positives can disproportionately impact multilingual and neurodivergent students, leading to unwarranted academic penalties and emotional distress[41]. This issue underscores a broader concern: AI systems trained on limited or biased datasets often reinforce existing inequities rather than solving them, especially when used for high-stakes decisions like grading or discipline. As AI becomes more embedded in classrooms, these real-world cases highlight the urgent need for transparent, fair, and context-aware systems that do not inadvertently disadvantage vulnerable student populations.

Across academia, research teams leverage IRBs and multidisciplinary advisory boards—drawing on expertise in pedagogy, ethics, and data science—to oversee pilot studies of AI tutors and adaptive platforms. These boards review proposed data collection methods, assess potential biases in training sets, and mandate transparency measures (such as model explainability reports) before any classroom rollout.

Practical considerations for schools and developers include:

- **Distinguish roles**: Recognize that commercial engineers and educational technologists have complementary strengths—one excels at engineering scale, the other at pedagogical integrity—and foster collaboration between them.

- **Embed stakeholder voices**: Use ethical review boards, public listening sessions, and educator focus groups early and often to identify risks and design for realworld diversity.

- **Document and share protocols**: Publish dataauditing procedures, fairness metrics, and usertesting results so the entire field can learn and iterate.

By clarifying these distinct pathways—and ensuring commercial vendors, university labs, and nonprofits alike adopt shared ethical practices—AI in education becomes a truly collaborative endeavor, guided not just by regulation but by the collective expertise and values of all stakeholders.

Furthermore, schools should actively work to identify and correct AI systems that may produce biased results. Transparency in AI decision-making is critical, enabling educators and students to understand how AI systems arrive at particular conclusions or decisions. It helps to anchor our ethical commitments in three interlocking actions to ensure fairness. First, every AI system must undergo rigorous, ongoing audits to uncover and correct bias before it can harm students. Second, educators themselves must be empowered to interrogate and, if necessary, override AI decisions—because no algorithm should ever go unchallenged in the classroom.

---

40 AI detection tools falsely accuse international students of cheating – the Markup. (2023, August 14). https://themarkup.org/machine-learning/2023/08/14/ai-detection-tools-falsely-accuse-international-students-of-cheating
41 AI biases in educational technologies and the classroom. (2025, January 6). https://www.onlineeducation.com/features/artificial-intelligence-biases-in-education

And third, those building these tools must commit to truly inclusive design: training models on richly diverse datasets and bringing together educators, ethicists, sociologists, and data scientists at every stage. Only by weaving these practices together can we ensure that AI in education not only drives innovation but also does so with fairness, transparency, and respect for every learner.

Algorithmic accountability and transparency

In education, an AI system is accountable when its owners can trace, explain, and justify how the model produces decisions that affect learners, and when students, parents, or regulators can challenge those decisions. Accountability, therefore, rests on two technical pillars: explainability (clear, human-interpretable reasons for an output) and auditability (independent checks that the model behaves as claimed). Without both, even wellintentioned AI can erode trust.

In April 2023 *The Washington Post* tested Turnitin's new AIwriting detector[42] with five U.S. highschool students[43]. The tool falsely flagged one student's original essay as AIgenerated, yet neither the vendor nor the school could explain how the score was produced or offer a clear appeals process. The episode illustrates what happens when an algorithm's conclusions cannot be justified to stakeholders: confidence collapses, and innocent learners may suffer academic penalties.

A few months later, *Vanderbilt University* disabled Turnitin's detector campus-wide, citing the model's blackbox nature and an inability to audit its accuracy, especially for multilingual writers[44]. Administrators concluded that any AI service used in assessment must provide verifiable evidence of reliability and a transparent pathway for contesting errors.

Why are explainability and auditability non-negotiable? Explainability enables educators to translate an algorithm's output into pedagogical action. If a recommender lowers a student's reading level, teachers must know why—was it vocabulary errors, pacing, or something else? Auditability lets districts and inspectors verify that AI behaves consistently with policy and antidiscrimination law.

Some practical steps for schools and vendors include:

1. **Demand transparent documentation**: Before adoption, require vendors to supply model cards or equivalent reports detailing training data, performance limits, and known biases.

---

42 Turnitin. (n.d.). Plagiarism Detector: Prevent Academic Misconduct | Turnitin. https://www.turnitin.com/

43 Fowler, G. A. (2023, April 14). We tested a new ChatGPT-detector for teachers. It flagged an innocent student. The Washington Post. https://www.washingtonpost.com/technology/2023/04/01/chatgpt-cheating-detection-turnitin/

44 Coley, M. (2023, August 16). Guidance on AI detection and why we're disabling Turnitin's AI detector. Vanderbilt University. https://www.vanderbilt.edu/brightspace/2023/08/16/guidance-on-ai-detection-and-why-were-disabling-turnitins-ai-detector/

2. **Pilot and compare**: Run smallscale trials and compare AI outputs with human judgments to surface discrepancies before full rollout.

3. **Set up an internal review board**: Include teachers, data specialists, and community representatives empowered to audit highstakes AI decisions (grading, placement, discipline).

4. **Embed contestability**: Publish clear procedures so students and parents can request a manual review and see the evidence behind any algorithmic flag.

Accountability is, therefore more than a legal checkbox; it is the shell that keeps AI aligned with educational values. By pairing explainability with systematic audits, schools move algorithmic accountability from principle to practice, ensuring that AI tools support, rather than undermine, fair and transparent learning environments.

To operationalize this commitment, schools must distinguish between internal audits, which offer ongoing self-assessment, and third-party reviews, which provide independent validation and public trust—each playing a distinct but complementary role in responsible AI oversight. Internal audits are conducted by an organization's own staff to regularly evaluate and improve internal processes, risk management, and compliance with policies, offering actionable insights for management and continuous improvement[45]. In contrast, third-party (external) reviews are performed by independent auditors or organizations, providing an objective assessment that assures external stakeholders—such as regulators, partners, or the public—of the institution's compliance, credibility, and security[46]. In the context of AI in education, a best practice is to conduct internal audits at least semi-annually to promptly identify and address emerging risks, while third-party reviews should be scheduled every 1–2 years or after major system updates to ensure independent validation and maintain stakeholder trust[47]. This dual approach helps balance ongoing oversight with the credibility and objectivity needed for responsible AI governance in schools.

Role of educators, students, and parents or guardians

As AI becomes more embedded in educational tools and practices, its ethical use becomes a shared responsibility. Educators play a central role in ensuring that AI technologies are used in ways that align with educational values and support students' wellbeing. Educators must be able to critically assess AI tools, understand their limitations, and ensure they do not reinforce harmful biases.

---

45 MindBridge. (2025, May 2). Internal vs. External Audit: Key Differences, Use Cases, and Strategic Alignment. MindBridge. https://www.mindbridge.ai/blog/internal-vs-external-audit-key-differences-use-cases-and-strategic-alignment/

46 What is auditing? (n.d.). ASQ. Retrieved July 12, 2025, from https://asq.org/quality-resources/auditing

47 HighRadius. (2024, August 2). External Audit vs Internal Audit: Key Differences. HighRadius Resource Center. https://www.highradius.com/resources/Blog/external-vs-internal-audit/

Students, on the other hand, need to be educated about the ethical implications of AI. Empowering students with the knowledge of how AI works, the potential risks it poses, and how to use AI tools responsibly is a key part of fostering an ethical AI culture. AI-driven assessment tools and plagiarism detection systems are important in maintaining academic integrity. However, ethical AI ensures that these tools do not wrongly accuse students because of algorithmic errors.

Similarly, parents or guardians should be active participants in this conversation, ensuring that AI technologies used by their children are ethical, secure, and beneficial to their learning.

Teacher and student autonomy

AI's role in education raises questions about the balance between technology and human decision-making. The integration of AI tools must ensure that teachers retain their professional autonomy and that students' agency is not diminished by the overuse of technology.

AI has the potential to significantly support teachers by automating administrative tasks, offering personalized learning experiences for students, and providing real-time feedback. However, AI should not replace human teachers or undermine their authority in the classroom. Teachers must be empowered to make ethical, pedagogical decisions, even in AI-driven environments.

AI systems must respect students' learning choices and autonomy. AI should enhance the learning experience rather than dictate it, providing students with options for self-directed learning and fostering critical thinking. Over-reliance on AI could undermine students' ability to make independent decisions or develop problem-solving skills. Explore these practical considerations:

- AI tools should be designed to support and augment teachers' abilities, not replace them.

- Ethical AI should empower students by providing options for self-paced learning and promoting their decision-making skills.

- Schools and educators should maintain control over AI systems and ensure they align with the school's educational goals.

Addressing the ethical challenges of AI in education requires a concerted effort from students, teachers, developers, and policymakers to ensure that AI is used in ways that promote fairness, privacy, and accessibility. By mitigating bias, safeguarding privacy, and ensuring equity in access, we can create a future in which AI not only enhances education but also serves the best interests of all students.

Global AI policies in education

AI has the potential to address some of the biggest challenges in education today, innovate teaching and learning practices, and accelerate progress towards UNESCO's Sustainable

Development Goals[48] (more concretely, SDG 4[49], Quality Education). However, rapid technological developments inevitably bring multiple risks and challenges, which have so far outpaced policy debates and regulatory frameworks. Governments and international bodies are now racing to establish policies that harness AI's benefits for learning while managing risks to students and educators. This section provides a global perspective on AI regulations in education, covering existing policies across regions, legal and ethical considerations, emerging governance trends, upcoming regulations, and real-world case studies of policy implementation.

Existing policies by region

In this subsection, we will explore, in depth, policies from different regions around the world. You will be able to compare and contrast how different locations are managing to integrate AI in education and view emerging trends.

European Union and the EU member states

The European Union is a frontrunner in AI regulation. The EU AI Act[50] is a comprehensive regulation on AI, a risk-based law that assigns applications of AI to four risk categories, which include[51]:

- **Unacceptable-risk AI systems**[52]: Systems considered a threat to individuals, such as those manipulating vulnerable groups, engaging in social scoring, or using biometric identification and categorization. The regulation on this risk category is that these systems are banned, including real-time and remote biometric identification like facial recognition, except under strict law enforcement conditions, which must first gain court approval.

- **High-risk AI systems**[53]: Systems impacting safety or fundamental rights, including AI in toys, medical devices, critical infrastructure, education, employment, essential services, law enforcement, migration, and legal interpretation. The regulation on this risk category is that these systems must be registered in an EU database, thoroughly risk-assessed, and regularly reported on to ensure strict compliance and oversight. Assessment will have to be conducted prior to high-risk AI systems being put on the

48 Artificial intelligence in education. (n.d.). unesco.org. Retrieved March 5, 2025, from https://www.unesco.org/en/digital-education/artificial-intelligence
49 United Nations. (2020, June 29). Sustainable Development Goals (SDG 4) | United Nations Western Europe. United Nations Western Europe. https://unric.org/en/sdg-4/
50 EU Artificial Intelligence Act | Up-to-date developments and analyses of the EU AI Act. (n.d.). https://artificialintelligenceact.eu/
51 AI Act. (2025, March 4). Shaping Europe's Digital Future. Https://digital-strategy.ec.europa.eu/en/policies/regulatory-framework-ai
52 Chapter II: Prohibited AI Practices | EU Artificial Intelligence Act. (n.d.). https://artificialintelligenceact.eu/chapter/2/
53 Chapter III: High-Risk AI System | EU Artificial Intelligence Act. (n.d.). https://artificialintelligenceact.eu/chapter/3/

market and then throughout their lifecycle. People will also have the right to lodge complaints against AI systems to their designated national authorities.

- **Limited-risk AI systems**[54]: The limited-risk category includes generative-AI models like ChatGPT[55]. These are not high-risk per se, but must meet transparency obligations and comply with EU copyright law. The regulation on this category states that providers of limited-risk AI models and applications must disclose to users that their content is AI-generated, must prevent illegal content generation, and must also publish summaries of copyrighted data used for training. High-impact AI models must undergo thorough evaluations and report serious incidents to the European Commission. AI-generated or modified content (e.g., deepfakes) must be clearly labeled as such.

- **Minimal-risk AI systems**[56]: These applications are already widely deployed and make up most of the AI systems we interact with today. Examples include spam filters, AI-enabled video games, and inventory-management systems. The regulation on this category is that most AI systems in this category face no obligation under the EU AI Act, but companies can voluntarily adopt additional codes of conduct. Primary responsibility will be shouldered by the providers (developers) of AI systems, though any business that utilizes them should remain vigilant of their compliance obligations.

The EU AI Act explicitly addresses education as an area of focus: using AI to infer emotions in educational settings is banned as an unacceptable risk, and most other AI systems in education are deemed high-risk, subject to strict compliance (e.g., transparency, human oversight).[57] This means AI tools that monitor students' facial expressions or biometrics to gauge emotions cannot be used in schools within the European Union, while adaptive learning or grading systems must meet high standards for safety and fairness. Also, as providers of AI systems, EdTech vendors will need to provide detailed technical and functional documentation on their AI models to EU-based schools by August 2025, which they will likely do via an update to their terms and conditions.[58]

Although the EU AI Act is a regulation implemented by the European Union, its impact extends far beyond the EU's 27 Member States. It also governs companies operating internationally, including those in the United States, that market AI products within the EU or develop AI systems whose outputs are utilized there.

---

54 Chapter IV: Transparency obligations for providers and deployers of certain AI systems | EU Artificial Intelligence Act. (n.d.). https://artificialintelligenceact.eu/chapter/4/

55 ChatGPT. (n.d.). chatgpt.com. Retrieved March 5, 2025, from https://chatgpt.com/

56 Chapter V: General-Purpose AI Models | EU Artificial Intelligence Act. (n.d.). https://artificialintelligenceact.eu/chapter/5/

57 AI in education: What approach are regulators taking to AI? (n.d.). https://www.9ine.com/newsblog/ai-in-education-what-approach-are-regulators-taking-to-ai#:~:text=aware%20of%20their%20obligations%20as,higher%20levels%20of%20compliance%20requirements

58 AI in education: What approach are regulators taking to AI? (n.d.-b). https://www.9ine.com/newsblog/ai-in-education-what-approach-are-regulators-taking-to-ai#:~:text=In%20contrast%20to%20the%20EU%2C,governance%3B%20and%20contestability%20and%20redress

United Kingdom

The **United Kingdom** (**UK**) has opted for a cross-sector, principle-based framework focusing on safety, transparency and explainability, fairness, accountability, and contestability.[59] Regulators in different sectors (education, health, etc.) are encouraged to apply these principles. For example, Ofsted (the UK education inspectorate) announced it will evaluate schools' use of AI through existing inspection frameworks, ensuring schools have assessed and mitigated AI-related risks.[60] Furthermore, school inspections will now include evidence of risk assessments for any AI tool in use, explicitly checking that leaders can justify algorithmic decisions in plain language and log corrective actions when errors occur. This marks a shift from abstract principles to concrete inspection criteria. The UK is considering more prescriptive rules, but at the time of writing this chapter (March 2025), it leans on existing laws (like data protection laws) plus guiding principles to govern AI in schools

North America

The United States has no federal law dedicated solely to AI in education yet. Instead, it relies on a patchwork of existing protections and emerging guidelines. Federal privacy laws such as FERPA[61] and COPPA[62] already apply to AI tools handling student information. The U.S. Department of Education has emphasized that it can use existing authorities to address AI risks in schools. Several AI-related bills have been proposed in Congress, but none have passed as of 2025. However, some U.S. states are taking initiative. For instance, Colorado enacted the first comprehensive state AI law[63] (effective 2026), which will set up frameworks for transparency and accountability in automated systems, including those used in education. In practice, U.S. schools are guided by non-binding federal recommendations (discussed throughout this chapter) and must comply with general laws (e.g., anti-discrimination, data security) when deploying AI.

Canada, similarly, does not have an education-specific AI law. Canada's first attempt at comprehensive AI regulation, Bill C-27[64], which introduced the **Artificial Intelligence and Data Act** (**AIDA**)[65], was halted in January 2025. Provinces like Ontario are advancing their

59 A pro-innovation approach to AI regulation. (2023, August 3). GOV.UK. https://www.gov.uk/government/publications/ai-regulation-a-pro-innovation-approach/white-paper
60 Ofsted's approach to artificial intelligence (AI). (2024, April 24). GOV.UK. https://www.gov.uk/government/publications/ofsteds-approach-to-ai/ofsteds-approach-to-artificial-intelligence-ai
61 FERPA | Protecting Student Privacy. (n.d.). https://studentprivacy.ed.gov/ferpa
62 Children's Online Privacy Protection Rule ("COPPA"). (2023, February 3). Federal Trade Commission. https://www.ftc.gov/legal-library/browse/rules/childrens-online-privacy-protection-rule-coppa
63 Consumer Protections for Artificial Intelligence | Colorado General Assembly. (n.d.). Colorado General Assembly. https://leg.colorado.gov/bills/sb24-205
64 C-27 (44-1) - LEGISinfo - Parliament of Canada. (n.d.). LEGISinfo. https://www.parl.ca/legisinfo/en/bill/44-1/c-27
65 The Artificial Intelligence and Data Act (AIDA) – Companion document. (2025, January 31). https://ised-isde.canada.ca/site/innovation-better-canada/en/artificial-intelligence-and-data-act-aida-companion-document

own AI regulations[66], making it the first province or territory in Canada to establish guardrails for the responsible use of AI in the public sector.

China

AI governance in the Asia-Pacific region is varied. China is a clear frontrunner, with an active regulatory regime for AI. It was among the first to require registration of AI algorithms and to issue specific measures governing AI applications (for example, rules on recommendation algorithms and generative AI services and provisions on deep synthesis)[67]. China's national AI strategy also pushes AI education initiatives[68] (coding and AI literacy in schools) while tightly controlling data and content for student-facing AI applications.

Singapore and Hong Kong

Singapore and Hong Kong have taken an approach of regulating AI through existing laws (like data protection acts) supplemented by sector-specific frameworks that provide guidance without binding force. Singapore's Ministry of Education even developed an AI in Education Ethics Framework[69] for schools, outlining principles of agency, inclusiveness, fairness, and safety to guide the use of AI in teaching and learning. This framework builds on Singapore's model AI governance principles, ensuring that AI tools in classrooms augment (not replace) teachers and uphold student choice, fairness, and data protection.

South Korea

South Korea's AI Basic Act (passed in 2024 and effective in Jan 2026) is one of Asia's first comprehensive AI laws, aligning with the EU AI Act and adopting a similar risk-based approach[70]. It aims to foster AI development responsibly, including provisions on fair and transparent AI, which would cover education technology as well.

---

66 Ontario's Trustworthy Artificial Intelligence (AI) framework. (n.d.). ontario.ca. https://www.ontario.ca/page/ontarios-trustworthy-artificial-intelligence-ai-framework
67 Navigating the complexities of AI regulation in China | Perspectives | Reed Smith LLP. (2024, August 7). https://www.reedsmith.com/en/perspectives/2024/08/navigating-the-complexities-of-ai-regulation-in-china
68 陈笛. (n.d.). China launches AI campaign to empower education. https://english.www.gov.cn/news/202403/29/content_WS6606302bc6d0868f4e8e5941.html
69 AI in Education Ethics Framework. (n.d.). https://www.learning.moe.edu.sg/ai-in-sls/responsible-ai/ai-in-education-ethics-framework/#:~:text=The%20MOE%20AIEd%20Ethics%20Framework,Agency%2C%20Inclusivity%2C%20Fairness%20and%20Safety
70 Wang, A. R. E. L. J. (2024, December 31). Korea's Won? South Korea's AI Basic Act: Asia's first comprehensive AI legislation. Passle. https://techinsights.linklaters.com/post/102js56/koreas-wonsouth-koreas-ai-basic-act-asias-first-comprehensive-ai-legislatio#:~:text=Korea%27s%20Won%3F%20South%20Korea%27s%20AI,AI%20Basic%20Act

Japan

Japan does not yet have an AI-specific law, but its government issued guidelines for AI in schools (e.g., encouraging educators to use generative AI as a teaching aid under supervision) and is updating its national curriculum to include AI literacy[71].

Australia

Australia published, in September 2024, the Voluntary AI Safety Standard[72], to help organizations develop and deploy AI systems through 10 voluntary AI guardrails[73] after recognizing gaps in the initial approach launched in 2019. In the legal landscape[74] for AI in Australia, this standard and the 10 guardrails are voluntary, with the standard not seeking to create new legal obligations for organizations. Australia's education authorities are in consultation on how to apply upcoming AI regulations to educational contexts, ensuring tools meet standards for safety and non-bias.

Middle East

There is no single unified AI regulation across the Middle East, but several countries have national strategies. The **United Arab Emirates** (UAE) is a regional leader; it established the world's first Ministry of State for Artificial Intelligence (2017) and a national AI strategy[75] (for 2031) that promotes education[76] and workforce development while imposing ethical standards[77]. The UAE's strategy includes introducing AI into school curricula and training, alongside guidelines to ensure algorithms are fair and transparent. With schools in the UAE already implementing metacognitive techniques to revolutionize educational experiences of

71 New School Guidelines in Japan Emphasize AI Education. https://theaitrack.com/school-guidelines-in-japan-ai-education/

72 Department of Industry Science and Resources. (2024). Voluntary AI Safety Standard. https://www.industry.gov.au/publications/voluntary-ai-safety-standard

73 Department of Industry Science and Resources. (2025). The 10 guardrails. Voluntary AI Safety Standard | Department of Industry Science and Resources. https://www.industry.gov.au/publications/voluntary-ai-safety-standard/10-guardrails

74 Department of Industry Science and Resources. (2024a). The legal landscape for AI in Australia. Voluntary AI Safety Standard | Department of Industry Science and Resources. https://www.industry.gov.au/publications/voluntary-ai-safety-standard/legal-landscape-ai-australia

75 UAE National Strategy for Artificial Intelligence 2031. (n.d.). United Arab Emirates Minister of State for Artificial Intelligence, Digital Economy & Remote Work Applications Office. Retrieved March 5, 2025, from https://ai.gov.ae/strategy/

76 UAE National Strategy for Artificial Intelligence 2031. (n.d.). United Arab Emirates Minister of State for Artificial Intelligence, Digital Economy & Remote Work Applications Office. Retrieved March 5, 2025, from https://ai.gov.ae/strategy/

77 UAE AI and Blockchain Council. (2022). AI Ethics: Principles and guidelines (pp. 1–44). https://ai.gov.ae/wp-content/uploads/2023/03/MOCAI-AI-Ethics-EN-1.pdf

both teachers and students, institutions are leading the way in integrating AI into the school digital ecosystem.[78]

Saudi Arabia has issued draft AI Ethics Principles[79] and Generative AI Guidelines (via its Saudi Data and AI Authority, SDAIA[80]) to steer AI development in all sectors, including education. These emphasize data privacy, non-discrimination, and ethics rooted in Islamic traditions[81]. At the time this chapter is being written, March 2025, many countries in the region are in early stages of publishing their national AI strategies that will likely include education technology governance.

Africa

Across Africa, governments are recognizing the need for an AI policy framework. The **African Union** (**AU**) has taken steps to develop a common African stance on AI and establish an AI think tank as part of the continental Africa-centric AI strategy[82]. This continental blueprint[83] encourages member states to adopt AI in ways that advance social good (like expanding educational access) while safeguarding human rights. Some countries (e.g., South Africa, Mauritius) are still consulting stakeholders on AI governance, and others have yet to announce plans. Overall, existing AI-in-education policies in Africa often focus on capacity-building (training teachers in AI, investing in infrastructure) rather than strict regulation, but there is growing interest in developing ethical guidelines (often informed by UNESCO and other global principles).

Latin America and the Caribbean

Latin American countries are actively developing AI strategies with components on education. For example, Brazil's national AI strategy[84] (2021) identifies education as a priority area for

---

78 Sircar, N. (2025, February 10). UAE: How schools are using AI, metacognition to develop self-monitoring skills in students. Khaleej Times. https://www.khaleejtimes.com/uae/education/uae-how-schools-are-using-ai-metacognition-to-develop-self-monitoring-skills-in-student

79 Kingdom of Saudi Arabia develop AI ethics principles. (n.d.). SaudiPressAgency. https://www.spa.gov.sa/2383900

80 Saudi Data & AI Authority. (2024). AI Adoption Framework. https://sdaia.gov.sa/en/SDAIA/about/Files/AIAdoptionFramework.pdf

81 Navigating the intersection of AI and Islamic ethics: opportunities, challenges, and collaborative pathways. (n.d.). International Qur'an Research Association. https://iqra.study/navigating-the-intersection-of-ai-and-islamic-ethics-opportunities-challenges-and-collaborative-pathways/#:~:text=This%20article%20explores%20the%20multifaceted%20relationship%20between%20AI,the%20harmonization%20of%20technological%20progress%20with%20Islamic%20p

82 Continental Artificial Intelligence Strategy | African Union. (n.d.). https://au.int/en/documents/20240809/continental-artificial-intelligence-strategy

83 Continental Artificial Intelligence Strategy. (2024). In United Nations Educational, Scientific and Cultural Organization, Continental Artificial Intelligence Strategy. https://au.int/sites/default/files/documents/44004-doc-EN-_Continental_AI_Strategy_July_2024.pdf

84 I Inteligência artificial. (n.d.). Ministério Da Ciência, Tecnologia E Inovação. https://www.gov.br/mcti/pt-br/acompanhe-o-mcti/transformacaodigital/inteligencia-artificial

AI investment[85] and calls for ethical use of AI, respecting privacy and non-discrimination. Chile, Argentina, Colombia, Mexico, and others have drafted or approved national AI policies that, while not education-specific, set broad principles (human rights, transparency, inclusion) that apply to educational uses of AI. In October 2023, officials from across Latin America and the Caribbean adopted the Santiago Declaration[86], signaling a commitment to jointly shape AI policies suited to the region's needs. The declaration proposes establishing a regional AI council and aligns with UNESCO's Recommendation on the Ethics of AI. This means Latin American countries intend to influence global AI governance while tailoring regulations to local educational, social, and cultural contexts. As of early 2024, several countries (like Mexico[87] and Costa Rica[88]) have AI bills in discussion that include education-sector guidelines, though few binding laws specific to AI in schools have been passed by this time (March 2025).

Looking ahead, we may see more formal international agreements affecting AI in education. The G7 nations launched the Hiroshima AI Process[89], in mid-2023, to harmonize approaches to AI governance among advanced economies; education is not the sole focus, but any G7 consensus on AI ethics or safety will trickle down into national education policies. The **Global Partnership on AI (GPAI)**[90], an international initiative, has a working group on AI and the future of work and education that might propose global guidelines or even a certification scheme for trustworthy educational AI products.

All these ongoing efforts and many more not listed here mean that over the next few years, the regulatory environment for AI in education will become more robust and interconnected, guided by both national laws and international norms.

85 Inteligência Artificial Estratégia - Eixo 4. (n.d.). Ministério Da Ciência, Tecnologia E Inovação. https://www.gov.br/mcti/pt-br/acompanhe-o-mcti/transformacaodigital/inteligencia-artificial-estrategia-eixo4
86 Cumbre Ministerial y de Altas Autoridades de América Latina y el Caribe. (2023). DECLARACIÓN DE SANTIAGO.
87 Pascu, M. (2024, August 18). A closer look: Mexico's proposed artificial intelligence bill. INQ Consulting. https://www.inq.consulting/post/a-closer-look-mexico-s-proposed-artificial-intelligence-bill
88 Times, T. (2023, June 2). Harnessing AI: Costa Rican legislators lead the way in regulation : The Tico Times | Costa Rica News | Travel | Real Estate. https://ticotimes.net/2023/06/02/harnessing-ai-costa-rican-legislators-lead-the-way-in-regulation#:~:text=The%20primary%20objective%20of%20the%20bill%20is%20to,ability%20through%20the%20rapid%20processing%20of%20internet-extracted%20data.
89 The Hiroshima AI Process: Leading the global challenge to shape inclusive governance for Generative AI | The Government of Japan - JapanGov -. (n.d.). The Government of Japan - JapanGov -. https://www.japan.go.jp/kizuna/2024/02/hiroshima_ai_process.html
90 The Global Partnership on Artificial Intelligence. (n.d.). gpai.ai. Retrieved March 5, 2025, from https://gpai.ai/

In the following table, you will see comparative regulatory information highlighting global differences:

Region	Data rights	Algorithmic transparency	Ethical guidelines	Regulatory enforcement	Policy maturity
Europe	Strong legal protections (e.g., GDPR ensures strict student data privacy and user consent)	Emerging mandates for transparency (the EU's AI Act will require disclosure and oversight of high-risk educational AI)	Comprehensive ethics frameworks (EU published educator guidelines on AI ethics in education)	Active enforcement (data protection authorities enforce GDPR; AI Act introduces hefty fines for non-compliance)	Advanced and cohesive (most countries have national AI strategies and EU-wide policies guiding AI in education)
North America (US/Canada)	Moderate protections (sector-specific privacy laws like FERPA/CCPA; no blanket data law at the federal level)	Limited transparency requirements (reliance on voluntary industry standards and agency guidelines)	Guidance-driven approach (non-binding frameworks such as the US AI Bill of Rights blueprint, which emphasize ethics, but no unified code)	Piecemeal oversight (regulation via existing laws; federal agencies adapt old authorities to AI, but no dedicated AI law)	Evolving (high innovation capacity but fragmented policy; Canada aligns with EU principles, while the US develops frameworks instead of formal regulation)
Asia-Pacific	Variable protections (some nations have robust laws like China's PIPL or Japan's Act on Personal Data, others lag)	Developing transparency norms (China imposes algorithmic disclosure and content labeling under state oversight, whereas others are nascent)	Present but uneven (many countries endorse AI ethics principles; China's policy stresses a balance of security and development over individual rights)	Mixed enforcement (China enforces strict AI controls, e.g., approval required for new AI services, while enforcement in other countries is weaker or just emerging).	Progressing (about 25% of Asia-Pacific countries have national AI strategies, led by China, Japan, Singapore); strong innovation agendas with gradually expanding governance.

Region	Data rights	Algorithmic transparency	Ethical guidelines	Regulatory enforcement	Policy maturity
Latin America	Growing protections (Brazil's LGPD mirrors GDPR, mandating stringent consent and data handling in AI systems)	Emerging focus on transparency (existing laws like Mexico's data protection require companies to safeguard data and encourage algorithmic accountability)	Guided by global norms (regional initiatives and draft laws emphasize ethical AI and human rights, e.g., Argentina's proposed AI laws on accountability and fairness)	Limited AI-specific oversight (few dedicated AI regulations yet; enforcement mainly through data protection authorities and general ICT laws)	Moderate but uneven (only ~19% of countries have a national AI strategy); collaboration networks like the AI Latin America Network foster shared development).
Africa	Nascent frameworks (several countries have recently adopted data privacy laws influenced by global standards; continental efforts to harmonize data rights)	In infancy (the new African Union AI Strategy calls for transparent and inclusive AI governance, but concrete transparency rules are mostly still in draft stages)	Principle-based approach (the AU strategy advocates AI governance rooted in ethical principles, human rights, and the rule of law)	Minimal so far (AI-specific regulators largely absent; a few data protection authorities have acted on AI issues, but broad enforcement is yet to develop)	Early-stage (only ~4% of Sub-Saharan African countries had national AI plans by 2024, though this number is slowly growing)

Table 10.2: *Comparative table on AI in education policy by region (as of March 2025)*[91,92]

Cross-regional reflections and lessons

Despite being at different stages of development, all regions face common challenges in leveraging AI for education responsibly, from ensuring data privacy and addressing bias to training educators and providing equitable access. Europe's experience demonstrates the

---

91 Shaping the future: Higher education's impact on national AI policies. (2025, March 20). Unesco. https://www.iesalc.unesco.org/en/articles/shaping-future-higher-educations-impact-national-ai-policies#:~:text=,but%20still%20in%20early%20stages

92 Daly, K. (2025, April 9). The Geopolitics of AI Regulation - The Yale Review of International Studies. The Yale Review of International Studies. https://yris.yira.org/global-issue/the-geopolitics-of-ai-regulation/

value of strong legal frameworks: its rigorous data protection laws and EU AI Act have set transparency and accountability benchmarks that can inspire other regions[93]. These frameworks help build public trust in educational AI tools by safeguarding rights and requiring oversight. Policymakers elsewhere (for example, in Latin America or Africa) might adapt elements of Europe's approach, such as clear transparency standards or enforcement mechanisms, to bolster their own governance, even if tailored to local contexts.

The other way around, innovation-oriented strategies offer transferable lessons in flexibility and inclusion. Latin America's focus on using AI to expand educational opportunity, for instance, deploying AI-powered platforms to reach remote learners and underserved communities, provides a model for under-resourced regions[94]. This approach emphasizes practical solutions like personalized learning and remote teaching support to bridge gaps where infrastructure or staffing is limited. Such successes illustrate that even without extensive resources, policy can encourage innovative uses of AI to promote equity. Common hurdles remain (infrastructure, teacher training, ethical use), but by sharing experiences, Europe's rule-setting and Latin America's inclusive innovation, policymakers across regions can learn from each other. These cross-regional insights help in crafting balanced AI in education policies that protect learners while also fostering innovation, ultimately guiding all regions toward more ethical and effective AI integration in education.

Legal and ethical considerations in AI for education

Student data protection is a cornerstone of AI policy in education. As discussed earlier in this chapter, many AI-driven educational tools rely on collecting personal data (from learning analytics to biometric data in proctoring), raising serious privacy concerns. Governments are addressing this through general data privacy laws and specific rules for schools. For instance, Europe's GDPR[95] and related laws mandate strict data consent, security, and oversight for any system processing student personal data. This has tangible effects: educational AI vendors operating in the EU must build in privacy by design or face hefty penalties. In the United States, existing laws like FERPA[96] restrict the sharing of student records with AI providers without parental consent, and COPPA[97] requires parental consent for online services (including AI tutors or apps) used by children under 13. Some regions have gone further: Italy's data

---

93 Daly, K. (2025, April 9). The Geopolitics of AI Regulation - The Yale Review of International Studies. The Yale Review of International Studies. https://yris.yira.org/global-issue/the-geopolitics-of-ai-regulation/
94 Lynch, M. (2024, September 25). The AI education leapfrog in the global South - pedagogue. Pedagogue. https://pedagogue.app/the-ai-education-leapfrog-in-the-global-south/#:~:text=platforms%20powered%20 by%20AI%20can,down%20geographical%20and%20socioeconomic%20barriers
95 Regulation - 2016/679 - EN - gdpr - EUR-Lex. (n.d.). https://eur-lex.europa.eu/eli/reg/2016/679/oj
96 What is FERPA? | Protecting Student Privacy. (n.d.-b). https://studentprivacy.ed.gov/faq/what-ferpa
97 Children's Online Privacy Protection Rule ("COPPA"). (2023b, February 3). Federal Trade Commission. https://www.ftc.gov/legal-library/browse/rules/childrens-online-privacy-protection-rule-coppa

protection authority temporarily banned ChatGPT in 2023 due to privacy concerns (in part because it had no age verification to protect minors' data), forcing the AI provider to implement new safety measures[98]. Likewise, some countries in the EU now station trained IT and **data protection officers (DPO)** in schools to ensure compliance when new AI tools are introduced[99]. Ensuring student privacy also means limiting intrusive data practices: for example, the EU AI Act will require that any high-risk AI system used in education keep detailed logs and documentation to facilitate audits[100]. To summarize, legal frameworks worldwide insist that educational AI tools comply with data protection principles, obtain informed consent, minimize data collected, securely store data, and allow parents or students to access or delete their information.

Fairness is a critical ethical concern, as AI systems can inadvertently amplify biases (e.g., against certain genders, ethnicities, or disabilities) if not carefully managed. Policymakers are responding by embedding fairness requirements into AI guidelines. The UK's AI principles explicitly list fairness as key[101], meaning schools and edtech providers should ensure AI models do not treat students inequitably (for example, an algorithm that recommends advanced coursework should not systematically favor one demographic over another). The United States Department of Education echoed this in 2023, urging that AI used in schools should advance equity and not widen achievement gaps[102]. One cautionary tale comes from the UK's 2020 exam grading algorithm[103]: when exams were canceled due to COVID-19, an algorithm was used to predict students' grades. It ended up systematically downgrading students from historically underperforming schools, with ~40% of grades lower than teacher predictions, disproportionately affecting disadvantaged students. The public outcry and legal challenges led to the algorithm's abandonment, underscoring the need for fairness and transparency in any AI decision-making in education. In response, many countries now emphasize algorithmic accountability[104]: AI tools that impact student outcomes should be regularly tested for bias

98 Satariano, A. (2023, March 31). ChatGPT is banned in Italy over privacy concerns. The New York Times. https://www.nytimes.com/2023/03/31/technology/chatgpt-italy-ban.html

99 EU Artificial Intelligence Act: Key considerations for data protection officers. (2024, July 1). Andersen. https://de.andersen.com/en/insights/article/eu-artificial-intelligence-act-key-considerations-for-data-protection-officers

100 Article 12: Record-Keeping | EU Artificial Intelligence Act. (n.d.). https://artificialintelligenceact.eu/article/12/

101 Fairness in AI: A View from the DRCF. (2024, April 15). www.drcf.org.uk. https://www.drcf.org.uk/publications/blogs/fairness-in-ai-a-view-from-the-drcf

102 U.S. Department of Education publishes recommendations for AI use. (2023, July 18). California School Boards Association. https://publications.csba.org/california-school-news/july-2023/u-s-department-of-education-publishes-recommendations-for-ai-use/#:~:text=Foundational%20elements%20for%20building%20ethical,promoting%20transparency%20%E2%80%94%20are%20critical

103 CousensEV, & CousensEV. (2022, November 10). "F**k the algorithm"?: What the world can learn from the UK's A-level grading fiasco - Impact of Social Sciences. Impact of Social Sciences - Maximizing the impact of academic research. https://blogs.lse.ac.uk/impactofsocialsciences/2020/08/26/fk-the-algorithm-what-the-world-can-learn-from-the-uks-a-level-grading-fiasco/#:~:text=For%20those%20who%20haven%E2%80%99t%20followed,exams%20gone%20forward%20as%20planned

104 Cheong, B. C. (2024). Transparency and accountability in AI systems: safeguarding wellbeing in the age of algorithmic decision-making. Frontiers in Human Dynamics, 6. https://doi.org/10.3389/fhumd.2024.1421273

and subject to human review. The EU AI Act requires providers of high-risk AI systems to disclose key characteristics of their models, including the training data, model architecture, and performance metrics. In the United States, the proposed Algorithmic Accountability Act of 2023 was reintroduced as a bill that would require impact assessments for high-risk automated decision systems used in sensitive domains such as schools or colleges. Non-discrimination laws (e.g., Title VI and Title IX in the U.S.[105], equality acts in the EU[106]) also provide a legal backstop; if an AI system in education results in biased outcomes against protected groups, schools could be held liable under existing anti-discrimination statutes.

Ensuring AI in education is accessible to all students, including those with disabilities and those in underserved communities, is a growing policy focus. On one hand, AI offers huge potential benefits for accessibility: for example, speech recognition and text-to-speech AI can assist students with visual or hearing impairments, and adaptive learning software can support multilingual learners or those with learning disabilities[107]. Governments are encouraging these uses; many national edtech plans include AI tools for special education support. On the other hand, policymakers stress that AI should not exacerbate the digital divide; if only wealthy schools have access to advanced AI tutors, inequality could worsen. Several countries (like India) frame AI-in-education policies around *AI for All*[108], aiming to provide equitable access to AI resources in public schools and training teachers in rural or low-income areas to use them. Legally, accessibility requirements (such as the **Americans with Disabilities Act (ADA)**[109] in the U.S. or the EU's accessibility act[110]) apply to digital educational tools. If an AI-powered educational app is not usable by a student with a disability (and no accommodation is provided), the school could be violating disability rights laws. Thus, governments are pushing developers to ensure educational AI tools meet accessibility standards and that no student is left behind as AI transforms pedagogy.

105 Section IV- Interplay of Title VI with Title IX, Section 504, th Fourteenth Amendment, and Title VII. (2021, February 3). https://www.justice.gov/crt/fcs/T6manual4

106 Know your rights in the EU: Equality. (n.d.). European Commission. https://commission.europa.eu/aid-development-cooperation-fundamental-rights/your-fundamental-rights-eu/know-your-rights/equality_en

107 U.S. Department of Education publishes recommendations for AI use. (2023b, July 18). California School Boards Association. https://publications.csba.org/california-school-news/july-2023/u-s-department-of-education-publishes-recommendations-for-ai-use/#:~:text=Educators%20are%20exploring%20opportunities%20to,adapt%20lesson%20plans%20and%20more

108 All, A. F. (n.d.). AI For All | Self learning online program. https://ai-for-all.in/#/home

109 Americans with Disabilities Act of 1990, As Amended. (n.d.). ADA.gov. https://www.ada.gov/law-and-regs/ada/

110 European accessibility act. (2025, January 29). European Commission. https://commission.europa.eu/strategy-and-policy/policies/justice-and-fundamental-rights/disability/union-equality-strategy-rights-persons-disabilities-2021-2030/european-accessibility-act_en

Transparency is a common demand in AI ethics policies; students, parents, and teachers should know when AI is being used and how it reaches decisions. Many governments urge or require transparency in educational AI systems. For instance, the UK calls for appropriate transparency and explainability as a core principle[111], implying that schools using AI should be able to explain an algorithm's role in, say, grading or recommendation. The EU AI Act mandates that users are informed when they are interacting with an AI (rather than a human) in certain contexts, and it requires detailed technical documentation for high-risk AI, effectively forcing transparency for regulators and users[112]. In practice, this could mean a student writing an essay with an AI co-authoring tool should be informed of the AI's nature and limitations, or a university deploying an AI admissions screener must disclose that and explain the criteria.

Accountability mechanisms are also critical. Policies often assign responsibility to either the AI provider or the educational institution (or both) for outcomes. For example, New Zealand's Generative AI guidance[113] suggests that human teachers must take responsibility for students' learning when using AI. Some countries are creating oversight bodies: France has an education data guardian and is considering an AI ethics committee for education, while China requires human oversight for AI tutoring systems and holds companies accountable for content and outcomes.

Additionally, contestability and redress[114] are emerging principles, students or parents should have the right to a human review of an AI-made decision (like a grading or disciplinary action). This is reflected in several AI frameworks (e.g., the Blueprint for an AI Bill of Rights[115] in the United States, lists notice and explanation[116] and human alternatives, consideration, and fallback[117] as rights). Ensuring transparency and accountability is legally tricky, but regulators are leaning on tools like algorithmic audits, impact assessments, and compliance reporting to keep AI use in education trustworthy.

---

111 Implementing the UK's AI regulatory principles: initial guidance for regulators. (2024, February 6). GOV. UK. https://www.gov.uk/government/publications/implementing-the-uks-ai-regulatory-principles-initial-guidance-for-regulators/implementing-the-uks-ai-regulatory-principles-initial-guidance-for-regulators

112 Key issue 5: Transparency obligations - EU AI Act. (n.d.). https://www.euaiact.com/key-issue/5

113 Generative AI. (n.d.). Ministry of Education. https://www.education.govt.nz/school/digital-technology/generative-ai

114 Mishcon de Reya. (n.d.). Contestability and Redress | EU AI ACT & UK AI Principles Navigator. Mishcon De Reya LLP. https://www.mishcon.com/eu-uk-ai-navigator/principle-5

115 The White House. (2022, October 4). What is the Blueprint for an AI Bill of Rights? | OSTP | The White House. https://bidenwhitehouse.archives.gov/ostp/ai-bill-of-rights/what-is-the-blueprint-for-an-ai-bill-of-rights/#:~:text=What%20is%20the%20Blueprint%20for%20an%20AI%20Bill,American%20public%20in%20the%20age%20of%20artificial%20intelligence.

116 The White House. (2022a, October 4). + Notice and explanation | OSTP | The White House. https://bidenwhitehouse.archives.gov/ostp/ai-bill-of-rights/notice-and-explanation/

117 The White House. (2022a, October 4). + Human Alternatives, Consideration, and Fallback | OSTP | The White House. https://bidenwhitehouse.archives.gov/ostp/ai-bill-of-rights/human-alternatives-consideration-and-fallback/

Based on what we have seen, the legal or ethical consensus is that AI in education must be used transparently, everyone involved should understand its role, and there must be clear accountability for one's decisions and mistakes.

Case studies

To illustrate how these policies play out, here are a few examples of both successful and challenged implementations of AI regulations in educational contexts:

- **UK A-level grading algorithm fiasco (2020)**[118]: This case became a textbook example of the importance of fairness and transparency. When the UK's **Office of Qualifications and Examinations Regulation (Ofqual)** used an algorithm to moderate high school exam grades (due to exam cancellations in the pandemic), the result was widespread student disappointment and allegations of bias. On results day (13 Aug 2020), nearly 40 % of teachers'predicted grades were downgraded, the algorithm disproportionately lowered grades for students in larger, historically lower-performing schools, while seemingly inflating some grades for small elite schools. The public backlash was swift; within hours, thousands of students gathered outside the Department of Education to protest (chanting *F*** the algorithm!* which became a rallying cry[119]), pointing out the lack of transparency in how grades were decided and accusing ministers of class bias[120,121]. Legally, there were even threats of lawsuits on grounds of discrimination. In less than a week, the government Uturned, scrapping algorithmic grades in favor of teacher assessments. Prime Minister at that time, Boris Johnson, later blamed a mutant algorithm, and the Department for Education's top civil servant resigned[122].

118 CousensEV, & CousensEV. (2022b, November 10). "F**k the algorithm"?: What the world can learn from the UK's A-level grading fiasco - Impact of Social Sciences. Impact of Social Sciences - Maximizing the impact of academic research. https://blogs.lse.ac.uk/impactofsocialsciences/2020/08/26/fk-the-algorithm-what-the-world-can-learn-from-the-uks-a-level-grading-fiasco/#:~:text=For%20those%20who%20haven%E2%80%99t%20followed,exams%20gone%20forward%20as%20planned

119 Ammara. (2024, May 31). "F*ck the Algorithm": a Rallying Cry For the Future. Medium. https://medium.com/digital-diplomacy/fuck-the-algorithm-the-rallying-cry-of-our-youth-dd2677e190c

120 Busby, M. (2020, August 17). A-level students speak: "I always dreamed of going to Cambridge." The Guardian. https://www.theguardian.com/education/2020/aug/15/a-level-students-protest-at-classist-government-algorithm

121 Team, G. C. (2020, August 17). Have you been protesting against A-level downgrading? The Guardian. https://www.theguardian.com/education/2020/aug/17/have-you-been-protesting-against-a-level-downgrading

122 Walker, A. (2024, September 25). UK coronavirus live: Department for Education's most senior civil servant to step down in wake of exams row – as it happened. The Guardian. https://www.theguardian.com/world/live/2020/aug/26/uk-coronavirus-live-news-covid-19-latest-updates-boris-johnson-u-turn-face-masks

The outcome of this failure prompted regulators to be extremely cautious about automated decision systems in education. The UK government and Ofqual faced inquiries about why warning signs of bias were ignored[123]. In response, the UK has since emphasized that any future use of AI in high-stakes assessment must be transparent and subjected to bias evaluation. In 2021, the UK Cabinet Office launched the **Algorithmic Transparency Recording Standard (ATRS)**[124], requiring public bodies (including exam regulators) to publish plainlanguage documentation on any algorithm used in decisions affecting citizens. It also reinforced the idea in the UK's AI principles that contestability is key; students effectively did contest the algorithmic decisions and were heard. The fiasco, while a negative experience, ultimately strengthened the resolve to regulate algorithmic fairness in education. The Alevel algorithm was not merely a technical error; it became a crisis of public trust that mobilized students, parents, and the media. The episode cemented algorithmic accountability—transparency, explainability, and appeal rights—as non-negotiable principles for future AI deployment in UK education and, by extension, for any jurisdiction seeking to protect learners from automated harm.

- **Italy's temporary ban of ChatGPT (2023):** When generative AI hit mainstream, Italy became the first Western country to directly restrict it on data protection grounds. In March 2023, Italy's data protection authority (Garante) suspended ChatGPT nationwide[125], citing violations of EU privacy law—particularly, the lack of age controls to prevent under-13s from using it and the unlawful processing of personal data without proper notice. This ban had immediate effects in education: Italian schools suddenly lost access to a tool that some teachers and students were experimenting with, raising awareness that even popular AI must comply with privacy rules. ChatGPT's OpenAI scrambled to implement measures to address the regulators' concerns (such as an age-gate and better privacy disclosures) and within a few weeks, ChatGPT was reinstated in Italy[126].

123 CousensEV, & CousensEV. (2022, November 10). "F**k the algorithm"?: What the world can learn from the UK's A-level grading fiasco - Impact of Social Sciences. Impact of Social Sciences - Maximizing the impact of academic research. https://blogs.lse.ac.uk/impactofsocialsciences/2020/08/26/fk-the-algo-rithm-what-the-world-can-learn-from-the-uks-a-level-grading-fiasco/#:~:text=This%20incident%20has%20shone%20the,decisions%3A%20There%20can%20be%20no
124 Government Digital Service. (2024, December 17). Algorithmic Transparency Recording Standard Hub. GOV.UK. https://www.gov.uk/government/collections/algorithmic-transparency-recording-standard-hub
125 Milmo, D. (2023, April 4). Italy's privacy watchdog bans ChatGPT over data breach concerns. The Guardian. https://www.theguardian.com/technology/2023/mar/31/italy-privacy-watch-dog-bans-chatgpt-over-data-breach-concerns#:~:text=Italy%27s%20privacy%20watchdog%20bans%20ChatGPT,on%20which%20the%20platform%20relies
126 McCallum, B. S. (2023, April 28). ChatGPT accessible again in Italy. https://www.bbc.com/news/tech-nology-65431914

The outcome of this case is viewed as a successful assertion of regulatory authority. It signaled to AI providers that compliance with data privacy, especially regarding minors, is non-negotiable. For educators, it was a reminder that using a new AI tool in class carries legal responsibilities. The ban also spurred discussions in Italian schools about how to harness generative AI safely. Eventually, Italy fined the AI provider[127] and set a compliance schedule, essentially enforcing privacy-by-design in a generative AI system. This proactive stance has encouraged other jurisdictions to review generative AI under privacy laws (Spain and France also launched investigations). As a result, schools globally are now more cautious: many began requiring parental consent for student use of AI tools or opting for education-safe versions of AI with stricter privacy controls.

- **Estonia's nationwide AI education initiative (2024–ongoing)**: Estonia, a small but digitally advanced nation, is currently implementing an ambitious program to integrate AI (specifically a customized version of ChatGPT) into all high schools, which offers a glimpse of a tightly managed rollout. Partnering with an AI company, Estonia is providing an AI assistant to every secondary student and teacher by September 2025[128]. Crucially, this is happening under a policy framework that ensures compliance and ethics: the government negotiated data usage terms to protect student privacy and is overseeing teacher training on how to use AI pedagogically and safely[129]. The implementation includes ongoing evaluation by Estonia's education technologists to watch for any biases or issues the AI may introduce.

The outcome, while still ongoing at the time of writing (March 2025), could become a success story if it manages to scale AI across an entire nation's school system with minimal problems. Early emphasis on ethics (teachers were told AI is an aid, not a replacement, reinforcing human agency[130]) and equity (the tool is provided to all schools to avoid disparities) shows the impact of good governance. It also demonstrates policy innovation: by working directly with the AI provider, Estonia set conditions (like data

---

127 I Pollina, E., & Armellini, A. (2024, December 20). Italy Fines OpenAI over ChatGPT Privacy rules breach. Reuters. https://www.reuters.com/technology/italy-fines-openai-15-million-euros-over-privacy-rules-breach-2024-12-20/#:~:text=Italy%20fines%20OpenAI%20over%20ChatGPT,after%20closing%20an%20investigation

128 Global Affairs. (2025, February 25). Estonia and OpenAI to bring ChatGPT to schools nationwide. OpenAI. https://openai.com/index/estonia-schools-and-chatgpt/

129 Ferguson, M. (2025, February 27). Estonia Launches Cutting-Edge AI Education in Collaboration with US Tech Titans! Estonia Launches Cutting-Edge AI Education in Collaboration With US Tech Titans! https://opentools.ai/news/estonia-launches-cutting-edge-ai-education-in-collaboration-with-us-tech-titans

130 Err. (2025, February 25). President Karis spearheads AI-driven transformation in Estonia's high schools. ERR. https://news.err.ee/1609614773/president-karis-spearheads-ai-driven-transformation-in-estonia-s-high-schools

must be stored locally in Europe, certain unsafe features disabled for minors, etc.). This public-private cooperation model might inform upcoming regulations, essentially writing the rules through contracts and pilot conditions before formal laws catch up. Other countries are closely watching Estonia: its outcomes could influence EU policy implementation and global best practices for scaling AI in education under regulatory oversight.

Each of these stories vividly demonstrates how the six ethical pillars of responsible AI are not abstract ideals but practical necessities in real-world education policy. The UK A-level grading fiasco exposed the consequences of neglecting fairness and transparency, as the opaque algorithm disproportionately harmed students from less advantaged backgrounds and offered little recourse or explanation, ultimately forcing a reckoning with accountability and the need for contestability. Italy's temporary ban on ChatGPT underscored the centrality of privacy and security in AI deployment, especially for minors, while also highlighting the importance of transparency in how data is handled and accountability in regulatory enforcement. Meanwhile, Estonia's nationwide AI education initiative illustrates a proactive approach to inclusiveness, ensuring equitable access for all students while embedding privacy, security, and transparency through contractual safeguards, teacher training, and ongoing oversight. Together, these cases show that when AI policy in education is anchored in all six principles, it is far more likely to foster trust, equity, and positive outcomes for learners.

These case studies illustrate as well that implementing AI in education is a learning process for policymakers too: early missteps (like biased grading algorithms or invasive proctoring) have led to stronger safeguards, while proactive strategies (like Estonia's) show promise in integrating AI responsibly. In essence, the world is moving toward an educational future where trustworthy AI is a baseline requirement; AI systems must be as ethical, transparent, and inclusive as the teachers and institutions that deploy them. Policymakers are not only reacting to today's challenges but also anticipating tomorrow's, working to ensure that as AI evolves, it aligns with our educational values and legal standards. With ongoing oversight and international cooperation, AI can remain a tool for empowering learners and educators, rather than a source of new inequities or risks. The coming years will be critical in refining and enforcing these AI policies in education, ultimately shaping how the next generation learns in the age of intelligent machines.

Responsible use of AI by students

AI literacy refers to the ability to understand, use, evaluate, and critically reflect on AI technologies and their applications[131]. Unlike digital literacy, which focuses broadly on using digital tools and navigating online environments, AI literacy emphasizes grasping how

---

131 Milberg, T. (2025, June 3). Why AI literacy is now a core competency in education. World Economic Forum. https://www.weforum.org/stories/2025/05/why-ai-literacy-is-now-a-core-competency-in-educa-tion/

AI systems work, recognizing their outputs, and understanding their ethical and societal implications. This deeper competency equips learners not only to interact effectively with AI but also to question its limitations, biases, and impacts, preparing them to engage responsibly in an AI-driven world.

AI is revolutionizing education, and with these powerful tools comes the responsibility of using them ethically and wisely. For students, who are often among the first to interact with AI-powered educational systems, understanding their role in the responsible use of AI is paramount. Much like any other transformative tool throughout history, whether it was the printing press, the compass, or the early use of computers, AI presents opportunities but also requires careful consideration of its implications.

In many ways, AI in education mirrors the early days of the printing press. When books became widely available, they transformed the way people accessed knowledge. However, their use also required new skills: critical reading, analysis, and discernment. Similarly, AI offers students unprecedented access to personalized learning experiences, tools for self-assessment, and resources to expand their knowledge. Since students use AI to aid their education, they must also learn to navigate the complex ethical landscape it creates.

Today's students are engaging with AI tools that can analyze their learning patterns, suggest resources tailored to their individual needs, and even offer real-time feedback on assignments. Tools like adaptive learning platforms and AI-driven tutoring systems provide students with resources designed to optimize their learning, responding to their strengths and weaknesses. However, with this personalized support comes a greater need for students to use AI tools responsibly and critically.

Understanding the responsibilities of students with AI tools

AI is a powerful tool, but it is not infallible. For students, understanding the limits of AI is essential. While AI can suggest helpful resources or correct grammar mistakes, it cannot think critically for students, nor can it provide the nuance and context that a human teacher or peer might offer. The use of AI in learning requires that students retain control of their education and not relinquish decision-making to technology.

One of the most important responsibilities students have when using AI tools is to maintain their critical thinking skills. Just as students in medieval times learned to engage critically with religious texts or scientific works (when knowledge was scarce and hard to access), students today must learn to ask questions about the information AI presents to them. What biases might exist in the algorithms that generate these recommendations? How accurate is the data used to assess my performance?

The role of AI should be to augment learning and not replace it. While AI can offer assistance, it is ultimately the student's responsibility to analyze, interpret, and question the insights provided by AI systems. This mirrors the shift in history when the printing press gave people access to books. While books expanded knowledge, they also placed the onus of interpretation and critical analysis on the reader. Similarly, AI tools require students to engage with them actively and not passively accept their conclusions.

Similarly, just as the advent of the printing press required the protection of intellectual property and the careful management of information, today's students must understand how their data is being used by AI systems. AI systems track students' progress, monitor their behaviors, and collect vast amounts of personal data to tailor the learning experience. It is crucial for students to be aware of how their data is collected, why it is collected, and who has access to it. Ensuring that this data is handled responsibly is key to protecting students' privacy.

Moreover, students must be aware of the informed consent process and must take an active role in consenting to the collection and use of their personal learning data. Educating students about the implications of sharing their data with AI tools and platforms fosters a sense of ownership over their learning experience and encourages responsible participation in an increasingly digital education system.

Potential for misuse and the ethical dilemma

While AI holds significant promise for enhancing education, students must also be aware of the ethical dilemmas that arise from AI misuse. One of the most prominent concerns is academic integrity. AI systems designed to assist with research or assignments may unintentionally encourage academic dishonesty. For example, AI-powered essay generators or tools that assist with homework could easily be misused by students to complete assignments without engaging in the actual learning process.

Throughout history, tools that made knowledge more accessible have had their share of misuse. In the early days of the printing press, people feared that widespread access to books would undermine oral traditions or even spread false information. In a similar vein, today's students need to navigate AI tools thoughtfully, understanding that while these technologies offer convenience, they must be used to augment and not replace the process of learning.

The ethical dilemma is not new; every technological leap in education has brought with it concerns over the potential for misuse. Just as students once faced the temptation of plagiarism through copying from books, now they face the challenge of engaging with AI systems that can do the work for them. Students must be taught the value of academic honesty and the responsibility that comes with using AI tools in their education.

Developing responsible AI use habits

The ultimate goal for students is to use AI as a collaborative partner, a tool that enhances their education, not one that diminishes their personal growth or critical thinking.

Students can develop responsible AI use habits by practicing ethical learning. This includes using AI tools to supplement their learning, but not allowing AI to take the place of independent study, and asking critical questions about the AI's outputs: How is this conclusion being drawn? What data is being used to generate it? There is always a continuous need for monitoring AI interactions, ensuring that AI recommendations or feedback are fair, unbiased, and aligned with the student's personal goals.

AI can be a powerful tool for fostering collaborative learning among students. Just as early universities encouraged the exchange of ideas, AI can facilitate peer-to-peer learning, allowing students to interact with one another, share resources, and collaborate on projects with the help of AI-driven platforms. Ethical AI can help students connect with diverse perspectives, broadening their educational experience.

Supporting student learning

Educators and parents alike share a common goal: to foster curiosity, resilience, and critical thinking in students. While critics may worry that AI could erode these values by offering an easy way out, the reality is far more nuanced. When used responsibly, AI becomes a dynamic partner in the learning process. It serves not as a crutch, but as a launchpad for creative exploration, helping students brainstorm, structure their ideas, and refine their writing. In this way, AI challenges students to delve beneath the surface, to ask better questions, and to build robust problem-solving skills.

This perspective transforms the debate. Instead of labeling AI as a tool for cheating, we should see it as a means to shift the focus from mere memorization to meaningful understanding and application. AI supports collaborative learning by enabling students to analyze data together, explore diverse perspectives, and engage in discussions that mirror real-world problem-solving. In an era where AI literacy is becoming essential, restricting access to these tools only limits students' potential to adapt, innovate, and thrive in the modern workforce.

Ultimately, the ethical use of AI is not about substituting human thought but about empowering it. It is about embracing technology that can help bridge the gap between knowledge and understanding, and that can prepare students to meet the challenges of the future with confidence. Instead of fearing AI, we must guide our students in harnessing its capabilities responsibly and creatively, ensuring that it serves as a bridge to deeper learning rather than a barrier to academic integrity.

Guidance for educators in security and ethical AI use

As AI increasingly integrates into the educational landscape, educators find themselves at the forefront of ensuring that AI data is secure and used ethically, responsibly, and effectively in the classroom. AI holds immense promise for transforming education, but its benefits must be tempered with a strong commitment to equity, security, privacy, and transparency. To support this, a number of organizations, including Monsha.ai[132], ICTEvangelist[133], and Witness.AI[134], offer practical, ready-to-use ethical AI policy templates specifically designed for schools. These resources are designed for direct adaptation and provide a strong foundation for educators to establish clear guidelines and best practices, develop and update their own ethical use policy for AI in education, making it easier to implement responsible AI use and safeguard student interests as technology evolves.

Focus on security

Choosing the right AI-based educational tools and service providers requires due diligence and a focus on security, privacy, and ethics. Whether it is a K–12 district evaluating a new adaptive learning service or a university adopting an AI-driven tutoring system, administrators must apply rigorous vetting before adopting. This involves not only assessing the application's educational merits but also scrutinizing vendor and service provider practices and contractual terms to ensure they meet the institution's standards.

Districts must begin by aligning any prospective AI tool with educational goals and values. Administrators and educators should ask themselves, and students, teachers, and parents, *Does this technology genuinely address an instructional need or problem?* rather than being technology for technology's sake. It is wise to pilot new AI tools with small pilot experiments and gather feedback from teachers and students. Additionally, consider the service provider's background—was the tool developed with input from students, educators, and learning science research? A vendor who understands the education context is more likely to deliver a beneficial product.[135]

Educators as ethical stewards of AI

Educators are uniquely positioned to guide AI use in the classroom, ensuring that these tools serve students' best interests. Just as teachers have historically been trusted to foster a culture of honesty, integrity, and respect in the classroom, today's educators must also become stewards of ethical AI use, advocating for the fair and responsible application of AI-powered tools.

132 AI Policy Guide for Schools: Templates, Examples & Best Practices (2025). (n.d.). https://monsha.ai/guides/ai-policy-guideline-for-schools
133 Anderson, M., & Anderson, M. (2025, February 24). AI Policy Template for Schools (2025 update) - ICTEvangelist. ICTEvangelist -. https://ictevangelist.com/ai-policy-template-2025/
134 WitnessAI. (2025, July 9). AI Policy Template Guide: Build a Responsible AI Usage Policy - WitnessAI. WitnessAI. https://witness.ai/blog/ai-policy-template/
135 O'Hagan, J. (2025, April 14). Before your school buys AI, ask these 4 questions | Chalkdust & Silicon. *Medium*. https://medium.com/chalkdust-silicon/before-your-school-buys-ai-ask-these-4-questions-or-pay-for-the-mistakes-later-590c581b23d0

Educators are role models for students, and this extends to the ethical use of technology. When educators introduce AI tools, they should demonstrate how to engage with them critically, questioning the outputs of AI and considering the broader implications of their use. For example, when using AI to assess student progress, educators should always check the AI-generated feedback for fairness and ensure that it aligns with their personal observations of student work.

Teachers can encourage students to question the AI's decisions, whether it is a grade suggestion or a learning recommendation. Showing students how to critically assess AI-driven insights can foster a sense of digital literacy and ethical engagement that is crucial as students navigate an increasingly AI-powered world.

Teachers must be adequately trained to evaluate AI tools from an ethical perspective. Professional development programs should go beyond just understanding how AI tools work and should include training on the ethical implications of these tools in their classrooms. This includes how AI systems handle student data, how they make decisions, and how to ensure AI tools align with principles of fairness and educational integrity.

Ensuring fairness for all students

AI systems are only as good as the data they are trained on. If the data used to train AI models is biased, whether intentionally or unintentionally, it can lead to biased outcomes. It is essential for educators to question and understand how these systems are making decisions.

Teachers can audit AI systems regularly to ensure they are not reinforcing discriminatory patterns, particularly when it comes to minority students, students with disabilities, or students from low-income backgrounds. For example, if an AI-based learning system suggests learning paths that do not align with the needs of diverse student groups, it is crucial to intervene and adjust.

One important aspect is the promotion of inclusiveness in AI. AI tools must be designed to account for diverse learning styles, backgrounds, and accessibility needs. Educators can ensure that AI tools used in their classrooms cater to a variety of learning needs. This includes ensuring that AI-driven platforms are adaptive, offering different learning pathways for students with special needs or those who may need additional support, such as language learners or students with cognitive disabilities.

Teachers can advocate for the use of AI tools that are designed inclusively, ensuring that all students, including those with learning disabilities, are equally supported. **Universal Design for Learning (UDL)** principles[136] can guide teachers in selecting AI tools that accommodate students' diverse needs.

---

136 CAST, Inc. (n.d.). The UDL guidelines. https://udlguidelines.cast.org/

Protecting students' information

Just as students trust educators to protect their personal information in a physical classroom, they must trust that AI tools will handle their data ethically and securely.

AI tools often collect a wide range of data and as an educator, it is essential to understand what data is being collected, how it is being used, and who has access to it. Educators must ensure that AI systems used in their classrooms comply with privacy laws, such as FERPA (in the U.S.) or GDPR (in Europe), and ensure that students' personal data is never misused.

In the same way, students need to be aware of their rights when using digital platforms, educators must ensure that informed consent is obtained before AI tools are introduced. Schools and institutions should provide both students and their families with transparent explanations of the data use policy, explaining exactly what data is collected, how it will be used, and how long it will be stored, and obtain explicit permission. This fosters trust and gives students and their families control over their personal data. Schools can also offer students the option to opt out or limit the data collection, respecting their right to privacy.

Teacher autonomy and the role of human judgment

AI has the potential to automate many tasks within education, and while these systems can save teachers time, AI should never replace the role of human judgment. Educators are not just administrators; they are mentors, guides, and leaders in the classroom.

AI can handle repetitive administrative tasks, but teachers must remain the ones who make important pedagogical decisions, using their expertise and intuition to guide their students' learning journeys. For example, AI might recommend a learning path for a student struggling in a particular area, but it is the teacher's responsibility to assess whether this path fits the student's unique learning style.

Teachers should also remain central in fostering emotional intelligence, critical thinking, and collaborative skills, aspects of learning that AI cannot replicate. Encouraging open discussion, creative problem-solving, and a safe environment for social-emotional learning are all areas where AI cannot replace the teacher's role.

Critical responsibility for educators

Teachers should actively evaluate the AI tools they use in their classrooms, ensuring that these tools align with the ethical standards of fairness, transparency, and data security. Regular assessment is key to making sure that AI remains a supportive, rather than intrusive, presence in the classroom.

Educators must be critical consumers of AI technologies. They should investigate how AI tools were developed, who developed them, and how data is being used. It is important to select tools that are transparent about their algorithms and data usage.

Teachers should not only assess AI tools before introducing them but also regularly evaluate how well they are working. They should gather feedback from students about their experiences with AI tools and adjust their use as necessary. If AI is found to be causing issues, such as bias, inaccuracy, or a lack of engagement, educators must be ready to recommend alternatives or call for improvements.

As stewards of ethical AI in the classroom, educators are responsible for ensuring that AI tools are used effectively, fairly, and transparently. With proper training, critical thinking, and a commitment to ethical standards, educators can use AI to support and enhance learning, empowering students to navigate an AI-driven world with integrity and responsibility.

Role of parents or guardians in ethical AI use

As AI continues to shape the educational landscape, parents or guardians have an increasingly important role in guiding their children through the ethical challenges posed by these powerful technologies. Parents, guardians, and other primary caregivers are often the first line of defense when questions about educational AI and privacy arise. Their responsibilities reach well beyond signing consent forms; they include monitoring how children's data is used, advocating for equitable access, and helping young learners develop critical AI literacy.

The first step for any parent or guardian in this journey is to understand what AI tools are being used in their child's education, how they work, and what data they collect. AI-powered tools are increasingly used for a variety of purposes, and while AI holds tremendous potential to enhance learning, it is crucial that parents are fully informed about the systems their children are interacting with. Not all AI tools are equal in terms of their educational value, data security, and ethical design and parents need to understand whether the AI tools their children use are inclusive, transparent, and fair.

In July 2024, the U.K. **Information Commissioner's Office (ICO)** reprimanded *Chelmer Valley High School* for rolling out **facialrecognition technology (FRT)** in its canteen without a full dataprotection impact assessment or explicit parental consent[137]. After parents raised privacy objections, the school hurriedly issued letters offering an opt-out, allowing families to switch their children back to PIN or card payments. Several parents chose that option, arguing that biometric scanning for lunch payments was disproportionate and risked normalizing surveillance. The incident illustrates how a single family's decision—*No, we do not want our child's face stored in that database*—can surface wider accountability gaps and force institutions to rethink deployment.

---

137 Opiah, A. (2024b, July 24). UK school reprimanded by ICO for using facial recognition without DPIA. Biometric Update | Biometrics News, Companies and Explainers. https://www.biometricupdate.com/202407/uk-school-reprimanded-by-ico-for-using-facial-recognition-without-dpia

A contrasting example comes from U.S. districts using AI-powered monitoring tools such as Gaggle[138] or GoGuardian[139]. Investigations by *The Seattle Times* and Associated Press in March 2025 found that many parents had no way to opt out once the district enabled 24/7 surveillance of student devices; some were not even informed that thousands of sensitive documents were being scanned and stored[140]. The stark difference between Chelmer Valley's postbacklash opt-out and the nochoice reality in many U.S. districts shows how local policy determines whether families have genuine agency.

Here are some examples of what parents or guardians should pay attention to regarding AI use:

- **Data privacy and consent**: Parents or guardians should ensure that they are fully informed about what data is being collected, how it is being used, and who has access to it. Just as parents have historically been guardians of their children's personal and educational records, they must now take an active role in ensuring their children's digital data privacy. Questions such as *What type of data is being collected?* and *How long is it stored?* should be asked of schools or the providers of AI tools.

- **Supporting digital literacy and critical thinking**: While AI offers the potential to enhance learning, it also places an increased responsibility on students to engage with technology critically. As their primary guides, parents or guardians can help their children develop the necessary skills to think critically about the AI-driven content and suggestions they encounter. Empowering children to question AI recommendations, asking questions like: *How did the AI come to this conclusion?* or *What are the implications of this suggestion for my learning?* These are questions that help foster critical thinking and AI literacy in children, ensuring that they understand AI as a tool, not a substitute for their own judgment and intellectual engagement.

  Several school systems already embed AIethics modules into their digitalliteracy programs:

  o MIT RAISE's Day of AI curriculum[141] offers free, hands-on lessons (Grades K-12) that walk students through how recommendation engines work, where bias creeps in, and why transparency matters[142]. One activity asks learners to audit a movierecommendation algorithm and debate whose voices were excluded—an exercise parents can replicate at the dinner table.

---

138 Gaggle.Net, Inc. (n.d.). Gaggle | K-12 Online Safety Management Software. https://www.gaggle.net/
139 GoGuardian | Engaging Digital Learning for Schools. (n.d.). https://www.goguardian.com/
140 Lurye, S., & Times, C. B. O. S. (2025, March 12). AI surveillance on school Chromebooks has security issues, investigation shows | AP News. AP News. https://apnews.com/article/ai-school-chromebook-surveillance-gaggle-investigation-takeaways-381fa82978f27eb85f20d03236820711
141 MIT RAISE: Responsible AI for Social Empowerment and Education. (n.d.). https://raise.mit.edu/
142 Breazeal, C. (n.d.). Grow with Google launches a new generative AI course for educators in collaboration with MIT RAISE – MIT Media Lab. MIT Media Lab. https://www.media.mit.edu/articles/grow-with-google-launches-a-new-generative-ai-course-for-educators-in-collaboration-with-mit-raise/

- o Common Sense Education's AI Literacy Lessons (Grades 612)[143] include 20-minute grab-and-go modules on chatbots, algorithmic bias, and deepfakes, complete with family discussion guides. Schools in California's San Mateo County have adopted the set, and parents receive take-home prompts that encourage questions like *How did the AI reach that answer?*

- o In 2024, the New Zealand Ministry of Education released *Introduction to Artificial Intelligence*[144], a resource that weaves AI concepts—accuracy, fairness, and data consent—into the national curriculum and supplies reflection sheets for parents to use at home.

While AI can be a powerful tool, it is not infallible. Parents should help their children recognize the limitations of AI, including potential biases in decision-making, inaccuracies in predictions, and the inability of AI systems to provide the full context or understanding that a human educator can offer. By helping children understand the difference between what AI can and cannot do, parents can cultivate a more balanced relationship with technology.

- **Ensuring fairness and equity in AI use**: As AI continues to be integrated into educational settings, it is critical that all students have equal access to these tools. However, the digital divide, the gap between those who have access to technology and those who do not, remains a significant issue. Parents must ensure that AI tools are used to promote fairness and equity in their children's education, advocating for fair access to AI tools in schools and ensuring that students from lower-income backgrounds or rural areas are not left behind due to a lack of resources. Parents must also be aware of the potential for bias in AI systems. Parents should advocate for the use of AI systems that are fair, inclusive, and transparent. They should ask schools whether AI tools are regularly tested for bias and how the tools ensure equitable outcomes for all students, regardless of their background.

- **Guiding ethical AI use at home**: As parents or guardians become more aware of the growing presence of AI in education, they also have a role in setting healthy boundaries and ensuring ethical use of technology at home. Parents or guardians can help guide their children in using AI tools responsibly and ensure that these technologies do not replace human interaction, creative thinking, or physical activity. AI-powered tools can be beneficial, but they can also lead to over-reliance or screen time overload. Research

---

143 Millennium@EDU. (2025, February 12). AI Literacy lessons for grades 6–12 | Common Sense Education. Millennium@EDU SUSTAINABLE EDUCATION. https://millenniumedu.org/ai-literacy-lessons-for-grades-6-12-common-sense-education/
144 NZC - Resource. (n.d.-b). https://newzealandcurriculum.tahurangi.education.govt.nz/introduction-to-artificial-intelligence/5637235331.p

by the *Special Olympics Global Center* (2024)[145] [146] shows that when parents discuss AI's limits and possibilities, students are more likely to view technology as a tool—not an infallible authority—thereby increasing engagement and reducing over-reliance. Parents or guardians should set clear boundaries on how and when their children use AI tools for educational purposes, ensuring a balance between AI-assisted learning and offline activities, such as physical play, reading, and social interaction. Encouraging children to use AI tools as a supplement to their learning, rather than as a replacement for thinking and problem-solving, will help them develop independent thought. AI can guide them toward solutions or can be great companions for brainstorming, but it is the critical thinking that parents or guardians encourage at home that will allow them to truly learn and grow.

- **Advocating for ethical AI in education**: Parents or guardians also have a role in advocating for ethical AI policies in schools. As educational stakeholders, parents or guardians can join efforts with educators, administrators, and policymakers to ensure that AI is used in a way that benefits all students fairly and equitably. Individual opt-outs can trigger broader change, but systemic safeguards require collective action: schoolsite councils and PTAs can demand transparency reports and routine bias audits before procurement, and regional parent coalitions (i.e., *New York Civil Liberties Union* parents who secured the 2023 state ban on facial recognition in schools) demonstrate that organized advocacy can shift statewide policy[147].

Parents are crucial in navigating the ethical challenges of AI in education. By staying informed, advocating for fairness, promoting digital literacy, and guiding responsible AI use at home, parents can help their children engage with AI in a way that maximizes its benefits while minimizing its potential risks. The role of parents is not just to monitor AI use but to empower their children to use it ethically, responsibly, and critically, ensuring that they are prepared to thrive in an AI-enhanced future. By exercising their consent rights and fostering open dialogue with educators, families ensure that AI enhances rather than undermines children's learning and wellbeing. Everyday choices—opting in, opting out, or pushing for better guardrails—are a powerful check on the ethical deployment of AI in schools. AI will not make learning obsolete; it will magnify whatever values, good or bad, we embed in our schools.

Throughout this chapter, we have returned to five ethical pillars that must guide every AI decision:

145 Langreo, L. (2024, August 1). AI's potential in special education: What teachers and parents think. Education Week. https://www.edweek.org/teaching-learning/ais-potential-in-special-education-what-teachers-and-parents-think/2024/08

146 No one left behind: Landmark Special Olympics study reveals concern about disability representation in development of AI technologies. (2024, July 22). SpecialOlympics.org. https://www.specialolympics.org/about/press-releases/no-one-left-behind-landmark-special-olympics-study-reveals-concern-about-disability-representation-in-development-of-ai-technologies?locale=en

147 New York bans facial recognition in schools after report finds risks outweigh potential benefits | AP News. (2023, September 27). AP News. https://apnews.com/article/facial-recognition-banned-new-york-schools-ddd35e004254d316beabf70453b1a6a2

- **Fairness**: Systems must not disadvantage any learner.

- **Transparency**: Students, families, and teachers deserve to know how algorithms work.

- **Accountability**: Institutions must be able to trace, explain, and correct AI decisions.

- **Inclusiveness**: Tools should adapt to diverse languages, cultures, and abilities.

- **Privacy and data security**: Rigorous safeguards are non-negotiable when children's information is at stake.

Restating these pillars is more than a summary; it is a reminder that ethical literacy is now as urgent as digital literacy. AI use in schools is accelerating faster than many policies can keep pace. If educators, parents, and technologists do not master these principles quickly, we risk normalizing biased or opaque systems before we fully understand their impact.

To translate principles into practice, every stakeholder should act now by taking three high-priority steps, so that these safeguards become well established. These steps include:

1. Conduct an **ethical impact assessment (EIA)** before adopting any high-stakes AI tool.

2. Provide targeted AI training for educators.

3. Implement clear student and family consent (and opt-out) protocols.

Conclusion

In many classrooms today, AI is often dismissed as a shortcut, a tool that undermines genuine learning and is equated with cheating. Yet, such a narrow view misses the transformative potential of AI in education. Rather than replacing thought, AI can amplify it, acting as a catalyst for creativity, critical inquiry, and deeper engagement with learning materials.

By acting on these commitments now—auditing impact, empowering educators, and honoring family consent—we signal that AI is welcome in our classrooms only when it advances equity, transparency, and student wellbeing. The path ahead is bright, but only if we walk it with clear ethics and shared accountability.

In the next chapter, we will explore the future. The future of AI in the classroom is one of promise, innovation and vision. How human and AI solutions come together to offer students a comprehensive roadmap to academic and social-emotional growth. With strong adherence to privacy and security standards, instructors, policymakers and educational institutions will offer students personalized learning experiences, building resilience and shaping the future.

Questions

1. If AI systems make educational decisions—like grading, intervention targeting, or even admissions—who holds the moral accountability: the algorithm, the developer or vendor, the school, or the teacher?

2. Is it ethical to use AI systems that provide personalized learning only to students with access to devices and high-speed internet, leaving behind the underserved? Will this technology widen the digital divide?

3. Should students and parents be given the right to opt out of AI-powered educational tools, if doing so might disadvantage the student academically or socially? What are the regulatory implications?

4. If AI can analyze student emotions through facial recognition or other biometric data (e.g., heart rate, blood pressure) should emotional privacy and security of biometric data be considered a fundamental right in the classroom?

5. Are schools at risk of outsourcing moral and pedagogical decisions to algorithms, and if so, how will educators co-exist and reclaim their agency while still benefiting from AI support?

Exercises

1. **Accountability role play- The AI decision fallout**: Explore accountability in AI decision-making.

    a. **Create an example scenario**: An AI grading system incorrectly flags a student as at-risk and denies them access to an advanced course. Assign participants different roles:

        i. Student

        ii. Parent

        iii. Teacher

        iv. Principal

        v. Vendor

        vi. Individual AI system developer

        vii. School board member

    b. Have each role defend or challenge the AI's decision, and discuss:

        i. Who is ultimately accountable?

        ii. What is justice for the student?

        iii. What safeguards and guardrails should exist?

    c. Reflect on how a shared responsibility can work in reality.

2. **The data control simulation**: Explore ethical data ownership and consent.

    a. Break into groups and distribute fictional profiles of students used by an AI learning platform. Each group must:

      i.   Decide what data should be collected or provided, who owns it, and who can access it.

      ii.   Draft a one-paragraph *Permission for AI Data Use Agreement* from the student's perspective.

      iii.   Present it to the class and explain the rationale.

  b. **Prompt for reflection: `What would informed consent look like in a classroom powered by AI?`**

3. **Bias diagnostic lab**: Learn how AI systems might reinforce inequity.

  a. Use a case study (e.g., the UK A-level grading algorithm scandal)[82]. In small groups, identify:

      i.   The source(s) of bias.

      ii.   Who was most harmed by AI, and who benefited.

      iii.   What should have been done differently.

  b. **Challenge**: Each group must redesign the system using ethical principles (transparency, fairness, equity, and inclusion). Share discoveries with the larger group.

4. **AI in the classroom**: Set community boundaries on the role of AI in the classroom.

  a. Create a continuum from 0 to 10:

      i.   0 = No AI used in classrooms

      ii.   10 = Fully AI-run classrooms (grading, teaching, disciplining)

  b. Ask participants to signal where they believe the ethical line should be. Then, facilitate a discussion:

      i.   What kinds of classroom decisions should **never** be made by AI?

      ii.   Where does AI support autonomy? Where does it threaten?

5. **Parent-teacher town hall- The AI transparency challenge**: Encourage community-wide dialogue on transparency and inclusion.

  a. Simulate a school town hall. Assign roles (parents, teachers, admin, students, AI developers, tech vendors). Present this prompt: **`Your school is deploying a new AI-powered learning analytics system that uses emotional recognition and predictive analytics`**.

b. Each role must:

   i. Raise questions, propose policies, or resist implementation or deployment.

   ii. Draft a one-slide *Community Transparency Charter* on acceptable AI use.

6. **Ethics draft board: build your own AI bill of rights**: Engage with and develop core ethical principles.

   a. Using large chart paper, teams draft an **AI Bill of Rights for Students**, selecting 5–7 non-negotiable rights (e.g., transparency, right to contest AI decisions, right to understand how data is used).

   b. Compare your charter with real-world policies like the U.S. AI Bill of Rights or the EU AI Act. What is missing?

7. **Fk the algorithm- Protest design studio**: Examine the role of student voice and resistance.

   a. Study the UK student protest after the biased A-level grading algorithm. Then:

      i. Design a creative protest campaign (slogan, visuals, social media strategy).

      ii. Present the ethical and emotional case behind it.

   b. Debrief:

      i. When should students push back against AI systems?

      ii. How can schools create space for respectful resistance?

      iii. How should schools respond to a protest? What forums can be used for healthy discussions?

Join our Discord space

Join our Discord workspace for latest updates, offers, tech happenings around the world, new releases, and sessions with the authors:

https://discord.bpbonline.com

CHAPTER 11
Future of AI in the Classroom

The best way to predict the future is to create it.

-Peter Drucker

Introduction

As we conclude this journey through **artificial intelligence** (**AI**) in education, this chapter looks ahead, beyond today's tools and practices, to what lies on the horizon. We are entering a pivotal era where artificial intelligence, when implemented thoughtfully, can profoundly elevate learning experiences, empower educators, and open doors for students worldwide. It is no longer a question of if AI will shape education, but how, by whom, and to what end.

The integration of AI into learning environments is an unfolding reality that is reshaping how we teach, learn, and envision the future of education. In the coming years, classrooms are poised to blend human teaching with powerful AI support. Rather than replacing teachers, AI will handle routine tasks and personalize learning in real-time, freeing educators to focus on mentorship and complex, social aspects of teaching. According to a 2025 World Economic Forum report[1], 60% of teachers report using AI to grade quizzes, track student progress, or generate practice exercises, allowing them to spend more time giving meaningful feedback

---

1 Haoyang, D. L., & Towne, J. (2025, January 9). How AI and human teachers can collaborate to transform education. World Economic Forum. https://www.weforum.org/stories/2025/01/how-ai-and-human-teach-ers-can-collaborate-to-transform-education/

and leading discussions. In this same report, education experts widely agree that the future is about human–AI collaboration: the future of education is not about choosing between human teachers and AI, but rather harnessing the best of both worlds. This vision sees AI tutors, immersive simulations, and real-time data insights enhancing lessons, all under the guidance of skilled teachers.

Crucially, educators remain at the center of this future classroom. Research and policy perspectives emphasize that AI cannot replicate the empathy, inspiration, and judgment a human teacher provides. Instead, AI is viewed as a tool to empower teachers and students alike. For instance, a 2024 Financial Times editorial[2] noted AI is unlikely ever to be able to substitute for the judgment, motivation, guidance and pastoral care a teacher can provide, but it can give teachers more time to do what they do best by taking over administrative work.

Likewise, since today's students will enter AI-rich workplaces, schools have a responsibility to prepare them for that world. Surveys[3] reflect this urgency: in 2023, 71% of K–12 teachers and 65% of students agreed that AI tools will be essential for student success in college and careers. In short, the stage is set for AI to become an integral, transformative part of education, provided it is implemented thoughtfully, with teachers and schools steering the way.

This final chapter invites educators, policymakers, school leaders, and readers of all backgrounds to imagine the next frontier: a world of classrooms powered by AI tutors, translated in real time, personalized to every learner's needs, and emotionally aware. But more than imagining, we focus on preparing with strategies, case studies, and critical reflections on what readiness truly looks like, such as a forward-looking roadmap.

This is not a passive future to be observed; it is one we must co-create with intent, ethics, and humanity at the center. Let us look ahead and ask: *What comes next with AI in the classroom?*

Structure

This chapter covers the following topics:

- Projecting future trends in educational AI
- Preparing students as innovators and ethical stewards
- Empowering educators for the road ahead
- Evolving school and district ecosystems
- Building global partnerships and collaboration
- Bridging AI with social-emotional growth

---

2 The future of the AI-enhanced classroom. (2024, August 26). Benton Foundation. https://www.benton.org/headlines/future-ai-enhanced-classroom#:~:text=As%20students%20return%20for%20a,equipped%20 workplaces
3 Haoyang, D. L., & Towne, J. (2025, January 9). How AI and human teachers can collaborate to transform education. World Economic Forum. https://www.weforum.org/stories/2025/01/how-ai-and-human-teach-ers-can-collaborate-to-transform-education/

- Looking to the horizon and disruptive possibilities
- Future led by humanity and vision

Objectives

This chapter aims to equip readers with a forward-looking understanding of how AI is likely to evolve within educational contexts and what it will take to ensure these developments are inclusive, ethical, and impactful. Readers will learn about emerging technologies and pedagogies, examine real-world examples of innovation in action, and consider the broader cultural and institutional shifts required to adapt. The chapter emphasizes how educators, students, leaders, and policymakers can all play a role in shaping this future—developing not just technical fluency but also ethical awareness, resilience, and creative agency. By the end of the chapter, readers will feel inspired and better informed to help lead the next phase of education's transformation. The following figure highlights a global AI future:

Figure 11.1: *AI and human students will partner together in the future*

Projecting future trends in educational AI

What key trends are likely to emerge as AI becomes more fully integrated into the educational landscape? One immediate development has been the surge of interest in generative AI tools (like large language models) since late 2022. To illustrate the remarkable growth of this technology, let us review the user adoption statistics for ChatGPT: it achieved 100 million users within two months, marking it as one of the fastest-growing apps in history. It took 4.5 years for Facebook to reach the same number of users, and 11 years for Spotify[4].

---

4 Singh, S. (2025, April 16). ChatGPT Statistics (2025): DAU & MAU Data Worldwide. DemandSage. https://www.demandsage.com/chatgpt-statistics/?utm_source=chatgpt.com

The public debut of tools like ChatGPT in 2022 marked a tipping point that took educators by surprise and prompted intense debate about how to respond[5]. In early reactions, some school systems banned such tools out of concern for academic honesty, only to reverse course months later as the educational potential became clearer[6]. Indeed, by 2023, many educators began experimenting with AI to enhance lessons, provide feedback, or save time on planning. According to a national survey[7] by the *RAND Corporation* and the *Center on Reinventing Public Education*[8], 18% of K-12 teachers reported using AI in their classrooms as of 2023, and about 60% of school districts planned to start training teachers in AI by the end of the 2023–2024 school year. These data points illustrate a rapidly growing adoption curve: what was novel yesterday is quickly becoming mainstream practice.

Personalized learning at scale is emerging as one of the most promising trends. Around the world, there is a clear trend toward customization of education through AI, with countries seeking to tailor learning to individual students' needs. For example, AI-powered tutoring systems are being piloted to give every student access to one-on-one help. By late 2024, Khan Academy's AI tutor Khanmigo, built on a ChatGPT engine, was already being trialed in 266 school districts in the United States[9]. These AI tutors can guide students through problems step-by-step and answer questions in a conversational manner, much like a personal tutor would. Early pilots in public schools (such as a trial in Newark, NJ, aiming to combat pandemic learning loss) show AI tutors acting as on-demand support for students while also assisting teachers with tasks like lesson planning and tailored recommendations[10]. Across Asia, governments are investing in similar tools: South Korea, for instance, is rolling out personalized AI tutor systems that adapt homework to each child's level and learning behaviors, with plans for each child to have a personalized AI tutor alongside access to online

5 Admin, C., & Admin, C. (2024, November 14). Shockwaves and innovations: How nations worldwide are dealing with AI in education – Center on Reinventing Public Education. Center on Reinventing Public Education. https://crpe.org/shockwaves-and-innovations-how-nations-worldwide-are-dealing-with-ai-in-education/#:~:text=Rapid%20developments%20in%20artificial%20intelligence%2C,use%20of%20AI%20in%20schools

6 Klein, A. (2024, October 24). 180 degree turn: NYC District goes from banning ChatGPT to exploring AI's potential. Education Week. https://www.edweek.org/technology/180-degree-turn-nyc-schools-goes-from-banning-chatgpt-to-exploring-ais-potential/2023/10#:~:text=That%20development%E2%80%94announced%20Oct,other%20districts%20to%20follow%20suit

7 Diliberti, M. K., Schwartz, H. L., Doan, S., Shapiro, A., Rainey, L. R., & Lake, R. J. (2024, April 17). Using artificial intelligence tools in K–12 classrooms. RAND. https://www.rand.org/pubs/research_reports/RRA956-21.html

8 Williams, S. (2025, April 11). Penn program offers artificial intelligence training to Philadelphia school district teachers. WHYY. https://whyy.org/articles/university-of-pennsylvania-ai-training-teachers/#:~:text=According%20to%20a%202023%20national,using%20AI%20in%20their%20classrooms

9 CBS News. (2024, December 16). Meet Khanmigo: the student tutor AI being tested in school districts I 60 Minutes. https://www.cbsnews.com/video/khanmigo-ai-tutor-60-minutes-video-2024-12-08/

10 Gómez, J. (2024, October 30). Newark Public Schools considers new AI tutor chatbot for districtwide use after pilot testing. Chalkbeat. https://www.chalkbeat.org/newark/2024/05/13/artificial-intelligence-khanmigo-chatbot-tutor-pilot-testing-districtwide-expansion/#:~:text=Newark%20Public%20Schools%20wants%20to,up%20from%20pandemic%20learning%20loss

learning platforms[11]. Such examples suggest that the 1:1 tutor for every student model, long a dream for educators, may become a practical reality through AI. Research has shown that individualized tutoring can dramatically boost student outcomes (with tutored students performing better than 98% of those in traditional classes[12]), but providing a human tutor for every child has been economically unfeasible. AI offers a potential solution to bridge that gap by making personalized support scalable.

Another trend is the use of AI-driven analytics and early warning systems. Modern education produces a wealth of data, from quiz results to classroom behavior observations, and AI can analyze this data to identify patterns or problems that might otherwise go unnoticed. Education systems are beginning to deploy AI to flag students who may need extra help or are at risk of falling behind. For instance, the **Organisation for Economic Co-operation and Development (OECD)** reports that data-driven AI systems can help with early identification of at-risk students and enable timely interventions, especially to support disadvantaged or struggling learners[13]. In practice, this might mean an AI system monitoring a student's progress across subjects and alerting teachers if it detects a consistent difficulty with, for example, reading comprehension or if a normally engaged student's participation drops off. School districts have started piloting such uses; in one case, a few districts in *New Mexico* experimented with an AI platform to automate tracking of student attendance and promptly identify patterns of absenteeism so staff can follow up[14]. Going forward, we can expect more schools to adopt AI tools that help personalize assessment, providing teachers with rich, real-time insights into each student's strengths and weaknesses. This can make assessment more formative, guiding learning in real time, rather than just summative. It also raises new questions about data privacy and ethics, which we will touch on later.

Importantly, educational AI policy and governance are also evolving as a parallel trend, as discussed in *Chapter 10, Data Security and Ethical Considerations in AI*. The initial lack of policy guidance is giving way to more structured approaches by education leaders and governments. A noteworthy example occurred in New York City: after initially banning generative AI, the NYC Department of Education not only lifted the ban but established an *AI Policy Lab* in 2023 to proactively shape how AI is used in teaching and administration[15]. This initiative, launched in partnership with researchers and other school districts, is focusing on human-centered

11 Admin, C., & Admin, C. (2024, November 14). Shockwaves and innovations: How nations worldwide are dealing with AI in education – Center on Reinventing Public Education. Center on Reinventing Public Education. https://crpe.org/shockwaves-and-innovations-how-nations-worldwide-are-dealing-with-ai-in-education/#:~:text=South%20Korea%20has%20implemented%20AI,teachers%20to%20focus%20on%20social
12 Milberg, T. (2024, April 28). The future of learning: How AI is revolutionizing education 4.0. Weforum. https://www.weforum.org/stories/2024/04/future-learning-ai-revolutionizing-education-4-0/#:~:text
13 Herbert. (2023, December 19). OECD: Guidelines for effective use of AI in education. Griffl.org. https://griffl.org/oecd-guidelines-effective-use-of-ai-in-education/#:~:text=,avoid%20narrowing%20curricula%20or%20prioritizing
14 Mexican, A. S. S. F. N. (2025, January 12). School districts pilot AI tool to improve attendance. Yahoo News. https://www.yahoo.com/news/school-districts-pilot-ai-tool-043400558.html?guccounter=1
15 Banks, D. C. (2024, February 4). ChatGPT caught NYC schools off guard. Now, we're determined to embrace its potential. Chalkbeat. https://www.chalkbeat.org/newyork/2023/5/18/23727942/chatgpt-nyc-schools-david-banks/

AI implementation with an emphasis on equity, safety, ethics, and transparency. It signals a broader trend of education systems shifting from reactive stances to proactive planning. We see nascent networks of districts collaborating (as NYC is doing with ~15 districts nationwide) to develop shared guidelines, address cybersecurity and privacy issues, and define best practices for classroom AI. On the national level, some governments and organizations are issuing guidelines: the U.S. Department of Education released a policy report[16] in 2023 on AI in teaching and learning (its first major guidance on the topic), teacher unions like the **American Federation of Teachers (AFT)** adopted resolutions[17] on AI ethics, and the European Union is moving forward with the EU AI Act[18] that classifies educational uses of AI as high risk requiring strict oversight. All these developments indicate that infrastructure, policy, and ethical frameworks are catching up with technological advances—a necessary evolution if AI is to realize its potential safely.

Looking ahead, educators and experts broadly agree on a few key points. First, AI in education should augment human teachers and learners, not replace the human element. AI's greatest promise lies in automating the mundane tasks—grading simple assessments, compiling lesson materials, and organizing data, to free up teachers for the creative and relational parts of teaching. In parallel, AI can offer students more adaptive pathways through content, but it should not diminish the importance of peer interaction, critical thinking, and hands-on learning. Second, with AI enabling such personalization and automation, the role of the teacher is likely to shift (a trend we discuss in detail in the *Empowering educators for the road ahead* section in this chapter). Teachers may increasingly act as coaches and mentors, using AI insights to guide each student's progress in a more individualized way. Third, issues of equity, bias, and access will remain front and center. Without deliberate action, there is a risk that only well-resourced schools benefit from the latest AI tutors and analytics, while others are left further behind. We explore this challenge more in the Global Partnerships section, but it is worth noting here as a dominant theme: the future of AI in the classroom must be one where *AI for all* is more than a slogan; it is backed by concrete efforts so that every student and teacher, regardless of geography or background, can share in the benefits.

Here is a quick recap of the top six AI trends reshaping education[19]:

- **Personalized learning ecosystems**: AI-powered systems analyze individual student data to tailor content, pacing, and instructional approaches, ensuring that each learner's unique needs are met. This personalization enhances engagement and

16 Cardona, M., Rodríguez, R. J., Ishmael, K., & U.S. Department of Education. (2023). Artificial intelligence and the future of teaching and learning. https://www2.ed.gov/documents/ai-report/ai-report.pdf

17 Social media, artificial intelligence and generative artificial intelligence. (2023, June 1). American Federation of Teachers. https://www.aft.org/resolution/social-media-artificial-intelligence-and-generative-artificial-intelligence

18 EU Artificial Intelligence Act | Up-to-date developments and analyses of the EU AI Act. (n.d.-b). https://artificialintelligenceact.eu/

19 Lee, S. (n.d.). 5 AI Trends Reshaping Education: Data & Applications. https://www.numberanalytics.com/blog/5-ai-trends-reshaping-education?utm_source=chatgpt.com

improves learning outcomes.

- **Intelligent tutoring systems (ITS)**: Leverage AI to provide one-on-one guidance, simulating the benefits of human tutors. These systems use natural language processing and machine learning to interact with students, offering real-time feedback and support.

- **Automated assessment and feedback**: AI-driven assessment tools are transforming how educators evaluate student work. From automated essay scoring to real-time analysis of problem-solving approaches, these technologies reduce teacher workload and provide students with immediate, personalized feedback, fostering a more responsive learning environment.

- **Augmented and immersive learning environments**: The integration of AI with **augmented reality** (**AR**) and **virtual reality** (**VR**) is creating immersive learning experiences. These technologies allow students to engage with interactive simulations and virtual environments, enhancing understanding and retention of complex concepts. Such experiential learning approaches are becoming increasingly prevalent in educational settings.

- **AI for accessibility and inclusion**: AI technologies are playing a crucial role in making education more accessible. Tools like speech-to-text, text-to-speech, and AI-powered translation services assist students with disabilities and those who speak different languages, ensuring a more inclusive learning environment. These advancements help bridge gaps and provide equal learning opportunities for all students.[20]

- **Ethical considerations and AI literacy**: As AI becomes more integrated into education, ethical considerations are paramount. Educators and students must be equipped with AI literacy to understand the implications of AI use, including data privacy, algorithmic bias, and the importance of human oversight. Developing curricula that address these topics is essential for the responsible integration of AI.

The road ahead points to classrooms that are smarter and more responsive to individual needs, supported by emerging policies and a growing comfort level among educators. The trends suggest a vision of education that is more personalized, data-informed, and efficient–but achieving that vision will require careful preparation of both students and teachers, robust support from school systems, and collaboration across borders. Let us now delve into what it means to prepare our students to thrive as innovators and ethical stewards in an AI-augmented world.

---

20 Hollingsworth, H. (2024, December 26). AI is a game changer for students with disabilities. Schools are still learning to harness it | AP News. AP News. https://apnews.com/article/artificial-intelligence-students-disabilities-ff1f51379b3861978efb0c1334a2a953

Preparing students as innovators and ethical stewards

One of the greatest responsibilities of education is to prepare the next generation not just to cope with the future, but to create it. In the context of AI, this means helping students develop the skills, mindset, and ethical grounding to innovate and flourish in a world where AI is ubiquitous. As we look forward, future-ready students will need a strong foundation in digital and AI literacy alongside the timeless skills of creativity, critical thinking, and collaboration. AI literacy is a blend of technical understanding (not necessarily deep engineering, but conceptual grasp) and ethical reasoning, enabling informed and responsible participation in an AI-driven world. Many educational leaders have recognized this and are integrating AI concepts into curricula to ensure students are not merely end-users of intelligent systems, but informed shapers of technology. Building on the previous section's example, South Korea has embarked on an ambitious plan to introduce AI education across all grade levels of its national curriculum by 2025[21]. Starting with high school and moving down through elementary, Korean students will progressively learn about AI concepts, from basic principles to practical applications, as part of their formal schooling. This goes hand-in-hand with Korea's deployment of AI tutors in classrooms—the idea is that students not only benefit from AI-supported learning in subjects like math and reading but also gain meta-understanding of how these AI systems work and how to use them responsibly. Such integration of learning with AI and learning about AI is critical. It echoes the World Economic Forum's recommendation that teaching about AI is equally crucial as teaching with AI in schools[22]. When students understand the basics of algorithms, data, and ethical issues, they are better positioned to navigate AI tools critically and even create their own.

At the same time, countries with high-performing education systems are emphasizing broad digital skill programs to reach all learners. Finland, for instance, has embraced AI education not only in K-12 schools but for the public at large. A bold national commitment offers free online AI courses to all citizens (including a popular *Elements of AI* course), reflecting the philosophy that widespread AI knowledge underpins a competitive and equitable society[23]. Within Finnish schools, nearly half have adopted a platform called ViLLE that gives students

21 Admin, C., & Admin, C. (2024, November 14). Shockwaves and innovations: How nations worldwide are dealing with AI in education – Center on Reinventing Public Education. Center on Reinventing Public Education. https://crpe.org/shockwaves-and-innovations-how-nations-worldwide-are-dealing-with-ai-in-education/#:~:text=South%20Korea%20is%20investing%20heavily,is%20designing%20and%20piloting%20extensive

22 Milberg, T. (2024, April 28). The future of learning: How AI is revolutionizing education 4.0. Weforum. https://www.weforum.org/stories/2024/04/future=-learning-ai-revolutionizing-education4-0-/#:~:text-,experience

23 Admin, C., & Admin, C. (2024, November 14). Shockwaves and innovations: How nations worldwide are dealing with AI in education – Center on Reinventing Public Education. Center on Reinventing Public Education. https://crpe.org/shockwaves-and-innovations-how-nations-worldwide-are-dealing-with-ai-in-education/#:~:text=Finland%2C%20long%20admired%20for%20its,and%20analytics%20on%20student%20assignments

immediate feedback and analytics on assignments using AI-driven learning analytics. This not only supports personalized learning but also familiarizes students with how AI can be a tool for improvement and reflection. Even as Finnish educators use such platforms, a parallel initiative called *AI in Learning* (involving researchers and companies globally) is focusing on equity and ethics in AI for education. Among its projects is the design of an intelligent system to gauge student wellness and provide insights to learners and teachers, showing a forward-thinking approach that blends technical innovation with wellbeing and ethical considerations. The lesson here is that preparing students for the future is not just about technical content; it is about modeling the values and responsible use of technology in the learning process.

Many schools are beginning to introduce age-appropriate AI and coding activities to spark curiosity. In earlier grades, this might involve simple exercises in which students train a basic model (for example, teaching a computer to recognize patterns or categorize objects) or discuss how a recommendation system works in everyday apps. By high school, students might engage in projects like building a rudimentary chatbot, analyzing a dataset for a science project with AI tools, or debating the ethics of facial recognition. Such activities cultivate an innovator's mindset—students learn to see AI as something they can tinker with and improve, not just something pre-made that they consume. They also learn by doing, which demystifies AI. A notable initiative supporting this is MIT's *Day of AI* program[24], a free curriculum designed to introduce K-12 learners to AI through hands-on lessons and games. *Day of AI* provides materials for elementary, middle, and high school students, and it's accessible even to classrooms with no prior coding experience. Teachers around the world can pick and choose modules (from understanding how AI recognizes images to exploring how AI affects society) and even participate in an annual *Day of AI* celebration where students share projects and ideas. This program and others like it have engaged countless students globally to date, illustrating how we can build AI awareness and skills at scale in fun, participatory ways.

In cultivating student innovators, educators are placing a strong emphasis on creativity and critical thinking. AI, by its nature, can automate routine tasks and provide information, so the human skills that will stand out in the future are the abilities to think originally, ask the right questions, and use AI as a tool for creative expression. In practice, this means encouraging students to leverage AI in imaginative projects. For example, an art teacher might have students use a generative AI image tool to brainstorm ideas for a painting, and then critically evaluate and refine those ideas by hand. A STEM teacher might guide students to design an experiment where an AI predicts an outcome (i.e., the trajectory of a rocket) and the students test and discuss any discrepancies. In this article[25], one educator described AI as Artificial Inspiration, telling students that their own ideas are more powerful than AI and that they can use AI to help those ideas grow. This perspective flips the script: instead of fearing that AI will make

24 MIT Open Learning. (2023, February 3). Day of AI is back! - MIT Open Learning - Medium. Medium. https://medium.com/open-learning/day-of-ai-is-back-e15ab52c4f55#:~:text=About%20Day%20of%20 AI%20Day,access%20to%20the%20curriculum%20and

25 AI + SEL & the Mental health crisis: How can we leverage new tech to meet the moment? (and what are the risks?) - CASEL. (2024, July 31). CASEL. https://casel.org/blog/ai-sel-the-mental-health-crisis-how-can-we-leverage-new-tech-to-meet-the-moment-and-what-are-the-risks/#:~:text=One%20thing%20I%20 know%20for,expression

human creativity obsolete, it frames AI as a catalyst for human creativity. In classrooms that have adopted this approach, students are producing inventive work—from writing stories collaboratively with AI, to composing music using AI suggestions, to building prototypes of apps that use AI for social good. Such experiences prepare students to be adaptive, lifelong learners. They learn how to learn with emerging tools, which is arguably one of the most important skills in a rapidly changing world.

Underpinning all of this is the commitment to ethical education and social responsibility. Today's students are tomorrow's AI developers, policymakers, and informed citizens. Thus, discussions about bias, fairness, privacy, and the impact of AI on society are being brought into the classroom. Educators are finding age-appropriate ways to explore these topics— for instance, having students analyze scenarios where an AI decision might be unfair, or reflect on how relying on AI for answers can affect one's own learning. The **United Nations Educational, Scientific and Cultural Organization** (**UNESCO**) has been actively guiding such efforts. In 2024, UNESCO introduced AI competency frameworks[26] for students (and teachers) to help countries ensure young people understand the potential as well as risks of AI and can engage with AI safely, ethically, and responsibly. These frameworks outline not just technical competencies, but also awareness of issues like data privacy, the importance of human oversight, and the ability to seek help or speak up if an AI tool seems to be causing harm. By incorporating these principles, schools can nurture empathetic innovators and ethical stewards—students who are excited by technology but also mindful of human values.

Preparing students as innovators in the age of AI involves a multi-faceted approach: integrating AI literacy into curricula, encouraging creative use of AI, ensuring a grounding in ethics, and making learning experiential and student-centered. It is heartening to see real-world momentum: from Asia to Europe to the Americas, initiatives are underway to AI-enable curricula and empower students. In India, for example, the ed tech company *Embibe*[27] is using AI in education not only via products (such as an app that lets students scan textbook passages and view 3D AI-generated visualizations of complex concepts) but also by launching innovation challenges to involve students in solving community problems with AI. Such global efforts send a clear message—the next generation should not be mere passengers in the AI revolution, but co-pilots who can steer technology toward positive ends. If we succeed in this, our students will indeed be the innovators who shape a better future with AI, rather than being shaped by AI.

Empowering educators for the road ahead

Every step toward an AI-enhanced classroom must go hand-in-hand with empowering educators. Teachers are the anchor of educational transformation; no technology can succeed in schools without teachers who are confident, competent, and supported in using it. The coming years will place new demands on educators: they will need not only basic digital

26 Artificial intelligence in education. (n.d.). unesco.org. Retrieved March 5, 2025, from https://www.unesco.org/en/digital-education/artificial-intelligence
27 EMBIBE - The most powerful AI-powered learning platform. (n.d.). https://www.embibe.com/

skills but also an understanding of how AI tools work, how to integrate them pedagogically, and how to address ethical issues that may arise. This represents a significant shift in teacher preparation and ongoing professional development. The good news is that many efforts are already underway to equip teachers with the knowledge and support they need to thrive alongside AI.

As discussed in previous chapters, a priority area is **professional development (PD)** and training focused on AI. Recognizing the urgency, some school districts and universities have launched specialized training programs for in-service teachers. A notable example is the **Pioneering AI in School Systems (PASS)** program[28] in Philadelphia. In 2024, the University of Pennsylvania's Graduate School of Education, in collaboration with the city's school district, created PASS as a free professional development pilot to train teachers and administrators on effectively using AI in classrooms. The district's superintendent highlighted that bridging the digital divide and equipping educators with AI tools is essential for helping students graduate ready for college or careers. This reflects a broader trend highlighted earlier in this chapter: according to a 2023 national survey[29], while only about one in five teachers had started using AI in teaching, a solid majority of districts (approximately 60%) anticipated beginning teacher AI training by 2024. Thus, we are likely to see an expansion of workshops, courses, and certifications aimed at helping current teachers build AI fluency. These can range from short webinars on using AI for lesson planning to intensive summer institutes, where teachers might learn the basics of machine learning or develop AI-enhanced curriculum units.

In addition to in-service training, there is growing attention on pre-service teacher preparation –ensuring new teachers enter the workforce AI-savvy from day one. Traditional teacher education programs have begun to update their curricula to include educational technology and AI components. For example, the **International Society for Technology in Education (ISTE)** and ASCD (a global educators' association) partnered with Microsoft in 2024 on an initiative called *Transforming Teacher Preparation*[30]. This project, supported by a Microsoft grant, is developing a sustainable training module for teacher preparation programs that will be available in multiple languages (English, Spanish, Arabic). The aim is to give every pre-service teacher a foundational understanding of how to use AI tools to enhance teaching and learning, and how to do so safely, responsibly, and innovatively. As AI becomes integral to learning and life, it is critical that new teachers are prepared to thrive in an AI-infused world: tomorrow's educators should view AI not as a threat or an afterthought, but as one of the core components of their teaching toolkit. We can expect to see more universities emulate these efforts, updating

28 Williams, S. (2025, April 11). Penn program offers artificial intelligence training to Philadelphia school district teachers. WHYY. https://whyy.org/articles/university-of-pennsylvania-ai-training-teachers/#:~:text=The%20pilot%20program%2C%20Pioneering%20AI,free%20for%20school%20district%20personnel

29 Diliberti, M. K., Schwartz, H. L., Doan, S., Shapiro, A., Rainey, L. R., & Lake, R. J. (2024, April 17). Using artificial intelligence tools in K–12 classrooms. RAND. https://www.rand.org/pubs/research_reports/RRA956-21.html

30 ISTE and ASCD Awarded Grant from Microsoft to Advance AI in Teacher Preparation Programs. (2024, June 24). ISTE. https://iste.org/news/iste-and-ascd-awarded-grant-from-microsoft-to-advance-ai-in-teacher-preparation-programs#:~:text=Together%2C%20Microsoft%E2%80%99s%20investment%20and%20knowledge,based%20instructional%20design%20principles

standards for teacher competencies. In fact, UNESCO's 2024 AI competency framework for teachers[31] serves as a guide, emphasizing continuous professional growth so teachers can engage with AI in a safe, ethical and responsible manner and support student learning with AI. This global framework outlines key areas teachers should develop, from understanding AI's basic functions and limitations to using AI-assisted teaching resources, to managing data privacy and bias concerns in the classroom.

In a real-world case[32] from a classroom in a small New York district, two 6th grade teachers— *D'Aurio* and *Donaghy*—used AI tools to dramatically reduce lesson preparation time and enhance student learning experiences. Traditionally, they spent hours searching for lesson materials and creating differentiated resources. By integrating AI platforms such as Canva and Diffit, they transformed this process quickly, generating visual aids and reading passages tailored to different student levels, while also generating multiple-choice and short-answer questions. Students completed reading and comprehension tasks in Google Classroom, receiving immediate, level-appropriate feedback, allowing teachers to focus on creative projects and deeper discussions. This approach saved the teachers several hours each week while improving student engagement and learning outcomes.

An empowered educator in the AI era is not only one who has technical knowledge, but also one who has pedagogical strategies for AI integration. That means teachers need models of how to use AI to enrich learning rather than distract or detract from it. Professional communities and early adopters have begun sharing success stories and lesson ideas, which is helping to build a repertoire of AI-informed teaching practices. For instance, teachers are finding that generative AI can help differentiate instruction: a teacher might ask an AI tool to generate reading passages at different difficulty levels on the same topic, to match each student's reading ability better. Others use AI as a creative partner, i.e., having students brainstorm questions and then using a chatbot to get initial answers, which the class then fact-checks and elaborates on, thereby teaching research and critical thinking. Early experiences suggest AI can save teachers considerable time on administrative and routine tasks. This resonates with anecdotal reports from classrooms: some educators use AI tools to draft parent newsletters or generate ideas for activities, which frees up precious time to focus on student interaction and planning more engaging lessons.

However, training must also address the challenges and anxieties teachers may have. One common concern is: will AI replace teachers? The answer from experts is a resounding no; instead, AI is seen as augmenting teachers' roles. As one OECD review put it, while AI can automate certain tasks, it will augment teachers' work rather than replace them and is best suited to providing personalized feedback and administrative streamlining, not the nuanced human

---

31 Artificial intelligence in education. (n.d.). unesco.org. Retrieved March 5, 2025, from https://www.unes-co.org/en/digital-education/artificial-intelligence

32 D'Orio, W. (2024, April 15). Case Study: How 2 Teachers Use AI Behind the Scenes to Build Lessons & Save Time. The74. https://www.the74million.org/article/case-study-how-2-teachers-use-ai-behind-the-scenes-to-build-lessons-save-time/

connection that real teaching requires[33]. Teachers in training are being reassured and shown evidence that their role remains absolutely crucial. In fact, with AI handling some drudgery, a teacher's human skills—mentoring, motivating, empathizing, and inspiring students—become even more prominent. Another concern is how to maintain academic integrity when AI can produce answers or essays. Educators are being prepared with new assessment strategies (like more oral exams, in-class writing, project-based learning) and taught how to discuss academic honesty in the age of AI with students, setting clear guidelines for when AI use is appropriate or not. Some school districts have even created resource kits: New York City's aforementioned AI Policy Lab is producing sample letters to families explaining AI tools and developing clear policies for educators on AI use[34]. Empowering educators means giving them not just tools, but confidence and clarity—clear rules of the road, ethical guidelines, and a support network to troubleshoot issues as they arise.

Supportive infrastructure is another aspect. To effectively use AI, teachers need reliable technology access in their classrooms, from devices to internet connectivity, as well as tech support. Districts that are early adopters of AI often invest in instructional technology coach positions or AI lead teachers who can mentor colleagues. In 2023–24, some innovative districts appointed small committees or task forces of teachers to experiment with AI tools and share findings. For example, one district in *Utah* (Jordan District) participated in a pilot where teachers voluntarily tried out AI apps and met to discuss what worked, feeding their insights to the district for broader implementation planning[35]. These stories highlight that empowering educators is not a top-down mandate; it often grows from bottom-up engagement. Teachers, given the time and encouragement, often become the best champions and trainers of their peers.

Finally, we must acknowledge the importance of teacher wellbeing and mindset. Learning a new technology can be daunting, especially one as hyped (and sometimes hyped-up) as AI. Effective professional development around AI, therefore, also focuses on mindset: helping teachers adopt a growth mindset for themselves as learners of new tools, fostering collaboration (so no teacher feels alone in figuring this out), and even addressing the stress or tech fatigue educators might feel. Encouragingly, educators in various parts of the world have voiced optimism once they get hands-on experience with AI, noting that it could actually reduce burnout by saving time, tools that might help manage workload, or provide on-demand

33 Herbert. (2023, December 19). OECD: Guidelines for effective use of AI in education. Griffl.org. https://griffl.org/oecd-guidelines-effective-use-of-ai-in-education/#:~:text=While%20AI%20could%20potential-ly%20replace,and%20social%20aspects%20of%20learning
34 Klein, A. (2024, October 24). 180 degree turn: NYC District goes from banning ChatGPT to exploring AI's potential. Education Week. https://www.edweek.org/technology/180-degree-turn-nyc-schools-goes-from-banning-chatgpt-to-exploring-ais-potential/2023/10#:~:text=New%20York%20will%20make%20any,any%20district%20that%20needs%20guidance
35 Jordan District teachers give AI a try | West Jordan Journal. (2023, September 11). https://www.westjor-danjournal.com/2023/09/11/465161/jordan-district-teachers-give-ai-a-try

coaching for teachers themselves[36]. Imagine an AI assistant that helps a teacher prioritize tasks for the week, or a system that analyzes a teacher's lesson and offers tips to better engage a quiet student; these ideas are on the table, and some are being prototyped. When teachers see AI as something that helps them be the best version of themselves professionally, the adoption becomes much smoother.

Empowering educators in the AI era involves robust training (both pre- and in-service), strong community support, clear policies and ethical guardrails, and a narrative that teachers are, and will remain, irreplaceable leaders of learning. The period from 2023 onward is already demonstrating what is possible: teachers are attending AI workshops in record numbers, higher education institutions are redesigning teacher prep, and cross-sector partnerships (like universities, nonprofits, and companies working together) are yielding accessible training resources. By investing in our educators and urgently equipping them with AI skills, we ensure that the integration of AI into classrooms is guided by wisdom, ethics, and pedagogical sense—in other words, guided by the heart and expertise of teachers.

Evolving school and district ecosystems

While individual teachers and students are the daily actors in classrooms, the broader school and district ecosystem sets the stage for how successfully AI can be implemented. Ecosystem here refers to the infrastructure, policies, culture, and organizational structures that support teaching and learning. As we move forward, schools and districts will likely undergo significant evolution to accommodate AI, from upgrading technology infrastructure to rethinking data policies to creating new roles or teams focused on digital innovation. This section explores those systemic changes and the challenges and opportunities they present.

A fundamental piece of the ecosystem puzzle is infrastructure, having the technological capacity for AI-supported learning. Many exciting AI tools require reliable internet connectivity, adequate devices (computers or tablets), and in some cases, advanced computing power or cloud services. Yet, a sobering reality is that not all schools are currently equipped for this. Globally, only about half of schools have internet access: as of 2023, roughly 40% of primary schools and 50% of lower-secondary schools worldwide were connected to the internet for educational purposes, according to a report by UNESCO[37]. Even at the upper-secondary level, about one-third of schools lack connectivity. And in some regions, basic infrastructure like electricity is not guaranteed in every school. Bridging this gap is an urgent priority if we want AI in education to be an equitable innovation rather than one that widens existing divides.

---

36 AI + SEL & the Mental health crisis: How can we leverage new tech to meet the moment? (and what are the risks?) - CASEL. (2024b, July 31). CASEL. https://casel.org/blog/ai-sel-the-mental-health-crisis-how-can-we-leverage-new-tech-to-meet-the-moment-and-what-are-the-risks/#:~:text=Taking%20that%20thought%20a%20step,%E2%80%9D

37 UNESCO, Alcott, B., Al Hadheri, S., April, D., Barakat, B. F., Barrios Rivera, M., Barry, M., Bekkouche, Y., Caro Vasquez, D., D'Addio, A. C., Davydov, D., Endrizzi, F., Flynn, S., Gil, L., Jain, C., Dwivedi, I., Joshi, P., Kaldi, M.-R., Kiyenje, J., . . . Weill, E. (2023). Global Education Monitoring Report Summary 2023: Technology in education: A tool on whose terms? In Global Education Monitoring Report [Report]. UNESCO. http://creativecommons.org/licenses/by-sa/3.0/igo/ (Original work published 2023)

Initiatives like UNICEF and ITU's Giga project[38] are emblematic of the efforts needed—Giga is mapping schools worldwide using AI and satellite imagery to identify connectivity gaps, aiming to connect every school to the internet and every student to digital opportunity[39]. As these partnerships expand access, districts must plan for sustainable infrastructure: investing in broadband, networking hardware, and regular maintenance. Some countries have made bold moves, such as installing nationwide education cloud platforms or central AI servers that schools can tap into securely. In the years ahead, we might see more regional or national education data centers offering AI services (like language translation, text-to-speech, or adaptive learning engines) that individual schools can use without each having to host complex systems locally.

Alongside infrastructure, policy and governance frameworks at the school or district level will evolve. Earlier, we discussed how districts are starting to form AI task forces or labs (like NYC's) to create usage policies. We anticipate that most school boards and education departments will craft formal guidelines around AI in education. These may cover questions such as: Which AI applications are approved for use (academic, administrative, or both)? How is student data protected when using AI tools? What transparency is required from AI vendors about how their algorithms work and what data they collect? For example, a district might mandate that any AI software used undergo a privacy review and that parents are informed if an AI will be interacting regularly with their child (such as a tutor bot). The **Consortium for School Networking** (**CoSN**), which brings together district technology leaders, has been advising districts to ask tough questions of vendors: what are you allowing and not allowing, and what questions are you going to ask vendors is absolutely critical[40]. This reflects a shift to more assertive procurement policies; schools will need to vet AI tools for bias, inclusiveness and accessibility, transparency, accountability, privacy and security, reliability, and alignment with learning goals. In Europe, we see movement on this through compliance with broader regulations (the EU's AI Act requires risk assessments for educational AI). In Japan[41], the government has issued guidelines specifically for AI in schools after piloting them in select schools to see what regulations made sense before scaling up. Districts in other countries may not wait for national mandates; many are already hungry for specifics on AI policy and beginning to draft their own, as evidenced by superintendents increasingly considering AI policies even if few have them finalized yet[42]. We can imagine that in a few years, an average school district might have an AI Acceptable Use Policy akin to the internet acceptable use policies of the early 2000s.

38 Project Connect. (n.d.). https://projectconnect.unicef.org/about
39 GigaMaps. (n.d.). https://maps.giga.global/map
40 Klein, A. (2024, October 24). 180 degree turn: NYC District goes from banning ChatGPT to exploring AI's potential. Education Week. https://www.edweek.org/technology/180-degree-turn-nyc-schools-goes-from-banning-chatgpt-to-exploring-ais-potential/2023/10#:~:text=families%20explaining%20AI%20tools%20or,any%20district%20that%20needs%20guidance
41 New School Guidelines in Japan Emphasize AI Education. https://theaitrack.com/school-guidelines-in-japan-ai-education/
42 Klein, A. (2024, October 24). Schools want guidance on AI use in classrooms. states are not providing it, report says. Education Week. https://www.edweek.org/technology/schools-want-guidance-on-ai-use-in-classrooms-states-are-not-providing-it-report-says/2023/09

The organizational culture and roles within schools might also change. Just as many schools today have IT coordinators or instructional tech coaches, tomorrow's schools might have AI integration specialists. These could be staff who help teachers use AI tools, maintain AI systems, and analyze data from AI platforms to inform school improvement. Some districts may form committees that include teachers, administrators, parents, and even students to continuously evaluate how AI is impacting learning and well-being. In terms of roles, we might see positions like a Chief Innovation Officer or Data Privacy Officer become more common in education systems as technology's role grows. For teachers, the redistribution of time due to AI (less time grading, more time mentoring) could influence staffing models. If AI tutors handle a lot of direct instruction and practice for students, schools might choose to reduce class sizes or assign teachers to smaller mentoring groups, focusing on higher-order skills and personalized help. Or perhaps schools will adopt team-teaching models where a group of educators collectively oversee a larger cohort of students who are often working on individualized AI-supported tasks. One teacher might monitor the AI dashboards and flag issues, another leads group discussions, and another focuses on socio-emotional check-ins.

School and district leadership will need to champion a vision that balances innovation with prudence. The most successful examples we have seen involve leaders who actively learn about AI and involve stakeholders in planning. In Singapore's Ministry of Education, for example, a dedicated research center, **AI Center for Educational Technologies (AICET)**[43], was established in partnership with the national AI initiative to pilot projects aimed at improving the education system with AI. They are taking a measured approach: running experiments, collecting evidence on what works, and using that to guide larger-scale implementation. Similarly, Finland's approach of involving multidisciplinary researchers via the AI in Learning project[44] brings external expertise into the ecosystem. In local school districts, this could translate to partnerships with nearby universities or EdTech startups, creating a pipeline from research to practice. A principal or superintendent might initiate a small pilot with volunteer teachers using an AI tool, rigorously evaluate outcomes (did student engagement improve? did it save teacher time? were there any equity issues?), and only then expand usage. This evidence-based, iterative approach will be crucial to avoid pitfalls and ensure AI adoption is genuinely enhancing learning.

We cannot talk about evolving ecosystems without mentioning ethics and equity structures. School systems will likely need to establish ethical guidelines or review boards for AI usage. For instance, if a district considers using AI that monitors student emotions via webcam or analyzes student essays for mental health indicators, these raise serious ethical questions. An ethics committee could review such proposals, include community input, and perhaps require opt-in consent. Equity committees might monitor whether AI is benefiting all student groups or if gaps are widening. The OECD has emphasized that guidelines should ensure inclusive

43 AI Centre for Educational Technologies (AICET). (2024, October 7). Home - AI Centre for Educational Technologies (AICET). AI Centre for Educational Technologies (AICET) - Expanding the Possibilities of Education Through AI. https://aicet.comp.nus.edu.sg/
44 AI in learning. (n.d.). https://blogs.helsinki.fi/ai-in-learning/

education, transparency, explainability, and human alternatives for AI systems[45]. What might that look like in a district? Possibly a requirement that any AI-driven decision (like placement into a remedial program) can be appealed and reviewed by humans, or a requirement that AI recommendations in high-stakes contexts are always considered with human judgment rather than blindly followed. Another practical step is providing opt-out paths; for families not comfortable with a certain AI tool, is there a non-AI alternative curriculum or activity? Ensuring such flexibility could become part of policies, much like how parents can opt out of certain media or topics for their children in some schools.

Communication and community engagement form a pillar of the ecosystem. Schools will need to educate parents and students about the AI tools being used, the benefits and risks, and how data is handled. Transparency builds trust. We saw a hint of this with NYC's lab planning to create sample letters to families explaining AI tools. A district might hold informational nights on AI, showcase student projects involving AI, or publish an AI handbook that explains in plain language what tools are in use and why. Engaging students in forming AI usage norms can also be powerful. For example, a student council could work with teachers to develop an honor code regarding AI (when it is okay to use tools like ChatGPT for help and when it is not).

The school and district ecosystem is the support structure that will either enable AI innovations to flourish or, if neglected, cause them to fail. As we look to the road ahead, it is clear that investing in infrastructure (so all schools can plug into digital learning), updating policies (to set guardrails and expectations), evolving organizational roles, and fostering a culture of continuous learning and ethical vigilance will be key. Education systems that proactively adapt will be better positioned to harness AI's benefits—improving administrative efficiency, enriching curriculum, and targeting resources where they are needed most. Those who are slower may find themselves scrambling to respond to changes or facing backlash from unaddressed issues. The encouraging fact is that even in the early 2020s, we are already seeing many green shoots: national strategies, district labs, international guidelines, and collaborative networks. These efforts are helping educational ecosystems become more agile and resilient, which sets a strong foundation for navigating whatever changes the AI revolution may bring.

Building global partnerships and collaboration

Education has always been a global concern, and the advent of AI in the classroom is no exception. In fact, the challenges and opportunities of educational AI are so vast that they transcend national borders. Issues like equity, ethics, and quality in AI-assisted learning are being addressed worldwide. This is where global partnerships come into play. Collaborations between international organizations, countries, researchers, and industry aim to ensure AI benefits all of humanity's learners, not just a privileged few. In this section, we highlight how global entities and alliances are shaping the road ahead and why such cooperation is

45 Herbert. (2023, December 19). OECD: Guidelines for effective use of AI in education. Griffl.org. https:// griffl.org/oecd-guidelines-effective-use-of-ai-in-education/#:~:text=,useful%2C%20used%20appropriate-ly%20and%20effectively

indispensable.

One of the leading voices in this domain is UNESCO, the United Nations' agency for education and culture. UNESCO has positioned itself as a champion for a human-centered and ethical approach to AI in education. As early as 2019, it gathered consensus on guiding principles (the *Beijing Consensus on AI in Education*[46]), and more recently, it has been actively rolling out resources to help countries navigate AI. In 2023 and 2024, UNESCO introduced new competency frameworks[47] for both students and teachers regarding AI, as mentioned earlier. These frameworks are not abstract guidelines; they are meant to be practical tools that ministries of education can adapt into curricula and training programs. UNESCO's message emphasizes inclusion and equity: it urges that the promise of *AI for all* must be that everyone can take advantage of the technological revolution and ensure AI does not widen the divides within and between countries. This principle of AI for all is guiding global initiatives to bridge digital divides (like the Giga project we discussed) and to share AI innovations freely (for example, by open-sourcing educational AI software or sharing translations of content into low-resource languages).

Another key player is the OECD, which has been researching and advising on AI in education among its member countries. The OECD's Digital Education Outlook 2023 report[48] is one landmark, providing opportunities, guidelines, and guardrails for effective and equitable use of AI in education. One of the OECD's contributions is highlighting the dual nature of AI's impact—its ability to help (improve outcomes, personalize learning) and the risks it poses (inequity, bias, privacy issues)—and then offering evidence-based recommendations on how to maximize the former and mitigate the latter[49]. In practice, OECD facilitates working groups and expert networks. Countries like Finland, Singapore, and others often share pilot results through OECD channels. The organization has also proposed policy guidelines, such as ensuring teacher agency in AI adoption (teachers should have a say and be co-designers, not just end-users of new systems). We are likely to see the OECD continue to play a coordinating role, perhaps helping to benchmark AI integration progress in education across countries or to develop common metrics for AI literacy.

Beyond UNESCO and OECD, multilateral and multi-stakeholder partnerships are flourishing. The World Economic Forum's Education 4.0 Alliance[50] is one example, bringing together public and private sector leaders to advance new models of education for the Fourth Industrial

---

46 UNESCO. (2019). Beijing Consensus on Artificial Intelligence and Education. In UNESCO (ED-2019/WS/30). Retrieved April 30, 2025, from https://unesdoc.unesco.org/ark:/48223/pf0000368303
47 What you need to know about UNESCO's new AI competency frameworks for students and teachers. (2024, September 3). https://www.unesco.org/en/articles/what-you-need-know-about-unescos-new-ai-competency-frameworks-students-and-teachers?hub=32618
48 OECD (2023), OECD Digital Education Outlook 2023: Towards an Effective Digital Education Ecosystem, OECD Publishing, Paris, https://doi.org/10.1787/c74f03de-en.
49 Herbert. (2023, December 19). OECD: Guidelines for effective use of AI in education. Griffl.org. https://griffl.org/oecd-guidelines-effective-use-of-ai-in-education/#:~:text=,effectiveness%20with%20explainabili-ty%20and%20alternatives
50 Reskilling Revolution - Education 4.0. (n.d.). https://initiatives.weforum.org/reskilling-revolution/education-4-0

Revolution, including AI integration. In 2024, this alliance released a report on *Shaping the Future of Learning: The Role of AI in Education 4.0*[51], which outlined key promises of AI (like supporting teachers, refining assessment, personalizing learning) and crucial factors for implementation (like designing for equity and co-designing with stakeholders). What is significant is that such alliances mix perspectives: tech companies, governments, educators, and **non-governmental organizations** (**NGOs**) work together. For instance, companies might provide AI tools or funding for pilot projects, while researchers evaluate outcomes and international bodies ensure results are shared widely, not kept proprietary.

There are also inter-country collaborations, such as the ones in Latin America, where countries are collaborating to develop AI education strategies. The **Organization of American States** (**OAS**), along with other regional partners, has been involved in initiatives to promote AI in education, focusing on sharing resources and best practices among member states[52]. High-income countries are also providing technical assistance and grants to lower-income countries to build capacity in AI education. The **Global Partnership for Education** (**GPE**) has started considering technology, including AI, in its grant programs. For example, the GPE **Knowledge Innovation Exchange** (**KIX**) Africa 21 Hub has been instrumental in facilitating regional collaboration and knowledge sharing on AI in education among Francophone and Lusophone African countries[53].

A particularly urgent focus of global partnerships is addressing the global equity gap so that AI does not become a new agent of inequality. As mentioned earlier, connectivity and infrastructure are one challenge, and another one is content and language. A lot of AI educational content today is in English or a few major languages. UNESCO and others are pushing for localization: ensuring AI tutoring systems or educational content are available in many languages, including indigenous languages, so that children can learn in their mother tongue. This might involve partnerships with local universities to create language data sets for AI, or with companies to add more languages to their tools. It is notable that some AI chatbots can now function in dozens of languages—an opportunity to bring quality resources to places where good textbooks or teachers in certain subjects are scarce. For example, an AI mentor that can speak and understand Kiswahili or Bengali could help millions of students in Africa or South Asia practice and learn in those languages, provided the tools are made accessible.

Global knowledge exchange is perhaps the simplest but most powerful aspect of partnerships. The experiences of one country can be invaluable to another. Consider that by 2025, China will likely have had several years' head start using AI at scale in education, albeit with a very

51 World Economic Forum. (2024). Shaping the Future of Learning: The role of AI in Education 4.0. In I N S I G H T R E P O R T. https://www3.weforum.org/docs/WEF_Shaping_the_Future_of_Learning_2024.pdf
52 Artificial intelligence can contribute to transforming development models in Latin America and the Caribbean to make them more productive, inclusive and sustainable. (n.d.). Economic Commission for Latin America and the Caribbean. https://www.cepal.org/en/pressreleases/artificial-intelligence-can-contribute-transforming-development-models-latin-america?utm_source=chatgpt.com
53 Sub-regional seminar for Francophone and Lusophone countries in Africa on digital and AI competencies. (n.d.). UNESCO. Retrieved April 30, 2025, from https://www.unesco.org/en/articles/sub-regional-seminar-francophone-and-lusophone-countries-africa-digital-and-ai-competencies?utm_source=chatgpt.com

exam-focused lens[54]. By learning from each other, nations can avoid duplication of effort and steer clear of known pitfalls.

As we have explored, global partnerships act as the connective tissue that links individual efforts into a larger movement. They ensure that the road ahead is not travelled in isolation by each educator or each nation, but as a collective journey where we share maps and jointly clear obstacles. The human-centered, ethical, and equitable use of AI in classrooms is a grand vision; too grand for any single entity to achieve alone. However, as the examples in this chapter show, when international agencies, governments, academia, and industry collaborate, real progress is made. This global solidarity in reimagining education gives hope that AI's benefits can truly extend to every learner, while its risks are contained by our shared wisdom and mutual support.

To truly harness the benefits of global knowledge exchange, as a call-to-action local educators are encouraged to actively connect with these international efforts. By engaging with open educational resources, online forums, and collaborative platforms, teachers can both contribute their insights and learn from peers around the world. Joining this global movement not only enriches local practice but also ensures that every classroom benefits from the collective wisdom and shared innovations of a worldwide community. It is imperative that educators embrace this opportunity to collaborate across borders, thereby helping to shape a more equitable and effective future for education.

Bridging AI with social-emotional growth

Amid all the technological change, educators and parents continue to prioritize something very fundamental: the social and emotional development of students. SEL—encompassing skills like empathy, self-awareness, relationship-building, and emotional regulation—remains a cornerstone of holistic education. A pressing question for the road ahead is how AI and SEL might influence each other. Can AI tools support SEL in positive ways? Can they help address the student mental health crisis or better personalize emotional support? Conversely, what safeguards are needed to ensure AI does not undermine human connection or wellbeing in schools? In this section, we explore the nuanced synergy (and tensions) between AI and SEL. The following figure depicts the partnership between AI and students:

---

54 Davis, M. R. (2024, July 18). Global artificial intelligence boom predicted in education, particularly in China. Marketbrief. https://marketbrief.edweek.org/education-market/global-artificial-intelligence-boom-predicted-in-education-particularly-in-china/2019/06

Figure 11.2: *Students and AI will partner closely*

On one hand, AI offers new tools to enhance SEL activities and access to support. AI's ability to handle personalization and natural language interaction can be leveraged to practice and reinforce social-emotional skills. For example, role-playing exercises are a common technique in SEL, where students might act out how to resolve a conflict or how to stand up to bullying. AI can enrich this by generating scenario-based learning prompts tailored to students' backgrounds. Educators have found that with well-crafted prompts, AI chatbots can produce culturally relevant and relatable scenarios for students to discuss or act out[55]. This can make SEL lessons more inclusive and impactful. AI can also adapt SEL activities for various developmental levels or learning differences, ensuring every student can participate meaningfully.

Another promising synergy is using AI as a force multiplier for mental health support and counseling, especially in the face of shortages of school counselors or psychologists[56]. While AI is *not* a replacement for professional mental health care, it can help triage needs and provide some level of support when human help is scarce. One real-world example is a chatbot called Alongside[57], designed as a Tier 1 mental health support for secondary students. Alongside, it uses conversational AI to check in on students, providing a non-judgmental listening ear and coping strategies for common issues like stress or anxiety. Its CEO notes that AI can make brief and early interventions widely accessible, essentially offering a first line of support that can either resolve minor issues or prompt a referral for more serious help. Interestingly, research over the years has shown that some people (teens in particular) might be more comfortable

---

55 AI + SEL & the Mental health crisis: How can we leverage new tech to meet the moment? (and what are the risks?) - CASEL. (2024, July 31). CASEL. https://casel.org/blog/ai-sel-the-mental-health-crisis-how-can-we-leverage-new-tech-to-meet-the-moment-and-what-are-the-risks/#:~:text=adapting%20an%20activity%20for%20various,playing%20variations

56 AI + SEL & the Mental health crisis: How can we leverage new tech to meet the moment? (and what are the risks?) - CASEL. (2024, July 31). CASEL. https://casel.org/blog/ai-sel-the-mental-health-crisis-how-can-we-leverage-new-tech-to-meet-the-moment-and-what-are-the-risks/#:~:text=adapting%20an%20activity%20for%20various,playing%20variations

57 Alongside | Mental Health AI for schools. (n.d.-d). https://www.alongside.care/

initially opening up to a chatbot than to a human counselor, especially if they fear stigma or have social anxiety[58]. Knowing this, some schools are exploring AI companion apps where students can journal their feelings or get guided meditations and resilience exercises. Importantly, when an AI detects signs of serious distress, it can alert a human counselor, making sure the student does not go unnoticed.

AI can also help break language barriers and foster inclusion, which is very much an SEL concern (making every student feel understood and safe). If a student is an English language learner struggling to express themselves in a second language, an AI translator or a multilingual chatbot can allow them to communicate in their native language. The Alongside chatbot, mentioned earlier, reportedly supports students in 30 languages, and they anticipate doubling that number. Imagine a newcomer student who speaks Arabic being able to describe their feelings or ask for advice in Arabic to an AI, and then get support while they continue to develop English skills. That student is far less likely to feel isolated or voiceless. Additionally, AI can tailor its interactions: a student on the autism spectrum might benefit from an AI coach that practices social scenarios with them repeatedly, adjusting complexity based on the student's comfort, something a busy teacher might not always have time for.

Perhaps the biggest way AI can synergize with SEL is by freeing up more time for human-to-human interaction in the classroom. We touched on this earlier: AI could shoulder administrative and routine instructional tasks, giving teachers more bandwidth to focus on students' emotional and social needs. Some forward-thinking applications even consider educator SEL and wellness as part of the equation. Stressed or burned-out teachers struggle to provide emotional support to students. AI tools that help manage teacher workload or even provide wellness resources (like an app suggesting mindful breaks based on a teacher's schedule) indirectly benefit student SEL by keeping teachers more balanced.

However, the synergy of AI and SEL comes with significant caveats and the necessity for safeguards, so any AI tool in this space must be approached carefully and ethically. There are legitimate concerns: privacy is paramount when dealing with personal feelings and mental health data. Bias is another; an AI might inadvertently give different responses to students of different backgrounds if not properly designed. The risk of dehumanization is real if schools lean too heavily on AI for counseling or monitoring; students might feel they are being watched by algorithms or receiving canned empathy, which could erode trust. This calls for strong safeguards: AI tools used in school settings must be engineered with protective factors (data encryption, anonymization, clear opt-outs) and thoroughly vetted for quality. Transparency with students is crucial as well: they should know if they are interacting with a bot versus a person, and how any information they share might be used.

Another risk is AI errors and limitations in a sensitive context. If a chatbot gave a student poor advice or failed to flag a serious issue, it could do harm. Therefore, experts recommend that AI in SEL be used as a supplement, not a sole resource. There should always be a human in

---

58 Abrams, Z. (2023, July 1). AI is changing every aspect of psychology. Here's what to watch for. American Psychological Association. https://www.apa.org/monitor/2023/07/psychology-embracing-ai#:~:text=It%20can%20be%20used%20as,performance%20on%20%20cognitive%20%20reframing%20%20exercises

the loop and feedback channels so students can report if an AI interaction was unhelpful or upsetting. It is a frontier that will require careful research. Early studies are promising in some regards (for example, AI therapy bots showing decent outcomes for mild anxiety), but more evidence is needed in school contexts. Many are calling for more human-AI teamwork in SEL: perhaps an AI does the initial intake (asks questions, gathers data) and a counselor reviews that and takes over the nuanced parts. Or an AI monitors patterns (like noting if a student's tone in written assignments suggests growing frustration) and alerts the teacher, who can then check in personally.

The synergy between AI and SEL is ultimately about leveraging technology to deepen our humanity, not detract from it. It is about using AI to create safer spaces and personalized support for students to grow emotionally. For English language learners, AI might be the bridge that lets them express their true feelings. For students hesitant to approach an adult, an AI buddy might be the first step that then leads them to an adult. Additionally, for teachers, AI might handle the busywork so they can be the caring mentor that each child needs. The overarching principle must be AI in service of human connection. Any time an AI application appears to reduce face-to-face interaction or empathy, we should pause and reassess.

In a world where AI is ever-present, helping young people develop strong social-emotional skills and a firm sense of self is arguably more important than ever. The tools may change, but the heart of education—nurturing healthy, compassionate, and resilient humans—remains constant.

Looking to the horizon and disruptive possibilities

As we gaze toward the horizon of AI in education, we must also entertain the bold, disruptive possibilities that lie beyond the immediate trends. History has shown that transformative technologies often prompt us to rethink long-established models. Just as the printing press redefined access to knowledge, or the internet reshaped how we find information, advanced AI could one day disrupt the fundamental structures of schooling. In this section, we consider some forward-looking, even speculative, scenarios of how education might change if AI's potential is fully realized, and what challenges and choices those scenarios present.

One disruptive possibility is the radical personalization of the curriculum, potentially leading to a move away from the one-size-fits-all grade-level system. If each student has an AI tutor and a tailored learning path, the traditional age-based cohorts and rigid curriculum sequences could become less relevant. Instead of all 8th graders following the same math textbook, each student might be progressing at their own pace, with AI systems ensuring they master each concept before moving on. Education futurists have long imagined competency-based models where time is a variable and mastery is the constant: AI could be the key to making that practical at scale. If such a model were to take hold widely, schools might shift to something like learning hubs where students of different ages work on different things, guided by AI and coaches, rather than age-segregated classrooms moving in lockstep. This raises numerous questions: How do you ensure social development in mixed-age, individualized settings? How do you manage scheduling if everyone is on a different lesson? And how do you certify learning for college admissions or employers if not by traditional grades? Those would be challenges to solve. But the upside could be enormous: far fewer students are bored because the material is too easy or lost because it is too hard, and perhaps a greater ability to nurture individual talents. However, this concept is still largely speculative and would require extensive pilot testing to validate feasibility and effectiveness. The following figure shows the promise of the future with AI:

Figure 11.3: *A bright future for AI and student partnerships*

Another potential disruption concerns the role of the teacher, not in the sense of replacement, but rather in its redefinition. In a future highly personalized scenario, a single teacher might oversee 50 or 100 students who are all doing different things with AI assistance. That teacher's day-to-day role might look more like a combination of mentor, project manager, and intervention specialist. They might spend mornings reviewing AI-generated analytics about which students need help with what, then schedule a series of one-on-one or small-group mentoring sessions to tackle those needs. The delivery of new content might be done largely by AI tutors or rich multimedia materials, while the teacher focuses on higher-order guidance: facilitating discussions, teaching critical thinking, supervising collaborative projects where students apply what they learned from their AI tutors, and providing the emotional encouragement and deeper explanations that only a human can. This concept of teacher-as-coach is not entirely new, but AI could accelerate it. It is possible that we see new teaching specializations. For instance, some educators might become expert AI curriculum curators who design and tweak the AI-driven learning pathways, while others become learning motivators, concentrating on student engagement and habits of mind. Education systems might hire more paraprofessionals or community mentors to support learners, given that subject-matter delivery is handled by technology.

We also should consider assessment and credentialing, which could be heavily disrupted by AI-driven solutions. If AI can generate essays or solve problems, the traditional exam system (already under strain from cheating facilitated by technology) might become untenable. This could force a shift to more authentic assessments: projects, performances, and portfolios. We might finally abandon the factory-like examination hall in favor of a distributed, ongoing assessment where AI helps record and measure learning as it happens. For example, an AI could track a student's progress through a science project, logging how they plan, experiment, and draw conclusions, and then provide a competency report. Blockchains or other technologies might be used to store verified credentials of skills that students have demonstrated (think of a digital transcript that lists critical thinking–proficient, collaboration–advanced, Python programming–intermediate, etc., earned through a combination of AI assessments and teacher validation). This is disruptive because it might reduce the emphasis on high-stakes standardized tests, changing how students are evaluated for college or jobs. Organizations like the World Economic Forum have been advocating for recognizing a broader set of skills in Education 4.0[59]; AI might provide the tools to do so at scale by assessing things like creativity or teamwork through simulation and interaction. However, widespread adoption would depend on overcoming challenges like ensuring fairness and accuracy in AI-based assessments, requiring rigorous piloting and stakeholder validation. AI also holds promise for anytime, anywhere learning. AI has the potential to liberate learning from the confines of physical school buildings and rigid daily schedules. We saw glimpses of this during the COVID-19 pandemic with remote learning. In the future, a student could learn from home, a library, or a community center with AI tutors and lessons, checking in with teachers, maybe only periodically. Future scenarios might see virtual reality and augmented reality combined with AI, enhancing immersive learning experiences, potentially transforming the concept of traditional schooling if such technologies become accessible and effective. Do you want to learn history? Put on VR and have an AI-driven tour through ancient Rome, conversing with historical figures. AR could turn the world into a classroom; a student on a nature walk could use AR glasses with an AI that identifies plants and explains ecosystems on the fly. We might still have physical schools, but they could be more like collaborative workshops or safe spaces for socialization, while much academic learning can happen independently. Homeschooling and traditional schooling might blend into new hybrid models. This raises big equity concerns: ensuring every child has access to these rich experiences, not just those with means. It also challenges the social role of schools: for many communities, schools are a place for childcare while parents work, a place for meals, and for social services. Any disruptive change must account for those functions.

AI might also bring about global classrooms and peer learning in unprecedented ways. Language translation AI is nearing the point where real-time, seamless translation is feasible. This could allow students from different countries to be in the same virtual class, each speaking their own language and yet understanding one another. Imagine a global history seminar for high schoolers, facilitated by AI translation and moderation, where students from 10 different

59 Milberg, T. (2024, April 28). The future of learning: How AI is revolutionizing education 4.0. Weforum. https://www.weforum.org/stories/2024/04/future-learning-ai-revolutionizing-education4-0-/#:~:text-,experience

countries discuss world events together. Such cross-cultural collaboration could become routine, greatly expanding students' worldviews and communication skills. It disrupts the insular nature of many education systems and might eventually reduce duplication of teaching effort (perhaps one amazing physics teacher, aided by AI, could virtually teach students across multiple small rural schools around the world who lack a local physics teacher). The Khanmigo pilot in hundreds of districts hints at scaling quality instruction widely[60], but global peer-to-peer learning would take it to another level.

A more radical idea is AI-driven adaptive grouping, where the composition of classes or study groups changes dynamically based on needs and interests, identified by AI. For example, on a given afternoon, an AI system might suggest: Group A (these five students) should meet with Mr. Lopez to do a hands-on experiment about Newton's laws because they all just reached that point and would benefit from a collaborative lab; Group B (these three students) should work together on a creative writing piece because they have complementary strengths and challenges; Group C (these four students) are struggling with a concept, so they should get a targeted mini-lesson. The schedule could become highly flexible, orchestrated by AI that optimizes learning opportunities. School bells signaling uniform periods might fade away in such a scenario.

There are also disruptive negative possibilities that we should address to be responsible. If implemented carelessly, AI could potentially exacerbate inequalities (i.e., wealthy families get human tutors + AI, while others get only AI), or it could narrow the curriculum (for instance, if something is not easily taught or tested by AI, might it be deemphasized?). There is also the dystopian possibility of over-monitoring, where a school uses AI to constantly surveil student attentiveness or emotions. This might optimize test scores, but at great cost to student privacy and autonomy, and create a pressure-cooker environment. Such paths would likely provoke pushback from parents and students, and rightfully so. It underscores that disruptive change, if it comes, must be guided vigilantly by human values and ethics. The technology will permit many things that we as a society might not want in our schools.

Lastly, as AI potentially automates more cognitive tasks, the very definition of being an educated person might shift. When knowledge is universally accessible and AI can solve standard problems, education may focus far more on the uniquely human: creativity, ethical judgment, leadership, emotional intelligence, and original research. Schools might put much less emphasis on memorization or routine skill practice (since AI can handle those) and far more on mentor-guided exploration, interdisciplinary projects, and building character and resilience. This would be a profound pedagogical shift. In essence, it means doubling down on human-centered learning because the machine-centered parts are taken care of by machines. It is an optimistic vision: imagine classrooms buzzing with art, debate, experiments, community service projects, and real-world learning, while AI quietly personalizes some background tasks for each student. If done right, AI's disruption could liberate education from drudgery and standardization, unleashing a renaissance of creativity and individual growth in schools.

60 CBS News. (2024, December 16). Meet Khanmigo: the student tutor AI being tested in school districts | 60 Minutes. https://www.cbsnews.com/video/khanmigo-ai-tutor-60-minutes-video-2024-12-08/

However, this pedagogical shift requires validation through pilot studies and ongoing stakeholder engagement.

Of course, these disruptive possibilities raise as many questions as they answer. They may unfold over a longer horizon (a decade or two) or not at all in some cases, depending on social choices and technical developments. The key is to stay proactive. As a global educational community, we should scenario-plan for these possibilities: pilot new models on a small scale, research outcomes, involve stakeholders in discussions about what kind of future we want, and set policies accordingly. The worst approach would be to let disruptive change happen to us unprepared; the best would be to shape it intentionally towards our highest educational ideals. In the final analysis, no matter how technology changes, we will always circle back to education's core mission: to empower individuals and uplift societies. That compass should guide us through whatever disruptions the future may hold.

Future led by humanity and vision

The road ahead is illuminated by the promise of smarter, more personalized, and more inclusive education powered by AI. From intelligent tutors that adapt to each child, to global collaborative learning networks, to teachers transformed into even more impactful mentors, the possibilities are inspiring. Real-world examples show that this future is already beginning: schools are piloting AI in ways that help struggling students catch up[61]. Teachers are gaining new superpowers through well-designed AI training, and international bodies are laying ethical guidelines to ensure our innovations align with human values. There is a sense of momentum, a recognition that, handled wisely, AI can accelerate progress toward the long-held goals of education, such as equity, quality, and relevance to life and work.

Yet, woven through this optimistic outlook is a clear message that emerged time and again in our exploration: we must put humans at the center of AI in education. The ultimate measure of success is not how advanced our algorithms become, but how well we nurture the minds and hearts of learners. We have emphasized ensuring inclusion and equity, echoing UNESCO's call that the promise of AI for all means leaving no one behind. This will require continued advocacy and action to close digital divides, connecting every school to the internet, investing in devices and skills for underserved communities, and sharing AI resources globally so that a child in a rural village has access to the same powerful learning tools as a child in a major city. It also means vigilance that AI tools are accessible to learners of all abilities and respect the diversity of languages and cultures in our world.

Let us envision what success looks like a decade from now. It is morning in 2035: a teacher begins class by greeting his or her students individually, thanks to AI having already handled administrative prep. Students dive into learning experiences tailored to them; one is exploring

---

61 Gómez, J. (2024, October 30). Newark Public Schools considers new AI tutor chatbot for districtwide use after pilot testing. Chalkbeat. https://www.chalkbeat.org/newark/2024/05/13/artificial-intelligence-khan-migo-chatbot-tutor-pilot-testing-districtwide-expansion/#:~:text=Newark%20Public%20Schools%20wants%20to,up%20from%20pandemic%20learning%20loss

a rainforest in VR with an AI guide, another is debugging a code project with AI hints, and a small group is engaged in a discussion facilitated by the teacher about the ethics of AI itself (a topic part of their curriculum). A student who was absent due to illness yesterday is quickly brought up to speed by an AI recap and some peer support. In the afternoon, the class connects to a joint session with students in another country, broadening their perspectives. At the end of the day, the teacher receives a dashboard (accessible to parents and students, too) that highlights not just academic progress but also notes how students are feeling and collaborating, allowing timely celebration of successes and support for struggles. School feels more personal, more relevant, and still full of the laughter, debate, and friendships that define childhood.

Achieving that vision will require work—investing in infrastructure, training millions of teachers, crafting wise policies, and iterating on technology design. It is within reach if we remain committed. The road ahead is not pre-determined; it is ours to build. Let us build it wide enough for all learners, well-lit by the light of knowledge and ethics, and leading toward a future where education empowers every individual to thrive in both heart and mind. With hope, wisdom, and collaboration, we can ensure that AI in the classroom becomes a force that uplifts education's human mission for generations to come.

Conclusion

As we conclude this exploration of AI in the classroom, we find ourselves at a juncture of profound opportunity and responsibility. We have underscored the importance of ethics and data privacy at every step. As AI systems become more embedded in schooling, trust must be earned and maintained. Students and teachers should feel confident that these systems are transparent, fair, and accountable. The coming years will likely see more refinement of these guardrails, potentially even international standards for AI in education. AI can only ever be a means to an end, with the end being the flourishing of human potential.

Throughout this chapter and the book, a theme of partnership and collaboration has been prevalent. The journey into the future of AI in the classroom is not one that any teacher or school should walk alone. Whether it is teachers teaming up in professional learning communities to share AI lesson ideas, or countries joining forces to solve common challenges, collaboration is our surest strategy. Many minds working together can spot blind spots, share workloads, and amplify successes. The global partnerships we discussed—UNESCO, OECD, the Education 4.0 Alliance, and numerous others—give cause for optimism that we will approach this transformation thoughtfully and inclusively. The road ahead crosses many landscapes, from high-tech innovation to deep ethical terrain, and collaboration will be the vehicle that carries us through.

As we venture forward, it is clear that we are writing the next chapter of education together with AI. There will be surprises, new AI capabilities we have not imagined, and perhaps societal shifts (in jobs, in geopolitics) that change what we need from education. Navigating this will require lifelong learning, not just for students but for all of us. The mindset we cultivate in students—adaptability, critical thinking, creativity, empathy—we must also embody as educators and leaders. In a sense, the education system itself must model the learner's mindset: continuously learning, iterating, and improving. Mistakes will happen, as with any innovation; what is important is that we learn from them quickly and keep our compass oriented toward the core values that do not change.

Now is the time for action. We call upon professional communities, teacher leaders, and policy influencers to take these ideas forward—to champion AI integration in classrooms, advocate for ethical frameworks, and lead the charge in building a future where AI serves as an ally in fostering the growth of every learner. Together, let us drive the transformation, ensuring that AI not only enhances education but also enriches the human experience for generations to come.

Questions

1. How might AI evolve and influence education in the next five to ten years? How about 20 years from now?

2. What skills will students need to thrive in an AI-integrated world and future workplace, and how can we help them develop these?

3. How can we reinforce the ethical and responsible use of AI in my classroom?

4. What role should human connection and emotional intelligence play in an AI-enhanced learning environment?

5. How can AI be leveraged to support personal and individualized learning without widening existing educational inequalities?

6. What policies or guidelines do we need to implement to ensure security, data privacy, and student safety when using AI tools?

7. What PD do we need so that we can stay current with emerging AI technologies in education?

8. How will we balance the power of AI with the humanity of teaching?

9. How can we use AI to encourage student creativity, not conformity?

10. What can we do to ensure AI has a positive influence on the future of learning?

Exercises

1. **Design your AI learning buddy**

   a. **Goal**: Encourage students to think critically about AI-powered tutoring.

   b. **Activity**: Have students design their ideal AI learning assistant.

      i.   What subjects can AI help with?

      ii.   What personality traits would it have?

      iii.   What boundaries would be important (e.g., privacy, accuracy, support vs. doing the work)?

  c. **Bonus**: They can sketch it or create a chatbot persona.

2. **AI future classroom design**

  a. **Goal**: Explore possibilities for how classrooms may evolve with AI.

  b. **Activity**: In groups, students draw or digitally map out a school of the future.

      i.   Include AI tutors, SEL zones, immersive learning pods, etc.

      ii.   Use metaphors and labels to highlight how humans and AI interact.

  c. **Wrap-Up**: Each group presents and explains how their map prioritizes ethics and equity.

3. **Bias detective lab**

  a. **Goal**: Build AI literacy and ethical awareness.

  b. **Activity**: Students review 2–3 fictional scenarios where an AI makes a biased decision (e.g., grading, recommending content).

      i.   They investigate what went wrong and propose solutions.

  c. **Discuss** how human oversight can help

4. **Chatbot conversations: Human or machine? The Turing test**

  a. **Goal**: Examine the limits of AI empathy and communication.

  b. **Activity**: Students are given a series of short dialogues. Some were written by AI, some by humans.

      i.   Can they tell which is which?

      ii.   Which responses feel more trustworthy or helpful, and why?

      iii.   Where do humans excel? Where do machines excel?

  c. **Reflection**: What does this say about how AI can or cannot support SEL?

5. **Create with AI, reflect as a human**

  a. **Goal**: Leverage AI as a creative partner.

  b. **Activity**: Students use a GenAI art or writing tool to generate something (a story intro, an image, a song, a visual prompt). Then, they remix it—drawing, writing, or building on the idea with their own creativity.

c. **Reflect**: What did the AI contribute? What did you add that made it uniquely yours?

6. **Global AI collaboration challenge**

   a. **Goal**: Practice global citizenship and collaboration.

   b. **Activity**: In small groups, students select a world issue (e.g., climate change, education equity) and design a basic AI-powered solution.

      i. Include how it would be accessible in different languages and cultures.

      ii. Pitch it like a group that is applying for funding to UNESCO or the World Economic Forum.

   c. **Bonus**: Use translation tools to write part of the pitch in a different language.

7. **Disruption scenario workshop**

   a. **Goal**: Prepare students for new and adaptive thinking and future planning.

   b. **Activity**: Each group receives a what-if disruption scenario (e.g., AI replaces traditional grades, or students learn at different paces using AI tutors). They must assess:

      i. What are the benefits?

      ii. What are the risks or concerns?

      iii. How would we adapt as students, teachers, or a community?

      iv. Present their response strategy to the class.

   c. **Bonus**: Rewrite the Headlines Mini-Project

   d. After presenting their disruption response, each student group creates two fictional future news headlines about their scenario:

      i. One optimistic (best-case) headline: What happens if the disruption goes well?

      ii. One cautionary (worst-case) headline: What could go wrong if we are not careful?

Examples:

- AI-based Tutors Help Every Student Graduate With Honors by 2030!

- Schools Lean Too Heavily on AI—Students Struggle With Critical Thinking, Says 2032 Report

These headlines help drive home the importance of thoughtful, ethical AI implementation and spark a fun, creative discussion.

Index